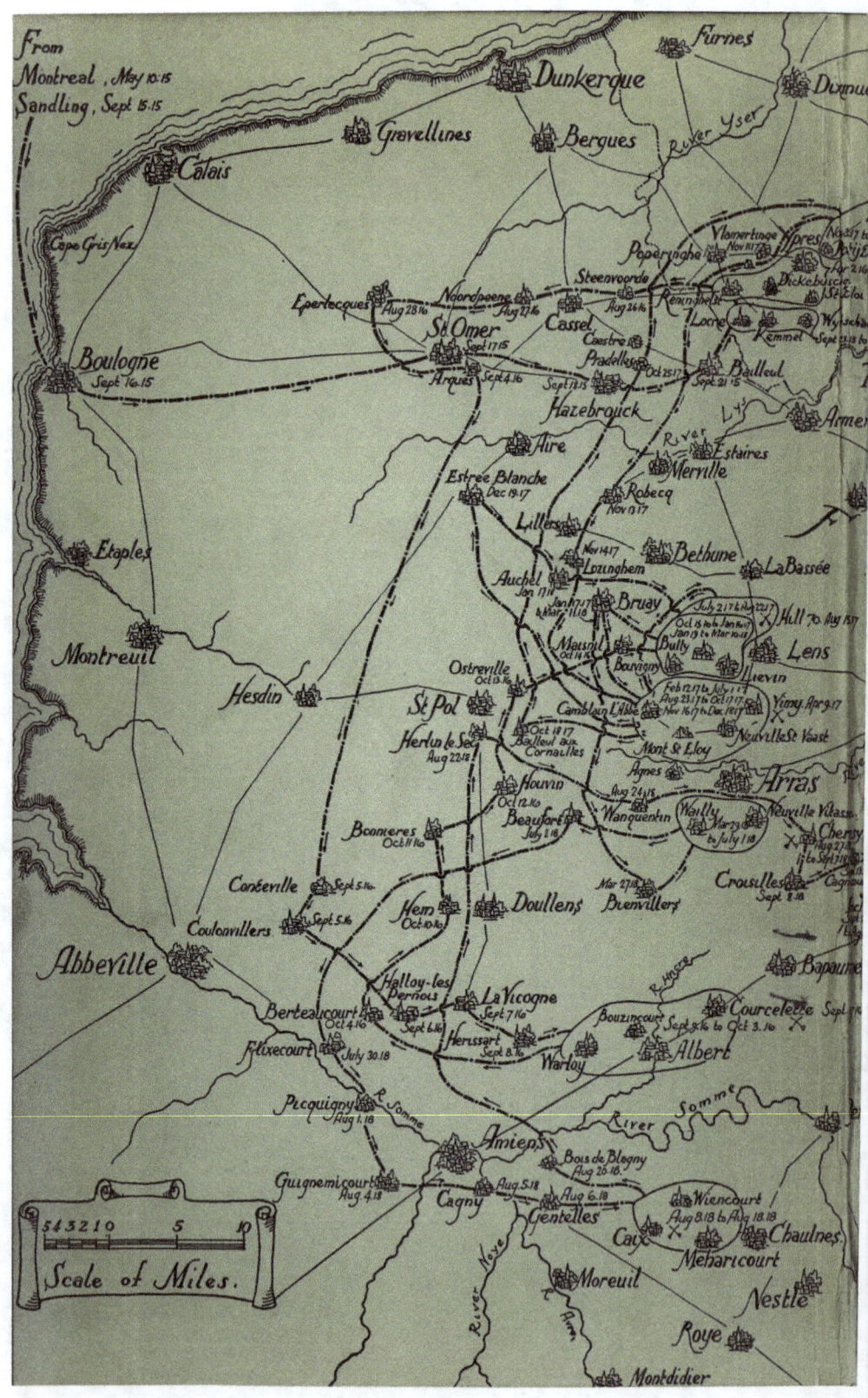

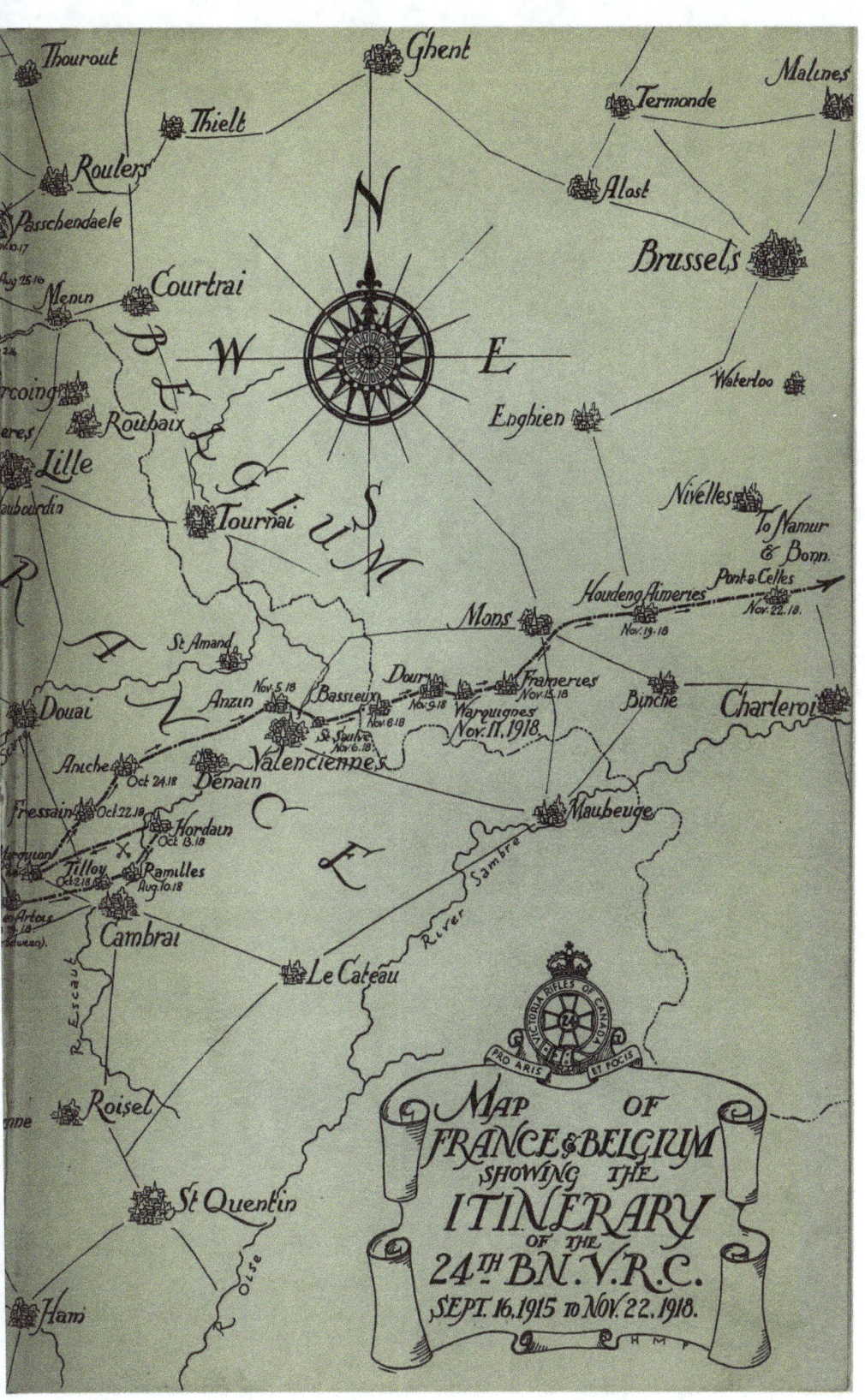

24TH BATTALION, VICTORIA RIFLES OF CANADA,
BATTLE PATCHES AND APPOINTMENTS

(1) Officers' Lapel Badge, (2) Shoulder Badge, (3) Final Cap Badge, (4) Other Ranks' Collar Badge, (5) Original Cap Badge, (6) Tunic Button, (7) Battalion Battle Patch, (8) Officers' Battle Patch.

THE 24th BATTALION, C.E.F., VICTORIA RIFLES OF CANADA 1914-1919

Edited and Compiled
by
R. C. FETHERSTONHAUGH

The Naval & Military Press Ltd

Published by

The Naval & Military Press Ltd
Unit 10 Ridgewood Industrial Park,
Uckfield, East Sussex,
TN22 5QE England

Tel: +44 (0) 1825 749494
Fax: +44 (0) 1825 765701

www.naval-military-press.com
www.nmarchive.com

In reprinting in facsimile from the original, any imperfections are inevitably reproduced and the quality may fall short of modern type and cartographic standards.

This Book is Dedicated
By Surviving Members
of
The 24th Battalion, C.E.F.,
Victoria Rifles of Canada
to
1006 Comrades Who Died
in
France and Flanders

In the preparation of this work the Department of National Defence has allowed the author free access to official diaries, orders, messages, maps and other documents.

MOUNT SORREL

SOMME, 1916-1918

FLERS · COURCELETTE · THIEPVAL · ANCRE HEIGHTS

ARRAS, 1917-1918

VIMY, 1917

ARLEUX · SCARPE, 1917 · 1918

HILL 70

YPRES, 1917

PASSCHENDAELE

AMIENS

HINDENBURG LINE

CANAL DU NORD

CAMBRAI, 1918

PURSUIT TO MONS

FRANCE AND FLANDERS, 1915-1918

PREFACE

IN the preparation of this history of the 24th Battalion, C.E.F., Victoria Rifles of Canada, the Regimental History Committee, under the chairmanship of Lieut.-Col. C. F. Ritchie, D.S.O., M.C., and with Major P. L. Hall, D.S.O., M.C., as Honorary Secretary, provided assistance of great value. The Committee, including at one time or another approximately thirty of the Battalion's former officers and other ranks, devoted many evenings to reviewing the manuscript and to supplying details of events not to be found in the Battalion's official War Diary, which was used as a base for the entire narrative.

The thanks of the Committee are here extended to those officers and other ranks, and to the next of kin of a number of the fallen, who generously placed in the author's hands private diaries, letters, and other documents, or, possessing no data of this nature, furnished the verbal reports which bridged many gaps in the story as presented in documents of an official character.

A special debt is also acknowledged to the Historical Section of the General Staff, Department of National Defence, Ottawa, and to the Records Section of the Department. These Sections, under Col. A. Fortescue Duguid, D.S.O., and Major Clyde R. Scott respectively, assisted with unfailing courtesy, the Historical Section checking the manuscript, verifying the facts, and pointing out where errors had occurred; and the Records Section supplying the extensive data from which the appendices of the book were compiled.

For arduous work in the preparation and production of sketches and maps on the part of Capt. F. W. Stenson and Lieuts. G. S. Bushe and H. M. Patterson the Committee also desires to record its deep appreciation.

R. C. F.

MONTREAL, NOVEMBER 11, 1930.

Contents

	PAGE

CHAPTER I
TRADITION AND TRAINING. September 20, 1861—September 15, 1915 3

CHAPTER II
TRENCH WARFARE ON THE KEMMEL FRONT. September 15, 1915—April 2, 1916 23

CHAPTER III
THE CRATERS AT ST. ELOI. April 2, 1916—May 30, 1916 . 43

CHAPTER IV
ZILLEBEKE. May 28, 1916—August 24, 1916 . . . 58

CHAPTER V
THE SOMME. August 24, 1916—October 3, 1916 . . . 76

CHAPTER VI
THE ANGRES AND LA FOLIE SECTORS. October 3, 1916—March 23, 1917 104

CHAPTER VII
THE CAPTURE OF VIMY RIDGE. March 23, 1917—April 16, 1917 116

CHAPTER VIII
TRENCH TOURS ON THE VIMY FRONT. April 16, 1917—July 22, 1917 137

CHAPTER IX
HILL 70. July 22, 1917—October 16, 1917 . . . 152

Chapter X

Passchendaele. October 16, 1917—November 11, 1917 . 175

Chapter XI

The Mericourt and Lens Sectors. November 11, 1917—
March 21, 1918 188

Chapter XII

Germany's Bid for Military Victory. March 21, 1918—
July 30, 1918 199

Chapter XIII

The Battle of Amiens. July 30, 1918—August 20, 1918 . 218

Chapter XIV

The Second Battles of Arras, 1918. August 20, 1918—
August 30, 1918 232

Chapter XV

The Pursuit to Mons. August 30, 1918—November 11, 1918 246

Chapter XVI

The March to the Rhine. November 11, 1918—January 25,
1919 269

Chapter XVII

The End of the Road. January 25, 1919—May 18, 1919 . 284

APPENDICES

A—Honour Roll 298
B—Honours and Awards (Regimental) 310
C—Honours and Awards (Non-Regimental) . . . 315
D—Commissions 317
E—Statistics 319

Illustrations

	PAGE
REGIMENTAL CREST AND BADGES	*Frontispiece*
CHANGING THE GUARD, PEEL STREET BARRACKS	10
INSPECTION BY H.R.H. THE DUKE OF CONNAUGHT	12
OFFICERS WHO PROCEEDED TO FRANCE	26
THE ST. ELOI CRATERS	44
THE BRICKFIELDS AT ALBERT	82
THE SUNKEN ROAD, COURCELETTE	88
THE BATTALION'S BATTLEFIELD AT VIMY RIDGE	132
THE SERGEANTS. ANICHE 1918	194
THE COMMANDING OFFICERS, 1914—1919	208
CROSSING THE RHINE BRIDGE AT BONN	278
PRESENTATION OF THE KING'S COLOUR	290
HOMEWARD BOUND	292
THE BATTALION'S LAST PARADE	294

Maps

BATTALION ITINERARY.	*End Papers*
(Map by Lieut. H. M. Patterson)	
COURCELETTE, 1916	90
(Map by Lieut. H. M. Patterson)	
REGINA AND KENORA TRENCHES, 1916	100
(Map by Lieut. H. M. Patterson)	
VIMY RIDGE, 1917	134
(Map by Lieut. G. S. Bushe)	
HILL 70, 1917	162
(Map by Lieut. G. S. Bushe)	
AMIENS, 1918	228
(Map by Capt. F. W. Stenson)	
ARRAS, 1918	242
(Map by Capt. F. W. Stenson)	
THE GERMAN CONCENTRATION, September, 1918	248
(Map by Lieut G. S. Bushe)	

Sketches

(By Lieutenant Paul Jensen, 24th Bn. V.R.C.)

	PAGE
VIA GELLIA COMMUNICATION TRENCH	28
THE STABLE AT SIEGE FARM	28
RED CHATEAU IN FRONT OF THE PETIT BOIS	36
THE V.C. ROAD	36

THE 24th BATTALION, C.E.F., VICTORIA RIFLES OF CANADA
1914-1919

CHAPTER I

TRADITION AND TRAINING

I

Nearly seventy years ago, at a time when the outbreak of war between the Federal Government of the United States of America and the seceding states of the South had aroused a martial spirit throughout the whole of North America, the young men of the Beaver Lacrosse Club of Montreal discussed seriously the suggestion that they should band themselves together to form a military organization capable of taking part in any operations which might involve the forces of Her Majesty the Queen in Canada. Lacrosse at this time was, in fact, as well as in name, Canada's national sport, and the Beaver Lacrosse Club included in its membership the sons of many of Montreal's most prominent mercantile and professional families. Meeting on September 20, 1861, the members of the Club formed the "Victoria Rifles Company" and appointed W. Osborne Smith, Esq., their captain.

A few weeks later, on December 13th, the number of authorized recruits was increased to 300, and the Company, now formed into a battalion of six companies, was re-named "The Victoria Volunteer Rifles." This was at the time when relations between Great Britain and the United States were strained as a result of the action of the United States in seizing from the British vessel *Trent*, on the high seas, the Confederate diplomatic representatives, Mason and Slidell. No one could foresee the result of this seizure, but it was clear that hostilities might ensue; accordingly, the Victoria Volunteer Rifles paraded on three afternoons and three evenings each week and drilled faithfully on the Champ de Mars, or, when bitter weather made this impossible, in the shelter of Bonsecours Market. So excellent were results, that the battalion, on January 10, 1862, was formally enrolled as a militia unit in the Government service, with the title "3rd Battalion (Victoria Rifles)." At that time, rifle regiments carried colours in the same manner as regiments of the line, and on August 30th the unit paraded on the old Montreal Cricket Grounds to receive colours from the ladies of the city. Following the order that rifle regiments should no longer carry colours, these banners, on November 17, 1901, were deposited in the Church of St. James the Apostle, Montreal, where they still remain.

Meanwhile, despite settlement of the case of Messrs. Mason and Slidell, eyes in Canada were turning with increasing anxiety to the United States' border, where Fenians presented a constant threat of invasion. The Fenians were American sympathisers with the cause of Irish Home Rule, who imagined that Ireland might be helped and Great Britain discomfited by an invasion of Canada from the United States. Fantastic as the plan seems in retrospect, it could not be so regarded at the time. Little chance of permanent success existed even then, but many of the Fenians had served in the war between the North and South, were familiar with military organization in consequence, and might, if afforded opportunity, sweep over the border and, for a time, spread death and ruin in settlements on the Canadian side. On Christmas Day, 1864, a company of the Victoria Rifles, under Capt. McGraw, left for Windsor, Ontario, where invasion threatened, returning to Montreal when the danger had passed.

Little of more than passing significance occurred in the following year; but in 1866 alarms were frequent. On March 10th the Victoria Rifles paraded with other units of the Montreal garrison; companies were sent out on several occasions; and others were held ready for action in the regimental armoury, then situated on Victoria Square. Later in the year, in June, the entire Regiment left for Hemmingford and Huntingdon, P.Q., and there remained on duty for more than two weeks, ready to oppose invasion by a force of Fenians which had gathered at St. Albans, Vermont.

On the Queen's birthday, May 24, 1870, the Regiment paraded to honour the day in ceremonial fashion, but a message, handed to the Commanding Officer, announced that the Fenians were once more threatening the frontier and called for prompt action. Without delay, a special service company of the unit, under Capt. J. W. Crawford, Lieut. E. B. Greenshields, and Ensign J. K. Oswald, left for the scene of action and on the following day, the five remaining companies, under Major E. A. Whitehead, entrained at Point St. Charles for St. Armand, P.Q. When the Fenians crossed the border, the Victoria Rifles assisted in driving them back and were rewarded by Her Majesty, who granted the Regiment the right to carry on appointments and colours the name by which the engagement is known, "Eccles Hill."

On several occasions after the Fenian Raids had passed into history, the Regiment was called out to aid the civil power, notably in 1875, during the Guibord Riots, and subsequently at the time of Guibord's burial; in 1877, as a guard for the Orange Procession; in 1878, to proceed to Quebec during the Ship Labourers' Riots, and again when feeling ran high between those who were determined to parade on Orange Day and those willing to shed blood rather than allow the procession to take place. On December 5, 1879, the name of the unit was changed to the "3rd Regiment (Victoria Rifles of Canada)."

In 1885, the Regiment was "next for duty" in the North-West Rebellion; and was called out during the Smallpox Riots in Montreal, to aid in the maintenance of order. No serious casualties occurred on this occasion as a result of lawless action, but Private J. H. Samuels, of No. 3 Company, was killed by the accidental discharge of a rifle in the hands of a sentry.

The following year was marked by the purchase of land on the north side of Cathcart Street, west of University Street, for a regimental armoury. Construction followed; the cornerstone being laid on December 4, 1886, by Sir A. P. Caron, K.C.M.G., Canadian Minister of Militia, and the armoury being formally opened on June 21, 1887. Funds for constructing the armoury were raised without Government assistance and title to the building was vested in the "Victoria Rifles Association," composed of officers, other ranks, and friends of the unit.

A few years after the armoury was completed, the Regiment provided 67 officers and men for service in the Canadian Contingents to the South African War. A number of these won distinction, particularly in the Battle of Paardeburg, on February 18, 1900, and at Hart's River, on March 31, 1902. Five members of the Regiment, Privates Harry Cotton, G. H. Bolt, C. H. Barry, A. R. Kingsley, and G. S. Racey, were killed in action, or died of sickness. A tablet, erected in the Church of St. James the Apostle, commemorates their sacrifice and the measure of their service to Canada and the Empire.

In 1902 the Regiment was called out for duty at Valleyfield, P.Q., where industrial trouble threatened; and in 1903 in Montreal, during riots precipitated by a strike of dock labourers and longshoremen. No further active duty fell to the Regiment until 1914, but training and preparation were faithfully continued. When the test of 1914 and subsequent years came, the unit owed much to the following officers, each of whom, in his period of command, had striven earnestly to maintain and foster the spirit which brought the unit into being in 1861.

Commanding Officers	Assumed Command
Lieut.-Col. William Osborne Smith	Jan. 31, 1862
Lieut.-Col. Augustus Heward	June 15, 1866
Lieut.-Col. Hartland S. MacDougall	Nov. 16, 1866
Lieut.-Col. William Henry Hutton	Nov. 22, 1867
Lieut.-Col. Angus R. Bethune	July 19, 1870
Lieut.-Col. Nathaniel J. Handyside	Aug. 24, 1873
Lieut.-Col. Edward Ashworth Whitehead	June 6, 1876
Lieut.-Col. John Molson Crawford	Oct. 3, 1884
Lieut.-Col. Charles Peers Davidson	April 7, 1887
Lieut.-Col. Fred. Clarence Henshaw	July 15, 1887
Lieut.-Col. George Ritchie Starke	June 10, 1892
Lieut.-Col. Edwin Botsford Busteed	Sept. 10, 1897
Lieut.-Col. George Arthur Sicotte Hamilton	July 23, 1900
Lieut.-Col. Erastus Winans Wilson	Sept. 25, 1903
Lieut.-Col. Robert Starke	June 5, 1907

Lieut.-Col. Frank William Fisher........Sept. 7, 1909
Lieut.-Col. W. Watt Burland.............Dec. 9, 1912
Lieut.-Col. Fred A. de L. Gascoigne......Dec. 8, 1914

Honorary Officers   Gazetted

Hon. Colonel the Right Honourable Lord
 Strathcona and Mount Royal, G.C.M.G.,
 G.C.V.O..............................Jan. 10, 1898
Hon. Lieut.-Col. E. A. Whitehead........Jan. 30, 1912

II

When Great Britain declared war upon Germany in August, 1914, Lieut.-Col. W. W. Burland, who commanded the 3rd Regiment, Victoria Rifles of Canada, at the time, volunteered at once for service in the Expeditionary Force which the Government of the Dominion of Canada had authorized. His services were accepted and he was appointed second-in-command of the 14th Battalion, Royal Montreal Regiment. This unit came in existence soon after the outbreak of war and served with distinction throughout. Thirteen of its original officers and 338 of its original men were provided by the Victoria Rifles.

When the First Canadian Contingent sailed from Gaspé Basin in October, 1914, the Dominion stood committed to participation in the Great War. The Government had previously announced that Canada would support Great Britain and would fight to the end. No one doubted the good faith of this declaration; nevertheless the First Contingent provided a pledge of flesh and blood more convincing even than the solemn resolutions of Parliament. Soon after the Contingent sailed, while it was at sea in fact, the Government announced that a Second Contingent would be raised forthwith. All Canada expected the announcement and approval was widespread. In these circumstances, the battalions of the new force began to mobilize the moment that authorization to recruit was received from Ottawa.

On October 22, 1914, Major J. A. Gunn, of the 3rd Regiment, Victoria Rifles of Canada, was notified officially by Headquarters of the Montreal Military District that he had been chosen to recruit and command a new battalion in that city. Major Gunn had seen long service in the Canadian Militia, first with the Queen's Own Rifles, of Toronto, which he joined as a private in 1897, receiving a commission in 1898, and later with the Victoria Rifles in Montreal. At the time of his appointment for overseas service, the battalion he was to command possessed no name, or number, but on October 31st it was announced that the unit would be the "24th Battalion, C.E.F.", and would bear the additional title "Victoria Rifles of Canada." A few days later, the 24th Battalion, Victoria Rifles of Canada, was assigned to the 5th Infantry Brigade, 2nd Canadian Division. With this brigade and division, the Battalion served throughout the war.

As soon as his appointment was announced, Lieut.-Col. Gunn began the work that lay before him. Recruiting for the new battalion was opened at once in the armoury of the Victoria Rifles on Cathcart Street, in that of the 5th Regiment, Royal Highlanders of Canada, on Bleury Street, and in the Government Drill Shed, on Craig Street. Recruiting at the time presented little difficulty, and soon to the old Montreal High School, on Peel Street, which had been taken over as a barracks, there flowed a steady stream of men, from all walks in life, but chosen for a high standard of physique and intelligence. From the beginning, Lieut.-Col. Gunn instructed his recruiting staff and Medical Officer to weed out ruthlessly applicants unable to meet, physically and mentally, the high standard desired.

While recruiting proceeded at the armouries, appointments to the commissioned establishment were announced from time to time, the officers named usually assuming duties at once and taking part in the further organization and training of the Battalion. Within a week, it was known that Major C. H. Hill, of the Royal Canadian Regiment, was to serve as Second-in-Command; Capt. R. O. Alexander, of the same regiment, as Adjutant; and the Reverend Allan P. Shatford, Rector of the Church of St. James the Apostle, as Chaplain, with the rank of Hon. Captain. Twenty-four additional officers had been appointed, though some only provisionally, by October 31st. Eight of these were graduates of the Royal

Military College, Kingston, and the remainder had been trained in the 3rd Regiment, Victoria Rifles of Canada, the 5th Regiment, Royal Highlanders of Canada, or in other units of the Canadian Militia. Lieut. C. F. Ritchie, Assistant Adjutant, and Battalion Sergt.-Major E. G. Lidstone came from the Victoria Rifles; Hon. Lieut. and Quartermaster H. D. Campbell from the Royal Canadian Regiment; and Lieut. C. G. Greenshields, taken on the strength at a later date, joined after service in France as a private in the French Foreign Legion. Nineteen of the officers who sailed eventually with the unit from Montreal enrolled from the Victoria Rifles.

Meanwhile, recruiting at the armouries and at the barracks on Peel Street proceeded rapidly, and by mid-November the unit was practically at full strength. Changes in personnel were frequent, as undesirables were replaced by men better fitted, physically or mentally, for the work that lay ahead. An impression of the high physical standard thus attained can be gained from the following comparison:

Physical Requirements (Army Standard)	Average Physique (24th Battalion)
Height—5 ft. 3½ inches	Height—5 ft. 7¼ inches
Chest—34 inches	Chest—37 inches

As has been stated, recruits were drawn from all walks of life; they came, too, from widely scattered parts of His Majesty's Homeland and Overseas Dominions. In order of number, the recruits claimed the following as the countries of their birth:

England	Wales	India	New Zealand
Canada	Newfoundland	Egypt	Australia
Scotland	Trinidad	Br. Guiana	Bahamas
Ireland	Jamaica	South Africa	Grenada
		Barbados	

The United States of America does not appear in the list compiled and published at the time, as, owing to the declaration of neutrality by President Wilson, such inclusion was considered inadvisable, but a number of

American citizens joined the 24th Battalion and served in France. On one occasion, a party of American soldiers in uniform appeared at the Peel Street Barracks and, presenting certificates of honourable discharge from the forces of the United States, asked to be taken on the strength. When told that the uniform they wore prevented such action, they disappeared, returning an hour later in ill-fitting clothes, purchased in a second-hand shop on Craig Street. No embarrassing questions were asked the oddly attired civilians and all, taking the service oath of loyalty to the King, were enrolled in the ranks of the Battalion.

The early days of the 24th Battalion's existence in Montreal were marked by news from the front which impressed upon all ranks, and upon the people of the city, the measure of sacrifice that participation in the Great War would involve. November 12th was the 100th day of the war; and on the 13th it was announced that casualties in the British Army had reached a total of 57,000. On the following day, the cables brought news that Field Marshal Earl Roberts of Kandahar, V.C., had died while visiting troops of the Indian Army in France. Somehow, the two announcements deepened the impression of bitter war ahead. Lord Roberts was not killed by enemy action; nevertheless his passing stimulated recruiting and affected the Nation profoundly. He, almost alone for a time, had believed unwaveringly that Germany would one day make war on the British Empire; and he died with German guns sounding from the distance in his ears.

A few weeks after the news of Lord Roberts's death was received, the 24th Battalion paraded on the Champ de Mars for inspection by the Canadian Minister of Militia and Defence, Major-General the Honourable Sam Hughes; and again, on December 7th, before the Prime Minister of the Dominion, the Right Honourable Sir Robert Borden. So far as incident goes, there was nothing on these occasions to distinguish them in the minds of officers and men from many reviews that followed, but they were the first in the Battalion's history and are remembered in consequence. The same applies to the first church parade of the Battalion on December

Changing the Guard at the Peel Street Barracks, 1914.

13th, when the unit attended service in the Church of St. James the Apostle. Few will forget the singing of the opening hymn, *Fight the Good Fight*, the solemn prayers for King and Empire, the short soldierly sermon, and the beautiful recessional hymn, *Soldiers Who Are Christ's Below*.

The earnestness of this service, more particularly in the invocation of Divine protection for the soldiers and sailors on active duty, was deepened by news from France, where the "Old Contemptibles" of the original British Expeditionary Force had been locked in battle with superior forces of the enemy. Ypres, after a long interval, was again a name familiar to British ears, and the agony of the Salient, destined to last until 1918, had begun. Despatches had also reported activity at sea, and from the far-off Falkland Islands had come news that British battle-cruisers, avenging the loss of H.M. Ships *Good Hope* and *Monmouth* in the Battle of Coronel, had destroyed the fleet of the German Admiral, Graf von Spee.

Four days after the service in the Church of St. James the Apostle, the Battalion was inspected on the Champ de Mars by Field Marshal His Royal Highness the Duke of Connaught, Governor-General of Canada, who later became the Battalion's Honorary Colonel. That night His Royal Highness honoured Lieut.-Col. Gunn and the officers of the Battalion by dining at the first formal assembling of the Officers' Mess. After the toast to the King, Lieut.-Col. Gunn proposed the health of the guest of honour and the Duke of Connaught, in reply, raised his glass to the success of the Victoria Rifles.

On the day of His Royal Highness's inspection, Lieut.-Col. Gunn received orders to reorganize the Battalion in accordance with the 4-company system adopted by the British Army. Each company was made up of four platoons, each 60 strong, the personnel of these, plus the Headquarters staff, giving the unit a total strength of 1,112 all ranks. The 24th Battalion was one of the first in Canada to effect the reorganization which this new system required, all the necessary formalities and transfers being completed by December 21st.

Christmas, 1914, and New Year's Day, 1915, passed without unusual incident, and the Battalion settled down to a winter of hard training. Organized field sports, as a relief from work, were impossible owing to the season, but boxing was popular and at a Garrison Tournament, held on January 30th, under the auspices of the Montreal Amateur Athletic Association, the 24th Battalion entries swept the lists, defeating their opponents at all weights and revealing marked superiority.

Despite the time of year and the consequent weather, the Battalion drilled in the open regularly and carried out manoeuvres on several occasions, with Mount Royal City as the scene of operations. Field kitchens, presented to the unit by Basil Magor, Esq., of Hamilton, Ontario, accompanied the troops on these occasions and gave good service. Incidentally, the kitchens went eventually to France with the Battalion and proved equal to all that the hardships of the campaign demanded. Band instruments, presented to the Battalion at this time, proved most valuable, and socks, scarves, and wristlets, knitted and presented by the Ladies' Committee, helped the troops in the cold weather that prevailed.

By this time, the Battalion had reached a high level of attainment in drill and discipline. Guards were mounted each day at the barracks and the accompanying ceremonial, carried out in a manner that would have reflected no discredit on any unit in the Army, drew hundreds of spectators. As an incentive, Major Hill inspected the guard each day and awarded "the C.O.'s stick" to the man who seemed the smartest in appearance and drill. The "stick," though existing in imagination only, gained a day's leave for the man who won it and was eagerly sought, the guard, in consequence, presenting an appearance well up to the standard Lieut.-Col. Gunn desired.

On February 10, 1915, Major-General the Honourable Sam Hughes dined in the Officers' Mess; and on the 13th the unit was inspected on Fletcher's Field by Major-General F. L. Lessard. Conditions underfoot hampered the men on this occasion and hundreds of rubber overshoes were lost in deep mud and slush, but the Inspector-General ignored the trying circumstances and inspected most carefully, afterwards complimenting officers and men on many aspects of their work, but pointing out, quite bluntly, where improvement was required. Taking

His Royal Highness the Duke of Connaught, Honorary Colonel, Victoria Rifles of Canada, inspecting the 24th Battalion on the Champ de Mars.

Major-General Lessard's comments in the spirit in which they were intended, the Battalion worked hard in the following weeks to reach a maximum level of efficiency. Manoeuvres were held, and on one occasion, in order that subordinates might benefit from the experience, all officers fell out, leaving command of the unit to the N.C.O.'s. Under the leadership of Battalion Sergt.-Major Lidstone, the N.C.O.'s handled the unit creditably and revealed entire fitness for the responsibility with which they had been entrusted.

As a means of testing the men's endurance and training them in quick movement, platoon races around Mount Royal were held. Platoons in full marching order would start simultaneously from Peel Street, one proceeding by way of Côte des Neiges Road and the other in the opposite direction, by way of Park Avenue. Points were scored according to the condition in which the platoons returned to barracks, with a heavy adverse score for each man late, or forced to drop out.

On the whole, the Peel Street Barracks provided good accommodation for the men. Officers slept at home, with the exception of those on duty, but reported at 6 o'clock each morning for physical training in the Y.M.C.A. building on Drummond Street. Food for the men was cooked and served in the barracks and was usually satisfactory. There was, however, the day when, at the bottom of a vast soup cauldron, someone found the body of the barracks cat. A few men were promptly sick, but knowledge of the cat's misadventure was withheld from the majority and no serious trouble resulted.

Early in March the Battalion was called upon to provide escort and a firing party for the body of Private Haynes, who had died of illness. At a later date, firing parties for the fallen were to become all too familiar a duty, but this was the first military funeral that many of the men had seen and the ceremony left an impression deeper, perhaps, than most of those that followed.

By this time it was known in Canada that the 1st Canadian Division was in France and had been in action with the enemy. Knowledge of the transfer of the 1st Division from England stimulated the 2nd Division and all ranks worked energetically, with the assurance that the time of leaving Canada for overseas was drawing near. In the 24th Battalion, the companies drilled faithfully; the signallers attempted to speed the delivery and reception of their messages; the officers strove at the tasks assigned to them; and all ranks sought earnestly to improve the Battalion's work. As a result, when the unit paraded for inspection by its Honorary Colonel, the Duke of Connaught, on March 23rd, its performance and bearing left little to be desired.

On Saturday, April 24, 1915, all Canada was stirred by news that the 1st Canadian Division had been heavily engaged near St. Julien in the Ypres Salient and, in a battle against odds, in most difficult circumstances, had maintained the finest traditions of the British Army. Sir John French, Commander-in-Chief of His Majesty's Forces in France and Flanders, reported that the Canadian Division had "saved the situation," the War Office adding the comment that "heavy casualties had been incurred."

For twenty-four hours, or a little more, Canada rejoiced in the glory of her sons, with faint appreciation of what the term "heavy casualties" implied. Monday, however, brought partial realization, when newspapers published long lists of killed and wounded. Canada's time of trial had come, and, on each succeeding day, as many names were added to those originally published, the War as a fascinating event disappeared forever, and war, as it must always be, saddened the hearts of the people.

Soon after news of the battle at Ypres was received, the 24th Battalion began to prepare for transfer overseas. No one knew when the order to move would arrive, but all in the Battalion realized that its coming would not be delayed much longer. The citizens shared the Battalion's belief, and when the unit paraded to St. Andrew's Presbyterian Church, Westmount, on May 9th, it was known that the service was the last the Battalion would attend in Montreal. After the singing of the opening hymn, *O God, Our Help in Ages Past*, Hon. Capt. the Reverend A. P. Shatford preached the sermon and the Scripture Lesson was read by the Reverend A. B. McLeod. All then joined in singing *Onward, Christian Soldiers*, followed by *God Save the King*.

As expected, the service in St. Andrew's Church marked the 24th Battalion's last public appearance before proceeding overseas. All day on May 10th, officers and men were engaged in the tasks occasioned by receipt of definite orders that the unit would embark on H.M. Transport *Cameronia* and sail at dawn on May 11th for a destination, unannounced at the time, but known to be Shorncliffe, England.

In order that the embarkation might be effected in an orderly manner, Capt. R. O. Alexander, the Adjutant, prepared careful embarkation orders. These were approved by Lieut.-Col. Gunn and issued, but all hope of carrying them out in detail was ruined by the determination of the citizens of Montreal to bid the Battalion a memorable farewell. In thousands, people crowded the streets leading to the docks and, when the men emerged from the Peel Street barracks, orderly progress was impossible. Realizing that the situation had passed beyond control and that a march in formation was impossible, Lieut.-Col. Gunn ordered the men to follow and, accompanied by Major-General Sam Hughes, who had come to Montreal to bid the unit farewell, led the way to the wharf.

Progress was difficult, but officers and other ranks, some in a semblance of formation, some without, made their way as best they could to the wharf. A few men were swallowed up in the crowd and failed to reach the dock, but these were sent to Quebec by train and rejoined the Battalion when the *Cameronia* docked there on the following day. It was seldom, even in the stirring days of the War, that Montreal witnessed scenes of emotion such as those which bade farewell to the 24th Battalion, Victoria Rifles of Canada. News of the Second Battle of Ypres had revealed what the men must endure when they reached the front; and news of the sinking of the *Lusitania* drew attention to the danger they must traverse on the way. Accordingly, Montreal gave rein to emotion and the men of the 24th left the city with the echo of a fervent ovation thundering in their ears.

III

With regard to the voyage to England of the S.S. *Cameronia*, bearing the 24th Battalion, Victoria Rifles of Canada, not a great deal need be said. All ranks enjoyed the run in beautiful weather down the St. Lawrence to Quebec, where, in addition to the few men who had been left behind in Montreal, the ship embarked about one hundred soldiers from Bermuda. These, with some 40 officers of the Royal Army Medical Corps, a Remount Corps, and the 42 officers and 1,082 men of the 24th, filled the ship's accommodation. Sir Montague Allan, Honorary Colonel of the 5th Regiment, Royal Highlanders of Canada, also travelled on the vessel.

After a short stay in Quebec, during which no troops were allowed ashore, the *Cameronia* proceeded downstream and soon the long roll of the Gulf took toll of officers and men alike. Many were sick for days, a fair estimate of the total being provided by "A" Coy., which, at roll call on the morning of May 14th, mustered 130 men, instead of 261. The remainder were too sick to stand on their feet.

On May 16th a test alarm brought all troops on the *Cameronia* to the life boats. The time taken to assemble was checked and found to be satisfactory. Two days later, as the ship entered the zone of enemy submarine activity, the Chaplain, Hon. Capt. A. P. Shatford, conducted a service of intercession for Divine protection, marked by the fine playing of the 24th band and by two solo numbers, sung by Battalion Sergt.-Major E. G. Lidstone and Sergt.-Major A. F. Crichton.

On entering the submarine zone, four machine-guns of the 24th Battalion were mounted on the *Cameronia's* boat deck, and armed lookouts were stationed at points of vantage. Just what service these were expected to render in the event of submarine attack is not clear in retrospect, nor was the point convincingly settled at the time. Letters written on the *Cameronia* state that the duty was regarded as slightly humorous, but was carried out as a result of orders from authorities qualified to decide whether the posting of parties was advisable, or not. The guards were concealed from view and, to deceive the eye at any possible periscope, a number of men were ordered to appear on deck in civilian attire.

Fog settled around the *Cameronia* as she approached the British Isles, and some anxiety was manifest as the ship circled about without apparent cause. At 3.15 o'clock on the afternoon of May 19th, however, a destroyer appeared dramatically out of the mist, and at 5 o'clock, when the fog lifted, the troops realized with satisfaction that the Royal Navy had assumed responsibility for their care. Though approximately three hundred miles from shore, two destroyers were escorting them to their unknown destination. Morning on May 20th revealed that Devonport was the harbour chosen for disembarkation, and by 7.30 o'clock the *Cameronia* had been warped to her pier. On deck the band of the 24th Battalion played the airs of Canada; and from the shore cheering gave the troops from the Dominion a welcome. Plymouth and Devonport, stirred by the gallant behaviour of the 1st Canadian Division at Ypres, welcomed all with the badge of the Maple Leaf as their emblem.

IV

When the *Cameronia* docked at Devonport, the men of the 24th Battalion disembarked with little delay and boarded two trains, which conveyed them, by way of London, to Sandling, in Kent. At all stations and wherever the trains passed through populated districts, cheering assured the troops of England's welcome. In return, the men waved greetings and, where children were encountered, scattered Canadian pennies as souvenirs. Late at night both trains reached Westenhanger Station, whence the troops marched about three miles to East Sandling Camp, where hut billets had been prepared. Settling down in camp, about four miles from Shorncliffe and six miles from Folkestone, the Battalion soon resumed the training interrupted by the voyage from Montreal. Accommodation was good and the men, accustomed by this time to military life and discipline, adapted themselves to camp routine without difficulty.

Soon after the Battalion arrived, the 2nd Canadian Division came officially into existence. On May 24,

1915, Col. Denison issued the first Divisional Standing Orders; and on the 25th Major-General S. B. Steele, C.B., M.V.O., assumed command. The 24th Battalion, Victoria Rifles of Canada, commanded by Lieut.-Col. J. A. Gunn, was confirmed in its position as a unit of the 5th Canadian Infantry Brigade, commanded first by Colonel J. P. Landry, and later by Brigadier-General David Watson, previously commanding officer of the 2nd Infantry Battalion, 1st Canadian Division. Brigadier-General Watson had been promoted following distinguished service in the Second Battle of Ypres, and the 5th Brigade was fortunate in his appointment. In addition to the 24th Battalion, the Brigade included the 22nd (French-Canadian) Battalion, under Lieut.-Col. F. M. Gaudet; the 25th (Nova Scotia) Battalion, commanded by Lieut.-Col. G. A. LeCain; and the 26th (New Brunswick) Battalion, under Lieut.-Col. J. L. McAvity.

At the time when Major-General Steele assumed command, the troops were deeply interested in Italy's declaration of war on Austria-Hungary. Rumours spread —as rumours will—that the Division, without further ado, would be despatched to the Italian front to co-operate in a drive through Austria into the heart of Germany. Few believed this report, but it offered a stimulating subject of conversation and spread accordingly. A few days later, detailed reports of heavy fighting by Australian and New Zealand troops at Gallipoli shifted the 2nd Canadian Division's imaginary destination further east, but the majority of the men rejected this suggestion too, and maintained the belief that they were destined to fight in France. Training continued along lines that indicated the Western Front, and the presence in France of the 1st Canadian Division made it almost certain that the 2nd Division would see action on French soil.

Training of the 2nd Division, begun when the formation received official recognition, continued throughout June and July. The weather was ideal; rifle ranges at Hythe were in action from 5 o'clock in the morning until 7 o'clock at night; machine-gun courses were inaugurated; practices and drills occurred at all hours of the day; and the Division acquired a reputation for thoroughness and efficiency. Authorities expressed the opinion that the

Division would make a fine partner for the 1st Canadian Division in France and, desiring no higher praise, the men of the 2nd Division worked to attain the utmost efficiency possible. In the 24th Battalion, few will forget "Agony Hill," outside the camp, whose steep slope was used over and over to test the endurance and mobility of the companies and platoons when loaded with full equipment.

About this time the Battalion was ordered to send 2 officers and 3 other ranks to the British Army School of Musketry at Hythe. Capt. B. H. T. MacKenzie, Lieut. M. Laing, Sergt. L. S. Cook, Sergt. R. H. Lamb, and Corp. H. Fraser were despatched and acquitted themselves well. In examinations and tests in competition with many units of the Army, the 24th Battalion entries passed with credit, Sergt. Lamb scoring a "D" mark, equalled only by one other soldier from the 2nd Canadian Division and by three from units of the Imperial Army.

Early in June, the training of officers suffered slightly when Major J. A. Ross developed scarlet fever and was moved to hospital. Eight officers, who had shared a hut with him, were quarantined, but no sign of the infection having spread appeared, and before long the quarantine was lifted.

On August 4, 1915, the first anniversary of Great Britain's entry into the war, evidence of hard and successful training was shown when the Division was reviewed by the Secretary of State for the Colonies, the Right Honourable A. Bonar Law, who was accompanied by Major-General the Honourable Sir Sam Hughes, K.C.B. Lightning flashed during the inspection and rain soaked the men, but their bearing and demeanour were of a high order and the march past clearly revealed their discipline.

Soon after the review, the Division carried out manoeuvres under service conditions, operations being directed by Major-General R. E. W. Turner, V.C., formerly General Officer Commanding the 3rd Infantry Brigade of the 1st Canadian Division, who had succeeded to the command of the 2nd Canadian Division on the appointment of Major-General Steele to command reserve troops of the Canadian Expeditionary Force in the

Shorncliffe area. Through the manoeuvres conducted under Major-General Turner's command, officers and men of the 24th Battalion, and their comrades in other units of the Division, learned much regarding conditions in France and the outstanding features of trench warfare. Attack and defence of positions were practised, bayonet fighting was taught, and attention was paid to the rapid digging of cover trenches, when imaginary fire brought assaults to a standstill.

In these operations Lieut.-Col. Gunn and his officers took part. A few injuries to officers and men occurred, but these were not serious and were treated on the spot by Capt. J. S. Jenkins, the Battalion Medical Officer. Live ammunition was issued to the men on one occasion when Zeppelins raided England, but no opportunity to use it offered, though a number of the men caught sight of one of the airships returning at a great height to her base after bombing London.

Late in August it was announced that, on September 2nd, His Majesty the King would inspect the Division before its departure for France. A marked distinction fell to the 24th Battalion on this occasion when, from all battalions of the Division, the unit was chosen to provide the guard of honour for His Majesty's reception. This guard of 100 men, under Capt. R. K. Robertson, Lieut. H. C. Kennedy, Sergt. J. W. Worthington, and Sergt. R. H. Lamb, was inspected by the King, who was accompanied by Field Marshal Earl Kitchener of Khartoum, British Secretary of State for War. After inspecting the guard at the wayside station where he detrained, His Majesty proceeded to Marlborough Grounds, where the Division was awaiting him. Under dark and lowering skies, the King inspected with care, being watched with interest by a large number of civilians, and by many wounded soldiers and nursing sisters from hospitals close at hand. At the conclusion of the march past, His Majesty congratulated Major-General Turner on the Division's excellent appearance.

Following the royal inspection of the 2nd Canadian Division, the 24th Battalion spent ten days in sports, completing equipment, drawing stores, and making final preparations for the move to France. All ranks believed that the time in England was drawing to a close, nor was their belief contradicted in fact, for, not long after the King's farewell, orders were received to embark. Marching to Folkestone on the night of September 15th, the Battalion boarded the S.S. *Queen* and sailed for Boulogne. Many of the men were destined never to set foot on British soil again. Knowledge that this must be so was shared by all, but none could read the future, and high spirits prevailed. At last, after a year of training, the men of the 24th Battalion, Victoria Rifles of Canada, were to prove their mettle in action. No one who knew how faithfully they had trained could doubt that in the trial which lay ahead they would maintain the reputation already gained by Canadian troops in France. Determined that this should be done, cost what it might, the men of the Battalion felt the engines of the *Queen* revolve and realized with a thrill of excitement that England had been left behind.

24th Battalion, Victoria Rifles of Canada, Officers' Roll—(September 15, 1915)

HEADQUARTERS

Commanding Officer	LIEUT.-COL. J. A. GUNN
Second-in-Command	MAJOR C. H. HILL
Adjutant	CAPT. C. F. RITCHIE
Machine-Gun Officer	LIEUT. S. W. WATSON
Signalling Officer	LIEUT. A. G. WOOLSEY
Transport Officer	LIEUT. H. A. MURRAY
Quartermaster	HON. CAPT. H. D. CAMPBELL
Paymaster	CAPT. G. F. FURLONG
Y.M.C.A. Officer	HON. CAPT. C. G. ARMOUR
Medical Officer	CAPT. J. S. JENKINS

COMPANY COMMANDERS

MAJOR C. B. PARR	MAJOR E. O. MCMURTRY
MAJOR R. O. ALEXANDER	MAJOR J. A. ROSS

COMPANY SECONDS-IN-COMMAND

CAPT. B. H. T. MACKENZIE	CAPT. F. T. BOWN
CAPT. R. K. ROBERTSON	CAPT. R. D. SUTHERLAND

SUBALTERNS

Lieut. D. H. Beckett
Lieut. W. D. Chambers
Lieut. H. G. Davidson
Lieut. V. E. Duclos
Lieut. C. G. Greenshields
Lieut. P. L. Hall
Lieut. J. C. Heaton
Lieut. H. D. Kingstone

Lieut. Murdoch Laing
Lieut. B. H. Languedoc
Lieut. A. L. S. Mills
Lieut. G. R. Robertson
Lieut. D. C. Skinner
Lieut. A. L. Walker
Lieut. W. R. Hastings
Lieut. C. S. B. White

CHAPTER II

TRENCH WARFARE ON THE KEMMEL FRONT

I

After sailing from Folkestone at approximately 10 o'clock on the night of September 15, 1915, the S.S. *Queen* proceeded directly across the Channel to Boulogne. No incident marked the journey, and those officers and other ranks of the 24th Battalion whose duties permitted an appearance on deck enjoyed the soft breezes of the late summer night and remarked upon the unusual brilliance of the stars. Disembarking soon after the ship docked in Boulogne, the Battalion marched uphill to Osterhove Rest Camp, where billets had been provided. Loaded down with equipment, weighing 60 lbs. or more apiece, the men found that the long hill to the camp tested their marching ability severely, but, stimulated by realization that French soil lay beneath their feet at last, few allowed the fatigue they felt to appear.

After a stay of less than twenty-four hours in the rest camp, marked only by the mounting of guards and routine, the Battalion paraded at 12.10 a.m. on September 17th, marched to Pont au Briques railway station, and there entrained for the front. Most of the men found accommodation in the famous "40 hommes 8 chevaux" French box-cars; others rode in open trucks with the Battalion Transport. Envied at first, the men in the open cars were the objects of joyous derision when, as the train puffed through a long series of tunnels, dense smoke half choked and blinded them.

In the box-cars, few men of the Battalion were able to sleep that night, nor was rest awaiting them when the train reached St. Omer at 7 o'clock in the morning. Instead, the unit was ordered to march to Hazebrouck forthwith. Proceeding, in accordance with these orders, the Battalion marched a few miles, halted for breakfast, resumed the march, halted for a mid-day meal, then marched the remainder of the 15-mile way. Realizing that the hard and unfamiliar cobbles of the French highway inflicted appreciable hardship upon men carrying a heavy load under a hot sun, Lieut.-Col. Gunn ordered the bandsmen to unload their instruments from the Transport wagons and play the Battalion over the last few miles of the road. Accordingly, to the tune of *The Victoria Rifles March*, the men swung in to Hazebrouck.

Before the unit reached the town, word spread that billets in Hazebrouck Hospital would be available for all ranks. Clean, hospital wards were implied and optimists dreamed of attendants equally attractive; but fancy proved misleading and the roofless "hospital," under construction when war broke out, was found to possess walls, a basement, and all the benefits of adequate fresh air.

At Hazebrouck, the 24th Battalion remained for four days, parading for Divine Service at 9 o'clock on the morning of Sunday, September 19th; and again at 4 o'clock that afternoon for inspection by Lieut.-General Sir E. A. H. Alderson, formerly Commander of the 1st Canadian Division, who, upon its formation, had assumed command of the Canadian Corps. General Alderson, who was accompanied by Major-General A. W. Currie, Major-General R. E. W. Turner, and His Royal Highness Prince Arthur of Connaught, inspected carefully and, addressing the men from a gun limber, assured them that they would see action without appreciable delay.

Two days after General Alderson's inspection, the Battalion paraded in Hazebrouck and marched to bivouacs not far from Bailleul. Proceeding on September 22nd, the unit marched to Locre, halting on the Bailleul-Locre Road when the 14th Battalion, Royal Montreal Regiment, of the 1st Canadian Division, was encountered. As the 14th Battalion included officers and men from the old 3rd Regiment, Victoria Rifles of Canada, it shared tradition with the 24th and the personnel of each unit had many friends in the other's ranks. Accordingly, greetings were exchanged and the men of the 14th welcomed their comrades of the 24th to France.

From Locre "A" Coy. of the 24th Battalion, under Major C. B. Parr, proceeded to Siege Farm and there remained until September 28th, acting as support to the battalions in the front line. Before rejoining the main body of the Battalion, a party of 300 men of "A" Coy., under Lieuts. A. L. S. Mills, D. H. Beckett, J. C. Heaton, and P. L. Hall, was detailed to carry a large number of "smoke bags" to the battalions of the 5th Canadian Infantry Brigade which had preceded the 24th Battalion into the front line. No casualties occurred in the Victoria Rifles' carrying party, but the men obtained a vivid impression of how the line appeared at night and how British and German flares, rising at irregular intervals, flooded No Man's Land with the brilliance and contrasting shadows of their unearthly light.

On the night when the men of the 24th Battalion carried the smoke bags forward, the front of the British Army in France was tingling with suspense. To the south, bombardment of the German line had been in progress for days; and reports of troop concentrations had spread, as such news will. Action seemed imminent; and hope for success on a major scale ran high. On the morning of September 25th the Battle of Loos began, and early reports encouraged the belief that substantial success had been attained; but before long it became clear that, though gallantry of a high order had been shown and some ground captured, Loos was not to rank as a British victory, but as a name made tragic by the heavy losses of severe defeat. By October 16th, in all phases of the engagement, 50,000 British officers and other ranks had fallen, killed or wounded, a ratio, as compared with enemy losses, of approximately 2 to 1.

II

While the British First Army was engaged to the south in the Battle of Loos, the 24th Battalion, Victoria Rifles of Canada, was carrying out, in the Mont Kemmel Sector, its first series of trench tours in the front line. After tests of gas helmets and equipment, and after the Commanding Officer, the Adjutant, and a group of company officers had spent a night in the front line to gain experience, the Battalion, less "A" Coy., paraded at 6 p.m. on September 28th and marched to relieve the 25th Battalion in the right sector of the 5th Canadian Infantry Brigade frontage. "A" Coy., from support positions at Siege Farm, proceeded to the front line in small parties and rejoined the Battalion there.

Lieut.-Col. Gunn's order for the move instructed "B" Coy., under Major R. O. Alexander, "C" Coy., under Major E. O. McMurtry, "D" Coy., under Major J. A. Ross, Battalion Headquarters, the Bombers, and Transport to parade for the 4-mile march opposite Locre church at 5.50 p.m. A grim touch was provided as the troops fell in, by the band of another unit playing the *Dead March* at a military funeral in the churchyard nearby. The significance of the omen was not lost by the men of the 24th, but, as they received the order to march, the funeral ended and the bandsmen played them away to the stirring strains of *The Victoria Rifles March*.

Rain was falling when the Battalion reached the front line, nevertheless Lieut.-Col. Gunn established his Headquarters in Rossignol Estaminet according to schedule, and at 9 p.m. the companies reported relief of the 25th Battalion complete in trenches G.4 to J.10 on the western slopes of Wytschaete hill. In view of the fact that the 24th Battalion companies had not been given a tour in the line with experienced battalions, as was the custom, the manner in which the relief was carried out reflected great credit on the two battalions concerned.

As a whole, the Battalion's first night in the trenches passed without noteworthy incident. Officers and men did not settle down with the promptness that distinguishes the veteran; indeed there were minor alarms as sentries, peering into the night, saw, or thought they saw, something moving in No Man's Land. Flares rose frequently, German machine-guns were active, and rifle fire occasionally crackled from the enemy parapet as well as from that of the 24th, but day dawned without casualties in the Battalion having been suffered.

For a time on September 29th, the good fortune continued. Snipers were active, and the men of the 24th retaliated by smashing a number of enemy trench periscopes and by dispersing a German working party sighted

OFFICERS WHO CROSSED TO FRANCE WITH THE BATTALION, SEPTEMBER 15, 1915.

Front row—left to right: Lieut. P. L. Hall, Lieut. A. L. Walker, Lieut. C. S. B. White, Lieut. D. H. Beckett, Lieut. W. D. Chambers. *2nd row*: Lieut. H. D. Kingstone, Capt. R. K. Robertson, Capt. D. H. Sutherland, Major C. B. Parr, Major R. O. Alexander, Major C. H. Hill, Lieut.-Col. J. A. Gunn, Capt. C. F. Ritchie, Major E. O. McMurtry, Major J. A. Ross, Capt. F. T. Bown, Capt. B. H. T. MacKenzie. *3rd row*: Hon. Capt. H. D. Campbell, Lieut. D. C. Skinner, Capt. J. S. Jenkins, Lieut. H. A. Murray, Lieut. W. R. Hastings, Lieut. H. C. Kennedy, Hon. Capt. C. G. Armour, Lieut. Murdoch Laing, Lieut. I. R. R. MacNaughton, Lieut. A. L. S. Mills, Lieut. V. E. Duclos, Lieut. J. C. Heaton, Lieut. C. G. Greenshields, Lieut. A. G. Woolsey, Lieut. H. G. Davidson. *Top row*: Capt. G. F. Furlong, Lieut. G. R. Robertson.

from Trench J.2. Rations were carried up to the line and in this work the unit suffered its first casualty, Private J. S. McBride, of No. 12 Platoon, being struck in the arm by machine-gun fire.

Early in the day the Battalion was visited by Major-General R. E. W. Turner, the Divisional Commander, and Brigadier-General David Watson, G.O.C. the Brigade. Some time later enemy artillery shelled the line, and at 10 p.m. guns again bombarded. Rifle fire was added, and Corporal B. M. Paterson, who was firing in reply, received a bullet in the head, injuring him so severely that he died of the wound not long after.

The roll of casualties thus begun mounted steadily in the days that followed. Private W. A. Ward of "B" Coy. was shot through the heart while on a working party; Private E. A. Clift was struck and died a quarter hour later; and Private C. W. Price of "C" Coy. was also killed. A number of others were wounded, most of the casualties occurring on October 1st, when enemy artillery was unusually active.

From letters and diaries written by officers and men of the 24th Battalion during this first tour of the unit in the line, it would seem that rats created a deep impression. Trench rats abounded; rats, as a German soldier has observed, "with shocking, evil faces and long nude tails," and the men of the 24th found no pleasure in their company. None complained, however, and officers, censoring letters, were struck by the men's determination to assure their families and friends that life in the trenches was far from disagreeable.

On the night of October 4th, after gaining invaluable experience from the 6-day tour in the front line, the 24th Battalion was relieved by the 25th Battalion and marched back to Locre, taking over Brigade Reserve billets, which were occupied until the night of October 10th. Though the Battalion as a whole was in billets for six days, the time was by no means devoid of incident. During grenade practice on October 7th, Lieut. V. E. Duclos and eight other ranks were injured by the premature explosion of a bomb. Lieut. Duclos' injury was not severe, but several of the other ranks were badly wounded.

More serious was the misadventure which befell a working party in J.10 Trench on the afternoon of October 8th. This party, under Lieut. P. L. Hall, was engaged in trench construction and suffered sharply from the belated explosion of a "dud" shell. Private W. O. Roberts was struck in the stomach by a flying piece of shell; Private F. J. Smith's leg was torn from his body; and Sergeant G. G. R. Taylor received a shattering injury. All three died of their wounds, Private Roberts almost at once, Private Smith on the way back to hospital, and Sergt. Taylor not long thereafter. A party engaged on similar work on another occasion was also caught by enemy gunfire so severe that Brigadier-General Watson ordered the officer in command to abandon work and withdraw the party to safety. This was done, but not before the German fire had inflicted sharp losses.

On the night of October 10th, the Battalion paraded at Locre church and for the second time marched to relieve the 25th Battalion in the front line, "A", "C", and "D" Companies taking over the actual front and "B" Coy. occupying positions at Siege Farm. Rain fell heavily during the move and passage through waist-deep mud in Via Gellia Communication Trench was effected with great difficulty, but this circumstance had been foreseen and delayed the relief no longer than had been expected.

On taking over the front, the men of the 24th Battalion took over also the duty of keeping the line in a reasonable state of repair. Enemy action hampered this work, but rain effected the most serious damage, parapets and trench walls collapsing repeatedly under the lashing water of the autumn storms. Life in flooded dugouts and in trenches deep with liquid mud was far from agreeable, but the men faced the situation courageously and endured, without complaint, the added hardship provided at intervals by brisk German fire. As a result of enemy fire on October 11th, the Battalion suffered its first officer casualty through the wounding of Lieut. Murdoch Laing.

Another incident of this period occurred when three scouts of the Battalion, Corporal A. A. Ecclestone, Private A. F. Mott, and Private S. J. Bethune, carried out a patrol in No Man's Land, from in front of Trench

VIA GELLIA COMMUNICATION TRENCH.

THE STABLE AT SIEGE FARM.

*Sketches on the Kemmel Front.
Two Scenes Memorable in the
   Battalion's Story.*

H.3 to the left of the Petit Bois. At one point, the patrol approached to within a few feet of the German front line and was challenged by a sentry, who called a number of comrades to his section of trench. Receiving no answer to his challenge, the sentry opened fire, and two of the 24th Battalion scouts withdrew towards their own line. Private Mott, however, was able to remain in position and, when a number of the enemy had gathered, threw a bomb over the parapet. The bomb exploded and, from cries that followed, it would seem that casualties were inflicted. Heavy rifle fire was opened by the enemy, but Private Mott crawled away and, rejoining his companions, returned with them in safety to the Canadian lines.

Undoubtedly, the chief event of the six-day tour in the line occurred on the afternoon of October 13th, when the Battalion, in co-operation with the Lahore Divisional Artillery, carried out a demonstration to distract the enemy's attention from more serious operations to the south. Opening fire at 2 p.m., the Lahore guns cut the enemy wire and hammered the German front line. While this shelling lasted, the men of the 24th occupied "slit" shelters cut in the sides of the communication trenches. As soon as the shelling ceased, they were ordered, in the words of one participant, "to dash forward to the fire trench, hurl a number of phosphorus bombs in the general direction of Germany, open rapid fire under cover of the resulting smoke, maintain this for five minutes, then gallop back to the slits to see what the enemy would do about it."

Though official accounts describe the operation in more formal terms, this version gives an impression of the men's point of view. They did not take the affair altogether seriously, but they enjoyed it and worked hard to make their share in it an entire success. As the writer quoted above continues: "The excitement was intense, especially when the phosphorus from the bombs blew back on us, and with gas helmets on and the barrels of our Ross rifles red hot, we continued our rapid fire at the enemy trenches. Altogether, it was an interesting and not very dangerous experience for our newly-broken-in battalion."

Though the action was "not very dangerous" when compared with the Battalion's later experiences, it was not concluded without losses, Privates William Brown and Arthur Jones, of "A" Coy., being killed and some 14 men wounded when retaliatory shelling struck the Canadian line. Other casualties suffered during the tour included Capt. B. H. T. MacKenzie, wounded on October 14th, and Private Edward James, of "C" Coy., killed while on duty in Trench J.4. Reminder that other units had suffered in the area was given to a party under Major C. B. Parr and Lieut. H. D. Kingstone, which patrolled in No Man's Land one morning when fog obscured all distant observation. Lying where he had fallen nearly a year before, the party found the body of a captain of the 1st Battalion, Gordon Highlanders. In his pockets were a purse of sovereigns, and letters which, though faded, enabled the officers of the 24th to establish his identity and forward to his kin his property and the details of his death.

After six days in the line, the 24th Battalion was relieved by the 25th Battalion on the night of October 16th and withdrew to Locre, where, on the following morning, Divine Service was conducted by Hon. Capt. the Reverend A. P. Shatford, who, after a period of service elsewhere, had resumed duties as the Victoria Rifles' Chaplain.

From October 16th to 22nd, the Battalion remained in Locre, furnishing parties for work in the forward area, particularly in J.10 Trench, where Private George Whiteford was killed at 12.30 a.m. on October 20th. Private Sunta Gougersing (Gunga Singh), who stated in advance that he knew he must die that night, was also killed in J.10 Trench by a bullet which struck him in the stomach on the night of October 19th. By October 22nd, the first anniversary of the Battalion's formation, the roll of the unit's killed in France had reached a total of 12.

Marching from Locre on the night of October 22nd, the 24th Battalion relieved the 25th Battalion and began its third tour in the front line. The Battalion Diary states that the tour was "exceptionally quiet" and this is confirmed by private records, so far as enemy activity above ground is concerned. There was, however, the uncomfortable knowledge that the Germans were tunnelling somewhere underfoot. Listening posts reported unmistakable sounds of mining, and counter-action was promptly begun.

On October 23rd, a party from "B" Coy., under Major R. O. Alexander, carried out a reconnaissance in the Canadian wire and exchanged shots with a German party, engaged on a similar mission. At one point, the Canadian party found a number of dead bodies of men of the Gordon Highlanders, again proving that the area had seen hard fighting in the past.

Some days later, at 1 o'clock on the morning of October 26th, a gas alarm sounded and the Battalion stood to. The enemy, however, took no action, which is not surprising, as marsh gas, which had overwhelmed a listening post, was responsible for the alarm. The next afternoon, the men of the 24th Battalion were ordered into the protection slits at 1.45 o'clock, as His Majesty the King was on Kemmel Hill, whence, it was said, he would witness an artillery demonstration against the enemy front line, but rain at 2 p.m. and low visibility forced this programme to be cancelled. No further incident marked the remainder of the tour, which ended on the night of October 28th, when the Battalion was relieved and marched back to Locre.

In its principal features, the month of November, 1915, so far as the 24th Battalion was concerned, differed in no essential from October. Three times the unit moved forward from Locre to take over Trenches G.4 to J.11, relieving the 25th Battalion, which, in turn, relieved the 24th at six-day intervals. Mud and rain provide a theme for letters and diaries covering the period, the resulting conditions making a deeper impression than all efforts of the enemy. The Germans were often active, but the mud and water of the front line provided hardship in comparison to which the suffering through enemy action seemed almost negligible.

On the night of November 2nd, Lieut.-Col. Gunn and his officers entertained a number of guests in the Officers' Mess at a dinner to celebrate completion of the Battalion's first year of existence. The following evening, the unit marched to relieve the 25th Battalion in the line and, on the way forward, realized what the late autumn rains had accomplished. In Via Gellia Communication Trench, men from an Imperial Army unit were found stuck fast in the waist-deep mud. Rescue was effected, but soon the men of the 24th were in equal difficulty. Capt. F. T. Bown sank to the shoulders at one point; Bugler R. E. Mundy sank similarly at another; and a third man, sinking fast, was released only by the use of force sufficient to tear the muscles of his thigh. Progress in such circumstances was slow and exhausting, but at last the line was reached and relief of the 25th Battalion completed.

In the front line, conditions were almost as bad, many trenches being impassable and a number of the Battalion posts being attainable only by proceeding overland. To get rations to these posts after dark was impossible and some of the men lived for days on tins of bully beef, which someone had left behind months previously. Throughout the six days of the tour, more time was spent in building parapets, revetting, and pumping water than in the usual details of trench routine. The enemy was similarly engaged, but his artillery shelled at intervals and his trench mortars were active. Corp. Albert Metzger was wounded by a sniper who fired from a tree in the Petit Bois on November 7th; and on the 8th Private C. J. Diver, of No. 5 Platoon, was struck in the head and fatally injured.

Casualties in the line, or while detachments of the Battalion served on working parties, mounted steadily as the month progressed, Lieut. C. G. Greenshields being wounded, and among the killed being Private R. C. W. Harris, who fell while carrying a wounded man to safety, Privates Brian Hards, T. J. Smyth, and W. D. MacDonald, and Lance-Sergt. E. E. Barnes, of "D" Coy., who was sighted by a sniper and killed by a bullet in the head. Patrols were frequent at this time, every officer of the Battalion, on one or more occasions, leaving the Canadian line and reconnoitring in No Man's Land. Capt. F. T. Bown presented a valuable report as a result of one patrol, and other parties found more evidence of the heavy fighting the front had witnessed nearly a year before. The bodies of men belonging to the 1st and 3rd Battalions of the Gordon Highlanders, the London Scottish, and the Liverpool Scottish were discovered, discs establishing their identity and the faded record in their pay books showing to within a week or two the date on which they died. A crimson sunrise, white hoar-frost upon the ground, and mist shrouding the movements of the Battalion's night patrols, marked the morning on which these bodies were found.

December 1, 1915, found the 24th Battalion, Victoria Rifles of Canada, carrying out a routine tour in the front line. Private A. Ste. Marie, of "A" Coy.'s Signal Section, was killed in Trench H.2 on this date and Private J. Syder, of "B" Coy., a few days later. Meanwhile, on the night of December 3rd, Lieut. A. L. S. Mills and two other ranks carried out a patrol and brought back valuable information regarding the enemy wire. Approaching close to the German line at one point, the party was challenged and fired upon, but hid until the alarm subsided and then, after securing the information desired, moved back in safety to the Battalion lines.

Returning to the front on December 12th, after a period in billets during which parties were supplied constantly for work in the forward areas, the companies of the 24th Battalion, commanded as during previous tours by Majors C. B. Parr, R. O. Alexander, E. O. McMurtry, and J. A. Ross, settled down for a six-day tour. Shelling, fairly heavy when the tour began, increased as the days passed, adding inevitably to the Battalion's roll of killed and wounded. Snipers became troublesome too, and Corporal J. J. Shannon, of the Machine-Gun Section, was wounded on December 16th when on duty in Trench K.1. Capt. J. S. Jenkins, the Battalion Medical Officer, dressed a gaping wound in the corporal's neck, but no human skill could avail and the wounded man died of the injury.

Even more promptly fatal was the wound received at 2.30 o'clock on the morning of December 17th by Private O. O'Keefe, who, with a party under command of Lieut. P. L. Hall, was in No Man's Land repairing the Battalion's barbed wire. Just when work in front of Trench J.3 had been completed, fire was opened on the party by the enemy, and Private O'Keefe fell with a bullet in the head.

Two days after this event, while the Battalion was in billets at Locre, an alarm sounded at 7.30 o'clock and for some time the smell of gas was discernible. Believing that this might indicate an enemy attack, the Battalion stood to, but by 10.30 a.m. the last trace of the vapour had disappeared and, as no German activity was reported, the unit received the order "stand down."

When concern over the possibility of enemy attack on the Divisional front had subsided, the men of the 24th Battalion turned with relief to celebration of the Christmas season. Company dinners, notable for the excellent music provided, were held as opportunity offered, and, as the Battalion would be in the line on Christmas Day, the Chaplain conducted Divine Service at 7.30 o'clock on the morning of December 24th, followed by a celebration of Holy Communion for all who desired to attend. Shortly after noon on the same day, Major-General R. E. W. Turner, the Divisional Commander, called at Battalion Headquarters to convey to Lieut.-Col. Gunn, Major Hill, officers, and men of the unit the greetings appropriate to the season.

That afternoon at 4 o'clock the Battalion moved forward from Locre and relieved the 25th Battalion in the line. Taking over the front in the light of a brilliant moon, the Battalion awaited the coming of Christmas Day, with curiosity as to how the enemy would mark the occasion. Sharp at midnight a shower of flares rose from German trenches to the left and, after these had been answered from the Canadian lines, the troops on both sides settled down to an uneventful night of trench routine.

Christmas Day dawned peacefully. Occasionally a shell burst within sight or hearing, a machine-gun chattered, or rifles cracked from the opposing parapets, but these evidences of war died down as the day advanced and the Chaplain, Hon. Capt. A. P. Shatford, touring the forward area with Christmas greetings and a message of good cheer, was able to reach all the men, except those in isolated posts to which access in daylight was impossible.

Early in the afternoon shelling and rifle fire ceased completely and soon German soldiers were seen lifting heads and shoulders cautiously over the parapet of their front line trench. Encouraged by the fact that no fire was opened by the men of the 24th, a number of the Germans climbed over the top, advanced in No Man's Land, and, making signs of friendship, invited the Canadians to join them and celebrate the occasion.

Regulations frowned on such action, but curiosity proved strong, and a group of Canadians, including a number from the 24th Battalion, moved out to see what the enemy looked like at close range. Conversation proved difficult at first, but a number of the Germans spoke English fluently and others, having rehearsed for the occasion, one must judge, endeavoured to establish their benevolence by constant repetition of the phrase "Kaiser no damn good."

For nearly an hour the unofficial peace was prolonged, the Canadians presenting the Germans with cigarettes and foodstuffs and receiving in return buttons, badges, and several bottles of most excellent beer. By this time, news of the event had reached authority, and peremptory orders were issued to the Canadians in No Man's Land to return to their own line forthwith. When all had reported back, a salvo of artillery fire, aimed carefully to burst at a spot where no harm to friend or foe would result, warned the Germans that the truce was over and that hostilities had been resumed. The majority accepted the warning and governed themselves accordingly, but a few decided to climb over the parapet again and desisted only when rifle fire from a unit on the 24th Battalion's flank proved that the time when this could be done with impunity had passed.

For some days after Christmas comparative quiet prevailed in the front line, but soon activity increased and the Battalion's losses indicated that normal trench warfare conditions again existed. Before the unit moved back to Brigade Reserve billets at R. E. Farm on December 30th, Private R. H. Driscoll, of "B" Coy., was killed, also Private H. C. Clendenning, of "C" Coy.'s Machine-Gun Section, who was shot through the head by a sniper while on duty in Trench K.1.

In billets at R. E. Farm the men of the 24th Battalion spent the last day of 1915, which was marked by the departure of Major C. H. Hill, Second-in-Command of the Battalion, to assume duties on the Staff of the 2nd Canadian Division. The 24th Battalion, Victoria Rifles of Canada, owed much to the manner in which Major Hill had assisted Lieut.-Col. Gunn in organization and command and all ranks regretted that his promotion must involve a severance of the tie. On Major Hill's departure, Major R. O. Alexander became Second-in-Command of the Battalion, being succeeded in command of "B" Coy. by Capt. F. T. Bown. Simultaneously, it was announced that, for valuable service, Battalion Sergt.-Major E. G. Lidstone had been promoted to the Regiment's commissioned establishment and attached to "B" Coy.

III

January, 1916, so far as the 24th Battalion, Victoria Rifles of Canada, was concerned, brought no great change from the routine of trench warfare which had marked the closing months of the previous year. Twice in the first few days of January the Battalion stood to, awaiting a possible call for help from the 25th Battalion, which was engaged in night bombing operations near the Petit Bois, but on neither occasion was help required. Strong working and carrying parties, however, were despatched frequently to assist units in the line and the men accordingly benefited little from the fact that, technically, they were "resting" in anticipation of hard work ahead.

In the course of a front line tour lasting from January 5th to 11th, the Battalion endured heavy shelling on occasions and suffered casualties, snipers increasing the total by effective fire on exposed sections of the front. A number of men were killed by the shell fire, or by snipers' bullets, but the enemy was subjected to retaliation, which undoubtedly inflicted a similar toll. Trench mortars co-operated with the Battalion in an organized shoot on the last day of the tour and smashed the enemy trenches in front of the Petit Bois, to the satisfaction of men of the 24th, who realized as kitchen utensils, corrugated iron, and planks shot into the air, that the enemy was taking punishment more severe than any he had recently inflicted.

THE V.C. ROAD AND THE PETIT BOIS.

THE RED CHATEAU, IN FRONT OF THE PETIT BOIS.

Sketches on the Kemmel Front.
Scenes familiar to the Battalion
in the autumn months of 1915 and
the winter of 1916.

On conclusion of the tour in the front line, the Battalion moved back to Divisional Reserve billets in Locre, whence a party of 11 officers and 500 other ranks was furnished on January 14th for work under the orders of the 6th Canadian Infantry Brigade. Parties almost as strong were ordered daily to the forward areas to carry out work which taxed the men to the limit of their physical endurance. Accordingly it was almost with satisfaction that they received orders, on January 17th, to take over from the 25th Battalion the familiar front line trenches facing the Petit Bois.

On the night of January 18th, the Battalion suffered for the first time the death in action of an officer, when Lieut. R. H. B. Buchanan, of "A" Coy., was killed by machine-gun fire while in charge of a wiring party in No Man's Land. Lieut. Buchanan, an original 24th Battalion officer, had served for a time with a reserve battalion in England, but had rejoined his own unit in December and, in the short period before his death, had earned as a front line soldier the regard of all with whom he served. It was amid expressions of deep regret, therefore, that Lieut. G. R. Robertson, who was in charge of a wiring party on the flank, moved to where Lieut. Buchanan had fallen and arranged for the conveyance of his body to the rear for burial.

That same night Corporal A. McKenna was hit while carrying rations between two mine craters opposite Trenches H.3 and H.4. Stretcher-bearers carried him to shelter, despite German snipers, who, seeing or hearing the party and not necessarily aware of its mission, maintained a steady fire. No bullets took effect, but Corporal McKenna's injury was severe and the gallant effort of the stretcher-bearers to save his life was made in vain.

For the remainder of the month of January, the 24th Battalion moved in and out of the front line at 6-day intervals, suffering frequent casualties and enduring the hardships inevitably involved by the conduct in winter of a trench campaign. Interesting events of the period included the first appearance in the unit of the steel helmet, adopted eventually by all armies on the Western Front; the promotion to commissioned rank of Sergt. E. M. Amphlett, of the Machine-Gun Section; the promotion to the rank of captain of Lieuts. W. R. Hastings and H. D. Kingstone; the temporary assumption of the Battalion command by Major R. O. Alexander, during a period when Lieut.-Col. J. A. Gunn was acting as commander of the 5th Brigade; the arrival of Capt. H. E. Cumming to act as Battalion Medical Officer; and a visit to the trenches by Capt. His Royal Highness the Prince of Wales.

Again in February, 1916, the Battalion carried out a series of tours in the front line and reserve. Again the period was marked by no incident of major importance, though it called in a high degree for courage and endurance owing to the proximity of the enemy, the necessity for constant vigilance, the arduous work on trench repairs, the misery of life in saturated clothing, and the absence, in the line, of any sleep other than uneasy hours snatched when routine or enemy inaction would permit.

Undoubtedly, the most outstanding incident of the month occurred in the early morning hours of February 16th, when Corporal E. A. Mott and Scouts W. J. Dwyer and P. F. J. Williams moved into No Man's Land to reconnoitre the German line. Soon after leaving the protection of their own wire, the scouts sighted an enemy patrol of three men, manoeuvred cleverly, seized the leader, and forced his comrades to retreat.

Disgusted at being taken prisoner, the captured German talked little at first, but, when examined by Lieut. I. R. R. MacNaughton, answered in excellent English and later, at Battalion Headquarters, replied satisfactorily to many questions. Lieut.-Col. Gunn had offered a reward for the first prisoner captured by the unit and to the delighted scouts promptly and cheerfully paid his private reckoning, at the same time bringing to the notice of higher authority an account of the service they had rendered.

Relieved by the 25th Battalion on the night following the capture of the German prisoner, the Victoria Rifles moved back to Brigade Reserve billets at R. E. Farm, for six days, then reoccupied the front line, with the 26th Battalion on the left flank and at first the 49th Battalion, then the Princess Patricia's Canadian Light Infantry, on the right. The tour that followed was marked by a number of casualties and by the fact that the 31st Canadian Battalion effected the relief. When this had been completed on the night of February 26th, the Battalion moved to La Clytte and came under the orders of the 4th Canadian Infantry Brigade, so remaining until the afternoon of the following day, when the unit marched to Divisional Reserve billets in Locre.

IV

At Locre, the 24th Battalion welcomed to France "A" and "B" Companies of the 60th Battalion, Victoria Rifles of Canada, under Lieut-.Col. F. A. Gascoigne, and a day later "C" and "D" Companies, under Major W. B. Evans. The 60th Battalion, recruited in Montreal largely by the 3rd Regiment, Victoria Rifles of Canada, had come to France with the 3rd Canadian Division, which was taking a place alongside the veteran 1st and 2nd Divisions in the Canadian Corps. It was appropriate that the 60th Battalion should receive training by the 24th, and "A" and "B" Companies of the new battalion were accordingly attached for instruction, "C" and "D" Companies being attached simultaneously to other units of the 5th Brigade.

On March 2nd, Operation Order No. 39, issued by Brigadier-General David Watson, C.B., over the signature of Major Malcolm McAvity, Brigade Major, instructed the 24th Battalion to relieve the 25th Battalion in Trenches M.1 to N.3, positions to the left of that section of the line which frequent occupation in previous months had rendered so familiar. Machine-gun fire threatened the relief and harassed the troops on the following day, among the casualties being Private A. Grenier, of the Bombing Section, who was killed while repairing the front line wire. Next day the Battalion suffered the loss of a valuable non-commissioned officer when Corporal E. A. Mott was shot accidentally and died of the wound. The first class work of this N.C.O. had previously been brought to the attention of higher authority by a report, which also mentioned the valuable services rendered by Lieut. P. L. Hall, Hon. Capt. and Quartermaster H. D. Campbell, Corporal Albert Metzger and Private A. F. Mott.

Snow fell heavily on the night of March 7th and remained on the ground for some days, complicating the night work of the Battalion by throwing into relief any movement above the level of the parapet, and adding to the difficulty of the 52nd Canadian Battalion, which came forward to relieve. One company of the 52nd Battalion moved into the line on the night of March 9th, and the remaining companies completed relief of the 24th Battalion on the night of March 10th.

March 12th was marked in the Battalion by inoculation of all ranks against paratyphoid fever; and by the arrival at Locre, where the unit was in billets, of newspapers from Montreal describing the part taken by the 24th Battalion in a purely imaginary battle not far from Ypres. The German attack on the French at Verdun indicated clearly that winter warfare was over and that action on the British front might soon be expected, but details of the Battalion's fighting at Ypres were premature, to say the least, and the men resented the unnecessary anxiety inflicted on their kindred and friends at home.

Indications of increased enemy activity were noted by men of the Battalion during a tour in the right section of the 5th Canadian Infantry Brigade front between March 14th and 20th. Casualties were light in the first 48 hours, but at 6.25 o'clock on the afternoon of March 17th the Germans opened a sharp bombardment with high explosive, killing Private W. Wightman, of "D" Coy., and wounding seven of his comrades severely. While conveying the wounded down the truck railway in V. C. Road, Private Arthur Gagnon, of "B" Coy., was struck in the throat by machine-gun fire and died a half-hour later.

Again on March 20th, the enemy chose the late afternoon to bombard heavily, his fire striking the front and support lines and wounding seven men severely. Later, when the bombardment had died down, the 25th Battalion effected relief and the men of the 24th moved back to Brigade Reserve billets near R. E. Farm. Here Hon. Capt. C. J. S. Stuart reported for duty as Chaplain, an office he filled, taking part in every engagement, for the remainder of the Battalion's service in the war.

Moving up again on the night of March 26th, the Battalion, 951 strong, took over the trenches occupied during the previous tour. Each night the Machine-Gun Section, under Lieut. E. M. Amphlett, carried out, in co-operation with the Canadian Artillery, a series of demonstrations designed by Lieut. S. W. Watson, the Brigade Machine-Gun Officer, to harass the enemy, and prevent him from making repairs to his front line wire.

In addition to the operations of the Machine-Gun Section, the Battalion, under command of Major R. O. Alexander, as Lieut.-Col. Gunn was absent on leave, took steps to carry out Brigade orders regarding the placing and firing of three Bangalore torpedoes in the enemy wire. Routes by which the torpedoes might be carried out and placed in position were reconnoitred by the Battalion scouts on the night of March 26th, and early on the morning of the 27th the effort to place them began.

One party achieved prompt success, planting a torpedo in the enemy's wire and returning safely to the Canadian line, whence, at 4.15 a.m., the torpedo was fired according to pre-arranged schedule. Unfortunately, other parties were unable to duplicate this success. Party No. 2 was sighted by the enemy, who opened fire with machine-guns, rifles, and rifle grenades, making the placing of the torpedo impossible and forcing the plan to be abandoned.

Party No. 3 was also checked, but renewed the attempt when it seemed that opportunity offered. Again the enemy drove the party back, but the Victoria Riflemen were undismayed and, for the third time, attempted to carry out their mission as soon as the German fire slackened. This effort was not successful and the party was caught in No Man's Land when, according to arrangement, a British artillery bombardment opened at 4.51 o'clock.

Scattering, the men of the party crawled to their own line as best they might, the majority reporting safely, but a check of personnel showing that Privates W. J. Dwyer and F. P. Juteau, of the Scout Section, were missing. At 6.30 o'clock, when the heavy shelling resulting from the night's operation had died down, Sergt. W. C. Westwater and Private F. P. Heckbert moved into No Man's Land in an attempt to find out what misfortune Privates Dwyer and Juteau had suffered and to help them if help were of need. Before long they found Private Juteau, minus an arm and with wounds in the head, hanging where he had fallen dead in the Battalion wire.

When Sergt. Westwater and Private Heckbert reported Private Juteau's fate, arrangements for recovery of the body were made. A second patrol, composed of Privates S. J. Bethune and E. G. Collins, then moved into No Man's Land and crawled in the shelter of a hedge to an old French trench, along which they travelled to within 15 yards of the enemy wire. Though daylight revealed them to the Germans, who sniped repeatedly, Bethune and Collins persisted in their work and were rewarded by finding Private Dwyer, who had taken cover and was waiting until night to return to his own lines. After consultation, the three men crawled cautiously back across No Man's Land, picking up a party, composed of Sergt. Westwater and Privates Heckbert, Mott, and Dolphin, and eventually reaching the Battalion's front line. Six days later, after a tour marked by activity more pronounced than usual, the Battalion was relieved by the 7th Battalion, Northumberland Fusiliers, and marched to reserve billets at Reninghelst.

CHAPTER III

THE CRATERS AT ST. ELOI

I

After the long and arduous experience of trench warfare in the autumn of 1915 and in the winter months of 1916, the 2nd Canadian Division, with no appreciable period of rest, became involved at St. Eloi in a series of operations larger, longer drawn-out, and more costly in casualties than any in which Canadian troops had been engaged since the stand of the 1st Division at Ypres in the previous year. The Second Battle of Ypres was fought on a wide front and, at least for a time, produced conditions with a semblance to those of open warfare; St. Eloi, on the contrary, was fought on a front of not more than one thousand yards, on ground blasted beyond recognition by high explosive shells, churned by constant rain, and distinguished from the surrounding morass only by St. Eloi mound and the series of mine craters on top.

These craters, seven in number, provide the key to the seemingly purposeless attacks and counter-attacks that marked the battle, for possession of them and of St. Eloi mound would give to the British, or to the enemy, a measure of observation over the country round about. It may be presumed, too, from the British point of view, that the action was maintained, at least in part, to suggest to the enemy that Ypres was to be the scene of a major Allied effort, thereby diverting German attention from Verdun and from preparations for the opening of the Battles of the Somme.

An unusual feature of the Battle of St. Eloi was provided by the confusion that existed for many days between Craters Nos. 2 and 3, and Nos. 4 and 5 and Craters Nos. 6 and 7. Had normal weather prevailed, the error would soon have been corrected by aerial reconnaissance, but conditions were abnormal, storms and fog prevented observation from the air, and for nearly two weeks troops reported in good faith that they held Craters Nos. 4 and 5, though actually what they held were Craters 6 and 7. This mistake deprived the infantry of supporting artillery fire and provided a factor in the Germans' favour which influenced markedly the course and result of the battle.

In the circumstances, the mistake, once made, was capable of correction only from the air. By the time that correction was effected, the battle was almost over, the Germans had achieved a measure of success, and the 2nd Canadian Division, though suffering severely, had established its reputation as a formation capable of fighting unfalteringly in a situation as trying as any that soldiers must face. When the battle died down, the territory for which both sides had fought was found by the Germans to be almost untenable and was partly abandoned. Thereafter, the crater area of St. Eloi remained for the most part in No Man's Land, its shell holes, debris, and shattered trenches revealing to the personnel of an occasional British or German patrol the manner in which many brave men had died.

As Lord Beaverbrook has observed in his *Canada in Flanders*, "the story of the craters is like that of most of the battles of St. Eloi, one of misfortune for the 2nd Division; but it is not one of blame. The successive regiments who held the outposts were from the very outset at a great disadvantage compared with their enemies. They were not, and could not be, properly supported by their own gunners, while the enemy's artillery was pounding them to pieces."

II

Immediately on transfer from the Kemmel front to the St. Eloi district, the 24th Battalion, Victoria Rifles of Canada, furnished strong parties for work in the forward area. The men knew that their tasks, under the orders of the 6th Canadian Infantry Brigade, would be hard and dangerous, nevertheless on the night of April 4th, when 8 officers and 300 other ranks moved up, under

The Craters at St. Eloi, 1916.

This aerial photograph conveys an impression of the shattered area in which the Battle of St. Eloi was fought.

command of Capt. H. D. Kingstone, all were eager to accomplish work that would prove of credit to the Battalion and the 2nd Canadian Division. They had seen, marching back after battle at St. Eloi, remnants of battalions of the Gordon Highlanders and the Royal Scots, whose bearing, despite mud and blood, had aroused deep admiration and had inspired in the Canadians the desire to prove that they too were troops who, in good times or bad, could be counted upon to carry out satisfactorily whatever task chance might place before them.

Soon after the working parties had left for the forward area, the Battalion stood to, in response to an order which stated that support to the units in the line might be required. Again at 4.15 o'clock on the morning of April 6th a "stand to" order was received, followed shortly by instructions in obedience to which the Battalion marched to a field near Dickebusch and there bivouacked awaiting orders, which, it was expected, would send the unit into action in support of the 6th Brigade. This Brigade, holding the St. Eloi crater front, had been attacked, and, despite hard fighting, had been forced in places to give ground.

Though the 24th Battalion as a unit was not called forward on this occasion, machine-gun teams from the four battalions of the 5th Brigade accomplished gallant work against the enemy. The 24th Battalion team, under Sergt. H. S. Naylor, and composed of Lance-Corporal J. Rose, Lance-Corporal E. E. Duley, and Privates A. W. H. Arundell, C. W. Burchell, and Clarke, fought courageously during the retreat, using effectively Lewis guns issued a few days before. Sergt. Naylor earned in the official account of the engagement a warm tribute for "great presence of mind in mitigating the confusion of mixed units and saving the majority of his team." For devotion to duty in circumstances most dangerous and critical, he received the Military Medal, a similar award to Lance-Corporal Duley acknowledging support given to Sergt. Naylor throughout the bitter hours of the whole engagement.

While Sergt. Naylor and his men were fighting in the crater area, the 24th Battalion, as mentioned, was awaiting orders at Dickebusch. In the afternoon, the officers played the other ranks at baseball, but the game lacked stability, for enemy shelling on one occasion forced its transfer to a less exposed field and on another wounded a supporter of the other ranks' team.

Next day, the situation in the crater area being less critical, the Battalion moved back to Reninghelst, but at 8 p.m. on April 8th, orders to march again to Dickebusch were received and at 9.25 o'clock the Battalion moved off, the men bivouacking in an open field when their destination was reached, but getting little sleep owing to unusual cold. All ranks shared in the discomfort, including Capt. A. H. Taylor, C.A.M.C., who reported to Lieut.-Col. Gunn to assume duties as Medical Officer of the unit.

After a night in the open, the 24th Battalion marched back on April 9th to Reninghelst, whence at night a party of 7 officers and 300 other ranks was supplied for work in the front and support line trenches. The 4th Canadian Infantry Brigade was harassing the enemy on this date and the Germans were retaliating with high explosive. Caught by the enemy fire, the working party of the 24th suffered severely, Sergt. John Williamson and six other ranks being killed and 20 other ranks wounded. In attending to the injured, Stretcher-Bearers Marchand and Walker, under the direction of the officers of the party, accomplished work of a high order, and Private M. Young, working under the direct orders of Major C. B. Parr, carried out his duties in a manner that earned an award of the Military Medal. Valuable service was rendered by others of the party, who faced the blast of the German guns courageously and strove, despite the heavy losses, to complete the task to which they had been assigned.

Two nights after the working party suffered so severely in the forward area, the 5th Canadian Infantry Brigade relieved the 4th Brigade in the front line, the 22nd Battalion taking over the right sector of the front from the 20th Battalion, the 25th Battalion relieving the 18th Battalion in the St. Eloi craters, and the 26th Battalion relieving the 19th Battalion on the left. The 24th Battalion, in Brigade Reserve, placed Battalion Headquarters, with "B" and "D" Companies, in Scottish Wood and "A" and "C" Companies in positions not far away. Some shelling occurred during the relief, one man of the Battalion being killed and two wounded.

Carrying parties were provided on April 13th; and on the 14th the Battalion relieved the 25th Battalion in the St. Eloi craters and neighbouring front line trenches. At this time, the situation in the crater area had not been cleared up by aerial observation. Confusion in reports written during the tour is therefore unavoidable. Indeed, it is doubtful even to-day if the positions occupied by some Battalion posts can be identified with any degree of conviction.

Some impression of the appalling condition of the district and the resulting difficulty in identification of trench positions can be gained from Lord Beaverbrook's *Canada in Flanders*. Describing the St. Eloi area, the book says "The 'high hills were laid low and the valleys were exalted,'" until the ground destroyed by man bore little resemblance to the ground designed by Nature. In the battered area all was mud and debris. Every shell hole was a pond, and by day, even more markedly by night, the prevailing mist hid landmarks from view, or, swirling suddenly aside, revealed them in a distorted form most difficult to identify.

No sooner had the 24th Battalion taken over this ill-omened area than the enemy, supported by heavy artillery fire, launched a bombing attack on Craters 6 and 7. For forty minutes the enemy strove courageously to force a way into the craters and to drive the Victoria Riflemen out, but the garrisons, under Capt. R. D. Sutherland and Lieut. R. H. Lamb, maintained their positions and defeated decisively the German efforts to dislodge them.

When the enemy artillery opened fire in support of the bombing attack on the craters, communication between the Victoria Rifles' front line positions and Battalion Headquarters was cut almost at once. Lieut.-Col. Gunn became uneasy as the minutes passed and Brigadier-General Watson, fearing that the front line had been overwhelmed, urged that every effort be made to ascertain how the situation stood. Responding splendidly to the Commanding Officer's orders, the Signal Section and runners of the Battalion strove repeatedly to repair broken wires, or to push through the enemy barrage to the front line, notable attempts being made amongst others by Privates A. Findlay and Gillespie, of the Signal Section. Before any efforts brought success, however, a pigeon, despatched from the front by Capt. R. K. Robertson, reached a point far behind the Battalion lines, whence, by telephone, Lieut.-Col. Gunn was informed that casualties had been severe, but that the crater positions remained definitely in Canadian hands.

Shelling of the area was renewed by the enemy on April 15th, Capt. H. D. Kingstone being wounded, but remaining at duty, and many casualties occurring in the ranks, including a number instantly killed. Losses were inflicted on the enemy, particularly on one occasion at night when a supply of German flares was ignited by a Canadian bomb. The silhouetted figures of many Germans afforded a marvellous target and the men of the 24th Battalion shot a large number down.

That night, several officers of the Battalion reconnoitred in No Man's Land and returned with reports which threw appreciable light on the obscure situation in the crater area. Moving out at 10 p.m., Lieuts. V. E. Duclos and G. R. Robertson approached to within 50 yards of enemy Crater No. 2, a bright moon, emerging from clouds, preventing a closer approach, but revealing many details of the German defences, regarding which a clear report was compiled.

Even more valuable to the Intelligence Department of the Division and the higher command was the result of a reconnaissance by Major J. A. Ross and Lieut. C. G. Greenshields of enemy Crater No. 3, in front of which a crater not previously identified was discovered. Between Craters 2 and 3 Major Ross and Lieut. Greenshields found that the enemy were completing a parapet eight to ten feet high. Other important details were noted, the report, corroborated by aerial reconnaissance which became possible on the following day, proving of the greatest value, which was recognized by award to Major Ross of the Distinguished Service Order.

April 16, 1916, for the men of the 24th Battalion, was a day of unremitting effort and trial, more particularly for the garrisons of Craters 6 and 7, who endured artillery and trench mortar shelling and constant machine-gun and rifle fire. As many of their posts were under observation from the enemy line, movement of any kind produced heavy fire, with an inevitable toll of killed and wounded. At White Horse Cellars, too, shelling was severe, the Germans drenching the area with tear-gas, by which a number of 24th Battalion men were affected. At last the day wore to a weary close, but night brought the men no appreciable relief, for shell fire continued, and at 10.40 p.m. the enemy advanced once more to attack, their assault driving against the 24th Battalion posts in Craters 6 and 7. As on the previous night, enemy bombers advanced courageously and strove repeatedly to force a way into the Canadian positions, but again the garrisons stood fast and drove the Germans back to the shelter of their own line.

Meanwhile, a number of men from the 24th Battalion had assisted stretcher-bearers of the 2nd Pioneers in removing from No Man's Land members of a working party who had fallen during the attack, or under the shelling that preceded it. A number of the Pioneers, badly shattered, were dug from a collapsed trench in which they had vainly sought shelter; and one of the stretcher-bearers, with a foot blown off, legs broken, and body mangled, expressed deep gratitude to the men of the 24th for his rescue. Their work, however, could not save his life and he died as they were carrying him back to the Canadian lines.

As soon as the waves of the German attack had been driven back from the approaches to Craters 6 and 7, a 24th Battalion patrol of 1 officer and 3 men moved towards the enemy line to discover if further action seemed imminent. Machine-gun and rifle fire was heavy in volume, but the patrol, covering a large part of the front, could find no indication that the Germans were preparing to renew the attack. Working parties of the enemy were dispersed by machine-gun fire, and a Canadian party, under Capt. R. K. Robertson, accomplished valuable work in wiring a sector of the crater position.

April 17th resembled in its main features the preceding day. Again the enemy shelled vigorously, again his rifles, machine-guns, and trench mortars maintained heavy fire, and again the Battalion suffered appreciable loss, 8 other ranks being killed and 29 wounded, many by a German gun firing from the left. This gun, as Lieut. J. N. Bales noted in his Intelligence report, breached the parapet of the 24th Battalion crater position and, firing through the breach, harassed the Canadian troops severely.

Successful as this field gun was, the Germans did not rely upon it alone. Aerial torpedoes were fired frequently on the crater positions and support trenches, and the Voormezeele—St. Eloi road was heavily bombarded. Battalion Headquarters was in danger on many occasions when high explosive shells burst all around, but, despite the frequency and accuracy of the bombardments, casualties were somehow avoided.

At 10.40 p.m. the enemy launched a bombing attack on the crater positions, renewing the effort some hours later and, for a time, halting the relief of the 24th Battalion by the 29th Battalion. By 3 a.m. the situation had cleared and the men of the 24th, worn out by their efforts in the crater area, began a long march back to rest billets in Camp D, Reninghelst. The toll of casualties for the tour had been heavy, but was not at the time quite complete, for, on the way back, near Voormezeele, high explosive shells struck a section of the unit, killing Private G. A. Webb, wounding two others, and forcing the remainder, after rescuing their fallen comrades, to scatter hurriedly for safety.

In billets at Camp D, the men of the 24th rested on April 18th, but prolonged opportunity to recover after their exhausting work in the line could not be afforded them, for action in the crater area developed and support, closer to the front line, was required. Accordingly, a "stand to" was ordered on April 19th and, at 8.20 p.m., a march to Camp "A," where billets were shared with the 25th Battalion.

Sleep was almost impossible that night. Shelling in the forward area was heavy and the thunder of the guns vibrated menacingly, the noise and flashes of the bursting shells being intensified, it seemed, by the soaking atmosphere of the cold and rainy night. The final curtain in the tragic drama of the St. Eloi craters was falling, but in the last scene the 24th Battalion took no active part, for on the morning of April 20th the unit was ordered back to Reninghelst.

At Reninghelst, Lieut.-Col. Gunn and his officers tendered a farewell dinner to Brigadier-General David Watson, who was relinquishing command of the 5th Canadian Infantry Brigade to assume command of the 4th Canadian Division. The dinner also served to welcome Brigadier-General A. H. Macdonnel, who had been appointed from command of the Royal Canadian Regiment to command of the 5th Brigade. He was succeeded in command of the Royal Canadian Regiment by Lieut.-Col. C. H. Hill, who had crossed from Canada as the 24th Battalion's Second-in-Command.

The dinner was a success, but did not pass without reminder of the serious situation in the crater area, for at 9 p.m. the new Commander of the Brigade rose from his chair and remarking, "Gentlemen, we have our duty to perform," announced that orders had been received for an immediate stand to. Leaving the dinner, officers hurried to their posts and prepared, as they had done so frequently in the immediate past, to advance as soon as further orders were received. No movement was required that night, but at 6.30 o'clock on the following afternoon the Battalion marched to Dickebusch, there to become Divisional Reserve.

Before the move took place, 10 officers and 500 men had been sent to serve as a working party under the orders of the 4th Canadian Infantry Brigade; or rather as a series of parties, assigned to work in accordance with the following table:

1 platoon. Reserve Line (Right)
                    Lieut. D. A. Ewan.

2 platoons Reserve Line (Left)
                    Lieuts. A. L. Walker and
                    R. H. Lamb.

2 platoons. (wiring) Reserve Line.
                    Lieuts. P. L. Hall and
                    G. V. Walsh.

1 platoon. (carrying) Reserve Line.
                    Lieut. C. G. Greenshields

1 platoon.   (digging) C.T. from Res. to Front Line.
               Lieut. V. E. Duclos.
1 platoon.   (wiring) C.T. from Res. to Front Line.
               Lieut. G. R. Robertson.
2 platoons. (carrying) for Battalions in Line.
               Lieuts. J. C. Heaton and
               I. R. R. MacNaughton.

These parties were picked up in Reninghelst and conveyed by bus to the forward area. In view of the urgent nature of the tasks they were to accomplish, Brigade Headquarters stated that fatigue must not reduce the quality or quantity of their effort and that in no circumstances, except under compulsion through enemy attack, must work cease before 2.30 a.m. Realizing that these orders called for an effort even greater than usual, officers and men of the 24th Battalion parties strove throughout the night to accomplish all that the Staff of the 4th Brigade desired.

Returning to Dickebusch with their tasks completed, the men of the working parties rejoined the Battalion, which, at 7.30 p.m. on April 24th, moved into Brigade Reserve, with "A" and "B" Companies in Voormezeele Defences and the remainder of the unit in Scottish Wood. Lieut.-Col. Gunn established his headquarters in the Wood, with Major J. A. Ross acting as Second-in-Command, during the temporary absence of Major R. O. Alexander, and Lieut. J. N. Bales as Adjutant, during the absence on leave of Capt. C. F. Ritchie.

Wiring parties of 1 officer and 40 other ranks were supplied to the 18th Canadian Battalion on April 25th, the companies in Scottish Wood moving out on the same date to garrison a position nearby, whence they returned at 6 o'clock on the morning of April 26th. This day brought misfortune to the Battalion when, before noon, a shell struck the officers' dugout, killing Lieut. I. R. R. MacNaughton and wounding Major E. O. McMurtry and Lieut. J. C. Heaton. The death of Lieut. MacNaughton, who had shown high courage and marked ability on the Kemmel front and in the more recent action at the St. Eloi craters, was an event which all ranks in the Battalion deeply deplored.

Shelling continued throughout the day; and was renewed at intervals on each of the closing days of the month. On April 27th Lieut. C. G. Greenshields, who had been wounded in November, 1915, was wounded for the second time, while carrying out a reconnaissance of the Covent Lane—Ecluse trenches; and on the 29th Lieut. J. N. Bales and 4 other ranks were wounded while engaged on a wiring party. Further casualties were suffered by the Battalion when enemy shelling struck near Brigade Headquarters at Covent Gardens, Dickebusch, killing Sergt. A. Rae and two young brothers, Privates Cyril and Horace Hill, popular members of the 24th, who, from the time of the formation of the Battalion in Montreal, had served as buglers. In addition to the killed at this time, 8 other ranks of the Battalion were wounded.

On May 1, 1916, Battalion Headquarters and "C" and "D" Companies of the 24th were relieved in Scottish Wood by the 31st Battalion, which also relieved "A" and "B" Companies in the Voormezeele Defences. Following relief, "A" and "B" Companies were employed as carrying parties until daybreak on May 2nd, when they rejoined the main body of the unit in Divisional Reserve in Reninghelst.

From billets in Reninghelst, 325 men of the 24th Battalion reported in the forward area on the night of May 4th to work under the orders of the Staff of the 2nd Canadian Division. Valuable work was accomplished, but the party paid a toll, Lieut. G. V. Walsh and 3 other ranks suffering wounds before the required labour was completed.

On the following day, Lieut.-Col. Gunn was appointed to act as Commander of the 5th Canadian Infantry Brigade during the temporary absence of Brigadier-General A. H. Macdonnel, and Major J. A. Ross succeeded for the time being to the 24th Battalion command. Major Ross left for England on leave on May 10th, command of the 24th Battalion then passing to Major C. B. Parr, who was in turn succeeded when Major R. O. Alexander returned from leave two days later. Meanwhile, on May 6th, the 24th Battalion Transport had paraded, under Lieut. H. A. Murray, for inspection by Major-

General R. E. W. Turner, the main body of the unit parading simultaneously to attend Divine Service, conducted by the Battalion Chaplain, Hon. Capt. the Reverend C. J. S. Stuart.

Working parties were supplied frequently to the 2nd Canadian Division in the days that followed, some being used to carry material to the forward area and others in the never-ending effort to pump water from flooded trenches and repair parapets washed down by rain. The majority of these parties carried out their work without losses, but in some instances casualties occurred. In the period between May 3rd and 14th, while so many parties worked in the forward areas, the main body of the Battalion was carrying out a comprehensive syllabus of training.

Moving forward on the night of May 14th, the 24th Battalion relieved the 21st Battalion in the Centre Sector of the line, with Battalion Headquarters at Voormezeele, two companies in the actual front trenches, and two companies in support. As soon as the line had been taken over, patrols of the Battalion moved out to cover parties engaged in digging, wiring, and revetting. No. 1 Patrol, composed of Scouts Dickson, Le Boutillier, and Weinberg, and 2 bombers, sighted a party of 3 Germans near Crater No. 2, and was sighted, it would seem, for heavy machine-gun fire from the lip of the crater forced the Canadian party to seek cover.

No. 2 Patrol, composed of Scouts Fuller, Gillians, and Poulter, protected a working party of the 24th Battalion, then, when protection was no longer required, carried out a reconnaissance in the direction of Crater No. 2. Returning to the Canadian lines at 2 a.m., the members of the patrol reported that the crater parapet appeared to have suffered severely from shelling, or rain, and that the Germans were working hard to repair it. Scouts Keating and Forbes, of Patrol No. 3, confirmed the report of the scouts of No. 2 Patrol, but it was impossible to take advantage of the information at the time as the presence of Canadian working parties in No Man's Land masked the German position and rendered effective action highly dangerous.

On the night of May 16th, at 8.30 o'clock, four platoons of the Battalion, 100 strong, reported to Lieut.

R. H. Lamb in Voormezeele and carried to the front line 50 coils of French wire, 50 coils of barbed wire, and 50 long screw stakes. The party then worked to strengthen the parapet and parados of Trenches 15 and 16, which had been found to afford insufficient protection. Casualties in the Battalion that day had not been severe, but included Sergt. West, of "A" Coy., who was wounded twice, once in the trenches and again when near the Dressing Station at Voormezeele.

All day on May 17th enemy artillery was active at intervals, a fair example being provided by the hour between 10 and 11 a.m. when eight heavy shells and eleven rounds from field guns burst in the Battalion area. Patrols and carrying parties were numerous at night, creditable work being accomplished by 106 other ranks of the 25th Battalion, who reported at Voormezeele to Lieut. Lamb, Works Officer of the 24th, carried 2,500 sandbags to the front line, and accomplished extensive trench repairs.

Patrols in the crater area were, perhaps, the chief feature of the Battalion's work on May 18th and 19th, Intelligence reports, compiled by the Acting Adjutant, Capt. P. L. Hall, showing that, under Lieut. P. I. Walker, Scouts Bethune, McDonald, Poulter, Fuller, Sagan, and Keating carried out noteworthy reconnaissances on the first of these dates; and Scouts Gillians, Collins, Smith, Poulter, and Weinberg on May 19th. The afternoon of the 19th was also marked by heavy shelling of Battalion Headquarters. The Germans had seven observation balloons in the air and these directed the enemy fire. Approximately 150 shells burst close at hand, and it seemed for a time that heavy losses amongst the Headquarters personnel would be unavoidable. Believing that his men were in serious danger, Lieut.-Col. Gunn ordered them away from the Headquarters dugout, while he, Major R. O. Alexander, and Capt. C. F. Ritchie remained and operated the Battalion telephones. One man of the personnel, struck by shell fragments in the arms, legs, head and shoulders, died in a few moments; one other was wounded, but the remainder escaped unhurt.

Shelling of Battalion Headquarters was followed on May 20th and 21st by heavy shelling of the whole front and support line positions. It is not possible to describe the effect of the bombardments in detail, but an impression of their continuity and of the severe strain they imposed, even when unsuccessful in causing casualties, may be derived from the table below, covering the hours from 4.49 a.m. to 3.50 o'clock p.m. on May 21st:

Time	Number of Shells	Type of Shell
A.M.		
4.49— 6.50	17	H.E.
5.20— 6.50	9	Heavy
6.57— 7.02	40	Light
7.00— 7.15	40	Light
7.00— 7.30	30	Light
9.15—10.00	4	Light
—11.00	2	H.E.
11.15—11.30	40	Light
11.15—11.45	43	Light
P.M.		
1.45— 1.55	37	
2.00— 2.30	20	H.E.
2.40— 2.47	11	Howitzer
2.59— 3.02	16	H.E.
3.00— 3.10	45	5.9's
3.40— 3.50	5	Light
3.30— 3.45	34	Light
Plus	74	Trench Mortars.

Bombardments corresponding in frequency to those listed above, averaging one round every three minutes all day, were endured by the Battalion throughout the whole tour. Sergt. W. H. Redmond, of "D" Coy., was killed on May 22nd and Lance-Sergt. J. L. Brereton, of "B" Coy., on May 23rd. The previous day was marked by the death of 8 other ranks and the wounding of 26 when between 4 and 5 o'clock in the afternoon, forty 5.9-inch shells crashed into the junction of Trenches R.18 and R.19.

Despite the battering to which the Battalion was subjected on these days, patrols moved out after dark as regularly as when the front was inactive. No contact with enemy patrols occurred, Lance-Corporal Dwyer and 3 men, who entered Craters 6 and 7 on the night of May 22nd, reporting that these sites of stirring combat in the past were silent and unoccupied. Scout Macdonald, however, reported that in Crater 5 the enemy was building defences, and a searchlight, playing on the 24th Battalion lines for more than an hour from the direction of Crater No. 3, indicated that here, too, the enemy was active.

After the tour in the line, during which casualties reached a total of 12 killed and 43 wounded, the Battalion was relieved on the night of May 23rd by the 29th Battalion. Relief was complete at 12.30 a.m., the men marching back and being conveyed, some by train and some in busses, to Camp "B," Reninghelst. Camp "B" was a model, with splendid hut accommodation, showers, and electric light, and the men enjoyed its advantages for a week. An endless call for working parties marred the period, but the men appreciated the contrast with life in the front line and, not without a measure of regret, received orders to move forward at night on May 30th, and relieve the 29th Battalion in Brigade Reserve.

CHAPTER IV

ZILLEBEKE

I

On May 28, 1916, Lieut.-General Sir E. A. H. Alderson relinquished command of the Canadian Corps and was succeeded by Lieut.-General the Honourable Sir Julian Byng, an officer of the 10th Royal Hussars, who, in the Sudan, in South Africa, as commander of the 3rd Cavalry Division of Sir John French's "Old Contemptibles," and as G.O.C. the IX Corps, had gained experience and shown unusual ability. Five days later, his experience and ability were tested to the utmost, for the enemy, driving furiously against the 3rd Canadian Division between Hooge and the Ypres-Comines railway involved the Canadian Corps in fighting more severe and costly in casualties than any in which the formation had previously taken part.

Regarding the Battle of Mount Sorrel, or, more familiarly, "The June Show," little is known outside of Canada. One may speak anywhere of the Second Battle of Ypres, the Somme, Vimy Ridge, or Amiens and the name will be recognized at once, but the Battle of Mount Sorrel, though it involved bitter fighting and furnished examples of courage and endurance unsurpassed in the record of the Canadian Corps, remained essentially a Canadian engagement, with few troops from other parts of the Empire involved.

It occurred, too, at a time when the eyes of the world, and more particularly of the Empire, were turned to the waters of the seas around the British Isles. For the first time in history, battleships of the British and German navies had fought a general engagement and details of the battle, emerging from the fog created by Nature and from that built up by man, caught and held the undivided attention of all, except those whose interest in the Canadian Corps was personal and direct. Before the Battle of Mount Sorrel was concluded, there arrived also news that served, so far as the world was concerned, to concentrate further attention on the sea, for the Admiralty announced that H.M.S. *Hampshire* had been sunk by a German mine, bearing to death the British Secretary of State for War, Field Marshal Earl Kitchener of Khartoum.

In German accounts of the War on the Western Front, the Battle of Mount Sorrel receives less comment than engagements of distinctly lower significance. At first, the reason was hard to discern, but, in addition to distraction from land fighting provided by naval action at Jutland, it now seems established that the Battle of Mount Sorrel represented an effort to secure distinction by an ambitious German corps commander, rather than an action emanating from the more lofty mental atmosphere of the German General Staff. The corps commander almost succeeded in clearing a path to Ypres, indeed, at one time, he had before him only the remnants of the battalions which his shell fire had destroyed; but the remnants fought with a courage that nothing could subdue, time passed remorselessly, the remains of the shattered battalions were at last reinforced, and, with the closing of the gaps in the broken Canadian line, the German's dream of an open road to Ypres faded forever.

Once the road to Ypres was barred, Lieut.-General Sir Julian Byng took prompt measures to restore his broken front. Troops of the 1st, 2nd, and 3rd Canadian Divisions were employed in immediate counter-attack and in establishing a new front line; and on June 13th the 1st Division, under Major-General A. W. Currie, was launched in decisive counter-attack. Supported by a weight of artillery comparable with that used by the Germans in opening the battle, the 1st Division drove resolutely forward, encountering heavy shell and machine-gun fire and, in some places, obstinate enemy resistance. All objectives were reached, except at Mount Sorrel, where trenches had been obliterated, but where a new line with improved command was established. Within a few hours the German gains of June 2nd were reduced to an unimportant minimum, and the Canadian Corps, having inflicted heavy losses on the enemy, could state beyond shadow of doubt that the agony of the 3rd Division on June 2nd had been avenged.

II

Though the 24th Battalion, Victoria Rifles of Canada, took no direct part in operations resulting from the forward drive of the German infantry on June 2, 1916, or in the brilliant counter-attack by the 1st Canadian Division on June 13th, the activity provoked by these operations involved the unit in front line work of a hard and costly nature. After the broken line had been stabilized in the early days of June, the new front had to be held while the decisive counter-attack was being mounted and, after the counter-attack, the restored front line had to be garrisoned and consolidated. In both these tasks, the 24th Battalion took a highly creditable part.

On the night of June 2nd, the Battalion, less two companies in Voormezeele Defences, stood to in Scottish Wood, awaiting possible orders to advance in support of the battalions of the 3rd Canadian Division. No orders to move were received, but, even in positions behind the front, the Battalion suffered from enemy action, for a shell, falling in Voormezeele, severely wounded six other ranks, including Private J. S. McBride, who, previously, on the Kemmel front, had been the first man in the Battalion to suffer wounds in action. Private McBride had rejoined the Battalion after recovering from his injuries in England, but on this occasion, with one leg blown off and other shattering wounds, recovery was impossible and he died almost at once.

June 3rd, the birthday of His Majesty the King, was marked by the publication of a list of honours granted for service to the State. In the 24th Battalion, at or about this time, those to whom recognition of their work in France was afforded included Major J. A. Ross, who was awarded the Distinguished Service Order for his invaluable reconnaissances of the St. Eloi craters; Capt. P. L. Hall, who received the Military Cross, for courageous leadership in the front line; and Private A. F. Mott, who was awarded the Military Medal for his fine work with the Battalion Scouts.

After standing by all day on June 4th, Headquarters of the 24th Battalion was relieved by Headquarters of the 13th Battalion, King's Liverpool Regiment, of the 9th British Infantry Brigade, and moved to Camp "D," Reninghelst. "A" and "B" Companies were simultaneously relieved in Scottish Wood by companies of the British unit, which also took over from "C" and "D" Companies the duty of garrisoning the Voormezeele Defences. When the reliefs were completed, the 24th Battalion joined the other units of the 5th Canadian Infantry Brigade in Corps Reserve.

Two days later, at 7.45 p.m., the Battalion embussed in Reninghelst and drove to a point not far from Vlamertinghe, whence, after passing through Ypres on foot, the companies relieved the 2nd Battalion, of the 1st Canadian Division, in front line trenches between Armagh Wood and Maple Copse. When relief had been completed, Battalion Headquarters was situated in Valley Cottages, the four companies occupied the front line and immediate supports, and three platoons of the 22nd French-Canadian Battalion, under 24th Battalion orders, were available to reinforce any section of the front where need might arise.

On the way to the front line from Ypres, the Battalion was harassed severely by enemy fire. At approximately 11.45 p.m., "B" Coy., under Lieut. C. S. B. White, was passing in single file along the road in front of the church in Zillebeke when a heavy shell burst in the midst of No. 5 Platoon, no warning preceding it, as the sound of its approach had been drowned by the noise of a field battery clattering huriedly towards the front.

When the shell burst, the company commander was hurled into the roadside ditch, but soon recovered his feet and dazedly sought his men. For a moment it seemed that No. 5 Platoon had disappeared, but eventually, from a carnage of torn and riven bodies on the road, Lieut. G. V. Walsh and Company Sergeant-Major L. A. Sewell reported themselves unwounded. Lieut. Walsh was suffering from severe concussion, but was able to report the disaster and summon assistance from the rear.

Meanwhile, Lieut. White and Company Sergeant-Major Sewell strove to move the wounded from the road, which was threatened by further shells and along which the battery of field guns was waiting to advance. Twelve men lay dead on the road, including two of "B" Company's Signallers, and eleven severely wounded lay amongst them. Arms and legs were strewn around and in the darkness the nightmare task was to separate the wounded and dying from the dead. The guns must await the clearing from their path of the wounded; exposed to destruction by enemy fire, they could not await removal of the dead.

At last, with the help of stretcher-bearers, summoned by Lieut. Walsh from the rear, the wounded were moved from the road. The guns then rumbled forward on their appointed mission; the dead were carried to the roadside to await the completion of arrangements for their burial; and Lieut. White and Company Sergt.-Major Sewell, after a last survey of a scene which neither will forget so long as life endures, proceeded to join the remaining platoons of "B" Coy. in the line.

Sunrise on June 8th marked for the men of the 24th Battalion the beginning of a day of anxiety and peril. Their positions, in shallow ditches dug hastily after the check of the German onslaught on June 2nd and 3rd, were under enemy observation from Mount Sorrel and were subject to galling enfilade. Movement was almost impossible; and there was no escape from the continued battering of the German guns. Realizing that the Canadians' position was almost without defences, the enemy shelled vigorously all day. Trenches disintegrated under the constant fire and casualties mounted steadily; but at 1 o'clock on the morning of June 9th the men were cheered by an intense blast of retaliatory gun fire which played for half an hour on the German lines. This fire conveyed unmistakably the fact that, so far as the Canadian Corps was concerned, the German challenge of June 2nd had been accepted.

Shelling by the Canadian guns and counter-shelling by the enemy were again features of the engagement on June 10th. From 1.30 to 2.30 o'clock in the morning and from 6 to 6.30 o'clock in the afternoon, the bombardments increased to an intensity such as the men of the 24th had never previously witnessed. Before their eyes, the country around them was torn and rent, as it had been a week previously when the Germans and Canadians whose bodies were strewn about fought determinedly for its possession.

Again on the early morning of June 11th and at intervals throughout the day, whirlwind bombardments by the Canadian and German artilleries struck the devastated area between Armagh Wood and Maple Copse, and the 24th Battalion suffered severely. Shells battered the line from before dawn until after dark and casualties for the tour mounted to a total of one hundred and eleven.

Throughout the whole of this period, notable work was accomplished by the Battalion and company signallers, Private L. A. Bushe and his brother Private J. F. Bushe, in particular, gaining distinction for the manner in which the lines they supervised were over and over repaired in circumstances of the greatest danger. The Battalion and company runners, too, delivered messages unfailingly, despite fire under which the successful carrying out of their duties seemed almost impossible.

Early in the morning on June 11th, Lieut. G. S. LeMesurier, who had received a commission after service in the ranks of the 8th Canadian Battalion and had joined the 24th Battalion in May, was caught by the burst of a high explosive shell, which tore away one leg. For hours he lay without shelter, on the bottom of a shallow trench. Rain added to his misery, but he spoke no word of complaint, only, indeed, a few words of thanks to the Medical Officer, Capt. A. H. Taylor, who attended to his wounds, and of apology for causing trouble. Then, at 2 p.m., he remarked quietly "All is getting black," and in another moment his life ended. That night, with a number of officers and other ranks paying final honours, his body was buried near Battalion Headquarters.

On the day when Lieut. LeMesurier died so bravely in the line, the men of the 24th Battalion were notified that they would be relieved by the 2nd Battalion that night. The relief was completed at 12 p.m. and the 24th Battalion marched back to Camp "A," where the 5th Brigade was in Corps Reserve. Before leaving the line, Private E. H. R. Swift, of "A" Coy., captured a prisoner, Private G. Fischer, of the 121st Wurtemburg Regiment, who, though frightened almost beyond the power of speech, replied falteringly to questions at Battalion Headquarters and stated that the effect of the Canadian artillery on the German lines had been appalling.

After remaining in Corps Reserve on June 13th, the day when the 1st Canadian Division was counter-attacking successfully on the Hill 62—Mount Sorrel front, the 24th Battalion, at 7 p.m. on June 14th, was relieved in Camp "A" by the 2nd Battalion, Scots Guards, and moved forward to take over from the 4th Canadian Battalion the support line from Maple Copse to Armagh Wood, with Battalion Headquarters, as during the previous tour, at Valley Cottages. Three companies carried out this relief, taking over ground across which the 14th Battalion, Royal Montreal Regiment, had advanced so courageously ten days before; the fourth company, attached for orders to the 26th Canadian Battalion, occupied Halifax Trench, a position from which the Germans, on the previous day, had been ejected. Lieut. C. S. B. White, during the forward move of the Battalion, was attacked at Transport Farm by a Canadian soldier who had taken part in the fighting of the previous day. This man, crazed by his experiences in action, thought that White was a German and that those who rescued the 24th Battalion officer were also Huns. Shouting that nothing would make him reveal the position of his battalion, the madman was overpowered at last and led, under escort, to the rear.

Heavy shelling harassed the men of the 24th during the move to the forward area, in which morning revealed striking evidence of the fierce battles of June 2nd, 3rd and 13th. Dead lay everywhere; material of all types was half buried in the deep mud of the churned area; and in Sanctuary Wood, lay two "sacrifice" guns, which, on June 2nd, had become enshrined in Canadian military history forever, together with the name of Lieut. C. P. Cotton, who gave his life in serving them, and the reputation of the gunners, who died valiantly by his side, among them Gunner W. E. P. Bowie, an original member of the 24th Battalion.

Though the Battalion War Diary states that June 15th was "comparatively quiet," it was so only when compared with the days immediately preceding it. Shell fire was not intense, but additions were made to the never-ending roll of the Battalion's killed and wounded, among the casualties being Lieut. D. A. Ewan, wounded in the arm. Shells, striking Battalion positions from the rear, created for a time the impression that the supporting artillery was firing short, but investigation revealed that German heavy guns were responsible, the arc of the Ypres Salient explaining the apparent bombardment from the rear.

Moderate enemy shell fire permitted the men of the 24th to move about at night in the area they had taken over and to explore carefully the shattered dugouts which the enemy had at one time occupied. As a result, 6 wounded Germans were rescued and carried to Valley Cottages, where their infected injuries were cleaned and dressed. The majority of these wounded had suffered severe injury from the fire of the Canadian guns and, having been without food for days, were in a state exciting the compassion of those who took them prisoner.

Equally pitiable was the condition of Lieut. Karl Lieber, Machine-Gun Officer of the 120th German Regiment, who was rescued by the Canadians that same night. This officer, $19\frac{1}{2}$ years old, wounded in the legs, chest, and eye, had lain helpless for three days in a dugout in companionship with three of his unit's dead. Despite his sufferings and ghastly experience, he had maintained his fortitude and, when rescued, displayed admirable dignity and courage. No artificial hatred could lower the respect this brave man commanded and the Canadians, after dressing his wounds, sincerely wished him complete recovery.

Less tragic and more entertaining to the troops in consequence, was a man of the 125th Wurtemburg Regiment, found in a dugout that same day. This yokel, unwounded, but believing stories of the Red Indian tortures inflicted by Canadian troops upon their prisoners of war, had remained for days hidden below ground, trembling with fear when sounds from above indicated that someone was approaching. Starvation had undermined a courage none too robust and the man, when captured, was gibbering with fright. No harm could be offered in such circumstances and the prisoner, believing only that his fate had been unaccountably delayed, was bundled to the rear.

If June 15th was "comparatively quiet," no such description could apply on the day that followed. Shelling was persistent, the resulting casualties including Capt. B. H. T. MacKenzie, severely wounded for the second time; Corporal W. J. Hobday, killed; and approximately 20 other ranks killed and wounded.

That night an effort was made to repair damage done to the trenches by the German shells, but at 9 p.m. working parties were cancelled, owing to an increase in the volume of enemy fire. From 9.30 to 11 p.m. fire was heavy and persistent, but immediately thereafter it increased and a barrage fell between the companies in the line and Battalion Headquarters. Again between 2 and 3 o'clock on the morning of the 17th, barrage fire struck the area. For a time it was thought that this indicated a German attack on the front line, but no action developed. Again from 9.10 to 9.30 a.m. the enemy bombarded heavily, battering the Battalion's trenches and inflicting a few casualties, but achieving little of importance.

Though it might be said that the enemy fire on June 17th was "comparatively ineffective," Lieut. R. L. Weaver was wounded and the bombardments imposed on the weary men of the 24th Battalion the duty of repairing, under continued fire, the damage to their trenches that resulted. As soon as darkness fell every man available was set to work. Some improvement was effected, but shelling continued and, when day broke, the men were forced to admit that the net result of their arduous toil was disappointing.

After the heavy work on the night of June 17th, the men of the 24th were gratified when morning on the 18th brought no recurrence of the violent bombardments with which the enemy for some time past had greeted each new day. Again on the 19th no shelling of unusual intensity occurred, but intermittent fire inflicted a number of casualties, including the wounding of Lieut. J. C. Heaton, who had rejoined the unit after recovering from a wound received at St. Eloi in the previous April.

At night on the 19th the 24th Battalion was relieved by the 15th Battalion (48th Highlanders of Canada), Headquarters and one company moving to Railway Dugouts, one company occupying Woodcote House, and two companies moving back to Camp "H," Reninghelst. To Camp "H" the remaining companies moved on June 20th, the 5th Brigade being held at the time in Corps Reserve.

III

In Corps Reserve at Reninghelst the Battalion spent six days, marked by a visit from the new Corps Commander, Lieut.-General the Hon. Sir Julian Byng, on June 25th by Brigadier-General A. H. Macdonnel's inspection of the Transport, and, on the same afternoon, by highly successful sports. Next night, at 9 o'clock, the Battalion relieved the 29th Canadian Battalion in the centre sector of the St. Eloi trenches, with Battalion Headquarters in Bollartbeek Dugouts, "C" Coy. in Trenches 15 to 22 in the front line, "B" Coy. in immediate support, and "D" and "A" Companies respectively in the Voormezeele Switch and Voormezeele Defences.

On taking over from the 29th Battalion, the men of "C" Coy. found that no communication trenches gave access to the badly damaged front line, but that construction was under way and must be continued. The other companies, too, received orders to supply working parties each night and to bend every effort towards the improvement of the positions they occupied. On the whole, the following ten days were uneventful. Lieut. C. S. B. White was wounded in the shoulder and arm on the night of June 29th, but this was the only casualty amongst the officers. Casualties to other ranks were also light, totalling about 5 in all.

Patrols of the Battalion moved freely in No Man's Land on each night of this tour, approaching the German line repeatedly, but reporting little activity in the enemy trenches, which seemed to be garrisoned by forces appreciably weaker than usual. The enemy, too, had apparently withdrawn some batteries of artillery, for shell fire was light, though enemy aeroplanes, around Voormezeele, offset the low volume of artillery fire by bombing ration parties of the 24th whenever an opportunity was afforded.

On July 2nd all ranks of the Battalion were interested by news of the opening on the previous day of the Franco-British offensive at the Somme. At a later date the Battalion was to know the Somme, but in July the Canadian Corps was engaged in the Ypres Salient and news of the battle was received with no premonition that before it ended the 1st, 2nd, and 3rd Canadian Divisions, and the newly-formed 4th Canadian Division, would experience abundantly its agony and sorrow.

On the day when news of the opening of the Battles of the Somme was received, the 24th Battalion welcomed eight officer reinforcements. One of these, Lieut. M. Laing, rejoined after recovering from wounds received in the previous October; six reported from the strength of the 70th Canadian Battalion; and one from the 37th Canadian Battalion. A few days later, the commissioned establishment of the 24th was further strengthened when four more officers reported for duty from England.

By the time that the second group of officers arrived, the Battalion had been relieved on the night of July 6th by the 25th Battalion and had moved into Brigade Reserve, with Headquarters and two companies at Dickebusch, and two companies, plus the Machine-Gun Section, Bombing Platoon, and Battalion Scouts, in Scottish Wood. Corporal T. E. Dowse, who had completed a special course at Reninghelst, rejoined the unit at this time and assumed duties as Armourer Corporal.

For ten days 24th Battalion Headquarters and three of the companies remained in the positions taken up on the night of July 6th, but on the 8th "D" Coy. moved from Scottish Wood into the Voormezeele Defences, under the orders of the 25th Canadian Battalion. For all ranks of the 24th Battalion, the period was marked by frequent parties supplied to other units for carrying supplies, digging front line trenches, and burying cables. It would be monotonous to list these parties, to describe the work which each accomplished, or to detail the adventures of the personnel, but one party should be mentioned. This group, composed of 2 officers and 71 other ranks, reported to the 5th Canadian Infantry Brigade on July 10th for the duty of carrying into the front line gas cylinders to be used in a raiding, gas, artillery, and smoke demonstration against enemy position at Piccadilly Farm. Thirteen scouts of the Battalion guided G. S. wagons loaded with the cylinders from Micmac Camp to a point in the forward area, whence, under a guard also furnished by the 24th Battalion, the cylinders were carried into the line.

Though the carrying forward of the cylinders on July 10th was the principal military accomplishment of the Battalion's period in Brigade Reserve, July 15th was marked by the publication of the second number of *The Vic's Patrol*, a trench magazine produced, with the permission of Lieut.-Col. Gunn, by Hon. Capt. the Rev. C. J. S. Stuart, Editor-in-Chief; Private A. D. Smith of "D" Coy., Assistant Editor; C.Q.M.S. Lyon, of "D" Coy., Corporal A. S. Tracey, of the Signal Section, Sergt. G. S. Bushe, and Sergt. W. W. Wallace. At the time of publication, the Assistant Editor, who had been wounded, was in hospital in England, where, no doubt he heard of the magazine's success. On the first page appeared a sketch of Private ("Snowball") Darling, of "A" Coy., who at Zillebeke in the previous month had been taken from his duties as a cook to escort a German prisoner to the rear. At a point where a parapet blocked the way, Darling found that the bombs he carried impeded progress, so tossed them to his prisoner, remarking casually, "Hold these, Fritz, while I climb over." And the German, impressed by such overwhelming confidence, held the bombs as he was told.

In addition to a sketch of this incident, the magazine printed some good amateur verse; the results of competition in sport; details of the promotions and transfers of officers; and a paragraph of congratulations to Major J. A. Ross on his D.S.O., to Capt. P. L. Hall on his Military Cross, and to Battalion Sergt.-Major J. Hennessy, Sergt. H. S. Naylor, Corporal A. Metzger, and Lance-Corporal A. F. Mott on their Military Medals. Additions to the officer strength of the Battalion since its arrival in France were listed as follows:

Promotions:

Lieut. E. G. N. Lidstone, promoted from Battalion Sergt-Major (December 16, 1915).

Lieut. E. M. Amphlett, promoted from Machine-Gun Sergeant (January 7, 1916).

Lieut. D. A. Ewan, promoted from Sergeant (March 5, 1916).

Lieut. C. Dolphin, promoted from Sergeant (March 5, 1916).

Lieut. J. N. Bales, promoted from Battalion Sergt-Major (March 12, 1916).

Lieut R. H. Lamb, promoted from Sergeant (March 19, 1916).

Lieut. A. M. Dewar, promoted from Battalion Sergt-Major (June 26, 1916).

Lieut. G. Haddock, promoted from Sergeant. (June 26, 1916).

Reinforcements:

Lieuts. A. Fowlie, J. A. Parke, H. E. Scott, N. J. Marion, A. B. Campbell, R. L. Weaver (wounded), G. S. LeMesurier (killed in action), J. M. MacArthur, J. C. Carling, G. G. Garvey, N. L. LeSueur, G. A. McGiffin, J. F. Meek, J. C. Grant, E. G. Hart, K. S. Drummond, W. A. O'Hara, H. C. Mathias, C. A. Howell, S. Cowan, C. P. Smith, J. D. McIntyre, C. E. Hill, E. R. Wright and W. M. Rogers.

On July 15th, the 24th Battalion moved into Camp "H," Reninghelst, and there spent 9 days carrying out a syllabus of training, with special attention paid to bayonet fighting, bombing, squad drill, and arm drill. No outstanding incident marked the period, though sports were held, and on July 23rd a parade, at which Divine Service was conducted by the unit's Chaplain and the sermon preached by Hon. Capt. the Reverend A. P. Shatford, former Chaplain.

IV

On completion of the training at Reninghelst, the 24th Battalion moved forward on July 23rd and relieved the 31st Canadian Battalion in the right sector of the Vierstraat (M. and N.) Trenches, "C" and "D" Companies, 8 machine-guns, and one section of bombers taking over the actual front, with "A" and "B" Companies, the Scouts, and two bombing sections in dugouts near Battalion Headquarters.

Hostile artillery was not active during the relief, or immediately thereafter, but machine-gun fire was heavy and enemy trench mortars bombarded steadily. Early on the morning of July 24th, a trench mortar shell crashed into a dugout in the "N" section of the front, killing Coy. Sergt.-Major H. P. Sullivan, Sergt. G. H. Frampton, and one other man and wounding a number severely. Enemy artillery remained comparatively inactive thereafter, but the trench mortars continued their destructive work, until British Stokes guns undertook retaliation. The Stokes mortars, sighted with skill, hammered the positions of the German mortars and, by rendering these untenable, afforded the men of the 24th welcome relief from the fire they had previously endured.

On July 28, 1916, Lieut.-Col. Gunn, over the signature of his Assistant Adjutant, Lieut. A. Fowlie, issued orders for a small raid on the enemy position opposite the "M" trenches, to capture a prisoner, or otherwise obtain identification of the German unit holding the front. Movement of enemy troops to the Somme was suspected and it was important that the British Intelligence Staff should receive frequent and reliable reports on which knowledge regarding the transfer of German divisions could be based.

For the attempt to secure identification of the German unit opposing the 24th Battalion, Lieut. P. I. Walker and 9 other ranks were ordered to blacken their faces, equip themselves with 8 Mills bombs, 4 knobkerries, 4 revolvers, 2 pairs of wire-cutters and other accessories, and, at 1 o'clock on the morning of July 29th, to drive forward into the German line. Sergt. A. Geddes and 5 other ranks were ordered to advance as far as the point of entry into the enemy trenches and there to stand fast, ready to cover the attacking group when the time came to withdraw. Sergt. W. G. S. Egerton, 6 bombers, and 1 Lewis Gun crew were also ordered to move into No Man's Land to check any German attempt to rescue a prisoner or otherwise harass the Canadians' retreat. The Battalion Machine-Gun Officer was ordered to afford the attacking party still further protection by directing heavy fire against the German positions on both flanks.

Unfortunately, the careful organization of the raid and a determined effort on the part of Lieut. Walker and his men, failed to achieve substantial success. The raiding party advanced to a point not far from the German line, but the enemy had observed the previous cutting of his wire, was alert, and opened such heavy fire that further progress was impossible. Lieut. Walker waited for a time, hoping that an opportunity to complete the operation might still be afforded, but, at last, realizing that his hope was vain, he reluctantly gave the order to withdraw. Bearing the body of one man who had been killed and 2 men who had been wounded, the 24th Battalion parties returned without further losses to their own lines.

For two days after the attempt to raid the German trenches, the 24th Battalion remained in the front line. Enemy trench mortars became active on the afternoon of July 30th, but little damage resulted, none affecting the forward movement of the 22nd French-Canadian Battalion, which relieved the 24th on the following night. After relief, the men of the 24th moved to Brigade Reserve positions at La Clytte.

For half the month of August, 1916, the 24th Battalion, Victoria Rifles of Canada, remained in reserve, for four days at La Clytte, followed by three days at Ridgewood, and finally by 8 days at Camp "J," Reninghelst. At La Clytte, a change in the duties of officers was announced, when Capt. C. F. Ritchie took command of "C" Coy. and was succeeded as Adjutant by Lieut. A. Fowlie. A few days later, Lieut. A. L. S. Mills reported back to the Battalion from duty in England; Lieut. H. E. Scott reported from hospital, after recovering from a wound; and Major W. Butler, Major E. C. Woolsey, and

Capt. E. J. Griffith arrived from reserve battalions in England.

A week later, the Battalion paraded in heavy marching order for inspection by the Corps Commander, Sir Julian Byng. Careful training of the men, after their series of tours in the front line, had produced good results and the appearance and bearing of the unit proved highly satisfactory. General Byng expressed his approval to Lieut.-Col. Gunn, adding that the Battalion Transport was the equal of any he had seen in France.

Training was resumed after the inspection and for a time it was hoped that the Battalion might have the honour of parading before His Majesty the King, who passed through Reninghelst on August 14th and witnessed some sections of the unit at work, but whose engagements did not permit a formal review. Great as the pleasure of such an inspection would have been, more value, perhaps, attached to an experiment carried out in conjunction with aeroplanes on August 15th. In this operation, tin discs were fastened to the men's backs and the pilots of the planes, in varying conditions of light and shade, sought to discover in what degree the discs helped reconnaissance of an attack from the air.

After completing the period in Divisional Reserve, the 24th Battalion paraded on the evening of August 16th and advanced to relieve the 29th Canadian Battalion in the Centre Sector of the line at St. Eloi. Rain fell heavily during the relief, the resulting mud furnishing for Lieut.-Col. J. W. Warden and the officers and men of two companies of the 102nd Battalion, 4th Canadian Division, who were attached to the 24th Battalion for instruction, an example of the difficulties with which a relief in such circumstances was effected.

Despite the impediment of rain and deep mud, "A" and "B" Companies of the 24th, each with a platoon of the 102nd Battalion attached, moved without appreciable delay into the front line, "B" and "D" Companies, also with 102nd Battalion platoons attached, taking over simultaneously the support positions of the 29th Battalion in Trench R.16 and the Voormezeele Switch. Lieut.-Col. Gunn, Lieut.-Col. Warden, and their respective staffs established their Headquarters in dugout positions at Bollartbeek.

For three days, the men of the 24th Battalion and their comrades of the 102nd enjoyed comparative immunity from enemy fire. A few shells fell near Battalion Headquarters and at intervals desultory bombardments struck the front and support lines, one of these blowing about 10 feet of parapet on top of a half dozen men, without inflicting serious injuries.

Four minor casualties were suffered by the 24th Battalion in the first few days of the tour; but on August 19th, when the enemy opened a 5-hour bombardment at 10 a.m., the Battalion's position was battered to pieces with a heavy toll of killed and wounded. Severe though the bombardment was, the shattering of front, support, and communication trenches produced no situation with which, from bitter experience, the men of the 24th Battalion were unfamiliar. Undismayed, therefore, they gathered their dead, carried their seriously wounded to the Regimental Aid Post, and stood fast, as, in similar circumstances, they had done so often before.

To the men of No. 3 Coy. of the 102nd Battalion, the experience illustrated the suffering and horror that intense bombardment of a trench position involves. Before the German gunners ceased fire, 6 men of the 102nd had been killed and 12 seriously wounded. In circumstances more trying than mere recital of the facts can reveal, the men of the 102nd established the fighting reputation of their unit and proved that in the 4th Canadian Division were men equal in the essential qualities of a soldier to any in the Dominion's forces overseas.

That this should have been so was well, for the training of the 4th Division battalions in the line preceded by a few days only the relief of the 2nd Canadian Division by the 4th Canadian Division in the St. Eloi and adjoining sectors. On August 20th, the 25th Battalion took over the centre of the St. Eloi line from the 24th Battalion, which moved into reserve, with Headquarters, two companies, and all details at Micmac Camp, one company in Scottish Wood in immediate support, and one company in the Voormezeele Defences. Relief in these positions was carried out by corresponding elements of the 54th and 102nd Canadian Battalions, after which, on August 24th, the Battalion moved to Quebec Camp, Reninghelst.

CHAPTER V

THE SOMME

I

Of all the battles fought by the British Army on the Western Front in the Great War, none, with the possible exception of the Flanders Offensive in 1917, has produced more criticism of British methods and leadership than that series of great engagements now known officially as "The Battles of the Somme, 1916." Originally, in accordance with the plan agreed upon by Marshal Joffre and Field Marshal Sir Douglas Haig on February 12, 1916, the battles were to have been opened on July 1st by 39 French divisions on a front of 30 miles, with a subsidiary British attack, on a 15-mile front, with a maximum of 25 divisions participating. Primarily, the object of the battle was not to be geographical; the dominating purpose was to kill or capture men and guns, not to seize towns and villages. Before the battle opened, it had acquired the further vital function of relieving as rapidly as possible the well-nigh intolerable pressure on the French forces at Verdun.

It should not be inferred from emphasis on the primary purpose of the battle, that no strategic objective existed, for Marshal Joffre has stated that it was his intention to "carry a mass of manoeuvre against the group of German communications running through Cambrai, Le Cateau, and Maubeuge," but this purpose was secondary to the dominating plan of engaging the German Army and, in sustained fighting, wearing down its power of resistance. There was no serious thought of a "break through," with resulting defeat of the German Army, in the opening stages of the battle; on the contrary, Marshal Joffre, in his directive dated June 21st, explicitly stated that the engagement would be long and hard fought. In these circumstances, the final objectives were recognized as objectives to be attained by the full weight of the Allied Armies, not for the troops engaged at any one time.

As the date set for the opening of the battle approached and as French divisions disappeared into the furnace stoked by the fierce and sustained attack of the armies of the German Crown Prince at Verdun, the importance of the British attack at the Somme grew rapidly and that of the French diminished. By July 1st, the proposed rôles of the two Armies had been reversed and the major burden had shifted definitely to the shoulders of the British, the French front having been reduced to 8 miles from the 30 miles originally proposed and the number of attacking French divisions from 39 to 5. In addition, 11 French divisions, under General Ferdinand Foch, were prepared to engage as the battle progressed.

Opening the battle on the day and at the hour planned many months before, the French attack and the main British attack, on the 10-mile front between the Somme and the Ancre, achieved striking success, but north of the Ancre, a subsidiary British attack, which at one time reached Beaumont-Hamel and Serre, was later driven back with heavy losses. In the first five days of the battle, the British, on a front of six miles, drove for more than a mile into the German defences, capturing many guns and prisoners and inflicting a heavy toll of killed and wounded. North of the Ancre, however, the check was severe and offset, in a great degree, the notable success to the south.

Gathering his forces after the waves of the assault of July 1st had been brought eventually to a standstill, Sir Douglas Haig struck again at dawn on July 14th, gaining in three days of bitter fighting nearly four miles of the crest of the ridge dominating the Somme battlefield. For two months thereafter, the British and German Armies were locked fast in what the British Commander-in-Chief has described as "a real trial of strength and endurance," the British fighting doggedly for positions whence the advance on a major scale could be renewed and the enemy putting forth a supreme effort to retain trenches vital to the British plan.

By the end of the first week in September, German resistance on the whole front showed signs of weakening. To the north, in the Ancre sector, progress had been made in overcoming the result of the check in the opening engagement; on the main battle front practically the whole of the dominating ridge had been captured; and to the south the French, though somewhat behind the British, were in a position to co-operate in further action.

Accordingly, on September 15th, in an engagement notable as the first in which tanks were employed, Sir Douglas Haig struck on a 6-mile front astride the Albert-Bapaume Road and drove the enemy back for more than a mile. Renewing the attack on September 25th, the British again achieved success; but the French on the right were less fortunate, their failure impairing, to some extent, the success of the day's operations as a whole.

Despite the check on the right, British hope for a smashing victory ran high as September ended; but in October heavy and continuous rain washed away all possibility of decisive action. Disappointment in the result of the Battles of the Somme, 1916, was universal in the Allied countries and comment on the cost of what seemed a tragic failure was tinged with the bitterness of those whose kith and kin had paid the dreadful price.

High as the price was, the British Commander-in-Chief in his "Somme Despatch" and in all discussion to the end of his life maintained that it was not paid in vain. The Battles of the Somme, 1916, he claimed, and with his judgment many notable soldiers agree, yielded results far greater than at first appeared. When the battle ended, pressure on Verdun had been relieved so appreciably that the French were able to assume the offensive, capturing thousands of German prisoners; moreover, to quote General Ludendorff, the German Army on the Western Front was "completely exhausted." Ninety-eight German divisions and four brigades had been drawn into the fighting and had suffered losses so severe that defeat in 1916 had been narrowly averted; and defeat when the Allies should renew the battle in 1917 appeared evitable only if Fortune should grant to the Germans favour more pronounced than reason could lead them to expect. Through circumstances over which the British Army had no control, the battle was not renewed in the following year. Had it been, the result of the engagements of 1916 might more easily be weighed and valued.

Sir Douglas Haig stated in 1916 his belief that the losses of the enemy in the Battles of the Somme were greater than his own and those of the French combined. Critics have ridiculed this statement, and some have classed it as a falsehood, justifiable, possibly, on grounds of military advisability, but without basis in Sir Douglas Haig's mind. Owing to differing methods of compiling casualty returns, comparison of the actual losses is, even to-day (1930), a difficult matter and the results obtained represent opinion rather than established fact, nevertheless there is a growing body of thought supporting Sir Douglas Haig's view.

For example, with British, French, and German statistics available, Major-General Sir Frederick Maurice estimates (1928) that German casualties totalled 558,000, British 342,112, and French 143,072, giving an Allied total of 486,184. Though casualty estimates vary, there can now be no doubt that in the Battles of the Somme, 1916, Sir Douglas Haig brought the German Army perilously near to disastrous and irremediable defeat. No one can say what would have happened had it been possible to continue the battle on a major scale in October and November, 1916, or to renew it in the spring of 1917; but, from the measure of success which the New Armies of Great Britain, the Armies of the British Dominions, and the co-operating French Armies achieved from July to September, 1916, it would seem that victory on a major scale might have resulted.

II

In the latter part of August, 1916, when the newly-arrived 4th Canadian Division took over the St. Eloi and adjoining sectors of front line trenches, the 2nd Canadian Division joined the march of the 1st and 3rd Canadian Divisions towards the area in which were raging the mighty Battles of the Somme. Further effort to encompass the defeat of the enemy in these great engagements was clearly indicated, and the men of the 2nd

Division, as they marched away from Ypres, knew that a time of peril and sacrifice lay not far ahead.

In the 24th Battalion, Victoria Rifles of Canada, réveillé sounded at 2.30 o'clock on the morning of August 26th, and at 4.30 a.m. the Battalion marched to join the column of the 5th Canadian Infantry Brigade at a point on the Abeele-Poperinghe Road. Rain fell throughout the 9-mile march to Steenvoorde that followed, nevertheless the column, as it passed under the eyes of the Corps Commander in Abeele, presented a fine example of march discipline and well organized efficiency.

Parading again in the early morning on August 27th, the 24th Battalion marched about 14 miles to billets in Noordpeene, the men enjoying the lovely view as the unit swung through the outskirts of Cassel and noting the abundant harvest ripening on every side. After life in the war-torn fields of Flanders, the beauty of the quiet countryside created an impression which, in some instances, has remained vivid despite the passing of many years.

Again on August 28th, as the Battalion marched by way of Watten to Eperlecques, attractive scenery was encountered, especially from the top of a long hill near Watten. In the history of the Battalion, however, the day is marked not by memories of scenery and lovely views, but by the issue of Lee-Enfield rifles to replace the Ross rifles which the men had brought with them from Canada. Opinions on the service value of the Ross rifle may vary, but the Lee-Enfield was a weapon tested by the experience of war and the men welcomed its issue with unconcealed satisfaction. Officers, too, believing in the Lee-Enfield's efficacy, were not sorry to bid its predecessor farewell.

For a week after the issue of Lee-Enfield rifles, the 24th Battalion marched from Eperlecques each day to a special Training Area and carried out manoeuvres designed to prepare the men for the type of fighting they would experience at the Somme. Starting on the first day with the practice of "Section in Attack," followed by "Platoon in Attack," "Company in Attack," and "Battalion in Attack," the syllabus ended on the seventh day with manoeuvres embodying in detail the procedure laid down for attack on the enemy by an entire brigade. Throughout the period, attention was given to musketry, and the men were trained in the use of their new rifles, which they found highly satisfactory.

On completion of the period of training at Eperlecques, the Battalion paraded at 10.30 o'clock on the morning of September 4, 1916, and marched, by way of St. Omer, to Arques, where at 8.30 p.m. the men entrained. Leaving Arques fifteen minutes later, the train travelled all night, passed through Calais and Boulogne, and reached Conteville at 5.30 a.m. Unloading of equipment was completed by 6.20 a.m., and the unit marched, by way of Gramont, to billets in Coulonvillers.

After resting at Coulonvillers on September 5th, the Battalion marched 12 miles on September 6th to Halloy les Pernois, continuing the move on the following day by marching six miles to La Vicogne. From this village, Lieut.-Col. Gunn, his Bombing Officer, and the commanders of "A," "B," and "C" Companies proceeded to reconnoitre the area in which the Battalion would be employed, rejoining the unit that night. Even before the departure of this party, any lingering doubt regarding the scene of the Battalion's forthcoming endeavour had vanished completely, for, as the men marched on the preceding days, each mile had brought more distinctly to their ears the ominous thunder of the distant guns. British and enemy planes, too, by activity overhead, indicated approach to an area where bitter fighting must be expected.

Marching from La Vicogne on September 8th, the Battalion proceeded to Hérissart, where it was joined by Major R. O. Alexander, the Second-in-Command, and a group of officers, who, following in the footsteps of Lieut.-Col. Gunn and his companions, had reconnoitred the area from Albert forward to Contalmaison and Pozières. To the members of these two parties the deep sound of guns, as the Battalion marched on the morning of September 9th from Hérissart to Vadencourt Wood, occasioned no surprise. They had seen the massed batteries of the Somme and realized that when these opened fire their deep roar must surpass in volume even that to which the Canadians had become accustomed in the Salient.

Arriving in Vadencourt Wood at 11 a.m., the men of the 24th Battalion occupied hutments and were soon employed in sewing on the shoulders of their tunics the battle patches, which, for the remainder of the war, were to distinguish the formations of the Canadian Corps. The rectangular, oblong patch of the 2nd Canadian Division was dark blue; and above this the 24th Battalion mounted a small red semi-circle, the design and colour of the two patches enabling identification at a glance of the division, brigade, and battalion to which the wearer belonged.

On the morning following the issue of battle patches, Roman Catholic members of the 24th Battalion marched at 8.15 a.m. to attend Mass; and at 10.30 o'clock the Protestant majority attended Divine Service, conducted in the open by the Battalion Chaplain, Hon. Capt. C. J. S. Stuart. After a short sermon, preached from an altar of Red Cross packing cases, Capt. Stuart held a celebration of Holy Communion, in which more than 150 officers and men took part. Despite the passing of years, the sight of the troops kneeling before the rude altar in the open field is treasured in memory by many of those who, tasting soon thereafter the bitterness of the Somme, are numbered amongst its survivors.

At 5 p.m. on September 10th, the 24th Battalion, having marched from Vadencourt Wood, bivouacked in the Brickfields at Albert, whence, on the following day, two fatigue parties, each 125 strong, proceeded to the forward area to bury cable, a third party of the same strength being provided simultaneously to the 6th Canadian Infantry Brigade for trench construction in the line. Similar parties were employed in the forward area on September 12th, 13th, and 14th. The majority experienced no misadventure, but one party, caught by enemy shell fire while digging a communication trench, suffered casualties to other ranks totalling 2 killed and 9 wounded.

While parties of the Battalion were at work in the forward area, the main body at the Brickfields was practising attack in co-operation with contact aeroplanes. Simultaneously, Lieut.-Col. Gunn and senior officers of the unit were preparing for operations scheduled to take

The Brickfields at Albert.

place on the morning of September 15th, the first anniversary of the arrival of the Battalion in France. The 4th and 6th Canadian Infantry Brigades were to attack the Sugar Refinery near Courcelette and the 24th Battalion, attached for the time to the 4th Brigade, was to operate as Brigade Reserve.

While the Battalion was at the Brickfields, Lieut.-Col. Gunn and a number of officers proceeded to view a fleet of the new British weapons known eventually as tanks, which, for the first time, were to be tested in battle on September 15th. None of the officers had seen these monsters before; and opinion as to their probable value in action was sharply divided. As it happened, decision on this point was not reached on September 15th, and for a long time thereafter reports regarding the work of the tanks remained highly contradictory, each man governing his comment by what he had seen, or heard, and commending, or criticizing, the new weapons accordingly.

Actually, the tanks at Flers and Martinpuich demoralized some enemy units and contributed to a striking British success; in other instances they failed lamentably to accomplish what was expected of them, or even to reach their places of assembly. Statistics now available show that 49 tanks were engaged; 32 reached their jumping off positions; 9 broke down soon thereafter; 5 were promptly ditched; and 18 took a successful part in the battle.

Criticism of the British Command for permitting the secret of the tanks to be disclosed, when the few available were as faulty as the statistics indicate, has been voiced in definite manner; but the answer, that battle provides a test surpassing all others and that only in battle can hidden defects of personnel or material be revealed, cannot be dismissed as unworthy of consideration. Though the tanks were far from perfect on September 15, 1916, the British Army maintained throughout the war superiority in the construction of such weapons and, even more markedly, in methods of employing them.

Some impression of the fear they eventually imposed on enemy troops can be gained from the writings of the German soldier, Remarque, who says: "We do not see the guns that bombard us; the attacking lines of infantry are men like ourselves; but the tanks are annihilation—roaring, smoke-belching, invulnerable, steel beasts, squashing the dead and the wounded. Against their colossal weight our arms are sticks of straw and our hand grenades matches. From a mockery, the tanks have become a terrible weapon—and more than anything else embody for us the horror of war."

At midnight on September 14th, the 24th Battalion, under direct command of Lieut.-Col. Gunn, moved forward from the Brickfields at Albert to the Chalk Pits and there awaited the result of the attack on the morning of the 15th. Promptly at 6.20 a.m., the 4th and 6th Brigades drove into the enemy lines, and "C" Coy. of the 24th Battalion, under 4th Brigade orders, occupied the trenches from which the attack was launched. The 24th Battalion, some time later, received orders to move to Munster Alley, where Headquarters were shared with the Commanding Officer and Staff of the 19th Canadian Battalion.

While the main body of the 24th Battalion acted throughout the morning and early afternoon of Septerber 15th as Reserve to the 4th Brigade and remained comparatively inactive, "C" Coy. continued to garrison the 4th Brigade's jumping-off trenches, and "B" Coy., under Lieut. A. L. S. Mills, was employed in carrying material for the 4th Brigade battalions in the line, continuing this work all afternoon, all night, and again on September 16th. Casualties were severe, but officers and men, permitting nothing to interfere with the service they were called upon to render, earned warm commendation from the staffs of the battalions they assisted. Though command of the company was held by Lieut. Mills, who directed the entire operations, work of a valuable nature was also accomplished by Lieut. E. G. N. Lidstone, who displayed courage and resource in handling the tasks assigned to him, and by Lieut. E. G. Hart, who carried out his duties with marked success, until wounded on September 16th.

Meanwhile, shortly after 1 p.m. on September 15th, Brigadier-General A. H. Macdonnel, G.O.C. the 5th Canadian Infantry Brigade, pushed forward to a point near 4th Brigade Headquarters and summoned his

Battalion Commanders to hear the details of an attack to be launched forthwith against the village of Courcelette. Circumstances permitted only a brief reconnaissance, but the capture of the Sugar Refinery by the 4th and 6th Brigades in the morning had seriously affected the enemy's hold on the town and an attack by the 5th Brigade offered the possibility of a striking success.

Accordingly, it was arranged that the 22nd Battalion should attack on the right and the 25th Battalion on the left, with the 26th Battalion mopping up and thereafter remaining in close support, and the 24th Battalion, which came again under the orders of the 5th Brigade, carrying the supplies the attacking battalions would require. The 22nd and 25th Battalions were ordered to attack Courcelette, with the main street of the village as their dividing boundary, to clear their flanks as they pushed through the town, and to consolidate 300 yards beyond.

At 5 p.m., the attacking battalions advanced from their rendezvous in artillery formation and moved forward across open country, in the teeth of an enemy barrage, which threatened to annihilate them. It was a magnificent effort, and deserved the success that accrued. Driving into the enemy positions and using the bayonet freely, the 22nd Battalion inflicted heavy losses in killed and wounded and captured 300 prisoners, including the commanders of a German regiment and a German battalion. Sixteen officers and 320 other ranks of the French-Canadian unit fell in the attack, but nothing could daunt the ardour of those who survived and the Battalion, at 6.45 p.m., reported that its objectives had been attained.

Almost as noteworthy was the success of the 25th Battalion on the left. Seventeen officers and 241 other ranks of this unit were struck down by the enemy barrage, or in hand-to-hand fighting; but, in offset to these losses, 139 prisoners were taken and, in the wake of the unit's advance, the ground was strewn with enemy killed and wounded. For a desperate five minutes, the German troops tried to hold back the men of the 25th with the bayonet, but in this type of fighting they were no match for the Canadians, who drove to their final objective at 6.25 p.m.

Following behind the 22nd and 25th Battalions, the 26th Battalion encountered severe opposition in the village of Courcelette. That night, and even on the following day, parties of German troops emerged to fight from hidden positions in the town, or were routed from the dugouts and cellars where they lay concealed. Sharp casualties were suffered by the 26th as a result, but 600 German prisoners were captured and these numerically far exceeded the unit's losses.

All night on September 15th and all the following day, the men of the 24th Battalion were employed in carrying bombs, rifle ammunition, stretchers, signal lights, and rations to points near the Headquarters of the 22nd and 25th Battalions in Courcelette. Carrying parties are unassociated in the public mind with the glory that attaches to troops engaged in an attack, but the measure of success gained by assaulting waves is governed in a high degree by the success or failure of these unromantic auxiliaries. Knowing that this was so, the men of the 24th Battalion brought to their work determination, courage, and marked endurance. Though shelled and harassed by machine-gun fire, they permitted no circumstance to bar their path lest, in a moment of peril, the units in the line should find their urgent requirements unfulfilled.

It is not possible to follow the scattered parties of the Battalion back and forward amid the smoke of battle and the crash of bursting shells, but one party's story is remembered in the unit through the bravery and devotion to his men of Lieut. Murdoch Laing, the officer in charge. This party, laden with supplies, was working its way forward, when it was caught by the blast of a German barrage. Progress was impossible and shelter became a necessity if any of the party were to survive. Lieut. Laing, accordingly, ordered his men to withdraw to a trench and there seek cover until progress could be resumed. Word was passed to scattered members of the party, but the officer would not seek shelter for himself until assured that all his men were in. While standing so that he might see the men and so that they might rally to where he was, a shell blinded him, and inflicted wounds so severe that he died in hospital on September 18th.

Through the death of Lieut. Laing, the Battalion suffered the loss of an officer who had crossed with the unit from Canada and had rejoined, after recovering from wounds received on the Kemmel front in October, 1915. Nor was this the Battalion's only loss of a brave officer on that day, for Lieut. H. E. Scott, attached as Grenade Officer to the 5th Canadian Infantry Brigade, was killed while establishing a dump for bombs in the forward area.

That afternoon, the Battalion was ordered to carry rations to the companies of the 22nd and 25th Battalions in the front line and to the companies of the 26th Battalion in close support, and, on completion of these tasks, to relieve the 26th Battalion, permitting the 26th to advance and complete relief in the line of the 4th Canadian Infantry Brigade. In obedience to these orders, Lieut.-Col. Gunn saw that the duties of his carrying parties were carried out and then, at 6.30 o'clock on the morning of September 17th, advanced his Battalion Headquarters to a dugout at the Sugar Refinery, Courcelette. Later in the day, Brigade Headquarters ordered the Battalion, less "B" Coy., which was still attached to the 25th Battalion, to carry out an attack on the German front at 5 p.m.

While Lieut.-Col. Gunn and his staff were preparing plans for the attack, "B" Coy., under Lieut. A. L. S. Mills, reported to Lieut.-Col. Hilliam, of the 25th Battalion, and lined a ditch about 100 yards in rear of 25th Headquarters, just beyond Courcelette. Lieut.-Col. Hilliam, who had been wounded in the arm, sent for Lieut. Mills and ordered him to stand by, ready to assist in a forthcoming attack by the 25th, should this prove necessary.

Returning to the ditch where his men were waiting, Lieut. Mills found that shell fire had inflicted a number of casualties, among them being Sergt. A. Metzger, who was lying in a shell hole wounded. His injury did not appear serious, but, as Lieut. Mills bent over him to apply a bandage, a shell burst nearby and a splinter, passing under the officer's extended arm, ripped the sergeant's knee-cap wide open. Blood gushed from the wound, but Lieut. Mills used his necktie as a tourniquet and staunched the flow of blood until more skilled help could be provided.

Following the return of Lieut. Mills with Lieut.-Col. Hilliam's orders, "B" Coy. prepared to advance whenever the 25th Battalion should need their aid. No summons was received; but as the men waited, heavy shell fire battered the position and inflicted numerous casualties. At last a message from Lieut.-Col. Hilliam was received, stating definitely that in the operations his battalion was conducting active participation by the reserve company of the 24th would not be required.

Meanwhile, in the Sunken Road, with their right flank resting on the Albert-Bapaume Road and their left connecting with the flank of the 22nd Battalion, the main body of the 24th Battalion was completing preparations to attack the maze of enemy trenches to the east of Courcelette. Guns of the supporting artillery were firing in an effort to clear the way and orders for barrage fire at the zero hour had been issued, but the gunners had had little opportunity to register on their targets and the accuracy of their fire was seriously affected.

Prompt evidence that the barrage would prove of little value to the attack was forthcoming at 5 p.m., when in response to the sharp blast of a whistle, the three companies of the 24th climbed the bank of the Sunken Road and advanced against the enemy line. The barrage at the time was to have fallen on the German front line, thereby minimizing the volume of machine-gun and rifle fire the enemy could bring to bear; actually, it crashed approximately 500 yards to the enemy rear, serving possibly to prevent the Germans from reinforcing their forward positions, but leaving the strong garrisons of the front line trenches unhampered in their efforts to repel the Canadian attack.

Ignoring the enemy fire, though reminded at once of its danger by a bullet which tore his throat, Major J. A. Ross, D.S.O., led "D" Coy. against the enemy position on the right. With courage that no odds could daunt, he fought his way across the narrow strip of No Man's Land and the men of his company, inspired by his example, followed him straight to the German wire. Even when

The Sunken Road, Courcelette.

they found the wire uncut, no thought of abandoning the attack was entertained. Instead, the men strove desperately to force a way through; but no way through was found, and the Germans, with machine-guns and rifles, shot them steadily down. A few, wounded, dragged themselves back to the Battalion lines; the majority, including the officer who led the attack so gallantly, died in the positions where they fell.

With leadership equal to that on the right, "A" Coy., under Capt. H. D. Kingstone, drove forward in the centre and, despite bitter opposition, forced a way into its objective, attempting at once thereafter to get in touch with "C" and "D" Companies on the two flanks. On the right, a shower of bombs greeted the men as they moved along the trench, but it was not certain whence these bombs came, and the possibility that they had been thrown by men of "D" Coy. existed, "A" Coy. having no knowledge that "D" Coy. had perished almost to a man in the German wire.

Halting his men, Capt. Kingstone climbed to the parados of the trench to discover where the bombing originated and moved to the right to get a better view. Before he had advanced many yards, however, a shell hurled him to the ground, tearing off one hand and shattering his two legs. Simultaneously, a vicious bombing attack killed or wounded the members of his party at the spot where he had halted them.

Stunned and bleeding profusely, Capt. Kingstone lay for a few minutes unattended; but a stretcher-bearer who had seen him fall, came to his assistance, bandaged his wounds, and staunched the deadly flow of blood from the stump of his arm. Hardly had this task been completed, when a shell burst a few feet overhead and the stretcher-bearer, whose identity no man knows, sank to earth badly wounded in the back.

With one arm gone and both legs shattered, Capt. Kingstone's plight was serious, as no one living and unwounded knew where he lay, exposed to heavy shelling, which tore the area repeatedly. For a time he lay where he had fallen; then he crawled back towards the Sunken Road, dragging with him the wounded stretcher-bearer who had fallen at his side.

Imagination balks at contemplation of the slow and painful journey that followed. Inch by inch and yard by yard, it was accomplished, until at last, reaching their destination, the two men rolled down the embankment into the Sunken Road and were there discovered by survivors of the Battalion's attack. It would seem that on reaching the Canadian line, Capt. Kingstone might well have considered his duty complete; but one task remained for him to accomplish. Before morphia was administered and eased his pain, he dictated for Battalion Headquarters a clear report of the situation on "A" Coy.'s front up to the moment when the German shell had struck him down.

Meanwhile, in the German objective, the men of Capt. Kingstone's company had fought savagely to retain the position they had captured, but they suffered severely from shelling and from a series of vicious bombing attacks which the enemy pressed from in front and from the right rear. Slowly their strength waned, until it became clear that their ability to withstand the pressure of the enemy's repeated efforts had been exhausted. Realizing the situation, they attempted to withdraw. A few reached the Sunken Road alive; others fell before the goal could be attained; and a number, refusing to abandon all the ground they had captured, occupied an old communication trench in No Man's Land, barring the path of any German counter-attack.

Though uncut wire and determined fighting by the Germans deprived the 24th Battalion's attack of success on the right and in the centre, "C" Coy., under Capt. C. F. Ritchie, reached, held, and consolidated the final objective on the left. Advancing at the same time as their comrades, the men of "C" Coy. suffered appreciable losses as they drove across the 200 yards of No Man's Land, nevertheless they penetrated the German positions on a 170-yard front, only to find that the enemy garrisons had withdrawn to a line of shell holes about 50 yards away. As soon as the position of the Germans had been established, Capt Ritchie decided to attack and the men of "C" Coy., advancing with bomb and bayonet, quickly cleared the enemy out, occupied the shell holes from which the Germans had been ejected, and established, so far as

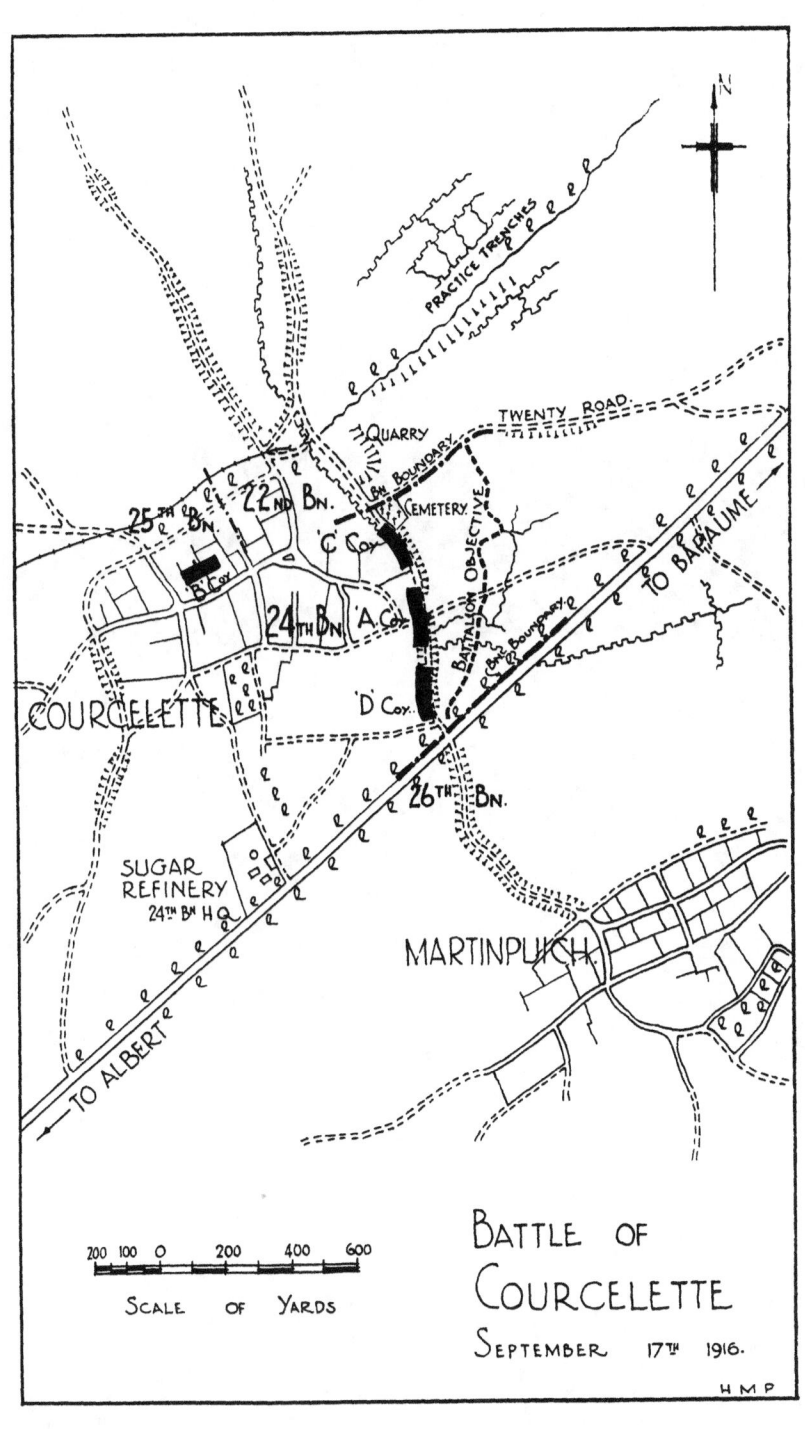

the circumstances permitted, a line capable of offering to any counter-attack a substantial measure of resistance.

In accordance with pre-arranged plans, the men of "C" Coy. should have been relieved that night in the position they had captured, but the relief could not be effected and Capt. Ritchie was ordered to stand fast. No water, food, or supplies could be forwarded to him, nevertheless his men stubbornly maintained their position until, twenty-four hours later, two platoons of the 4th Canadian Battalion made their way forward and carried out the delayed relief. As soon as the platoons of the 4th Battalion had taken over, Capt. Ritchie collected his weary men and, through the mud and wet of a cold and rainy night, led them back to the Brickfields at Albert. No attempt at orderly marching was possible; each man staggered along as best he might, falling sometimes in the treacherous mud, or sinking from sheer exhaustion, but, without exception, rising somehow and plodding on.

At the Brickfields, each man, after drinking a ration of rum, sank to rest beside a huge bonfire, which beckoned encouragingly to those still plodding in from the front. It was a strange scene; for the men, too weary to sleep, sat exchanging stories of their adventures in the line, or asking one another for news of comrades who had disappeared, the flames meanwhile shooting high into the air, offsetting by their genial warmth the cold discomfort of the driving rain.

While "C" Coy. was completing the prolonged tour of duty in the line "A" and "B" Companies of the 24th Battalion and what remained of "D" Coy. had been relieved on the night of September 17th, or on the morning of the 18th, had moved back to the Brickfields, and, at 1.30 p.m. on the 18th, had been conveyed by bus to Warloy. On the following morning they marched to Hérissart, where, in the afternoon, they were joined by Lieut.-Col. Gunn, Lieut. R. H. Lamb, who throughout the operation just completed had served as Battalion Adjutant, Capt. Ritchie, and the men of "C" Company, who arrived from the Brickfields by bus.

Upon the arrival of the Commanding Officer and the surviving officers and men of "C" Coy., the Battalion, with all companies and details present, could judge accurately the price paid in its first battle experience at the Somme. Ten officers it was found had fallen, killed or wounded, and casualties amongst the other ranks had reached a total of 320. "D" Coy. had suffered the most severely, but none of the companies or details had escaped, all mourning the loss of members, who, throughout the year since the Battalion's arrival in France, had served the unit faithfully and well.

Officer Casualties—September 15-18, 1916

Killed in Action

Lieut. C. P. Smith
Lieut. H. E. Scott (5th Brigade Grenade Officer)

Died of Wounds

Lieut. Murdoch Laing.

Wounded and Missing

Major J. A. Ross, D.S.O.
Lieut. Geoffrey Haddock.

Wounded

Capt. H. D. Kingstone
Lieut. G. A. McGiffin
Lieut. J. D. MacIntyre
Lieut. E. G. Hart
Lieut. P. I. Walker.

III

For six days after the companies and details of the 24th Battalion, Victoria Rifles of Canada, were reunited, following their attack on the German trenches east of Courcelette, the Battalion remained at Hérissart, checking casualties, re-equipping, and reorganizing. On September 20th and 21st, sections of the unit were conveyed by bus to Vadencourt, where the men bathed and received clean underclothing, previous to parading before the

Divisional Commander, Major-General R. E. W. Turner, who, on September 21st, inspected the Battalion and thanked the men for the gallant service they had rendered.

Two days later, the Battalion paraded again and the Commanding Officer read out the congratulatory messages which Battalion Headquarters had received. These referred in warm terms to the work the Battalion had accomplished, but none pleased the unit more than a message from Brigadier-General A. H. Macdonnel, who, with personal knowledge of what had occurred, commended the devotion to duty of the carrying parties in the operations against Courcelette and the gallantry of the attack to the east after the village had been captured.

Following the short period of reorganization at Hérissart, the 24th Battalion joined the column of the 5th Canadian Infantry Brigade on the morning of September 25th and, for the second time, marched towards the Somme. Moving from the starting point at 8.30 a.m., the Battalion marched approximately 12 miles and, at half-past four o'clock in the afternoon, bivouacked in the Brickfields at Albert, prepared, in accordance with orders received, to advance into the forward area on one-half hour's notice.

No orders to move were received that night, or on the following day, but, at 6 o'clock on the morning of September 27th, the unit marched to the forward area and bivouacked in Usna Valley. Divisional Orders ruled that, in any series of tours in the forward area at the Somme, the Commanding Officers of Battalions and their Adjutants should direct operations throughout the first tour and give place for the next tour to the Second-in-Command and Assistant Adjutant, taking over again should a third tour follow. In obedience to these orders, Lieut.-Col. Gunn and Lieut. R. H. Lamb remained at the Albert Brickfields on September 27th, Major R. O. Alexander leading forward the Battalion, 347 strong, with Lieut. A. M. Dewar as his Adjutant. Through the application of similar orders, which permitted employment in the line of only two company commanders at a time, the companies of the Battalion on September 27th were commanded respectively by Major C. B. Parr,

Capt. P. L. Hall, Capt. G. R. Robertson, and Capt. H. A. Murray.

Taking position in Usna Valley at approximately 8 a.m., Major Alexander and the men of the 24th Battalion remained inactive until shortly after noon, when the 2nd Canadian Division ordered the 5th Brigade to relieve the 3rd Brigade, the 24th Battalion being instructed to relieve the 15th Battalion, 48th Highlanders of Canada, in the front line. Preparations were made to carry out the relief, but a delay was ordered to permit the units of the 3rd Brigade to attain objectives in Regina Trench against which they were battering determinedly. Fighting continued throughout the night, complicating the effort of the 5th Brigade to relieve, but by 5 o'clock on the morning of September 28th the move had been carried out and 24th Battalion Headquarters had been established about 1,500 yards behind the front line. Forward Battalion Headquarters had also been established in Zollern Trench, contact with the 1st Canadian Mounted Rifles on the left and with the 25th Battalion on the right had been secured, and the companies had reported that relief of the 15th Battalion was complete.

On the morning of September 28th, 5th Brigade ordered the 24th Battalion to push out into Regina Trench that afternoon, and to work eastwards to connect with the left flank of the 26th Battalion, which, under the orders of the 6th Canadian Infantry Brigade, had attacked and occupied Regina Trench between the East and West Miraumont Roads. To assist the forthcoming operation, a company of the 22nd Battalion was attached to the 24th Battalion to hold the front line when the companies of the 24th advanced.

It was not to be a frontal attack. Instead, the Bombing Platoon, under Lieut. A. B. Campbell, was instructed to move up an old communication trench and enter Regina Trench on the left of Twenty-Three Road, thence bombing eastwards to the West Miraumont Road, and there establishing contact with the 26th Battalion. If the Bombing Platoon succeeded in entering Regina Trench, Capt. Hall was instructed to follow with "B" Coy. and occupy the positions captured. The remaining companies, facing Regina Trench, were ordered to move across No Man's Land into the German positions as soon as the bombing operations had cleared the enemy from their respective fronts.

In the interval before the attack of the Bombing Platoon could be launched, the companies of the 24th Battalion endured heavy enemy shelling, the effect of this being intensified by the short fire of a number of the supporting guns. Efforts to notify the supporting batteries that their fire was short were unsuccessful, and, up to the hour of the Bombing Platoon's advance, shells from the Canadian rear continued at intervals to strike in the Battalion lines.

Late in the afternoon, when all preparation had been completed, Lieut. Campbell led the bombers forward. Their advance drew a heavy barrage from the German guns, but they pushed along an old communication trench and, without serious losses, succeeded in crossing much of the wide No Man's Land opposite the positions of the enemy in Regina Trench.

For a time it seemed that Regina Trench might be reached and bombed in the manner that the plan of the operation ordered, but, as the bombers approached the German front, heavy machine-gun fire was opened by the enemy and progress was halted. Withdrawing his men to temporary shelter, Lieut. Campbell sought Capt. Hall, of "B" Coy., and with him made a reconnaissance to within 50 yards of the German line. This revealed a strong garrison in Regina Trench and the vital fact that uncut wire in front of the position would check the advance across No Man's Land of "A," "C" and "D" Companies, even if the Bombing Platoon could enter the trench as originally planned. Accordingly, the men of the Bombing Platoon were withdrawn, their retreat being covered by Private W. Buckley, who, with a machine-gun, courageously maintained a heavy fire on the German line until he was killed by a bullet through the head.

Meanwhile, officers and men of the companies in the Battalion front line were trying, through dense clouds of smoke from the explosion of British and German shells, to observe the operations of the Bombing Platoon and to judge when the moment for their own advance had come. In the circumstances, appreciation of the situation was impossible and knowledge that the Bombing Platoon had been forced to suspend its attack could not be gained by visual means. Accordingly, "D" and "C" Companies climbed from the shelter of their trenches to carry out the original plan. The bombers and "B" Coy., they believed, might be in possession of Regina Trench and, if so, might stand in urgent need.

As soon as the companies left their own trenches, heavy machine-gun fire proved that no friendly welcome in Regina Trench awaited them; but they were unwilling to abandon the attack while possibility of success existed and pushed across No Man's Land determinedly. Capt. Robertson displayed courage and leadership of a high order on this occasion and Lieut. G. S. Duckett, an original member of the Battalion who had joined as an officer only a few weeks before, led his men with bravery and skill. No leadership or fortitude, however, could find a way through the machine-gun barrage and the uncut wire, and the companies dug in about 75 yards in front of their original line.

Throughout the night that followed, the 24th Battalion held the positions taken up on the evening of September 27th. Casualties by this time included Capt. Robertson and Lieut. Duckett, wounded, and approximately 40 other ranks killed and wounded, the number being increased at 10 p.m. when heavy machine-gun fire and barrage fire by the German artillery suggested that a counter-attack was forming. Under the leadership of Major C. B. Parr, senior officer in the front line, the 24th waited confidently for the German effort, but, after a long bombardment, the barrage fire weakened and eventually it became clear that, if the Germans had contemplated an attack, some circumstance had rendered their plan abortive.

Though no counter-attack developed on the night of September 28th, the Battalion suffered appreciably from the fire of the German guns, nor was relief afforded on the morning of the 29th, for, as on the previous day, short firing by guns of the supporting artillery harassed the unit and threatened to inflict serious losses. No danger to morale is greater than that imposed by the short firing of supporting guns, and the men of the 24th grew bitter as the day passed, but permitted few signs of their exasperation to appear and no consideration whatsoever to affect their loyal attention to the duties they were called upon to perform. In the carrying out of these duties, highly creditable work was accomplished, noteworthy service being rendered, amongst others, by Sergt. A. Gunnell, Sergt. H. T. Rigg, Private J. E. Dodsworth, and Private C. Cooper.

At 4 p.m., Major Alexander, on instructions from the 2nd Canadian Division, relayed by the 5th Brigade, ordered scout patrols of the 24th Battalion, supported by bombers, to ascertain if the Germans in Regina Trench had retired, following a heavy bombardment of their position by the Canadian guns. Should the retirement of the enemy be found to have taken place, the companies of the Battalion were ordered to advance and consolidate the position. Attention, however, was directed to instructions from 5th Brigade, which stated emphatically that no attack was to be launched if the Germans held Regina Trench and were prepared to offer serious opposition.

Moving forward in obedience to Major Alexander's orders, the 24th Battalion scouts reached Regina Trench on the right flank, but were unable to approach on the left. They found that the trench had been battered in places by the fire of the British guns, but that strong garrisons of machine-gun crews were in possession and were protected by heavy belts of concertina barbed wire. From these reports it was clear that, on the 24th Battalion front, no unopposed occupation of Regina Trench could be contemplated. Accordingly, the operation order for the advance of the companies was unhesitatingly cancelled. Despite the fact that no action followed the report of the reconnoitring patrols, the Battalion casualties for the day totalled approximately 50.

Again on September 30, 1916, casualties in the 24th Battalion mounted, more particularly on the right flank, where a measure of disorganization resulted from the continued short firing of the supporting guns. At 2.30 p.m., the right company reported that the 25th Battalion had been compelled by this fire to evacuate trenches on the 24th Battalion's flank and that the company's flank was, in consequence, entirely in the air. This situation could not be permitted to remain unadjusted, and to remedy it Major Alexander ordered two of his companies to withdraw from their front line trenches to shell holes about 150 yards in the rear.

On the night following, Major Alexander was notified by Headquarters of the 5th Brigade that, on instructions from 2nd Canadian Division, the Brigade was to attack Kenora and Regina Trenches on the afternoon of October 1st, in conjunction with major operations of units on the flanks. After study of the situation, Major Alexander reported that, in the circumstances existing, high hope of success on the 24th Battalion front could not reasonably be entertained and that, on the contrary, a sharp reverse, with casualties disproportionate to the result achieved, seemed not improbable.

Had the attack involved the 24th Battalion only, or even the battalions of the 5th Brigade, consideration of the situation on the 24th Battalion front might have resulted in postponement of the contemplated attack until more favourable prospects could be obtained. The action, however, was more than local and circumstances compelled the attack on the 5th Brigade front to be carried out, despite the grave doubt as to its chances of success. With misgiving, therefore, but with every trace of this concealed and with all the care that his training in the Permanent Forces in Canada had taught him to employ, Major Alexander, with the assistance of Lieut. Dewar, prepared an operation order for the attack.

Though circumstances were not favourable and the prospect was undeniably dark, Major Alexander was encouraged by the fine demeanour of the officers who were to lead his attack. On the night of September 30th, Capt. P. L. Hall and Capt. H. A. Murray reported at Battalion Headquarters for orders and discussed details of the work that would be theirs. Capt. Murray had been painfully wounded in the arm and, in the normal course of events, would have been evacuated to hospital forthwith, but when he heard that an attack was planned and that, under serious disadvantages, his company was to take part, no argument or persuasion could stop him from returning to the line.

Later, at 9 o'clock on the morning of October 1st, Major C. B. Parr, who was to command the attack, arrived back from the line to arrange for the bringing forward of munitions and to discuss the actual assault. Cool and collected, though under no delusion as to the difficulty and danger of the task ahead, Major Parr received his final instructions, offered a number of valuable suggestions, and, without further delay, made his way back to the line. Convinced from these interviews that the attack would not fail through weakness in leadership, Major Alexander, at 11.35 o'clock, issued his final orders for the battle.

Some hours previously, that section of the 24th Battalion front which lay to the left of Twenty-Three Road had been taken over by the 5th Canadian Mounted Rifles, who were to participate in the forthcoming attack. Accordingly, no responsibility for action on this section of the front remained in 24th Battalion hands.

In brief, the duties falling to the lot of the 24th Battalion companies may be described as follows: "D" Coy., keeping in touch with the 5th Canadian Mounted Rifles, was to attack Regina Trench from Twenty-Three Road (exclusive) to the point where Regina and Kenora Trenches joined. At this point, about 140 yards from Twenty-Three Road, Regina Trench curved to the German rear and Kenora Trench became the German front line, with Regina running diagonally backward behind it and acting as a secondary stronghold, whence reinforcements could be furnished to the line and machine-guns operated with deadly effect.

To the right of "D" Coy., "C" and "A" Companies of the 24th Battalion were ordered to assault the junction of Regina and Kenora Trenches, and to drive forward past Kenora on the right to a point in Regina about 140 yards from the point where the two trenches joined. Here the objective of the 24th Battalion joined the objective of the 25th Battalion on the right flank. "A" Coy. was ordered to see that contact with the 25th Battalion attack was established and maintained. Three companies of the 24th Battalion were thus to take part in the assault. "B" Coy. was ordered to remain in support until the attack had reached its objectives, then to move forward and occupy the original front line. The Battalion bombers were ordered to take part in the attack on the junction of Kenora and Regina Trenches and later to proceed to "A" Coy.'s right flank, which they were ordered to secure and safeguard. Orders were also issued for the employment of the Battalion machine-guns and for the operation of a visual signal station from a point about 200 yards behind the front line.

At 3.15 p.m., Major Parr stood erect on the parapet of the 24th Battalion trench, and, after waiting a moment or two, signalled with a forward sweep of both hands, that the hour of the attack had come. Immediately, in battle patrol formation, the waves of the Battalion's attack followed him as he moved into No Man's Land and simultaneously the attack was launched by the units on both flanks.

As the Officer Commanding the 24th Battalion had foreseen, the attack of the 5th Brigade, though pressed with gallantry and resource, ended in costly failure. On the front of the 22nd Battalion, the advancing waves were caught in the blast of the German barrage and were also subjected to concentrated rifle and machine-gun fire from the front and flanks. Rapidly the force of the attack was spent, nevertheless survivors reached Regina Trench, where the majority were killed, or wounded and captured. A handful, wounded, including one man who had escaped after being captured, returned eventually to the Canadian lines, but the battalion, as a battalion, ceased to exist, and the 26th Battalion, in support, took over the sector whence the waves of the 22nd had been launched.

Similar in all but detail was the result on the front of the 25th Battalion. Despite short fire by supporting guns, which struck the unit's front ten minutes before the zero hour, the 25th Battalion stormed Kenora Trench and moved against Regina Trench beyond. It was an effort reflecting credit on the men who carried it out and on the whole 5th Brigade, but it did not achieve the success its gallantry deserved. Parties entered Regina Trench and others reached, but could not penetrate, the defending wire. They attempted to dig in facing the wire, but enemy machine-guns mowed them down and forced the few who by this time survived to retire.

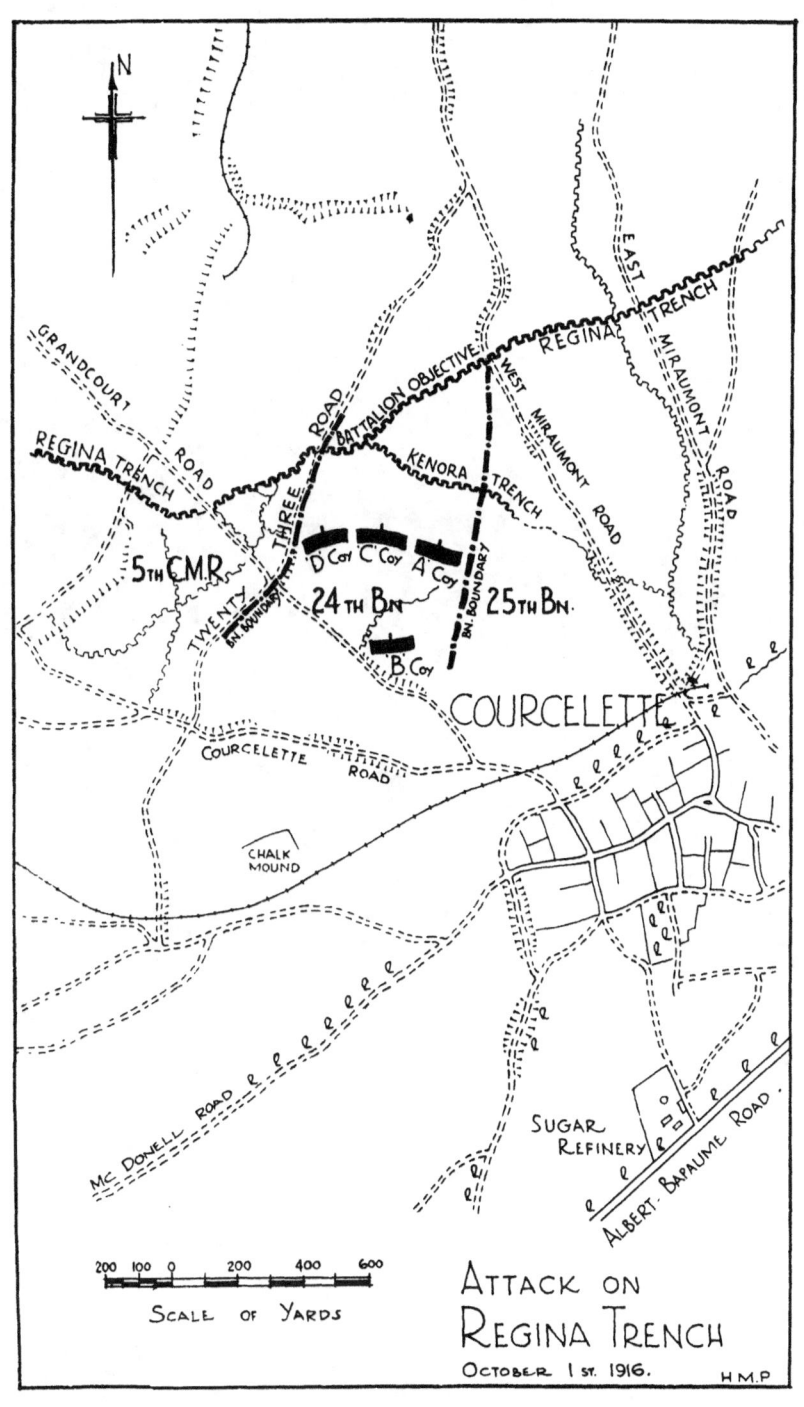

Meanwhile, on the 24th Battalion front, the companies had striven desperately to carry out the tasks assigned to them. No effort was spared; even batmen and cooks were thrown into the fight, also two fine attached platoons of the 22nd Battalion, but the final objectives could not be attained and held. On the right, "A" Coy., maintaining contact with the 25th Battalion, drove through Kenora Trench and fought a way into Regina Trench, attempting to hold the position gained and failing only when casualties wiped the company out of effective existence. In the centre and on the left, too, parties of "C" and "D" Companies battered their way to Regina Trench, but, despite their utmost efforts, could not hold much of the footing they had gained. Fighting of the bitterest type occurred in that section of Regina Trench between Kenora Trench and Twenty-Three Road, but beyond the road irresistible counter-attacks and deadly fire forced the 5th Canadian Mounted Rifles to withdraw. This exposed the flank of the 24th Battalion and contributed to the final enemy triumph in that area.

Slightly further to the right, however, men of the 24th Battalion succeeded in occupying a position near the junction of Regina and Kenora Trenches, where they established a double block 50 yards wide. Realizing that Canadian success at this spot would eventually imperil their whole line, the Germans strove repeatedly to wrench the position from the Battalion's grasp. To do so, however, was beyond their power, though their Marine troops fought doggedly, returning to the attack again and again. In repelling these enemy efforts, Lieut. A. B. Campbell and the Battalion bombers rendered service of a high order. Lieut. Campbell, though wounded, returned to the front line when his injuries were dressed and remained in action until, at 5.45 a.m. on October 2nd, the Battalion was relieved by the 28th Battalion.

Before the relief was completed, stretcher-bearers of the 24th Battalion had removed from the front line trenches and No Man's Land all the unit's wounded and had buried many of the dead. Lieut. Stewart Cowan, a gallant officer, had been killed in action, it was known, but no definite information could be gained regarding the fate of Capt. H. A. Murray, who, after being wounded, as mentioned previously, had returned to the front line to lead "D" Coy. forward. No trace of Capt. Murray's body was ever found, but it is certain that he died not far from Regina Trench. Many had seen him leading the attack on the left; but no survivor had witnessed his death, or seen his body after he had fallen. Accordingly, though with little doubt regarding his fate, his name was posted on the Battalion's roll of missing.

Major C. B. Parr, who led the attack, had fallen seriously wounded in the abdomen by a fragment of shell and had been carried to the rear, remarking to a stretcher-bearer, who encouraged him to keep his spirits up, "Thank you, but did you ever know me with my spirits down?" The Battalion never had known Major Parr with his spirits down and trusted, for a time, that high courage would enable him to recover from his dangerous wound. Courage was never lacking, but the injury was severe, and, to the deep regret of all ranks in the Battalion, Major Parr died in hospital on October 3rd. Capt. P. L. Hall, M.C., who had commanded "B" Coy., was more fortunate, though wounded severely, and lived to continue at a later date his faithful and devoted service with the Battalion. Lieut. J. F. Meek, who was wounded on September 28th, transferred to the Royal Air Force on recovery and was killed when his plane was lost in 1918.

Meanwhile, following relief by the 28th Battalion on the morning of October 2nd, the men of the 24th Battalion had marched to Usna Valley, where the units of the 5th Brigade were visited by Brigadier-General A. H. Macdonnel. With deep emotion, the Brigadier thanked the units for their devoted service in the line and deplored their heavy losses. In the 24th Battalion, more than 200 officers and men had fallen in the operations against Kenora and Regina Trenches, and more than 300 in the previous operations at Courcelette, the handful present at Usna Valley on the morning of October 2nd seeming but the ghost of the fine battalion which in September had arrived from the Ypres Salient to take part in the fighting at the Somme. In thanking the Headquarters Staffs of the units and as many of the men as circumstances would permit, Brigadier-General Macdonnel, confirming previous reports, stated definitely that the Brigade would be called upon for no further effort at the Somme, but would move to a less active front where opportunity to reorganize the shattered battalions would be afforded.

Officer Casualties—September 27–October 3, 1916

Killed in Action
Lieut. Stewart Cowan

Died of Wounds
Major C. B. Parr

Missing
Capt. H. A. Murray

Wounded
Capt. P. L. Hall, M.C.
Capt. G. R. Robertson
Lieut. A. B. Campbell
Lieut. G. S. Duckett
Lieut. J. F. Meek

CHAPTER VI

THE ANGRES AND LA FOLIE SECTORS

I

Following participation in the Battles of the Somme, 1916, surviving members of the 24th Battalion, Victoria Rifles of Canada, were conveyed by bus to Berteaucourt, where, without delay, the process of reorganizing the unit began; this being viewed sympathetically by a number of French soldiers on leave, who, from their own experiences at Verdun, could appreciate the difficulty involved. Somewhat to the good poilus' surprise, however, the process advanced more rapidly than had seemed possible; in fact, after a day's complete rest and a visit to the baths at St. Ouen, the Battalion appeared to the shrewd eyes of the observers not as a disorganized group of weary and bedraggled individuals, but as the remnant of a fine unit and the nucleus of a fine unit yet to be.

After some days at Berteaucourt, the strength of the Battalion was increased by the arrival from England of 218 other ranks; and 8 officers, Lieuts. C. G. Greenshields, G. Earnshaw, J. N. Bales, G. S. Bushe, A. F. Crichton, J. Donald, L. A. Sewell, and R. L. Weaver, who, as officers, or in the ranks, had served previously with the Battalion in France. Lieut. D. A. Ewan, who reported at approximately the same time, was also a former member of the unit, who had been wounded in the previous June.

Under Lieut.-Col. Gunn, who had appointed the rejoined officers to their respective commands, the Battalion paraded on October 9th for inspection by Major-General R. E. W. Turner, the Divisional Commander, and Brigadier-General A. H. Macdonnel, G.O.C. the 5th Brigade, the survivors of the Somme being accorded the honour of position on the right of the company, or section, to which they belonged. It would be untrue to state that the Battalion on this occasion resembled closely the efficient 24th Battalion of the days before the Somme; nevertheless, Major-General Turner was satisfied, and the Brigadier, who had seen the broken unit in Usna Valley only a week before, found a battalion not unworthy of trust and confidence. In thanking the unit for its services at the Somme and in decorating three other ranks with the Military Medal, Major-General Turner referred to the reconstruction which was taking place and complimented Lieut.-Col. Gunn on the rapidity with which, in so short a time, so much had been accomplished.

Parading in Berteaucourt on the morning following the inspection, the 24th Battalion marched at 10.30 o'clock, halted for a meal at mid-day, and, late in the afternoon, completed a distance of approximately 13 miles to Hem. No incident distinguished the march from others in the Battalion's story; but at night the officers gathered to congratulate Major C. F. Ritchie, who, for his outstanding service at the Somme, had been awarded the Military Cross. Further recognition of work accomplished by officers and other ranks at Courcelette and Kenora and Regina Trenches would, it seemed certain, be gazetted in due course, but this immediate award to an officer was highly acceptable, and the occasion was honoured in accordance with the established traditions of the Service.

Marching again on October 11th, 12th, 13th, and 14th, the Battalion proceeded first to Bonnières, then to Petit Houvin, thence to Ostreville, and finally to Maisnil les Ruitz. From this last village Lieut.-Col. Gunn, with the Officers of the Battalion Staff and the four company commanders, proceeded by bus to the forward area, Angres Sector, to reconnoitre trenches which the Battalion was to take over on the following day.

In accordance with arrangements previously announced, the 24th Battalion paraded at 8.30 o'clock on the morning of October 15th and, after marching about 12 miles, relieved the 6th Battalion, Bedfordshire Regiment, in the front line, which here ran through the mining suburbs of Lens. Daylight relief was possible in this sector and the 24th, accordingly, took over the front at 4.40 p.m., with "B and "C" Companies in the front line, "A" and "D" Companies in close support, and Battalion Headquarters in Forrest Hill Trench, about 300 yards to the rear.

After 6 uneventful days in the line, the Battalion was relieved by the 25th Battalion and moved back to Brigade Reserve positions in Bully Grenay and Mechanics Trench. Lieut.-Col. Gunn was absent on leave at this time and command of the Battalion, as from October 19th, had been assumed by Major R. O. Alexander. All in the Battalion expected that Lieut.-Col. Gunn would return, but, on October 31st, it was announced that his services had been retained in England and that Major Alexander, with the rank of lieutenant-colonel, would succeed to the 24th Battalion command. Major C. F. Ritchie, M.C., was simultaneously promoted to Second-in-Command.

Though the Battalion, through force of circumstance, was given no opportunity to bid its original Commanding Officer farewell, all ranks, remembering his services in the difficult period of recruiting and throughout more than a year of action in France, followed with interest his work in England and congratulated him, when opportunity offered, on his promotion to the rank of brigadier-general, on the award to him for his work in France of the Distinguished Service Order, and on his appointment, at a later date, to be a Companion in the Order of St. Michael and St. George. In addition to these honours, he was "Mentioned in Despatches" by the British Commander-in-Chief and, following his retention for duty in England, was twice "Brought to the Attention of the Secretary of State for War" for valuable services rendered.

Meanwhile, after six days in Brigade Reserve at Bully Grenay, whence working parties of 6 officers and 270 other ranks had reported daily to the Canadian Engineers, the 5th Canadian Trench Mortar Battery, or the 25th Battalion, the 24th Battalion had moved forward on October 27th and again occupied the Angres I Sector of the front line. One hundred and twenty other ranks from the 115th Canadian Battalion had reported to Major Alexander on October 23rd and the Battalion, having continued earnestly the reorganization work begun immediately after the engagements at the Somme, was regaining in appreciable measure the strength and *esprit de corps* of the days gone by. No little credit for what had been accomplished was due to Lieuts. E. M. Amphlett, A. L. S. Mills, C. S. B. White, and C. G. Greenshields, who, at the time, commanded the Battalion's companies.

Even before the Battalion moved into the line on October 27th, Lieut. A. B. Campbell had reported for duty, after recovering from the wound received at the Somme in September, and news had been received that, for gallantry in action, he had been awarded the Military Cross. All ranks of the Battalion were pleased by this award, also by the announcement that, for the splendid leading of his company in the attack beyond Courcelette, Capt. H. D. Kingstone had been similarly honoured; and that, for their work at the Somme, Sergt. John Donohoe and Pte. L. B. LeBoutillier had been awarded the Distinguished Conduct Medal.

Following relief of the 25th Battalion in the line on October 27th, the men of the 24th Battalion enjoyed a period of comparative quiet, made noteworthy, if private diaries can be trusted, more by orders permitting the shaving of the upper lip than by aggressive action on the part of the enemy. The calm did not continue throughout the tour, however, for on October 29th British trench mortars bombarded the German front and stirred the enemy into action.

On the afternoon of October 31st, ten officer reinforcements reported for duty from England, a number of these seeing action for the first time at 5 o'clock on the morning of November 1st, when, after a half hour's bombardment with trench mortars, about 20 Germans attempted to raid the Battalion's right flank. No casualties were suffered by the Victoria Rifles, but the Germans were less fortunate and, when driven back, left the body of their leader hanging limply on the Canadian wire. Scouts of the 24th Battalion reached the body soon after the German party withdrew and established that the dead soldier, a double Iron Cross man, was a member of the 17th Bavarian Regiment. Later, the body was brought in and buried behind the parados of the Battalion's front line trench.

Undismayed by the failure of their raid on the morning of November 1st, the enemy advanced in greater strength at 11.30 o'clock that night and again attempted to penetrate the Canadian wire. On the right, they reached a point whence a few bombs were thrown into the Battalion line, wounding one man, but this marked their maximum achievement, for the garrisons of the front line posts, warned of their coming by the report of a protective patrol, were everywhere alert and able, by heavy rifle and machine-gun fire, to drive them in confusion back to their own line.

A few minutes after noon on the following day, the Battalion was relieved by the 25th Battalion and moved back to positions at Fosse 10, where, for six days, it remained, carrying out the routine of Brigade Reserve. On November 4th, Major-General R. E. W. Turner inspected at 10 a.m., commending the Battalion's work in the line and pointing out where improvement in its organization and drill could be effected.

From November 8th to 14th, the Battalion again occupied the Angres I Sector of the front line. Rain had fallen heavily in the previous week and the trenches were deep in water and mud. The moon shone with unusual brilliance on the night of November 8th, but this did not mark a definite change in the weather, for, throughout the tour, little improvement in trench conditions was noted. Shelling by both sides was fairly heavy, the German bombardments damaging trenches on a number of occasions, but failing to inflict serious losses. No knowledge of the result of the British bombardments could be gained, but at least one German fell as a result of the Battalion's work, for, on the morning of November 13th, Private Johnson, a Battalion sniper, sighted a German Staff Officer and fired a shot which undoubtedly found its mark.

In the six days between November 14th and 20th, the Battalion, with Headquarters and two companies in Bully Grenay and two companies in billets in Mechanics Trench and Corons d'Aix, acted as Brigade Support. On successive days, the companies marched to the baths, and each day a party of approximately 7 officers and 300 other ranks was furnished for work in the forward area.

After the period in Brigade Reserve, the Battalion moved forward at 11.30 a.m. on November 20th and re-occupied the positions handed over to the 25th Battalion on November 14th. That night a party of Germans moved from their trenches, but were driven back by the fire of the 24th Battalion's machine-guns. No certainty that the party suffered from the Canadian fire could be established, but, following one burst of fire, a long scream of agony suggested that the machine-gun crews had not failed to find their target.

No outstanding incident marked the remainder of the six-day tour. Trench mortars were active and the British artillery shelled the enemy heavily, notably on November 22nd and 23rd, but the German retaliation was weak and the Battalion, when relieved on November 26th, had suffered no substantial losses.

In billets at Fosse 10, whither the Battalion moved following its relief in the line, Lieut.-Col. R. O. Alexander received Major-General R. E. W. Turner, V.C., who, on November 26th, called to bid the Battalion farewell. After nearly two years' service in France, first in command of the 3rd Canadian Infantry Brigade and then of the 2nd Canadian Division, Major-General Turner was leaving to assume supreme command of the Overseas Military Forces of Canada in England. It may be assumed that, though duty permitted him no alternative, he surrendered command of the 2nd Canadian Division with regret; it is certain that the units of the Division regretted his departure profoundly. For a time no one knew who would succeed him in France; but eventually, in mid-December, it was announced that Major-General H. E. Burstall, formerly commanding the Canadian Corps Artillery, had been appointed in his place. Though continuing to regret the departure of the soldier who had commanded them up to this time, all ranks of the 2nd Division accepted Major-General Burstall's promotion as deserved and were confident that, as in the past, experienced leadership would benefit them in the duties they would be called upon to perform.

For the men of the 24th Battalion, the work assigned in December, 1916, varied little from that carried out in the final weeks of October and in November. Three times the unit relieved the 25th Battalion in the front line, completed a 6-day tour, marked only by the normal incidents of winter trench routine, and, following relief, marched back to billets in Bully Grenay, or Fosse 10. At Fosse 10, 130 other ranks, who had reported for duty from the 148th Canadian Battalion, recruited under Lieut.-Col. A. A. Magee in Montreal, joined their comrades of the 24th Battalion in Christmas celebrations. All companies and details held dinners and at each Lieut.-Col. Alexander appeared, if only for a few moments, to convey to the men the greetings of the Headquarters Staff. It was also his agreeable duty to extend the unit's welcome to a number of guests, none more enthusiastically received than Capt. F. T. Bown, an original officer of the unit, who, at this time, was serving with marked ability as Traffic Control Officer of the 2nd Canadian Division. Capt. Bown appreciated the welcome his old unit extended and, after dining with "B" Coy. on the night of December 23rd, contributed effectively to the fine programme of old and new songs that followed.

II

New Year's Day, 1917, found the 24th Battalion, Victoria Rifles of Canada, occupying familiar trenches in the Angres I Sector of the front line. The new year was heralded at midnight on December 31st by a crash of gun fire from the supporting batteries of the British and German artilleries, but a few moments thereafter comparative quiet settled over the area and remained more or less unbroken for the remainder of the day. In one of the short spasms of enemy activity, however, three men of the 24th were wounded.

Though little action marked the opening of the new year on the Battalion front in France, officers and men of the unit were afforded recognition of their work in more arduous times in an honours list announced from London. For services at the Somme and on other fronts where the Battalion had been engaged, Lieut.-Col. R. O. Alexander was awarded the Distinguished Service Order, Lieut. G. R. Robertson received the Military Cross, and Major R. H. Lamb was Mentioned in Despatches. The work accomplished by other ranks was simultaneously recognized by the Mention in Despatches of Company Sergt.-Major G. H. Macario and Company Sergt.-Major F. H. Morgan, and the award of the Distinguished Conduct Medal to Quartermaster-Sergt. J. A. Donovan.

Two days after the honours to members of the unit were announced, the Battalion was relieved in the line and moved into Brigade Support in Bully Grenay, moving up after the usual 6 days and reoccupying the front line at 9.45 o'clock on the morning of January 9th. Quiet prevailed on the morning of the relief, but at 2 p.m. on January 10th the British artillery opened an intense 45-minute bombardment of the enemy line and, in a heavy retaliation which the enemy inflicted on the British front between 7 and 8 p.m., 3 other ranks of the 24th Battalion were killed and 7 wounded.

After the sharp bombardments on January 10th, quiet settled over the front once more, but the time was not entirely unmarked by incident, for on January 13th, the men of "B" Coy. captured in the Battalion support lines 3 German prisoners of war, who had escaped and were seeking a way through the Canadian lines to their own trenches. In the temporary absence of Lieut.-Col. R. O. Alexander and Major C. F. Ritchie, the prisoners were paraded before Major R. H. Lamb, who was commanding the Battalion, and afterwards despatched to the rear.

Two days later, orders for relief of the Battalion by the 25th Battalion were issued and the men carried out the routine of cleaning the trenches preparatory to handing over. As always when this work was under way, Sergt. A. J. Crabb, Sanitary Sergeant of the unit, was a busy man indeed. Though older than the majority of men at the front, Sergt. Crabb, by his hard work and willingness, set a fine example of devotion to the duties he was called upon to accomplish.

Leaving the front line at 8.30 p.m. on January 15th, the Battalion moved back to Brigade Reserve positions at Fosse 10, and at 9 o'clock on the morning of January 17th, marched, by way of Hersin, to Bruay. At Hersin, the unit was joined by a draft of 153 other ranks from the 2nd Canadian Divisional Training Battalion, also by the Transport, which, despite the handicap of falling snow and slippery roads, presented a most creditable appearance.

Throughout the remainder of January and for the first ten days in February, 1917, the Battalion remained at Bruay, carrying out a syllabus of training, with special attention paid to musketry and to the practice of companies in attack. Cold weather prevailed and the men trained frequently in fields hard frozen, or covered by snow, but, despite these conditions, progress was made each day, the Battalion showing marked benefit when, on February 7th, it paraded, under command of Major C. F. Ritchie, M.C., for inspection by the new Divisional Commander, Major-General H. E. Burstall.

For a further four days, the Battalion remained at Bruay, completing its training, enjoying some keenly contested football games, and preparing for a move forward into the line. At 9 a.m. on February 11th, the unit paraded in the Place Marmatton and marched approximately 12 miles to the Bois des Alleux, where the men occupied huts vacated by the Princess Patricia's Canadian Light Infantry. Next day, the Battalion, with a trench strength of 30 officers and 767 other ranks, marched at 5 p.m. and at 11 o'clock relieved the Royal Canadian Regiment in the La Folie right sub-sector of the front line. On the Battalion's left was the 42nd Battalion, Royal Highlanders of Canada, and on the right the 58th Canadian Battalion.

For a week after taking over the La Folie front, the 24th Battalion remained in the line. Shell fire was not severe, but enemy snipers were active and trench mortars bombarded frequently, inflicting casualties which, though not heavy on any one day, mounted before the end of the tour to a total of 3 other ranks killed and approximately 15 wounded. On February 19th, the Battalion moved to Brigade Reserve in Neuville St. Vaast and thence, after relief at midnight by the 22nd Battalion, to Divisional Reserve at Bois des Alleux.

Taken as a whole, the following five days at Bois des Alleux were marked chiefly by the appointing of "permanent" guards for a number of points in the neighbourhood, a "permanent" party of 21 other ranks for work at an ammunition dump in Petit Servins, and an equally "permanent" fatigue party of 1 officer, 10 N.C.O.'s, and 90 men. In addition, the period witnessed the selection of 200 volunteers to train for a raid on the enemy trenches.

Raiding at this time was a feature of trench warfare on the British front and the 24th Battalion party was left out of the line to complete its preparations on February 24th, when the unit again took over from the 25th Battalion the right sub-sector of the La Folie front. Anxious to gain information of value, members of the raiding party visited the 6th Battalion, Gordon Highlanders, of the 51st (Highland) Division, which, not long previously, had raided the enemy front and returned with 44 Bavarian prisoners. The Gordons, though suffering 45 casualties, including 1 officer missing, had wrought havoc in the German lines and had inflicted losses far outnumbering their own. They had advanced at 7 o'clock one morning and entered the German line, carrying grenades, petrol tins, fire bombs, and Stokes mortar shells. After bombing a dugout, their system was to jab a petrol tin with a bayonet, hurl the leaking tin down the dugout entrance, follow this with a bomb designed to set the escaped petrol on fire, and finally, when circumstance warranted, to destroy the dugout utterly with the Stokes gun shells. Methods similar to these were practised by the 24th Battalion party, but, before they could be used against the enemy, raid orders were cancelled and the members of the party were returned to battalion duty.

Meanwhile, in the front line, the Battalion had been carrying out a routine trench tour. At 3 a.m. on March 1st, the 4th Canadian Division on the left mounted a gas and artillery demonstration which produced in reply a 3-hour bombardment of the Canadian front. This bombardment was sharp, but not particularly effective, and the 24th Battalion suffered no casualties. At midnight, the Battalion was relieved by the 25th Battalion and moved to Brigade Support at Neuville St. Vaast.

Some shelling marked the period that followed and working parties of 4 officers and 300 men were supplied each day. Aeroplanes were unusually active on March 6th, the Germans being anxious to discover what action the Allies contemplated in the area and the British being determined to conceal, so far as was possible, their preparation for the Battles of Arras, 1917, including the attack of the Canadian Corps on Vimy Ridge.

After five days at Neuville St. Vaast, the Battalion, on March 6th, took over from the 25th Battalion the trenches occupied during the previous tour. Shelling was heavy throughout the period that followed and snipers on both sides were active. Lieut. K. B. Hawkins, of "D" Coy., and a German sniper carried out a shoot at Watling Crater one morning and Lieut. Hawkins hit his man, but another German, joining in the duel, sniped successfully and killed the Canadian officer with a bullet through the head. Private M. Peturson, of "B" Coy., also fell to a German sniper, who wounded him fatally with a shot in the back, and Private W. A. McCaskill, a sniper, was wounded by a neat shot, which, as he held binoculars to his eyes to study the result of his own shooting, passed through his left hand and through the edge of his steel helmet.

Apart from a number of heavy bombardments and the unusual activity of snipers, the chief incidents of the tour occurred in the early morning of March 11th, when an officer's patrol encountered an enemy patrol on the southeast lip of Watling Crater. Casualties were inflicted on the enemy in the exchange of shots that followed, but the 24th patrol did not escape unscathed, Lieut. P. I. Walker, whose work as Scout Officer in this period had been of a high order, suffering a wound that kept him from duty with the Battalion for several months.

That night "C" and "D" Companies and Headquarters of the 24th Battalion were relieved in the line by the 52nd Battalion and moved back to Neuville St. Vaast and Parallel 9, leaving "A" and "B" Companies in position on the right. At 8 p.m. next day an enemy patrol, taking advantage of an unusually dark night, approached a 24th Battalion post at Watling Crater and attempted to effect its capture. The effort was courageous and benefited by remaining undiscovered until a moment before its final assault was launched, but the men of the 24th held their own and drove the Germans to cover. An officers' patrol followed the retreating enemy, found 2 German dead in No Man's Land, and, from the bodies, established the identity of the 3rd Battalion,

263rd Reserve Infantry Regiment, to which the men belonged.

At 11 o'clock on the night following the German effort against Watling Crater, the units of the 24th Battalion were relieved by the 26th Canadian Battalion, marched back to Bois des Alleux, and there remained for ten days, first in Divisional, and then in Brigade, Reserve. Heavy working parties were supplied frequently in this period and each of the companies marched to the Divisional baths. Pay parades, attendance at the Divisional Gas School, a Battalion church parade, routine training, and sports, filled the remaining days until, at 9 a.m. on March 23rd, the Battalion marched to Maisnil Bouche, there to train intensively for the forthcoming operation of the Canadian Corps against the famous and hitherto impregnable German stronghold—the Vimy Ridge.

CHAPTER VII

THE CAPTURE OF VIMY RIDGE

I

In the history of the war on the Western Front in 1917, the capture by the Canadian Corps of Vimy Ridge on April 9th stands as an example of careful planning and complete success, rivalled only by the similar attack of Australian and British divisions on the Messines Ridge two months later. In November, 1916, Marshal Joffre and Field Marshal Sir Douglas Haig met at Chantilly and planned the following year's campaign; but Joffre was dismissed by the French Government and General Nivelle, who succeeded him, refused to endorse a continuation of the Somme offensive, upon which Joffre and Haig had agreed. Instead, he proposed a smashing and decisive blow by the French Army on the Aisne, with subsidiary British and French attacks between Arras and Rheims. The essence of his plan lay, in his own words, in the employment "de violence, de brutalité, et de rapidité." The Germans were to be defeated in twenty-four to forty-eight hours of intensive fighting and the Allies, thereafter, were to sweep the shattered enemy forces from the soil of France.

It is no secret that Sir Douglas Haig viewed this plan with profound misgiving. More experienced than General Nivelle, he realized more completely the trials through which the French Army had passed in 1916 and he doubted the ability of the French Army of 1917, or for that matter of any troops on earth, to carry out, with sufficient "violence, brutalité," and above all, "rapidité," the amazing schedule which General Nivelle's plan imposed. He voiced his doubts to the leaders of the British Government; but General Nivelle stated that the plan would almost certainly succeed and the British Commander-in-Chief was curtly ordered to conform to the French General's "directives."

Obeying, Sir Douglas Haig planned an offensive on the Arras front to precede by a few days the great smash forward of General Nivelle's armies on the Aisne. Informed by his Intelligence Staff that the Germans were likely to withdraw on a section of the front involved in his plan, Sir Douglas Haig extended the scope of his operation to include Vimy Ridge, lest, following the German withdrawal, his blow should encounter little opposition and waste its strength in the air. From the great bastion of Vimy Ridge, there was no possibility of the Germans withdrawing, unless compelled to do so by force of arms. Again and again, they had defended the position against the British and the French and there was no doubt that they would hold it with all the strength they could muster.

When notified by Sir Douglas Haig of the reasons for including Vimy Ridge in the front to be attacked by the British Army in April, General Nivelle criticized the plan severely. He refused to credit the statement of the British Intelligence Staff that the Germans were about to withdraw elsewhere to the Hindenburg Line and, remembering, perhaps, the unsuccessful attacks on the Ridge by the splendid first line regiments of France, prophesied that, if the attack were attempted, it would end in costly failure.

Despite the opposition of the French Commander-in-Chief, Sir Douglas Haig maintained his point and ordered Sir Julian Byng to attack on April 9th, with the four divisions of the Canadian Corps in line. South of the Scarpe, British divisions were to advance simultaneously, the combined operations, in addition to topographical objectives, having as a purpose the attraction to the British front of all possible enemy reserves, thus reducing the forces available to meet the assault of General Nivelle's armies on the Aisne.

Success attended the attack of the Canadian Corps on Vimy Ridge and, in a less striking degree, the operations south of the Scarpe, but the strategical value of the gains was offset by disaster on the Aisne. Throughout

April and in May, Sir Douglas Haig applied pressure to the German front beyond Vimy in an effort to assist the French and bring about a situation in which the Allied Armies might co-operate effectively, but the temper of the French Army, as a result of the Aisne failure, suffered severely and combined action could not be arranged. Accordingly, the British Commander-in-Chief broke off the engagement on the Arras front and concentrated his effort in Flanders. Vimy Ridge, however, remained in British hands and, in the following year, stood as the greatest physical barrier between the German Army and military victory. No direct attack was launched against it, but failure of an attempt to roll it up from the flank at the end of March, 1918, ruined the enemy plan of operation, which had opened a week previously with striking success against the front of the Third and Fifth Armies at the Somme. It might justly be said that, in ultimate effect, the capture of Vimy Ridge was as important to the Allied cause as any victory in the war; beyond peradventure the men who fell there in 1917 were not called upon to sacrifice life in vain.

II

In the 24th Battalion, Victoria Rifles of Canada, special training for the attack on Vimy Ridge began at Maisnil Bouche on March 26th, 1917, when unit commanders lectured to their men on the work that lay ahead. Next day, and again on March 28th, the Battalion proceeded to a special Training Area, where a replica of the battlefield was marked out to full scale, and there practised the attack, each company and detail carrying out a rehearsal of the movements and duties that would fall to its lot on the day of battle. Then, on March 30th and 31st, each battalion having similarly practised the work assigned to it, the 5th Canadian Infantry Brigade assembled at the Training Area and, as a brigade, rehearsed over and over the action that would be required when zero hour should send the battalion forward to success or failure.

Two days later, Major C. F. Ritchie, M.C., who was to command the Battalion in the absence on sick leave of Lieut.-Col. R. O. Alexander, D.S.O., issued, over the signature of his Adjutant, Capt. J. N. Bales, preliminary instructions for the offensive, and on April 7th Operation Order No. 72, with information regarding the scene of the forthcoming attack and with details of the Battalion's work more complete than had previously been available. In substance, Major Ritchie's orders and announcements were:—

Preliminary Instructions

(1) *Information*—The Canadian Corps has been ordered to take the Vimy Ridge, in conjunction with a larger operation by the British Third Army. The 5th Canadian Infantry Brigade will take part in the attack, with the 4th Canadian Infantry Brigade attacking on the right, and the 8th Canadian Infantry Brigade on the left.

(2) *Duty of 5th Canadian Infantry Brigade*—To capture and consolidate the Black Line (Swischen Stellung) and Red Line objectives.
When the 4th and 5th Canadian Infantry Brigades have captured these objectives, the 6th Canadian Infantry Brigade and the 13th British Infantry Brigade will pass through the captured lines and continue the attack against the Blue Line and Brown Line objectives.

(3) *Boundaries of 5th Brigade Attack*—[Indicated by reference to map locations.]

(4) *Plan of Attack*—The Brigade will attack (1) the German front line, (2) the German support line, (3) the Black objective (Swischen Stellung), (4) the Red objective.
The Brigade will attack with the 24th Battalion, Victoria Rifles of Canada, and the 26th (New Brunswick) Battalion in the front line, the 24th Battalion on the right.
The 25th (Nova Scotia) Battalion will be in reserve; the 22nd (French-Canadian) Battalion will be broken up into carrying parties and mopping-up parties.

(5) *Frontage*—The 24th and 26th Battalions will each have a frontage of approximately 350 yards.

(6) *Timing*—The leading waves of the 24th and 26th Battalions will go straight through to their objective in the Black Line, which they are timed to reach at zero plus 32 minutes. The 25th Battalion will follow, will pass through the Black Line to reform, and will recommence the advance at zero plus 75 minutes.

(7) *Procedure After Capture of Black Line*—If the 4th and 5th Canadian Infantry Brigades fail to capture the Red Line, the 6th Canadian and 13th British Infantry Brigades will be called upon to undertake this, before continuing their advance against the Blue Line.

(8) *Barrage*—The pace of the barrage up to the Red Line will be 100 yards in 3 minutes, with allowances [as indicated in barrage map] for crossing certain trenches.

(9) *Procedure in Event of a Check*—If any battalion, company, or platoon is held up, units on flank will on no account check their advance, but will form defensive flanks toward the unit held up and press forward themselves, thus enveloping the strong point which is impeding the advance. With this object in view, reserves will be pushed in to support successful parties rather than those held up.

(10) *24th Battalion Formation*—The 24th Battalion will attack with "B" and "C" Companies in the front line, "C" Coy. in support, "A" Coy. in reserve, and 1 company of the 22nd (French-Canadian) Battalion as moppers-up.

(11) *Battalion Boundaries*—"B" Coy.'s right will be on the right boundary of the 5th Canadian Infantry Brigade. "D" Coy.'s left will join up with the 26th Battalion's right.

(12) *Platoon Duties*—No. 11 Platoon will consolidate "B" Coy.'s front. No. 12 Platoon will consolidate "D" Coy.'s front. No. 10 Platoon will work as carrying parties and establish dumps in the Black Line, and will then assist in consolidating the front. No. 1

Platoon (assisted by 2 Sections of No. 1 Platoon, 22nd Battalion) will mop up the Volker Tunnel and will be responsible for holding the entrances and exits. Volker Tunnel is not to be damaged unless absolutely necessary. No. 1 Platoon will advance immediately in rear of the 1st wave of the Battalion's attack.

(13) *Other Duties of 22nd Battalion Platoons*—No. 2 Platoon (22nd Battalion) will mop up the German front line trenches and trenches between German front and support lines.

No. 3 Platoon and 2 Sections of No. 1 Platoon (22nd Battalion) will mop up German support line trenches and Grenadier Graben to Furze Trench.

(14) *Additional Duties of "A" and "C" Companies*— "A" Coy., if not otherwise employed, will occupy Grenadier Graben east of Furze Trench (the New Trench) as soon as the objective has been gained. When the 25th Battalion has cleared Furze Trench, "A" Coy. will occupy it and consolidate.

"C" Coy. will furnish 2 sections to follow the 1st wave and mop-up Furze Trench, after which they will rejoin their platoons.

(15) *Stokes Gun Fire*—2 Stokes guns will serve with the 24th Battalion. They will fire as follows: On the German front line, from zero to zero plus 1 minute. On the support line, from zero plus 1 minute to zero plus 6 minutes.

After zero plus 6 minutes, they will cease fire and advance immediately in rear of "B" and "D" Companies, notifying the Company Commanders and Battalion Headquarters of their position.

(16) *Tanks*—No tanks will advance with the 5th Canadian Infantry Brigade. 8 tanks will assemble in Elbe Trench and leave there at zero hour. They are timed to reach the Red Line at zero plus 4 hours and will advance from the Red Line with the infantry of the 6th Canadian and 13th British Brigades.

(17) *Assembly of 24th Battalion*—The 1st wave, moppers up, and No. 1 Platoon will assemble and jump off from the present British Observation Line.

The 2nd, 3rd, and 4th waves of the attack will assemble and jump off from a new trench dug 100 yards in rear of the present British Observation Line. Battalion Headquarters will be in old Right Company Headquarters [map location given].

(18) *Timing of Barrage and Advances*—At zero, barrage will open and troops will advance to the assault.
At zero plus 3 minutes, barrage will lift from the German front line.
At zero plus 8 minutes, barrage will lift from the German support line.
At zero plus 32 minutes, barrage will lift from the Black Line.
At zero plus 75 minutes, the Infantry will advance from the Black Line.
At zero plus 103 minutes, barrage will lift from the Red Line.
At zero plus 245 minutes, Infantry will advance from the Red Line.

(19) *Action of 24th Battalion after Capture of Black Line*—After capturing our objectives, "B," "D," and "C" Companies will consolidate same.
As soon as the barrage lifts and the 25th Battalion has passed through the Black Line, "C" Coy. will move forward and dig a new trench about 100 yards in front of the Black Line and will push out Lewis gun posts. The Black Line will be held until orders are received from Headquarters of the 2nd Canadian Division.

(20) *Communication*—
   (a) Before zero hour, buried cable will be extended from Brigade Headquarters, through the 24th and 26th Battalion Headquarters, to the tunnel exits at Lichfield Crater, where Lichfield Exchange will be established. The call for this exchange will be EX.
   (b) After zero hour, signallers of the 22nd Battalion will leave Lichfield Tunnel and follow the 24th and 26th Battalions, laying a ladder telephone line from EX to a suitable position in the Black

Line, which they will mark with a red flapper and where they will establish a signal station. The call for this station will be Z. A power buzzer will be set up at this station to communicate with Lichfield Tunnel to ensure communication if the telephone line is broken.
  (c) As soon as the Black Objective is reached, Lieut. G. S. Bushe will establish a Report Centre, marked with a white flapper. The call for this centre will be A. From this centre a ladder telephone line will be laid and kept in repair by 24th Battalion signallers to Signal Station Z.
  (d) Power buzzer messages will be acknowledged by EX by signals on a flapper at Lichfield Crater. If conditions prevent these signals from being seen, each message will be sent 3 times in succession.

(21) *Visual Signalling and Pigeons*—
  (a) The Battalion Signal Sections will carry visual signalling apparatus as follows:
  1 flapper per man hung on belt.
  1 pocket magnetic compass per man.
  1 French lamp for each report centre—flags if thought desirable.
  (b) A Brigade O.P. for visual signals will be established at Lichfield Crater. Call EX.
  (c) Signal Section will carry forward 2 pigeons to Report Centre. These will be used for URGENT messages only, and in case telephone or visual signalling cannot be maintained.

(22) *Runners*—Company runners will be employed between Company Headquarters and Battalion Report Centre. Battalion runners will be employed from Report Centre in the event that other means of communication fail.

(23) *Battle Flags*—Assaulting troops of the 2nd Canadian Division and the 13th British Infantry Brigade will carry the Divisional Battle Flag—A Yellow Disc with a Black Maple Leaf centre, reverse side khaki. Two flags per platoon will be carried. The 1st Canadian Division will carry a Dark Blue and Yellow Flag;

the 3rd Canadian Division will carry a Black and Red Flag; and the 4th Canadian Division will carry a Red Flag. These flags must be waved and not stuck in the ground.

(24) *Rations*—1 day's rations will be carried, in addition to the iron ration. 2 filled water bottles will be carried.

(25) *Wounded*—R.A.P.'s for Stretcher Cases—At Combow and Denis le Rock.
R.A.P.'s for Walking Cases—At Denis le Rock and Parallel VIII.
From the front, stretcher cases will be carried by the moppers up, after they have mopped up their area. These carrying parties will then report to Battalion Headquarters.

(26) *Burial of the Dead*—To ensure that all graves are registered, burials will be carried out under the direction of the Divisional Registration Officer, Lieut. G. O. MacKay, 2nd Canadian Pioneer Battalion, who has a special party already detailed for this work.

(27) *Prisoners*—Will be sent to the Divisional Cage at Aux Reitz Corner.
Prisoners should be given no opportunity to destroy or throw away documents in their possession at the time of capture. Officer Prisoners—All their papers and correspondence will be placed in sandbags and sent with the prisoners to the Divisional Cage.
Other Ranks Prisoners—Will retain their personal effects.
Enemy Dead—Documents will be collected from enemy dead, placed in sandbags, and forwarded to Battalion Headquarters.
Enemy Wounded—Will be treated in every way similarly to our own wounded.
Identity discs will never be taken from the living; discs from the dead will be turned in to Battalion Headquarters.

(28) *Escort for Prisoners*—Prisoners should be sent back in batches. The most convenient number to handle

is from 100 to 150. The escort should consist of about 15% of the strength of the prisoners. Receipts for prisoners will be issued at the Divisional Cage.

(29) *Salvage*—All steel helmets, rifles, ammunition, bombs, etc., whether British or German, will be collected and turned in to the Brigade Salvage Dump at Tram Head (Mowcop)—Denis le Rock.

Special Instructions

(1) *Equipment*—
Rifle Grenadiers will carry 10 rifle grenades.
Bombers will carry 10 bombs.
All others will carry 2 bombs.
Bombers, Rifle Grenadiers, Runners, Signallers, and Lewis Gunners will carry 2 bandoliers of small arm ammunition; all others will carry 2 bandoliers in addition to their 120 rounds.
Every man will carry 2 ground flares.
Every officer will carry 1 flare pistol and flares.

(2) *S.O.S.*
The S.O.S. signal will be any number of red lights in rapid succession.
Heavy rifle and machine-gun fire will also be taken as an S.O.S. signal.

(3) *Objective Gained Signal*—White flares will be fired when the objective has been gained.

(4) *Liaison*—
The leading waves of the attack must keep in touch with the units on their flanks; and must see that contact is maintained in the Black Objective.

Continuation of Preliminary Instructions

(Summarized)

(1) *Light Signals*—
(a) As soon as the Black, Red, Blue, and Brown Lines respectively have been captured, 3 white Very lights will be fired by the assaulting troops as a signal that they have reached their objectives.

These signals are to be fired only by the order of the Officers Commanding the Assaulting Companies. In addition, a special signal to denote the capture of Thélus or Hill 140 consisting of 3 Gold and Silver Rain Rockets will be fired by troops of the 6th Canadian and 13th British Infantry Brigades.

All observers are warned to keep a special lookout for these signals.

(2) *S.O.S. Signals—*
Canadian Corps—Red.
Third Army—Green.

(3) *Identification of Contact Patrols—*
The machine of No. 16 Squadron, Royal Flying Corps, working under the orders of the Canadian Corps, will have the following distinguishing marks:—
(a) 2 black bands under the right hand bottom plane.
(b) 2 streamers, one on each right rear interplane strut.

Operation Order No. 71

(Dated April 7, 1917)

(Summarized)

(1) *Concentration—*
The infantry concentration of the 2nd Canadian Division will be carried out on Y Day in 2 phases.
1st phase:—Concentration in Bois des Alleux.
2nd phase:—Move to Assembly Trenches after dark.

(2) *1st Phase—*
(a) The 24th Battalion, Victoria Rifles of Canada, will move from Maisnil Bouche to Bois des Alleux at 6.45 a.m.
(b) 200 yards intervals will be kept between companies and every effort must be made to conceal the movement from hostile aircraft.
(c) Cross country routes will be used if possible. If it is found necessary to follow the road, the route must be via: Gauchin Légal, Estrée Cauchie, and Camblain l'Abbé.
(d) Capt. E. G. N. Lidstone will report to the Staff Captain of the 5th Canadian Infantry Brigade at

7.30 a.m. on Y Day. He will also instruct Lieut. G. C. Smyth to move his special fatigue party to the 24th Battalion area in Bois des Alleux.
  (e) *Routine on Y Day*—
  Réveillé—4 a.m.
  Breakfast—4.30 a.m.
  Fall in—6.15 a.m.
  March—6.45 a.m.

(3) *Battalion Reserve*—
Officers and other ranks held in Reserve will move to Yukon Camp, under command of Major P. L. Hall, M.C.

(4) *2nd Phase*—
  (a) On arrival at Bois des Alleux, bombs, ammunition, and rations will be issued to the Battalion under the supervision of Hon. Capt. H. D. Campbell and Lieut. J. Donald.
  (b) At 7.30 p.m. the Battalion will move through the Wood to the Starting Point.
  At 8 p.m. the Battalion will pass the Starting Point and proceed up the St. Eloy—la Targette Road to Rietz Trench, and thence to the Assembly Trenches. Assembly will be completed at 3.45 a.m. on Z Day, and notification of completion will be reported to Battalion Headquarters by runners.

Operation Order No. 72

(Dated April 7, 1917)
(Summarized)

(1) *Information*—
On April 9th the Canadian Corps is attacking the Vimy Ridge. The 24th Battalion, Victoria Rifles of Canada, will attack in accordance with instructions already issued.

(2) *Zero Hour*—
Will be communicated later to all concerned.

(3) *Assembly*—
All troops will be in their assembly positions by 3.45 a.m. on April 9th.

(4) *Gas Protection*—
From 5 p.m. on April 8th and throughout the operation, all ranks will wear the box respirator in the gas alert position.

(5) *Contact Air Patrols*—
Contact planes will fly at the following times:—
For the Black Line—Zero plus 50 minutes.
For the Red Line—Zero plus 2 hours.
The leading infantry will be ready at the above hours to light flares as soon as the aeroplane calls for them.

(6) *Synchronization of Watches*—
The Battalion Signalling Officer will report to Brigade Headquarters at 4 p.m. and at 11 p.m. to-day and will synchronize watches with the Company Commanders and the Commanders of Regimental Units at 4 p.m. to-morrow (April 8th) in the Bois des Alleux. Battalion Headquarters will synchronize with Brigade Headquarters immediately after reaching Battle Headquarters.

Though the foregoing summary of the Orders issued by Major C. F. Ritchie for the participation by the 24th Battalion in the attack of the Canadian Corps on Vimy Ridge, conveys some impression of the care with which the operation was conceived and of the attention to detail paid by every unit under Lieut.-General Sir Julian Byng's command, no bare summarization of orders can describe the skill and enthusiasm with which the troops approached their task. For the first and only time, the four divisions of the Canadian Corps were attacking in line and each division, with supreme confidence in its own ability and implicit faith in the troops on its flank, believed that, beyond all doubt, Fortune would favour the Corps' assault. Even the announcement that the attack would be against the deadly Vimy Ridge served to raise rather than to lower morale. The men had seen the care with which the operation had been planned, had noted the massing of artillery in support, had observed the superiority of the British in the air, and were sure that in the day of battle victory would be theirs.

In the 24th Battalion, Victoria Rifles of Canada, preparation for the battle was continued at Maisnil Bouche throughout the first week in April, a period marked also by receipt of news that the United States of America had declared war on Germany. Ordinarily, news of such importance would have aroused enthusiasm; in the circumstances, the men received it without more than casual interest. Their concern at the moment lay definitely in the forthcoming attack, and events with no immediate bearing upon the assault on Vimy Ridge left them strangely unimpressed and disinterested.

Saturday, April 7, 1917, found the unit with its preparations complete. The following day would be Easter, but time would permit on that day of little regard to the observances of religion; accordingly, the Battalion Chaplain, Hon. Capt. C. J. S. Stuart, held Divine Service on the 7th. A bitter wind blew from the north as the Battalion paraded at 9 a.m., the lowering skies providing a sombre background for the figure of the Chaplain, who, after a short service and a solemn benediction, announced that, for all who desired to attend, a celebration of Holy Communion would be held in "A" Company's Headquarters. Despite the fact that "A" Coy.'s Headquarters was situated in an estaminet, whose dreary tap-room smelled sourly of malt, and mud, and sweat, many who partook of Holy Communion on that occasion have referred to the experience as one of the most solemn and impressive of their lives.

On the morning of Easter Sunday, April 8, 1917, réveillé sounded at 4 a.m. and at 6.45 o'clock the Battalion marched by companies across country, reaching Bois des Alleux about 9 a.m. and there bivouacking for the day. Until noon, the men were permitted to rest, but in the afternoon the camp was a beehive of activity as the men were equipped with ammunition, bombs, rifle grenades, rations, ground flares, and sandbags, according to the duties laid down for them in the orders for the forthcoming attack.

By 6 p.m., the last detail of preparation was completed and the Battalion Kitchens had provided the men with a hot and sustaining meal. No unforeseen event delayed the unit thereafter and at 7.30 o'clock Major Ritchie gave the command to march. Steadily and in high spirits, the Battalion moved off with platoons at 100-yard intervals to its battle position in the assembly trenches in front of Neuville St. Vaast.

Despite the obstacle presented by deep mud in communication trenches on the way forward, the 24th Battalion reached the front line by 1 o'clock on the morning of April 9th and stood by, while strong parties moved into No Man's Land to cut the Canadian wire and clear a path to the Observation Line, from which the waves of the attack were to debouch. Unfortunately, the communication trenches from the firing line to the Observation Line were impassable and the men of the 24th were compelled to move forward overland. This advance could not be concealed and the enemy, sighting it, called on his supporting artillery for S.O.S. fire. In reply, the German guns opened a sharp bombardment, which, though failing to deter the Battalion, killed or wounded about 15 men.

Soon after the 24th Battalion took position in the line, contact was established with the 26th Battalion on the left and the 19th Battalion on the right. The 25th Battalion, which was to act in close support in the first phase of the attack and later to carry the assault forward, was also found in position and prepared, as always, to carry out faithfully and efficiently the duties to which it had been assigned. With no fear, therefore, of ineffective action on the flanks or in the rear, Major Ritchie and the officers of Battalion Headquarters confidently awaited the hour when zero would send the companies forward.

As the hands of officers' watches approached the zero hour, 5.30 a.m., squalls of wind and snow and rain swept the crowded front line trenches, drenching the men, who, as their battle equipment permitted no greatcoats, were shivering and cold. In these circumstances, action was welcome and the men impatiently awaited the roar of the British barrage. Sharp to the moment, the guns opened fire, the infantry of the Canadian Corps and their comrades in the Imperial divisions to the south advancing simultaneously against the enemy trenches.

With "B" Coy., under Major A. L. S. Mills, on the right and "D" Coy., under Capt. V. E. Duclos, on the left, the first wave of the 24th Battalion's attack followed closely behind the rolling wall of the British barrage and, without serious opposition, stormed the front and immediate support line of German trenches, "A" and "C" Companies, under Lieut. A. M. Dewar and Capt. C. S. B. White, following in accordance with orders and taking an active part in the engagement. Machine-gun fire at this time was not hampering the attack as had been expected, and the German field guns, under the admirable counter-battery fire of the Canadian artillery, were being held effectively in check, but as the Battalion attack moved forward from the first lines of German trenches, opposition began perceptibly to stiffen and before long the unit was fighting hard to maintain the speed of its advance and the continuity of its attacking front.

As the German resistance increased, casualties in the assaulting companies began to mount, the Battalion losing two of its best subalterns when Lieut. J. P. MacArthur, who had joined in the previous year after service with the 70th Battalion, and Lieut. G. C. Smyth, an original member of the 24th Battalion who had received a commission for his fine work with the unit in France, were killed instantly while leading their platoons. Both were shot through the head and later, with the Chaplain of their own Battalion officiating, were buried side by side in the military cemetery at Ecoivres.

Meanwhile, in spite of stubborn resistance, the waves of the 24th Battalion's attack were driving resolutely toward their objective, each man, it seemed, setting for his comrades a fine example of determination to permit no obstacle to bar the unit's path. In front of the attack at one point, Private J. A. Bingley advanced, waving the Divisional Battle Flag to assist artillery liaison and displaying complete disregard for his own protection or safety. At another point, Lance-Corporal W. H. Chase was buried completely by the crash of a high explosive shell, but crawled to his feet and continued to lead his Section forward; at a third point, Corp. G. W. Croll seized a machine-gun from the hands of a dead or dying crew and brought it to bear against a German gun, while Sergt. A. L. Samson advanced to bomb the position where the gunners were concealed.

Though the individual efforts mentioned materially aided the Battalion's attack, hard fighting continued and the Germans contested bitterly each yard of the unit's progress. Enemy machine-guns by this time were sweeping the front and were subdued only after sharp encounters, sometimes by rifle grenades, in the use of which Private D. Campbell displayed marked ability; sometimes by counter machine-gun fire, as when Private A. A. Chapman and Private J. Walden successfully dispersed enemy crews; sometimes by bombing with Mills grenades, as when Sergt. W. G. Quirk, M.M., led a series of attacks on hidden enemy nests; and again by straight driving bayonet attacks in which many of the men participated.

As the enemy machine-guns were swept out of the Battalion's path on the left, Capt. Duclos led his men ever closer to their assigned objective, turning at intervals and throwing open his white-lined overcoat, thus indicating his position and helping his men to maintain correct alignment. Though wounded, he continued to lead his company, with no thought of leaving his men until the issue of the battle had been decided. Resistance was maintained by the enemy, but no effort that the Germans could put forth was successful in stopping, or even checking for more than a few moments, the power of "D" Coy.'s attack. Accordingly, at 6.02 a.m., white flares burning in the Black Line informed anxious observers in the rear and on the flanks that "D" Coy.'s objective had been attained.

Meanwhile, on the right, "B" Coy. had momentarily been checked by the fire of enemy machine-guns. German troops, also, lining the parapet of the Swischen Stellung, opened heavy rifle fire and inflicted sharp losses. Determined that these troops should not succeed in their brave attempt to halt the Canadian attack, Private V. Willett advanced in front of his comrades and opened fire, which assisted materially in driving the Germans to cover. He was seriously wounded just as Major Mills and the attacking waves reached his side, but his effort had not been in vain, for the men of "B" Coy. drove past him and at 6.14 a.m. fought their way to the final objective. Lance-Corporal S. O. Rose, of the

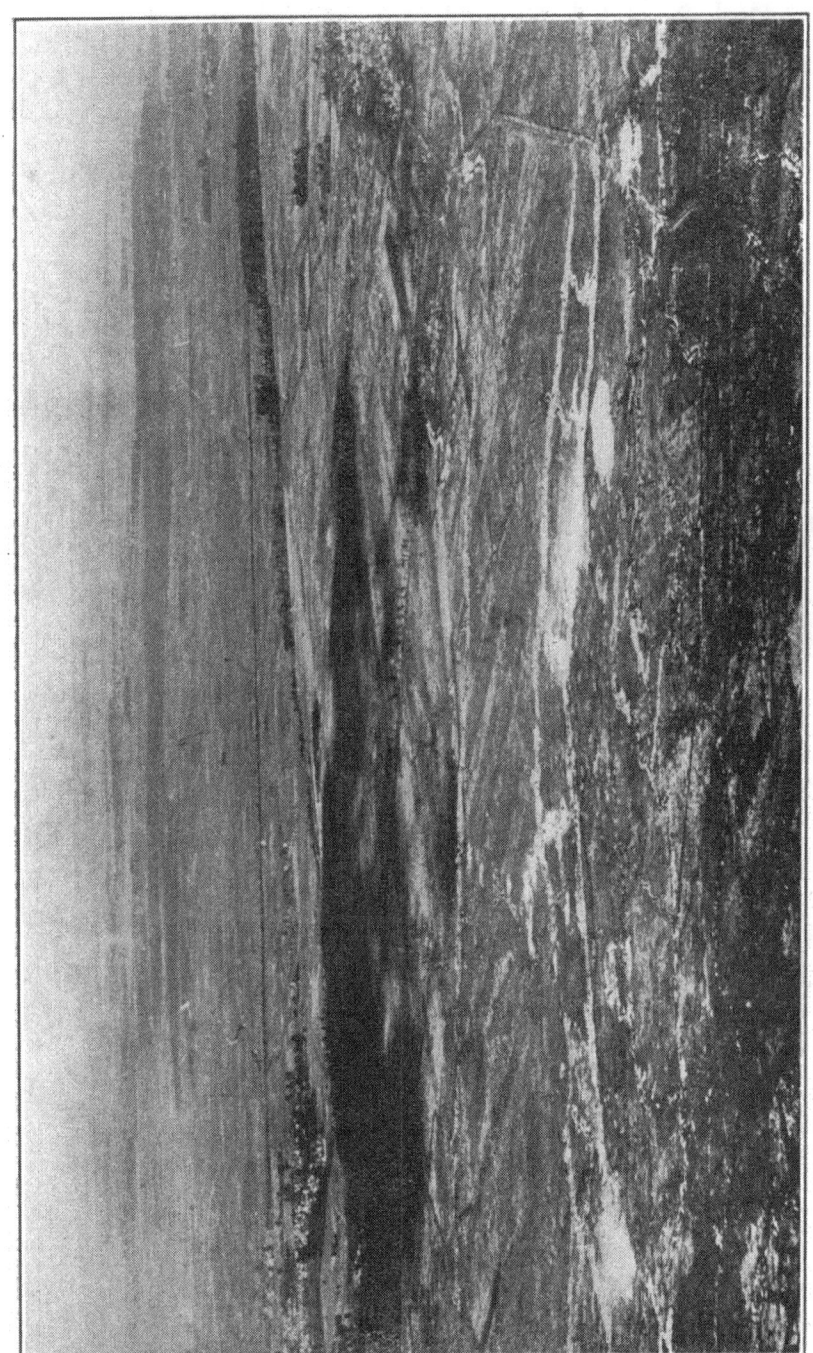

The Battalion's Battlefield at Vimy Ridge, April 9, 1917

Scout Section, who was killed in the moment of victory, was amongst those whose example of courage and determination contributed in a marked degree to the success which "B" Coy. won.

Occupation of the Black Line by "D" and "B" Companies did not mean that all enemy resistance had been overcome; on the contrary, parties of the enemy in the final objective, and in dugouts as far back as the original German front line, fought savagely with the parties of the 24th Battalion and the attached company of the 22nd Battalion, assigned to the task of mopping up.

At one spot in the Black Line, a German officer held a strong point with a party of his men and fought courageously until Private A. Abbey leaped at him, tore a revolver from his grasp, and forced him and his party to surrender; at another point, Private J. N. O'Reilly entered a dugout, attacked 9 Germans single-handed and subdued their spirited resistance; at a third point, Major Mills, with Company Sergt.-Major R. Mitchell, M.M., and two bayonet men supporting him, bombed a party of the enemy and, closing with them, effected their capture.

Even before these encounters had taken place and the companies had occupied the Black Line, the Signallers, the Stretcher-Bearers, and the carrying parties of the Battalion had advanced to accomplish their part in the unit's operation. Sergt. L. A. Wilson and his carrying platoon reached the Black Line on the heels of the actual assault and assisted in the work of consolidation. Similar prompt action by all consolidation parties, and by the parties engaged, under Lieut. G. S. Bushe, in establishing a Battalion Report Centre, meant that at 6.25 a.m., when a contact aeroplane flew low along the front, evidence that the line was safely in Canadian hands was clearly discernible. Twenty minutes later, the 25th Battalion, under Major J. A. De Lancey, advanced through the 24th Battalion's new front and, with two pipers leading, drove against the German positions in the Red Line, capturing these in a dashing manner, but losing the officer who had led the unit so bravely. Later, a battalion of the King's Own Scottish Borderers passed through the 24th Battalion lines to carry the attack down the eastern slopes of the Ridge.

Relieved through the 25th Battalion's advance of all danger of serious counter-attack on his front, Major Mills, as senior officer in the captured area, supervised the work of consolidation and notified Battalion Headquarters that "D" Coy. was in contact with the 19th Battalion on the right and with "B" Coy. on the left, the latter reporting simultaneously that contact with the 26th Battalion on the left flank had been established and was being maintained.

At 8 a.m. Major Mills reported the death of Lieut. MacArthur and stated that casualties had been fairly heavy, particularly at the time when the advance on the left had been subjected to heavy fire. He mentioned the bravery of Sergt. W. G. Quirk, M.M., also the fact that, in his bombing operations in the final objective, Lieut. Livingstone, of the 25th Battalion, had rendered brave and valuable assistance. He did not know at the time of Lieut. Smyth's death and was not certain with regard to the fate of a number of his most experienced and trusted N.C.O.'s.

Two hours later, Major Mills reported again, stating that, owing to a concentration of enemy fire on the Black Line, or Swischen Stellung, he had advanced his troops to a line less exposed to the pounding of the German guns. He stated that Lieut. A. M. Dewar, who was in command of "C" Coy., Lieut. E. P. Denman, and Lieut. R. B. E. Wilson were in the front line, that he still had no news of Lieut. Smyth, but that Sergts. A. Staples, C. G. Riley, and G. H. Walter had been killed.

Soon after this, as reports were received from all Battalion units, it became possible to estimate the Victoria Rifles' losses. When considered in relation to the success achieved, and to the fact that more than 200 prisoners had been passed back to the Divisional cage, the Battalion's numerical loss, which totalled 2 officers killed, 4 wounded, and approximately 230 other ranks killed and wounded, was not severe; but a balance struck in this manner fails to reflect accurately the character and value to the unit of the officers and men whose names make up the casualty total.

In the 24th Battalion, the wounded included two company commanders, Capt. C. S. B. White and Capt.

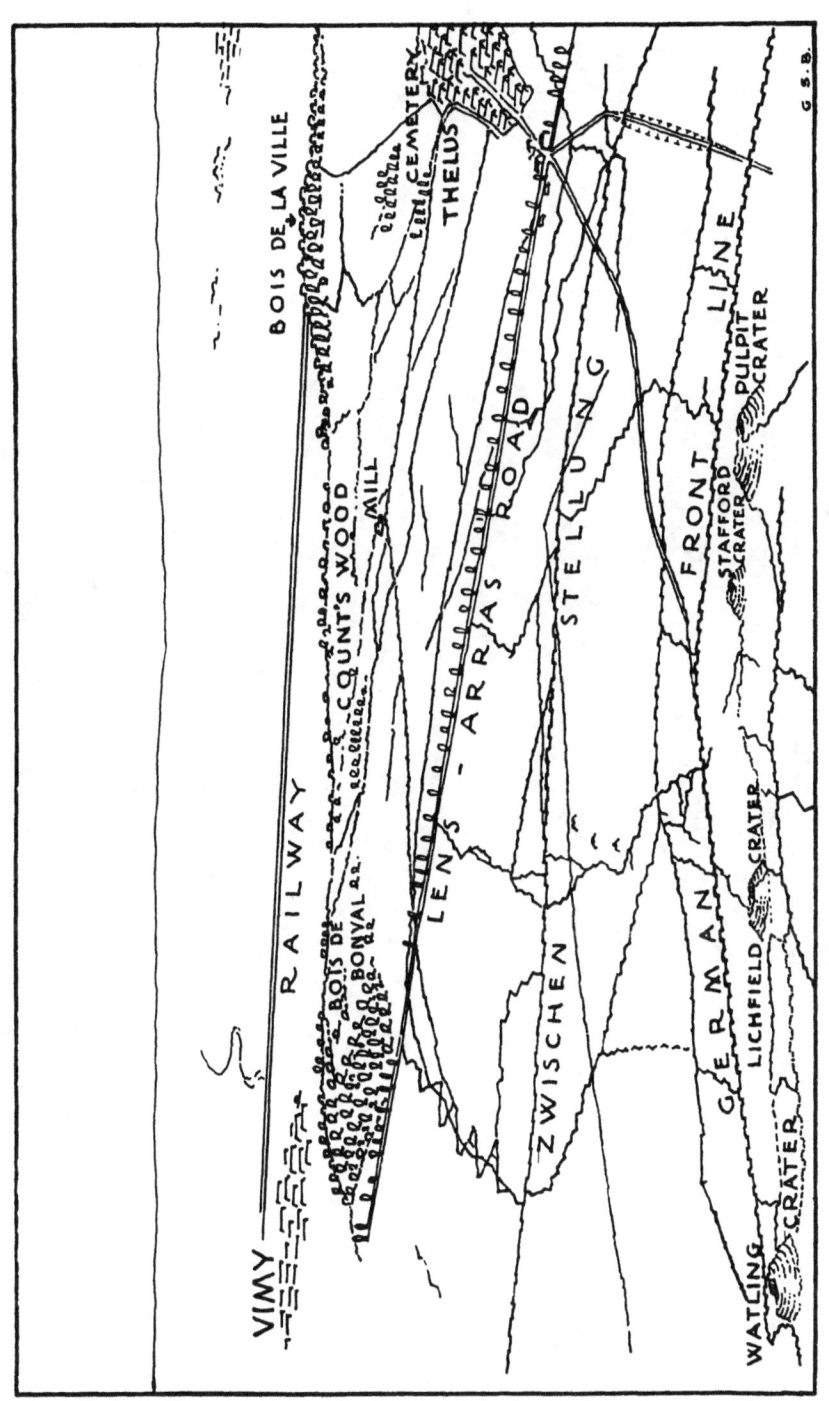

The 24th Battalion's Battlefield at Vimy Ridge—April, 1917.

V. E. Duclos, both original officers of the Battalion, who previously had suffered wounds and whose experience and ability in leadership had over and again proved of value; Lieut K. S. Drummond, who, despite severe injury, had led a bombing attack against a machine-gun which was holding up the assault of the Battalion on one flank; and Lieut. C. E. Hill, who had joined the 24th after service in the ranks of the Canadian Army Medical Corps. The wounding of these officers, together with the deaths of Lieuts. Smyth and MacArthur, inflicted a loss greater than mere enumeration can reveal; and through casualties to a large number of experienced N.C.O.'s the Battalion suffered a blow from which recovery could not easily be effected.

All day on April 9th, all during the bitter cold of that stormy night, and for three days thereafter, the 24th Battalion remained in the captured Black Line, consolidating the position against any possibility of enemy counter-attack. After the first few hours, as the Canadian assault drove deeper and deeper into the German lines, the danger of immediate counter-attack grew remote, but protection against enemy shelling was needed and the men worked hard to build the defences required. All casualties in the attack had been evacuated by the night of April 9th; and Major P. L. Hall, M.C., who had rejoined the unit in January after recovering from a wound received at the Somme, and Capt. E. G. N. Lidstone had arrived in the forward area to replace the wounded commanders of "D" and "C" Companies. At 10 a.m. on April 12th, Major Ritchie transferred his Headquarters to a position in the Swischen Stellung, whence he could control more effectively the consolidation work the Battalion was accomplishing.

On the following day, at 6 p.m., the Battalion advanced from the Swischen Stellung and relieved the 18th Canadian Battalion in front line and support positions in Goulot Wood, "A" and "C" Companies taking over the actual front, or outpost line, and connecting with troops of the 1st Canadian Division on the right and the 26th Battalion on the left. At 5 o'clock on the morning of the next day, April 14th, the 26th Battalion extended across the 2nd Canadian Divisional front and, after advancing some distance, dug a new front line, the 24th Battalion advancing simultaneously in support and digging in as follows:

"C" Coy. in outpost line, 400 yards beyond the Vimy-Arras railway line.
"A" Coy. along the Vimy-Arras railway embankment.
"B" Coy. 200 yards in rear of "A" Coy.
"D" Coy. in Goulot Wood.
Battalion Headquarters in a dugout at Vimy Station.

From these positions, "B" and "D" Companies moved out at 8 p.m. and dug a close support trench across the Brigade frontage, returning to their original positions at dawn and being succeeded in the digging work that night by "A" and "C" Companies. Heavy shelling of the area occurred on April 15th, but the fire was inaccurate, or, if accurate, was directed at unoccupied positions, and the Battalion, accordingly, had suffered few additional casualties when, at night, the 28th Battalion relieved. Following relief, the 24th Battalion moved back to support in Volker Tunnel and thence, at 12.30 p.m on April 16th, to rest tents at la Targette. Here the unit, which had suffered casualties in the line totalling 7 officers and 241 other ranks, including Lieut D. Colville, an original member of the Battalion, who was wounded on April 14th, was rejoined by Lieut.-Col. R. O. Alexander, D.S.O., who again assumed command.

Officer Casualties—April 9-16, 1917

Killed in Action

Lieut. G. C. Smyth
Lieut. J. P. MacArthur

Wounded

Capt. C. S. B. White
Capt. V. E. Duclos
Lieut. K. S. Drummond
Lieut. C. E. Hill

Lieut. D. Colville
Lieut. R. W. Casey (while attached to Canadian Trench Mortars).

CHAPTER VIII

TRENCH TOURS ON THE VIMY FRONT

I

At 6 o'clock on the morning of April 16, 1917, at a time when British operations at Vimy Ridge and Monchy-le-Preux had drawn to the Arras front many divisions of the German Army, General Nivelle launched his major offensive on the Aisne. In brief, his plan was that the French Northern Army Group, under General Franchet d'Espérey, should attack on the front between Harly and Alaincourt, in liaison with the main attack of the French Fifth and Sixth Armies of Reserve, under Generals Mazel and Mangin, on the Aisne. The Fifth and Sixth Armies were to rupture the German front and permit the passage through the resulting gap of the French Tenth Army.

In a letter to General Micheler, who was to command the group of armies of rupture and exploitation, General Nivelle repeated his instructions that the whole operation must be marked by "de violence, de brutalité, et de rapidité." These three qualities must govern the fighting; and of the three the greatest was the last. Again and again the French Commander-in-Chief had stated that rupture of the German line *must* be effected in the first 24 to 48 hours of the battle, and that his plan possessed no alternative.

On the front of the Fifth and Sixth French Armies, the first line of the first German positions was stormed and carried on April 16th, and in places a penetration of approximately 3 kilometres was effected; but before the Craonne plateau and on the slopes of Mount Sapigneul the driving attack of the French infantry was abruptly halted.

Throughout the day, the French Fifth Army strove desperately to effect the penetration vital to the whole plan of battle; but when night fell no outstanding success had been achieved. To the left, the French Sixth Army was equally unfortunate. By 8 a.m., coloured troops of the 2nd Corps had passed beyond the Chemin des Dames and reached the Ailette River; but on the plateau of Vauclerc concentrated machine-gun fire inflicted losses so severe that enemy counter-attacks drove the survivors back in confusion, and, after 10 hours of hard fighting, the Sixth Army halted. Many prisoners and great stores of material had been captured; but victory on a major scale was not even remotely in sight.

Meanwhile, the French Tenth Army had advanced to exploit the rupture which the Fifth and Sixth Armies had been expected to achieve. By 8 a.m., it had crossed the River Aisne and stood ready to fulfil its appointed mission, but, despite all efforts by the armies of rupture, no opportunity to advance further was provided; and at night the Army stood, chafing uneasily, on the ground taken up early in the day.

On April 17th, after his armies had been engaged for 30 hours, General Nivelle studied the reports from the right and left battle fronts and realized, beyond peradventure, that his great plan had failed. Sick at heart, it may well be believed, but greater, perhaps, in his hour of bitterness than when the tide of his success ran high, he ordered the attack of the Sixth Army to cease forthwith, and changed the direction of assault of the Fifth Army on the right.

Within 48 hours, the public in France realized with dismay that the battle was not going well. Rumours of a quarter-million casualties in the Fifth and Sixth Armies spread alarmingly. These were fantastic; but denial that casualties had been heavy was impossible, and the French, having accepted General Nivelle's optimistic promises of victory, were bitter when realization of their hope was denied.

On May 10th, the French Government demanded that General Nivelle resign. This request was refused; but the Government was determined, and on May 16th General Nivelle was dismissed and General Pétain appointed to succeed him. By this time, the full effect of General Nivelle's failure had appeared and mutiny, breaking out in certain French divisions, was a serious possibility in many more. Impressed by the danger, General Pétain visited Sir Douglas Haig, who, to assist so far as lay in his power, had maintained pressure on the enemy front at Arras, and stated that, for a time, the French Army must be relieved from all possibility of serious attack. Accordingly, Sir Douglas Haig broke off his operations at Arras and, concentrating the strength of the Armies of the Empire in Belgium, prepared to pin the enemy to the Flanders front.

II

Unaware of many details regarding the failure of the French Army on the Aisne, but conscious that, for some reason obscure at the time, the brilliant success at Vimy Ridge had not produced results in proportion to the opportunities it obviously had provided, the divisions of the Canadian Corps continued in action on the Vimy front for some time after the capture of the Ridge on April 9th. Sharp fighting occurred, as Sir Douglas Haig employed his forces to relieve pressure upon the French, but, despite local success, the character of the operations bore witness to the fact that they were diversions on an important scale rather than the determined drive forward of an army with ample reserves and far-flung major objectives.

In the 24th Battalion, Victoria Rifles of Canada, operations in the forward area were resumed on April 21st when, after a 5-day period in rest tents at la Targette, the unit relieved the 20th Battalion in trenches near the Swischen Stellung. Five days were passed in these positions without notable incident, though British and German planes were active over the area, working parties were frequent, and a few casualties were inflicted by enemy guns.

Moving from the Swischen Stellung on the afternoon of April 26th, the Battalion relieved the 18th Battalion in the Main Resistance Line, with Headquarters at Kramer Haus, three companies in the line, and "D" Coy. in strong-points nearby. Two new officers, Lieuts. R. M. Beckett and H. S. McGreevy, were with "D" Coy. on this occasion and both, soon after their arrival in the trenches, were struck by fragments of an enemy shell, Lieut. Beckett suffering a wound which required some days of hospital treatment.

Artillery was active on April 27th, when the Battalion moved from the Main Resistance Line and relieved the 22nd French-Canadian Battalion in the Observation Line, with Headquarters in Thélus Cave; and fire continued to be heavy on the 28th, when the 1st and 2nd Canadian Divisions conducted further operations against the German line. Twenty-one other ranks joined the Battalion on this date, being followed by 15 other ranks on April 29th, and by 6 officers, who reported for duty to Lieut.-Col. Alexander on April 30th.

Meanwhile, in the Observation Line, officers and men had witnessed the constant passing to and fro of British and enemy planes, and, on April 28th, had been startled by the crash of a British plane a few yards to the rear of trenches occupied by Major P. L. Hall and "D" Coy. On approaching the shattered plane, a party of men of the 24th found the two occupants dead and were shocked when one body proved to be that of Major E. O. McMurtry, an original officer of the 24th Battalion, who, after months of service in France, had recovered from a wound received in April, 1916, and had transferred to the Royal Flying Corps. Major McMurtry had completed training in England only ten days before his death, and the coincidence of his falling in the lines of the battalion with which he had sailed from Canada in 1915 attracted widespread attention. The Battalion, being on duty in the line at the time, could pay to his remains only the simple and affectionate tribute that circumstances would permit, but other troops assumed responsibility, when, with full military honours, he was buried at Bruay on April 29th.

For the 24th Battalion, the month of May, 1917, was marked by a series of trench tours on the Vimy front. No serious attack occurred in the period, but shelling, particularly gas shelling, was frequently heavy, communication was often possible only by runner, and supplies reached the front line only after carrying parties had toiled to the full limit of their endurance and, on some occasions, had suffered sharply from the fire of enemy guns. The Germans at the time were exasperated by the loss of Vimy Ridge and no opportunity of venting their irritation was allowed to pass through indifference or neglect. Solitary Canadian soldiers accordingly were sniped at on occasions by German field guns and a carrying party, if observed from the enemy lines, would attract the venomous attention of a battery or two, with heavy guns joining vindictively in the shelling from positions to the rear.

Some indication of the artillery activity that was to mark the month was noted on May 1st. Few casualties were suffered in the Battalion on this date, but members of the unit witnessed the destruction by a 12-inch naval shell of a neighbouring battalion headquarters and took part in removing from the debris some 35 living wounded and the dead bodies of an officer and 15 men.

That night, or rather at 5 o'clock on the following morning, the 24th Battalion was relieved in the Right Section of the 2nd Canadian Divisional Front line and proceeded back to the Observation Line, just below the crest of Vimy Ridge, where, as during a previous tour, Headquarters was established in Thélus Cave. Before the relief was completed, a ration party from the 69th German R.I.R. wandered by mistake towards the Canadian line, one man falling dead under fire opened upon the party and a second being captured when wounds prevented his escape.

After spending one day in the Observation Line, the Battalion moved up on May 3rd and took over from the 22nd Battalion the Left Sector of the Divisional Front, with "A" and "B" Companies in the line, "C" Coy. in support, "D" Coy. in reserve, and Battalion Headquarters in Mont Forêt Quarries. The trench strength of the unit included 18 officers and 463 other ranks when the relief began, but shelling was brisk and before long 5 other ranks had been wounded. Lieut. G. G. Garvey also suffered a wound, but was able to remain at duty.

Further reduction in the trench strength of the Battalion was suffered on May 4th when heavy shelling struck the front line, more particularly the position held by "A" Coy., and a barrage of gas shells enveloped ration parties immediately to the rear of Battalion Headquarters. No communication with the front line was possible during these bombardments, or at any time throughout the day, and casualties mounted to a total of 7 other ranks killed and 1 officer, Lieut. T. C. Courtenay, and 21 other ranks wounded.

Again on May 5th enemy batteries, firing from the direction of Mericourt and Martigny, enfiladed the 24th Battalion trenches, killing and wounding a total of 31 other ranks, including many in "A" and "D" Companies and a number engaged in carrying rations. Sergt. F. Willetts, in charge of a party carrying to Battalion Headquarters, was amongst those who suffered sharply from a bombardment with shells containing gas.

Shelling continued throughout the night, and was renewed in the morning hours of May 6th, when enemy planes were successful in directing the fire of the guns for which they observed. Three other ranks were killed by this fire and 5 were wounded. Major P. L. Hall, M.C., was also wounded, for the second time, when two shells burst simultaneously a few feet from where he stood. Later the 18th Canadian Battalion lost 3 company commanders and a number of other ranks while moving in to relieve the 24th Battalion in the line. The Victoria Rifles were more fortunate during the relief, but did not escape entirely, for a runner, sent by Major Mills to notify Lieut.-Col. Alexander that relief of "B" Coy. was complete, was killed while carrying the message to its destination.

After being relieved in the line on the night of May 6th, the 24th Battalion moved back to the Paynesley Area, halting there for a few hours and, at noon on May 7th, proceeding to the rest area at Aux Rietz. Two days were spent at Aux Rietz, the men bathing and receiving issues of equipment and supplies. Then, at 4.45 p.m. on May 9th, the Battalion, with a trench strength of 19 officers and 427 other ranks, moved again to the Paynesley Area, under Major A. L. S. Mills, who had assumed command owing to the illness of Lieut.-Col. R. O. Alexander and the absence on leave of Major C. F. Ritchie.

For four days the 24th Battalion remained in the Paynesley Area (near Neuville St. Vaast), supplying strong parties which were employed in burying cable, and then, on May 13th, relieved the 18th Battalion in the Forward Area. No outstanding incident marked the next few days; but on the night of May 16th guides, who were to lead the Battalion into the right sub-sector of the front line, missed direction and led their parties to the rear of British troops on the right. The error was recognized in time for the 24th Battalion to reach the positions to which it had been assigned before dawn, but not in time for the 25th Battalion to hand over and move out. All day, therefore, the two battalions crowded the front line, affording a target of which, fortunately, the enemy remained unaware. Desultory shelling occurred, but there was no blast of the shattering gun fire which all ranks dreaded, and at dusk the 25th Battalion withdrew to Brigade Support.

For two days more the 24th Battalion remained in the front line. Enemy planes were active overhead each morning and gun fire lashed the position at night, killing 4 other ranks and wounding 7 severely. To the regret of the Battalion, the killed included Private F. Y. Brown, whose name, on the day of his death, appeared in a list of those whose gallant service with the unit had won the Military Medal.

Withdrawing from the front line after relief by the 27th Battalion on the night of May 19th, the 24th Battalion proceeded to the rest area at Aux Rietz and there remained for a week, carrying out routine duties with the usual parades for bathing, pay, and replacement of deficiencies. The Battalion Transport paraded for inspection by the Brigadier; and sports were not neglected, the officers of the 24th defeating the officers of the 25th at baseball by a score of 24-5; and the other ranks, at football, playing a hard game with the 25th, in which neither side could score. Changes in the officer personnel of the Battalion at this time were effected by the arrival of Capt. G. L. Jepson from No. 4 Canadian Field Ambulance to replace Capt. K. F. Rogers, who, after some months of service as Battalion Medical Officer, was leaving to assume similar duties with the 2nd Battalion, Canadian Pioneers; and by the taking on strength of Lieuts. Vladimir Curtis and F. J. Montle from reserve battalions in England. Lieuts. E. E. Jones, N. W. Robins, M.M., and H. S. Ritchie, who joined at the same time, were all former members of the unit, Lieuts. Jones and Robins having enlisted before the Battalion left Montreal and Lieut. Ritchie, a brother of Major C. F. Ritchie, having served for a time in France, after crossing from Canada with the 12th Regiment, Canadian Mounted Rifles.

Following the short period in reserve at Aux Rietz, the Battalion moved forward on May 26th and relieved the 18th Battalion in the Ridge Line, "A" and "B" Companies with headquarters in Telegrapher Weg, "C" and "D" Companies further to the right, with headquarters at Kramer Haus, and Battalion Headquarters in Thélus Cave. In these positions the Battalion, on May 30th, received news that, for splendid leadership in the Battle of Vimy Ridge on April 9th, Major A. L. S. Mills had been awarded the Distinguished Service Order, and that for courage and resource in the same attack Lieuts. K. S. Drummond, F. de L. Clements, and R. B. E. Wilson had received the Military Cross. Lieut. Drummond had been seriously wounded in the engagement and Lieut. Clements, after displaying great bravery in the action, had fallen sick and had been transferred to England on May 13th. Major Mills and Lieut. Wilson, however, were on duty with the Battalion when news of the honours was received and were accorded by all ranks the congratulations which the awards so abundantly deserved.

Equally warm were the expressions of good-will a few days later when Hon. Capt. and Quartermaster, H. D. Campbell, Lieut. A. M. Dewar, Lieut. N. L. LeSueur, and Quartermaster-Sergeant H. T. Rigg were Mentioned in Despatches. Simultaneously, it was announced that Major-General R. E. W. Turner, V.C., General Officer Commanding the Canadian Forces in England, and Major-General David Watson, G.O.C. the 4th Canadian Division, formerly in command of the 5th Canadian Infantry Brigade, had been elevated by the King to knighthood in the Order of St. Michael and St. George, for their whole-hearted and valuable services in France.

A few days before news of the honours to Generals Turner and Watson was received, the 24th Battalion,

Victoria Rifles of Canada, had been relieved in the Thélus Ridge Line by the 13th Battalion, Royal Highlanders of Canada, of the 1st Canadian Division, had marched back to Aux Rietz for dinner, and on the same afternoon, June 1st, had proceeded to billets in Camblain l'Abbé. At Camblain l'Abbé, it was announced, the Battalion would rest for some weeks, re-equip after the losses that had occurred during the battle and trench tours on Vimy Ridge, and train for the fighting that lay ahead. To officers of the unit, an agreeable memory of the period that followed is provided by recollection of the hospitality afforded by Lieut. Crerar, Town Major of Camblain l'Abbé. This officer also worked hard to provide comfortable accommodation for the men and earned through his unstinted efforts the gratitude of all ranks of the Battalion.

A few days after· the unit arrived in the rest billets, Major P. L. Hall, M.C., Major R. H. Lamb, and Lieut. P. I. Walker reported for duty from hospital; and on June 5th and 12th strong drafts of reinforcements arrived from the 199th Battalion, Duchess of Connaught's Own Irish-Canadian Rangers, and from the 244th Battalion, Kitchener's Own, both recruited in Montreal. Though the Battalion was out of the line at the time, the draft arriving on June 12th suffered a loss on June 13th, when a private was killed by a runaway team of horses. At 5.30 p.m. this soldier was buried in Quatre Vents Cemetery by the Chaplain of the unit he had joined such a short time before.

Following their arrival, the men of the new draft assimilated from their veteran comrades of the 24th the details of life in billets in France. Some expressed surprise that appearances were maintained as rigidly as in the camps of England, or in barracks at home, but officers explained that the Battalion, though on active service, permitted no relaxation of morale and that the new arrivals would find it advisable to govern themselves accordingly. Pleased, it would seem, that Fortune had directed them to a unit in which they could serve with pride, the new men strove, not without success, to carry out the traditions which the 24th Battalion had established and was determined to maintain.

With the added strength provided by the new drafts, the Battalion, 1200 strong, paraded before Lieut.-Col. R. O. Alexander, D.S.O., on June 15th, again before the Brigadier on the following day, and for a third time before the Divisional Commander, Major-General H. E. Burstall, on June 25th. These inspections proved satisfactory and Lieut.-Col. Alexander was informed as a result that the Battalion had been chosen to represent the 2nd Canadian Division at an inspection to be held by Field Marshal His Royal Highness the Duke of Connaught at Canadian Corps Headquarters on June 27th.

Gratified by this honour, the Battalion, in full marching order, proceeded to Corps Headquarters on June 26th and, under the the watchful eye of Lieut.-General A. W. Currie, who, upon the promotion of Sir Julian Byng to command the Third British Army, had succeeded to the command of the Canadian Corps, rehearsed the morrow's inspection. Lieut.-General Currie, satisfied with the Battalion's work and appearance, stated his belief that the Duke of Connaught would find no cause to regret having accepted appointment as its Honorary Colonel.

The rehearsal was a success, but the inspection was even better. His Royal Highness reached Corps Headquarters at 5 p.m. and was received by the Corps Commander, a guard of honour from the Princess Patricia's Canadian Light Infantry, and the band of the Royal Canadian Regiment. Accompanied by the Army Commander, the Corps Commander, the Commanders of the four Canadian Divisions, and their respective staffs, the Duke of Connaught inspected the 24th Battalion and afterwards took the salute as the unit marched past. Steadiness and fine marching featured the occasion, His Royal Highness complimenting Lieut.-Col. Alexander and congratulating the company commanders on the manner in which all manoeuvres were carried out.

Pride in their work was taken at this time by all details of the Regiment and rivalry between platoons was keen. No. 1 Platoon and No. 12 Platoon were as fine as any, but to choose the finer was a difficult task. To decide the issue, and more particularly the factor of which was the cleaner, the two platoons paraded voluntarily in full marching order on the late afternoon of June 28th and asked the Commanding Officer and the Second-in-Command to inspect and settle a wager they had made. It was a hair-line decision, but when Lieut.-Col. Alexander and Major Ritchie counted the score, No. 1 Platoon gained the victory by a single point.

In the fortnight preceding the judging of the two platoons, the men of the Battalion had taken part in a varied athletic programme, starting with Battalion sports on the afternoon of June 16th, continuing with Brigade sports at Chateau de la Haie on June 20th, and culminating with Divisional competitions at Hersin Coupigny on June 23rd. The Battalion sports reminded veterans in the unit of the competitions held at Reninghelst a year before and the similarity in the two events became marked when, in the officers' 100-yards race, the Chaplain, Hon. Capt. Stuart, was defeated by inches by Lieut. E. E. Jones. In 1916, Capt. Stuart had been defeated by Major J. A. Ross, who, later, had fallen in action at the Somme.

In the Brigade sports at Chateau de la Haie, the Battalion track team was defeated by a margin of 6 points by a team from the 26th Canadian Battalion; but the Victoria Rifles' boxers maintained their old tradition of superiority and fought their way to the Brigade championship without serious difficulty. Three days later, at Hersin Coupigny, they met the finest boxers the 2nd Canadian Division could produce and emerged from a series of hard bouts with Divisional championships in two classes and a satisfactory standing in several more.

III

On July 1, 1917, the 50th anniversary of the Dominion of Canada's confederation, the 24th Battalion paraded in Camblain l'Abbé at 10 a.m. and marched to Bouvigny, where the men billeted in and about an old chateau, with stables, kennels, gardens, strawberry beds, and other attractions mentioned in many letters written at the time. Leaving this peaceful spot at 8 p.m. on July 2nd, the Battalion, with a trench strength of 23 officers and 687 other ranks, advanced into Brigade Support in Liévin, the Base Details moving simultaneously to billets in les Brébis.

On taking over Brigade Support positions from the 22nd Battalion, Lieut.-Col. Alexander established Battalion Headquarters in a cellar of the smashed and devastated town and saw to the accommodating of his companies in other cellars nearby. Shelling in this area was frequent, both with high explosive and gas, and casualties could not be avoided, one of the first occurring when Lieut. John ("Jock") Donald, an original member of the Battalion who had received a commission after fine service in the ranks, was struck in the abdomen by a fragment of shell and wounded so severely that he died a few hours later.

Meanwhile, shelling drenched the area at intervals with concentrations of poison gas, and high explosive threatened the cellar billets of the men repeatedly. Despite the difficulties, parties arrived regularly with rations and supplies from the rear and a special party carried to the front line 600 rounds of Stokes mortar ammunition. Casualties were not severe, but a half dozen other ranks were wounded and approximately an equal number affected by enemy gas, the wounded including Sergt. Cecil Thorpe, an original member of the Battalion, who was struck in the chest while making his way along the main street of Liévin.

On July 4th, Lieut.-Col. Alexander transferred Battalion Headquarters to a cellar less dangerously situated, the wisdom of the move appearing that night, when the old cellar was badly battered by German shells. Again on July 5th and 6th, the enemy bombarded heavily, blowing the Battalion cook-house to bits and killing or wounding a number of other ranks, among the former being Sergt. William Cottingham, of "A" Coy.

At 9.30 p.m. on July 6th, as the Battalion was about to move from Liévin to relieve the 25th Battalion in the Right Sub-Section of the Lens front line, intense fire held "B" Coy. underground for more than an hour. Shelling harassed the whole relief and Lieut. S. A. Rolland suffered sharply from poison gas when a shell burst amid the men of his platoon. Lieut. Rolland, who had joined the 24th Battalion from the 244th Battalion, Kitchener's Own, was experiencing his first tour in the forward area and was unwilling to admit that he would require medical attention, but Capt. P. I. Walker, in command of his company, ordered him to the rear and Capt. J. N. Bales, the Battalion Adjutant, knowing that in gas affection immediate treatment is essential, ordered his evacuation without delay.

In spite of serious interference by enemy shelling and gas, the Battalion pushed forward and, at approximately 2.30 o'clock on the morning of the 7th, completed relief of the 25th Battalion in the line. Lieut.-Col. Alexander established his headquarters in a cellar north of the Souchez River, at a corner of the Bois de Riaumont behind Hill 65; "D" Coy. took over the right front and established contact with Princess Patricia's Canadian Light Infantry; "B" Coy. joined up with the 26th Battalion on the left; and "A" and "C" Companies occupied positions in support.

For four days the Battalion remained in the front line, the period being marked by retaliatory shelling on July 9th, after troops of the 6th British Division had raided enemy trenches on the left; and, on the same night, by a brush between the 24th Battalion company on the right and an enemy patrol. The patrol encounter was inconclusive, as the men of the 24th, after driving the Germans back to their own line, could find no convincing evidence that casualties among the enemy had occurred.

On the night after this incident, the Germans opened a heavy fire on "D" Coy.'s front and Sergt. A. Findlay, of the Signal Section, entering a trench that had been blown in, noticed a steel helmet protruding from a heap of mud and debris. Some instinct compelled him to investigate and soon he realized that the owner of the helmet was underneath. No help was available at the moment, but Sergt. Findlay dug furiously and rescued Private Percy Ridge. Ten minutes later he uncovered two additional soldiers, both living, though unconscious and almost dead from suffocation.

Having dug his comrades from what had threatened to be their final tomb, Sergt. Findlay obtained assistance and, under the direction of Capt. P. I. Walker, of "D" Coy., worked all night in keeping repaired the signal lines linking the company with Battalion Headquarters and the units on the flanks. For his gallant services on this eventful occasion, Sergt. Findlay was commended by Capt. Walker, who reported his behaviour to Lieut.-Col. Alexander and recommended him for an immediate award. On July 21st, the award was gazetted and on the 23rd the Commanding Officer of the Battalion congratulated him and pinned on his tunic the ribbon of the Military Medal.

Meanwhile, at 11.30 p.m. on July 10th, relief of the 24th Battalion by the 19th Battalion had begun and, when this was completed, at 2.30 o'clock on the morning of the 11th, the Victoria Rifles had marched back to billets in Bully Grenay. Five days were spent in following the routine laid down for troops in billets, the Battalion then parading at 10 p.m. on July 15th, and proceeding forward to Brigade Reserve positions in Maroc, whence, on two consecutive days, parties of approximately 12 officers and 415 other ranks were supplied for the work of burying cable. Shelling throughout this period was brisk, and at intervals heavy, the Battalion suffering a total of 7 casualties, including a number seriously wounded. Despite shell fire, a large number of officers and men remember Maroc with satisfaction, for in the old reservoir of the town they swam and were refreshed in a manner that active service conditions seldom permitted.

On July 18th, the Battalion relieved the 25th Battalion in the Laurent Right Sub-Section of the front line, command of the unit being assumed on this date by Major C. F. Ritchie, M.C., vice Lieut.-Col. R. O. Alexander, D.S.O., who had been promoted to the Staff of the 2nd Canadian Division. Lieut.-Col. Alexander had crossed with the 24th Battalion from Canada in the spring of 1915, had served the unit as Adjutant, as a company commander, as Second-in-Command, under Lieut.-Col. J. A. Gunn, and finally as Commanding Officer. His work had been recognized by award of the Distinguished Service Order and by Mention in the Commander-in-Chief's Despatches, and the Battalion, aware of its indebtedness to him for honourable and faithful service, congratulated him on his promotion and sincerely wished him well. As he was to serve on the Staff of the 2nd Canadian Division, contact would not be entirely severed and he was assured that the Battalion would welcome him when duty, or inclination, brought him to its billets or position in the line.

After Lieut.-Col. Alexander's departure, the 24th Battalion remained for four days in the Maroc trenches. Shelling, as usual in the area, was brisk and the Battalion each day suffered a number of casualties, the losses being particularly sharp on July 20th when a German shell struck a machine-gun post in "A" Coy.'s line, killing or disabling the crew; and on the 21st, when shelling caught a party of the Battalion Scouts with equally unfortunate results. On the night following the second of these incidents, the Battalion was relieved in the line by the 28th Battalion and marched back to Noulette Wood, there to undertake training for the attack being prepared by the Canadian Corps against the enemy positions on Hill 70.

CHAPTER IX

HILL 70

I

At 4.25 o'clock on the morning of August 15, 1917, Lieut.-General A. W. Currie launched the 1st and 2nd Divisions of the Canadian Corps, commanded respectively by Major-General A. C. Macdonell and Major-General H. E. Burstall, against the German positions on Hill 70. In magnitude, the engagement that followed is not to be compared with the April assault by the Canadian Corps on Vimy Ridge, but care in preparation, similar to that which had preceded the Vimy attack, and splendid fighting by the troops engaged won a substantial victory, adding to the prestige the Corps possessed as a formation which could be relied upon to attack successfully, if success were within the power of human beings to attain.

Roughly speaking, the attack was launched on a front of 4,000 yards south-east and east of Loos, the objectives being Hill 70, which had been reached but not retained by the British in the Battle of Loos on September 25, 1915, the mining suburbs of Cité St. Elizabeth, Cité St. Emile, and Cité St. Laurent, the whole of the Bois Rasé, and the western half of the Bois Hugo. Observation from Hill 70 had been of value to the enemy and possession would help the British to hold command over the German defences of Lens. A secondary, though highly important, function of the battle was to distract German attention from the great battle which Sir Douglas Haig had opened two weeks previously in Flanders and, by presenting a strong threat to Lens, force the enemy to deflect to that area divisions which he might otherwise transfer to the scene of major operations in the north.

On the whole front of attack, with the exception of a short section of trench at the apex of the Corps' objectives west of Cité St. Auguste, the Canadian assault was highly successful. The Germans fought hard and counter-attacked bravely, but, with something approaching clockwork regularity, the Canadian battalions one after another reported that their final objectives had been attained.

In the late afternoon, the Germans, dissatisfied with the failure of local counter-attacks, brought a reserve division into action, but this unfortunate unit, caught in the open by the Canadian guns, afforded a target such as few batteries encountered in the war, and was demoralized before its attack could be driven home. In addition to the disastrous losses suffered by this formation, the Canadian attack, fighting its way through stubborn opposition, left a heavy toll of German killed and wounded in its wake, and the Canadian guns found many noteworthy targets. More than a thousand prisoners passed through the cages in the Canadian rear, and on the afternoon and night of August 16th the last of the objectives, the bit of trench west of Cité St. Auguste, was stormed and captured. Casualties in the Canadian Corps were severe; but not when considered in relation to the result achieved. German losses were heavy and were aggravated by the stinging sense of defeat. For the second time in 1917, the Canadian Corps had wrested from enemy grasp a position, strongly fortified, in which the Germans had believed they were secure. A third assault was to tear from the enemy the crest of Passchendaele Ridge; but in August this development lay shrouded in the future and the Canadian Corps, after the Battle of Hill 70, thought only of the possibility of attacking and capturing Lens. Operations with this end in view were planned and rehearsed, but circumstances drew the Corps to the Flanders front and forced the plans for an attack on Lens to be abandoned.

II

In the 24th Battalion, Victoria Rifles of Canada, training for the offensive by the Canadian Corps against the German positions on Hill 70 began immediately after the unit had been relieved in the line on the night of July 22nd and on the following morning had marched to huts in Noulette Wood. After resting on July 23rd, the men of the Battalion bathed on the 24th and a large group of officers and N.C.O.'s visited a special area where a taped reproduction of the trenches and positions to be attacked had been constructed. On the following morning, the Battalion marched to the taped area and practised the attack, officers and N.C.O.'s taking part in the operations and proceeding in the afternoon to the Headquarters of the 2nd Canadian Division, where a plasticine model of the German trenches revealed clearly the contours of the ground and the positions where German strong points would be encountered.

Training by the 5th Canadian Infantry Brigade was continued in the taped area on July 26th, 27th and 28th; but on the 29th the units were permitted to rest, Roman Catholics in the 24th Battalion taking advantage of the holiday to attend Mass in the morning, and the Protestant majority to attend Divine Service, conducted by the Battalion Chaplain, in the afternoon. To the deep regret of all ranks in the Battalion, the day brought news that a German naval shell had struck the Quartermaster's Stores in Bully Grenay, killing Private Albert Dakers and wounding severely Hon. Capt. H. D. Campbell, who died on the following day at a casualty clearing station in Noeux-les-Mines.

Capt. Campbell had served the Battalion in a manner revealed by the entry in the private diary of a senior officer which states: "He was a magnificent chap, a faithful soul, and one of the best soldiers I ever met." Circumstances prevented the Battalion attending the funeral on July 31st, but Major P. L. Hall, M.C., the Second-in-Command; Capt. J. N. Bales, the Adjutant; Hon. Capt. C. J. S. Stuart, and Capt. F. T. Bown, a former company commander, travelled to Noeux-les-Mines to pay the unit's respects to one who had served so faithfully and well. Canon F. G. Scott, of Quebec, also attended and took part in the service, which was conducted by Capt. Stuart.

Meanwhile, Operation Order No. 85, issued at 4.30 p.m. on July 27th, had informed the men of the 24th

Battalion with regard to the details of the work they would be called upon to accomplish in the attack on Hill 70. Summarized, Major Ritchie's orders were as follows:

(1) *Information*—
   With a view to forcing the enemy to evacuate Lens, the Canadian Corps will attack and capture Hill 70, on a date and at an hour to be announced later.

(2) *Attacking Troops*—
   The attack will be carried out by the 1st and 2nd Canadian Divisions; the 1st Division on the left and the 2nd Division on the right.

(3) *2nd Division's Attack*—
   The 2nd Canadian Division will attack with two brigades in line; the 4th Brigade on the right and the 5th Brigade (with 1 battalion of the 6th Brigade attached) on the left.

(4) *Boundaries*—
   [Map locations given]

(5) *5th Canadian Infantry Brigade's Objectives:*
   (a) *First Objective*—The Blue Line (Catapult Trench), which will be captured by the 25th Battalion on the right and the 22nd Battalion on the left.
   (b) *Final Objective*—The Green Line (Junction of Commotion and Carfax Trenches, thence along Commotion Trench to the junction with Nun's Alley, thence north up Nun's Alley and Norman Trench to the junction of Norman and Negro Trenches). This final objective will be captured by the 24th and 26th Battalions, with the 24th Battalion on the right and the 26th Battalion on the left.

(6) *Plan of Attack*—
   At zero, the 25th and 22nd Battalions will attack the Blue Line. Simultaneously, the 24th and 26th Battalions will move forward and reassemble on the east side of the German Front Line. The advance will then continue at zero plus 30 minutes. After the 1st Objective (Blue Line) has been captured by the

22nd and 25th Battalions, the 24th and 26th Battalions will pass through it and attack the Final Objective (Green Line). Should the 25th Battalion fail to capture the Blue Line, the 24th Battalion will be used to carry out this operation. Attack on the Blue Line will, therefore, be practised by the 24th Battalion in addition to attack on the Green Line.

(7) *Attack on Green Line—*
The 24th Battalion will attack the Green Line with "A" Coy., under Major E. M. Amphlett, on the right, and "C" Coy., under Lieut. G. G. Garvey, on the left. "B" Coy., under Major R. H. Lamb, will be in support (mopping up), and "D" Coy., under Capt. P. I. Walker, will be in reserve.
Should "A" and "B" Companies fail to capture the Green Line, "C" and "D" Companies will be used for this purpose.

(8) *Mopping up—*
Major Lamb and "B" Coy. will be responsible for the mopping up of all houses, buildings, and dugouts in the area over which the Battalion will advance.

(9) *Assembly:*
The 1st wave of "A" and "C" Companies, with 1 platoon of "B" Coy., will assemble in Martyr's Alley. The 2nd waves of "A" and "C" Companies, with 2 platoons of "B" Coy., will assemble in Marble Alley. "D" Coy. will assemble in Moat and College Trenches.

(10) *Headquarters:*
Major P. L. Hall, M.C., Second-in-Command of the Battalion, will move forward and select a location for Advanced Battalion Headquarters. This will be established as soon as possible after the Blue Line has been captured.

(11) *Consolidation:*
The general system of consolidation will be as follows:
(a) A front line of outposts.
(b) A line of machine-gun strong points supporting the outpost line.

(c) A reserve, or main, line.
The Blue Line along the whole Divisional front and the Green Line west of its junction with the Blue Line will be consolidated as a reserve, or main, line.

(12) *Strong Points:*
No. 15 Platoon will establish and hold a strong point at the southeast corner of Cité St. Emile. The 5th Canadian Machine-Gun Coy. will detail 2 guns for this strong point. A strong point will also be established at the eastern end of Fosse 14. These strong points will be joined up during the process of consolidation.

(13) *Consolidation of Green Line:*
The Green Line will be consolidated as the new British front line.
The Officer Commanding "A" Coy. will see to it that blocks are established well out in Commotion Trench and Nun's Alley.
The Officer Commanding "C" Coy. will see that a Lewis gun post is established to cover the Cutting and protect his left flank.

(14) *Strength of Companies in Attack:*
The Companies will each employ in the attack a maximum of 4 officers and 154 other ranks.
Minors on the Company strengths will not be used in the attack.
All personnel not to be employed in the attack will be left at the Brigade Training Camp.

(15) *S.O.S. Signal:*
The Corps S.O.S. signal is Red, either rockets or Very lights. In addition, heavy rifle or machine-gun fire breaking out after the capture of the Green Line will be recognized as an S.O.S. appeal.

(16) *Signal that Objectives have been Captured:*
Three white Very lights. These will be fired only by order of the Officer Commanding Assaulting Companies.

(17) *Communications:*
Before zero the buried cable will be extended forward from Brigade Headquarters. From the head of the buried cable, overland lines will be run to the 22nd and 26th Battalion Headquarters and thence to the 24th and 25th Battalion Headquarters. Lateral lines will also be run between these headquarters.
After Forward Headquarters of the 24th and 26th Battalions have been established, lines will be extended to these headquarters.

(18) *Power Buzzers:*
A power buzzer will be installed at 22nd Battalion H.Q. with an amplifier at 26th Battalion H.Q. The call on this buzzer will be C.B.F.
A second buzzer will be established in the Green Line if the earth is sufficiently damp to make it probable that signals can be transmitted.
Power buzzer messages will be sent three times to assure correct reception.

(19) *Visual Signalling:*
All visual messages will be sent three times.

(20) *Pigeons:*
The Battalion Signal Section will carry forward at least 2 pairs of pigeons, to be kept at Battalion Report Centre.

(21) *Runners:*
Company runners will be employed between Company Commanders and Battalion Report Centre. Battalion runners will be used if other means of communication fail. They should be informed of the location of all Signal Stations and Headquarters.

(22) *Prisoners of War:*
All prisoners will be sent under escort to Battalion Headquarters. Escorts should not exceed 15%.
All enemy equipment becomes Government property and should be turned in to Battalion Headquarters.
Prisoners should be given no opportunity to destroy or throw away documents in their possession at the time of capture.

(23) *Medical Arrangements:*
"B" Coy. will be responsible for the clearing of our wounded to our Regimental Aid Posts.

Bearing in mind the details mentioned in the foregoing paragraphs, as well as many which do not here appear, officers and men of the 24th Battalion, Victoria Rifles of Canada, continued their training over the taped reproduction of the Hill 70 trenches, their work being closely watched by Lieut.-General A. W. Currie, the Corps Commander; Major-General H. E. Burstall, Commanding the 2nd Canadian Division; and Brigadier-General J. M. Ross, who had succeeded Brigadier-General A. H. Macdonnel in command of the 5th Canadian Infantry Brigade. As a relief from the heavy work which these practices entailed, the Battalion in the afternoons engaged in varied sports. On August 6th, the Officers played the Other Ranks at cricket and, when rain interrupted the play, were striving to overcome a first inning handicap of 25 runs. They succeeded when play was resumed on August 7th; and took a substantial share in defeating a team from a neighbouring field ambulance on August 8th. The medical team scored 34, and captured 3 wickets for 6 runs when the Victoria Riflemen first went to bat, but Majors Amphlett and Lamb stood fast at this stage, their strong batting soon bringing the 24th Battalion total above that of the visitors.

Meanwhile, preparation for the attack had advanced steadily and each man possessed knowledge not only of his own duties, but of responsibilities which might be transferred to his shoulders by the toll which casualties were bound to inflict. By this time, allotment of commands had been completed and it was known that the Battalion, the companies, and details would attack under leadership as follows:

Officer Commanding the
    Battalion............Lieut.-Col. C. F. Ritchie, M.C.
Second-in-Command....Major P. L. Hall, M.C.
Adjutant..............Major J. N. Bales.
Scout Officer..........Lieut. G. S. Bushe
Signalling Officer.......Lieut. N. W. Robins

Medical Officer.........Capt. G. L. Jepson
Chaplain...............Hon. Capt. C. J. S. Stuart
O.C. "A" Coy..........Major E. M. Amphlett
O.C. "B" Coy..........Major R. H. Lamb
O.C. "C" Coy..........Lieut. G. G. Garvey
O.C. "D" Coy..........Capt. P. I. Walker
Battalion Sergt.-Major..Coy. Sergt.-Major A. Briggs

III

At 8.30 p.m. on August 13th, the 24th Battalion, Victoria Rifles of Canada, paraded with a trench strength of 21 officers and 572 other ranks and marched to relieve the 31st Canadian Battalion in support billets in the cellars of Cité St. Pierre, the Rear Details proceeding simultaneously to billets at Marqueffles Farm. All day on August 14th, Canadian guns, firing from Cité St.Pierre, battered the enemy line and tore the German wire to clear a way for the attacking battalions of the infantry. All day, enemy guns, in reply, bombarded the ruins where the 24th Battalion was billeted, but the men kept underground, so far as circumstances would permit, and, by running no unnecessary risk, avoided losses.

At 11 o'clock that night, the Battalion moved by companies to its assembly area for the attack. Gas shelling forced the men to use box respirators on the way up, but practice enabled them to move despite this handicap and at 3 a.m. on August 15th assembly was complete. At 4 o'clock the enemy shelled, and for a short time it seemed as though knowledge of the attack had reached the German lines, but, after approximately five minutes of heavy bombardment, the guns ceased fire without having inflicted serious harm.

Twenty minutes after the German bombardment died away, the zero hour of the Hill 70 battle was reached and, in the wake of a magnificent artillery and machine-gun barrage, the troops of the 1st and 2nd Canadian Divisions advanced against their assigned objectives. As the 24th Battalion occupied an area where the German counter-barrage would fall, the companies moved forward at zero without a moment's delay, difficulty in the manoeuvre being provided by a change in direction necessary to bring the Battalion's attacking formation into line for the final assault. The first three waves of the Battalion's manoeuvre passed through Cité St. Edouard in safety; but the 4th wave, composed of two platoons of "D" Coy., was caught in the blast of the German barrage, which wounded Capt. P. I. Walker, the Company Commander, killed Lieuts. W. M. Scougall and H. S. Ritchie, commanding Nos. 16 and 15 Platoons, and killed or wounded a number of their men. For a time, Lieut. Ritchie was posted as missing, but from the first little hope that he had survived could be entertained.

As a result of the heavy shelling in Cité St. Edouard, the death of two very gallant platoon commanders, and the wounding of Capt. P. I. Walker, a number of other ranks of the 24th Battalion lost direction and encroached on the front of the 4th Canadian Brigade to the right. Landmarks had been obliterated and boundaries were unidentifiable; accordingly, the men joined the 4th Brigade and bravely assisted in driving the attack forward.

At 5.21 a.m., the 24th Battalion passed through the 25th Canadian Battalion in the Blue Line and became the first wave of the Canadian attack in the advance to the Green Objective. In Cité St. Emile, "B" Coy., under Major R. H. Lamb, encountered stiff opposition in routing the enemy from strongly fortified cellars and houses, but the task was effectively accomplished and a substantial batch of German prisoners despatched under escort to the rear. In the mopping-up work, Lieut. D. M. Matheson was wounded, not, however, before he had encountered and exchanged revolver shots with a German officer, who fired and, missing, fell dead from the shot which Matheson fired in reply.

After passing through the 25th Battalion in the Blue Line and pausing in accordance with orders, "A" and "C" Companies attacked the German positions in Nun's Alley. Led by Major Amphlett, "A" Coy. drove forward, encountering fierce opposition, but maintaining steady progress towards the final objective. Under concentrated machine-gun fire from German strong points in the Green Objective, officers and men fell fast, Lieut. J. F. Wilkins being killed, Lieut. E. E. Jones suffering a serious wound, and the other ranks wilting away, until less than 20 remained. It might seem that 1 officer and 20 men would prove helpless in the face of a strong enemy position with ample machine-gun defences, but Major Amphlett and his party, with assistance from "C" Coy., fought a way into the German trench, killed or captured the majority of the garrison, and, before reinforcements could be sent to them, successfully defended the position they had seized against two bombing attacks by enemy survivors.

Meanwhile, on the left, despite the death in action of Lieut. J. H. Laird, who was first wounded and, when struck for the second time, killed by shell fire, "C" Coy. advanced in the face of similar opposition. On reaching the objective, Lieut. F. H. Morgan found himself in command of the company with approximately 30 men to support him. He drove into the Green Line with this party, assisted Major Amphlett on the right, and bombed and bayoneted the enemy garrison into submission, establishing firm contact with "A" Coy. and with the 26th Canadian Battalion on the left. "A" Coy., soon thereafter, established connection with the 20th Canadian Battalion on the right.

While the first waves of the Battalion's attack were driving forward to the final Green Objective, the mopping-up platoons and supporting units had continued their operations in the rear. At 6.41 a.m., Major P. L. Hall despatched Private Grant with a message to Lieut.-Col. Ritchie stating that he had found a dugout in Cité St. Laurent suitable for Battalion Headquarters and was employing 4 prisoners to remove enemy dead and wounded. He explained that his two runners had been killed, or wounded, but that Private Grant knew his situation and would be able to guide the Headquarters Staff forward.

Nine minutes after this message had been despatched, Private Sandford reached Advanced Headquarters and, on behalf of Major Lamb, reported that "B" Coy. had completed the mopping-up of its area and that No. 8 Platoon was engaged in consolidation. Less than half an hour later, "A" Coy. reported the capture of its final objective; and Lieut. Morgan reported that "C" Coy. also had seized and was holding the Green Line. These reports were satisfactory up to a point, but knowledge

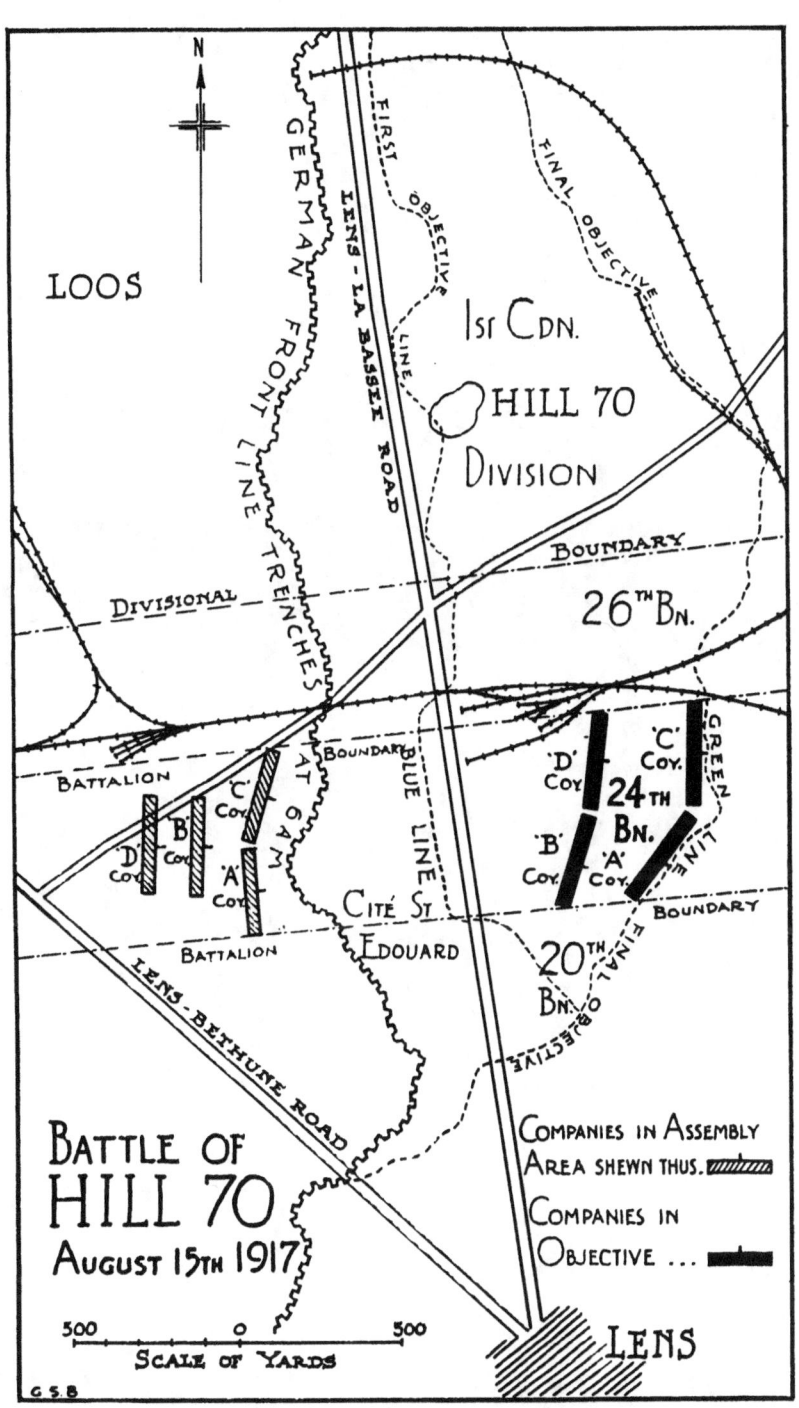

that the front line companies had been reduced to the strength of weak platoons caused Lieut.-Col. Ritchie acute anxiety, shared by Major Hall in Advanced Headquarters, where reports from the line were received at intervals.

At 10.07 a.m., Major Hall, knowing that all officers of "D" Coy. had fallen, ordered Sergt. S. Dunwoody, who had succeeded to the command, to advance without delay with a platoon and reinforce the front line. Similar orders were despatched to all support and reserve parties, with the result that, by 4 p.m., the entire remaining trench strength of the Battalion, 5 officers and 132 other ranks, was concentrated in the Green Line, the number increasing in some degree as soldiers who had lost direction in the attack reported back from the units with which they had been engaged. The security of the line was further assured when a company of the 25th Battalion, under Lieut. Fisher, advanced from the Blue Line, reported to Major R. H. Lamb, occupied positions in close support, and rendered to the 24th Battalion assistance of a most valuable order.

Several times on August 15th, German counter-attacks were seen massing, but on each occasion, when the enemy concentration was reported to the Canadian guns, shell fire shattered the German waves before they could carry out their obvious intent. At 7.45 p.m., a counter-attack approached the Victoria Rifles' line, but it lacked ability to drive through to its objective and was dispersed by artillery, rifle, and machine-gun fire.

Throughout the day, the Battalion Signal Section maintained communication in a manner that left little to be desired, Lieut. N. W. Robins, M.M., and Sergt. Arthur Beck rendering services that, even on a day of splendid effort, were outstanding. At one time, when the advance was checked by an enemy machine-gun, Lieut. Robins, who was advancing with the 2nd wave, threw his signallers and runners into action, leading them in a drive which forced the gun crew to shelter. He then took part in the final assault on the Green Line and, with the assistance of the three surviving other ranks of his section, established and maintained communication with Battalion Headquarters. In this work, he received support of the finest character from Sergt. Beck, an N.C.O. who at Zillebeke and the Somme in 1916, and at Vimy Ridge in 1917, had previously rendered distinguished service. Repeatedly, under heavy fire, Sergt. Beck left the front line trench and in the open repaired the wires on which success or failure in the operation might so easily depend.

Equal to the work of Lieut. Robins, and not dissimilar in character, was that accomplished by Lieut. G. S. Bushe, the Battalion Scout Officer, who, at Vimy Ridge, had previously rendered service of a valuable order. Hearing at Battalion Headquarters that on the right the attack of the Victoria Rifles had been slowed down by enemy machine-gun fire, Lieut. Bushe made his way through the German barrage, crossed the open under heavy machine-gun fire, reached the Green Objective in time to assist the attacking waves, then carried out with skill a reconnaissance of the whole front line, presenting to Battalion Headquarters a clear report of conditions as he found them. Only a few minutes after the Green Line was captured, Lieut.-Col. W. H. Clark-Kennedy and Capt. A. L. Walker, of the Staff of the 2nd Canadian Division, also carried out a most courageous and painstaking reconnaissance of the 5th Brigade front.

Gradually as reports reached Battalion Headquarters, Lieut.-Col. Ritchie learned from his officers of the gallantry with which the men had carried out the original plan of attack, or duties which had fallen to their lot through the death or wounding of comrades. Outstanding in courage and initiative was the action of Corp. F. J. Baillie, who, when his platoon commander was killed, led his men to their objective, where they were to establish a strong-point in rear of the newly captured front line. Realizing that the leading waves of the attack were in difficulty and almost checked, Corp. Baillie ordered his platoon forward, led his men by skilful rushes through heavy enemy fire, and, reaching the front line, set up a Lewis gun, assisted the men of the attacking waves to consolidate, and gained touch with the 20th Battalion on the right.

In the advance and in holding the line thereafter, Sergt. J. C. Mackie, Lance-Corporal N. T. Hammitt, and

Corporal G. D. Coughlin were conspicuous for bravery and leadership of a high order; and Privates P. R. Hurley, W. H. Pellow, Neill O'Reilly, G. S. Marsh, and Michael Doyle rendered courageous assistance in a manner that reflected favourably on the discipline and training the Battalion had undergone. In reporting on the engagement to higher authority, Lieut.-Col. Ritchie mentioned these men and drew attention to the service rendered by the Battalion Chaplain, Hon. Capt. C. J. S. Stuart. As at Zillebeke, at the Somme, and at Vimy Ridge, Capt. Stuart had voluntarily accompanied the Battalion into the forward area and, under heavy fire, had served as a stretcher-bearer, assisting the Medical Officer, Capt. G. L. Jepson, and setting an example of courage and calm confidence of great value to the unit's morale.

Lieut.-Col. Ritchie mentioned also the gallantry with which Major Amphlett led the attack and the splendid assistance rendered by the 5th Canadian Trench Mortar Battery, which, under Lieut. Arthur Durman, seconded from the 24th Battalion, came into action at the junction of Nun's Alley and Commotion Trenches and, by driving out an enemy machine-gun, cleared a path for the rush to the final objective of "A" Coy.'s first wave of assault. The Commanding Officer of the 24th Battalion has also placed on record his deep appreciation of the services rendered throughout the engagement by his Adjutant, Major J. N. Bales, who, without sleep or rest for days, strove successfully to co-ordinate and direct the difficult operations in which the unit was engaged.

After capturing the Green Objective on the morning of August 15th and, as mentioned previously, repelling a German counter-attack at 7.45 o'clock that night, the companies of the 24th Battalion remained in the front line on August 16th. Relief had been expected that night, but at 7.45 p.m. an S.O.S. signal rose on the Canadian front and the artillery, in response, opened a heavy fire, to which the Germans replied. For more than three hours the front was rocked by the fire of the opposing artilleries and the 22nd Battalion, which was to have relieved the 24th, was afforded no opportunity to come forward. Accordingly, the relief was cancelled and the 24th Battalion was ordered to stand fast in the line.

In obedience to these orders, the Battalion remained in position that night and all day on August 17th. No parties could be spared for the duty of carrying water, rations, and ammunition to the front line, but the 25th Battalion, assuming this task, carried it out determinedly, providing the men of the 24th with supplies adequate to meet their need. That night the 22nd Battalion effected the delayed relief and the men of the 24th Battalion moved back under heavy shelling to support positions in Cité St. Pierre.

In Cité St. Pierre, the Battalion rested on August 18th, but at night demand for a working party became urgent and 2 officers and 50 other ranks carried rations and ammunition to the front line. On August 19th, a party of double this strength was provided; and on the 20th, one officer and 40 other ranks worked their way forward and safely delivered 60,000 rounds of machine-gun ammunition to the battalions in the line. In the task of supplying material to the front line garrisons, Lieut. F. C. Billingsley and details from the Battalion Base accomplished most creditable work.

By this time, the Battalion was able to estimate with reasonable accuracy the casualties it had suffered in the attack on August 15th and in the subsequent holding of the Green Line. On August 20th, the Commanding Officer was informed that the body of his brother, Lieut. H. S. Ritchie, had been found, the discovery dissipating the slight hope that had existed that Lieut. Ritchie, dangerously wounded and unconscious, perhaps, had been conveyed unidentified to the rear. With the death of this gallant subaltern established, four officers were known to have died in action on August 15th and four to have been wounded.

In the ranks, 37 N.C.O.'s or privates had been killed, 36 were at this time missing, presumed dead, and 234 had been evacuated to hospital suffering from wounds. Accordingly, the Battalion, which had entered the attack with a strength of 21 officers and 572 other ranks, withdrew on the early morning of August 22nd, following relief by the Princess Patricia's Canadian Light Infantry, with 13 officers and 265 men. Strong drafts awaited the Battalion at Gouy Servins and soon the unit, despite the hard fighting at Hill 70, stood ready to carry out whatever duty the future might hold in store, all the more effectively because of the supreme confidence that the Hill 70 fighting had cemented between officers and men. Witness to the strength of this bond is a feature of those letters and private diaries which, written at the time, reveal clearly the unit's high morale. Vimy and Hill 70 proved beyond all doubt that the traditions established at St. Eloi, at Zillebeke, and at the Somme had not been forgotten.

Officer Casualties—August 15-22, 1917

Killed in Action	Wounded
Lieut. W.M. Scougall	Capt. P. I. Walker
Lieut. H. S. Ritchie	Lieut. E. E. Jones
Lieut. J. H. Laird	Lieut. D. M. Matheson
Lieut. J. F. Wilkins	Lieut. F. Gatenby

IV

For eleven days after participation in the Battle of Hill 70 and the subsequent holding of the Green Line, followed by a period in support in Cité St. Pierre, the 24th Battalion, Victoria Rifles of Canada, remained in Gouy Servins, re-organizing, re-equipping, and training a strong draft of men which had arrived to replace the losses sustained in action. Lieuts. J. G. R. Shuter and E. C. Platt had reported for duty on August 19th; and the commissioned roll received further reinforcement when Lieuts. G. R. Grenough, F. H. Hallam, J. J. Kavanagh, F. S. Leach, H. M. Alexander, and A. D. Smith, all original members of the Battalion who had seen service in France in the ranks, reported to Lieut.-Col. Ritchie from England on August 30th. Lieut. Wallace Watson, who reported at the same time, had been twice wounded while serving in the ranks of the 15th Canadian Battalion.

As a whole, the training of the Battalion at Gouy Servins was of a routine nature, but certain incidents are worthy of note. On August 23rd, Lieut.-General A. W. Currie called at Battalion Headquarters to express to Lieut.-Col. Ritchie his appreciation of what officers and men had accomplished in the Battle of Hill 70, when the unit had driven through to the Canadian Corps' final objective and firmly held the territory captured.

In the evening following the Corps Commander's visit, the Battalion attended a fine performance by the Concert Party of the 3rd Canadian Division. Two days later, the unit proceeded for musketry practice at the rifle ranges; and, in company with the 25th Battalion, paraded for Divine Service on August 26th. Bayonet fighting, platoon drill, bombing practice, machine-gun and signalling training, and the training of specialists in the use of rifle grenades were also features of this period. Contrary to what has sometimes been stated, there was no instruction in the use of the shovel as a weapon. The German soldier, Remarque, has stated: "The bayonet has lost its importance and now the fashion is to charge with bombs and spade only. The sharpened spade is a more handy weapon; not only can it be used for jabbing a man under the chin, but—if one hits between the neck and the shoulder, it easily cleaves as far down as the chest." Without denying the possible use of a spade in the manner the German soldier describes, the bayonet, so far as instruction in the British Army was concerned, remained at this time and until the war ended the main weapon to be used in hand-to-hand fighting.

While the 24th Battalion was in training at Gouy Servins, news arrived that Field Marshal Sir Douglas Haig, Commander-in-Chief of the Armies of the British Empire in France, would inspect the 5th Canadian Infantry Brigade at Maisnil Bouche on August 27th. Parading in Gouy Servins at 8 a.m., the Battalion was critically inspected by the Commanding Officer and then moved to Maisnil Bouche, taking position for the Commander-in-Chief's inspection at 9.45 o'clock. At 11.17 a.m., Sir Douglas Haig, on a white charger, cantered onto the parade ground and, after taking a general salute, rode down the lines of the battalions, accompanied by Brigadier-General J. M. Ross. The Brigade then marched past by double companies in fours, each battalion proceeding without further ceremony to its own billeting area.

For some days after Sir Douglas Haig's inspection, heavy rain and the resulting mud hampered the 24th

Battalion's out-door training, but an officer from No. 16 Squadron of the Royal Flying Corps lectured to all officers and N.C.O.'s on liaison between attacking infantry and contact aeroplanes; and lectures on Lewis gun work and the details of bombing and bayonet fighting were delivered to the men. Diversion from this routine was provided on the night of August 31st when 350 other ranks attended in the local theatre a performance given by the Concert Party of the Canadian Corps. On September 2nd, the weather having moderated meanwhile, Brigadier-General Ross inspected the Battalion Transport, under Lieut. V. Curtis.

On the day following Brigadier-General Ross's inspection of the Transport, the Battalion paraded in full marching order and proceeded, by way of Maisnil Bouche, to Villers Chatel and Mingoval, where training was continued. On September 4th, all officers, N.C.O.'s and Section Commanders attended a lecture at Brigade Headquarters on aeroplane liaison and, later, a group of officers visited No. 16 Squadron of the Royal Flying Corps, Major P. L. Hall, Lieut. S. A. Rolland, and Hon. Capt. C. J. S. Stuart each enjoying the experience of a half-hour's trip in the air. Starting from Camblain l'Abbé, the 24th Battalion officers were piloted up by Lens and Vimy Ridge and down to Arras at a height of about 3,000 feet, viewing thus many districts in which the Battalion had been employed and gaining an appreciation of the problem which satisfactory liaison with troops on the ground presented to officers of the Royal Flying Corps.

Further experience of value to senior officers of the Battalion was gained on the following day when Lieut.-Col. Ritchie, Major Amphlett, Major Hall, and Major Lamb visited the First Army's Schools of Musketry, Scouting and Sniping, and Trench Mortars. Through study of the work at these schools, the officers were enabled to visualize the problems which the schools sought to solve and to understand more clearly the relation of the teaching given to the work of battalions and other units in the line.

Meanwhile, at Villers Chatel, the men of the 24th Battalion were practising for Brigade Sports, to be held on September 6th and 7th, and for a Brigade boxing competition, to conclude on September 14th. In the sports, the 22nd Battalion won the baseball championship, the 24th Battalion won the sprints, an Indian in the 26th Canadian Battalion won the long distance running events, and the 25th Battalion scored a number of creditable successes. In boxing, the 24th Battalion maintained its old-time prestige, the winners including Privates E. Weaver and A. Chadwick, of "A" Coy., at 125 lbs. and 145 lbs. respectively, and Private W. Simpkins, of "B" Coy., who carried off the prize at 135 lbs.

Though sports occupied a generous share of the men's attention in the first fortnight of September, a competition to select the platoon which could carry out most satisfactorily the manoeuvres of "platoon in attack" resulted in keen rivalry, No. 13 Platoon finally winning a close decision. No. 10 Platoon, under Lieut. F. S. Leach, also earned distinction at this time when, on being chosen at random by the Brigadier, it demonstrated the highly effective organization which its section commanders had developed.

Rivalry between the companies was stimulated by a sham battle on September 10th when "C" Coy. was given a position on the main road near Bethonsart to defend, and "B" Coy. was launched to the attack from positions in Mingoval. "B" Coy.'s approach to its objective showed that its officers and men had gained in experience by the manoeuvres of the previous weeks, but "C" Coy. had gained too, and Major Hall, acting as referee, decided that the defence had won the day.

For a week after the sham battle, training continued, the period being marked by practice with live bombs, by comprehensive instruction in the use of machine-guns, so that any man in the Battalion could load and fire a Lewis gun if required, and by a notable smoker given by the Sergeants' Mess. This event, held on the night of September 14th, celebrated the second anniversary of the Battalion's crossing from England to France and the first anniversary of the Battle of Courcelette. Regimental Sergt.-Major J. Hennessy presided, the officers of Battalion Headquarters and the Company Commanders attended, and the guests included Capt. F. T. Bown, formerly in command of "B" Coy., whose presence assured the fine singing of the old ballads and the modern ditties without which no evening of celebration can be an entire success.

Two days after the Sergeants' smoker, the Battalion paraded at 9.30 a.m. and, with the band leading, marched by way of Cambligneul and Camblain l'Abbé to billets in Villers au Bois, proceeding thence on the following morning, September 17th, to the Neuville St. Vaast area and occupying the Goodman Tunnel and positions nearby. From these situations, the Commanding Officer, the Company Commanders, and the Scout Officer moved forward on September 19th to reconnoitre the right sub-sector of the Mericourt front line, which the 21st Canadian Battalion was holding and which the 24th Battalion was to take over on the night of September 20th.

Before the Battalion was relieved in the Goodman Tunnel position and moved forward into the Mericourt front line, it was announced that, for gallantry and distinguished leadership in the Battle of Hill 70, Major E. M. Amphlett, now Second-in-Command of the Battalion, had been awarded the Military Cross, that Lieuts. Arthur Durman, F. H. Morgan, and N. W. Robins, M.M., had been granted similar distinction, and that Sergt. F. J. Baillie had been awarded the Distinguished Conduct Medal.

Advancing at 7.50 o'clock on the night of September 20th, the Battalion relieved the 21st Battalion as arranged and established contact with the 26th Battalion on the left and the 42nd Battalion, Royal Highlanders of Canada, on the right. Six days were spent in the line, these being marked by some enemy activity and shelling, by working parties each day, and a few casualties, but by no incident other than to be expected in trench routine. Communication in this area was good and a telephone wire ran even into the "Gun Post Line," but, as there was strong reason to believe that German listening sets could tap this wire successfully, officers using the telephone were ordered, in reporting events, to employ code words as follows:

Enemy Artillery is firing on my line.........Antics
With 77 mm. shells......................Anti
With 42 mm. shells......................Apple
With 5.9-inch shells......................Beast

Retaliation wanted	Biff
Enemy is box-barraging my front	Bump
Our field artillery is firing short	Custard
Our heavy artillery is firing short	Damn
Situation normal	Engine
Situation satisfactory	Epi
Situation unsettled	Even
Send bombs	Idiot
Send flares	Ink
Send rifle ammunition	Ire
Send Lewis gun	Hungry
Send Lewis gun ammunition	Ham,
	Etc.

After the 6-day tour in the Mericourt front line, the Battalion was relieved on the night of September 26th and moved back to billets in Villers au Bois, where training for an operation to be undertaken by the Canadian Corps against Lens was continued until October 5th. As it happened, the attack on Lens was later abandoned in order that the Canadian Corps might take part in the great British offensive in Flanders, but this change of plan could not be foreseen and the 24th Battalion trained earnestly in full belief that the practice represented the rehearsal of a battle to take place not far in the future.

While at Villers au Bois, the Battalion, with sincere regret, bade farewell to its Scout Officer, Lieut. G. S. Bushe, an original member of the unit, promoted from the ranks for valuable and faithful service, who was leaving to assume duty with the Royal Flying Corps; to Lieut. Arnold Scobie, another original who had also transferred to the Royal Flying Corps; and to Major E. M. Amphlett, M.C., who, though expecting to return, was proceeding to take a Senior Officers' Course at Aldershot, England.

After bidding farewell to Lieuts. Bushe and Scobie on October 5th, the Battalion, with a trench strength of 16 officers and 531 other ranks, paraded at 4 p.m., marched to Le Pendu, entrained on a light railway which transported the men to Zivy, and marched thence to relieve the Princess Patricia's Canadian Light Infantry in support. Relief was completed at 8.30 p.m., the companies taking up positions in Montreal, New Brunswick, and Canada Trenches without untoward incident.

Working parties and visits by the companies in turn to the baths at Neuville St. Vaast marked the next few days; but on October 11th the comparative calm in the area was broken when the enemy shelled Montreal Trench, killing one man of the Battalion and obliterating about 50 yards of trench and parapet. That night, the Battalion moved forward and relieved the 25th Battalion in the front line from Quarries Road to Moose Jaw Road. Shelling hampered the movement, which, none the less, was completed at 9.30 p.m., with a loss of 1 man killed and 2 wounded.

Immediately on taking over the front, the Battalion despatched the usual patrols into No Man's Land to gather information and report on the condition of the enemy wire. Shelling was brisk and machine-guns were active at intervals, but the Battalion suffered no loss until, early in the morning on October 12th, Lieut. F. H. Hallam was killed by enemy fire while returning from a patrol towards the German line. Lieut. Hallam had received his commission after serving in the unit from the time when it was recruited in Canada and his death, less than two months after he had rejoined as an officer, was an event which all ranks in the Battalion deeply regretted.

At 10 o'clock on the morning of the following day, a Special Company of the Royal Engineers projected 100 drums of gas into the enemy's line opposite Montreal Trench. Retaliation for this operation was not heavy at the time, but at 4.45 o'clock on the morning of October 15th, fire of great intensity fell on the front and support lines of the Battalion's position. The Canadian artillery, after a 35-minute duel, subdued the enemy and forced his batteries to cease fire, but in the interval 8 men of the 24th Battalion had been killed and 13 wounded, the dead including Lieut. Arthur Durman, of "B" Coy., who, only a few weeks before, had been awarded the Military Cross for his gallant service in the Battle of Hill 70.

That night the Germans, continuing their activity, shelled Willerval with gas, a south-west wind bearing the poison fumes to the positions held by the men of the

24th, who were forced to use box respirators for protection. Believing, perhaps, that the gas had inflicted losses, the enemy advanced to raid the trenches of the battalion to the Victoria Rifles' right, but the garrison was alert and, with heavy fire, drove the German effort back to its own lines.

In view of the activity which the enemy was displaying in the area, the men of the 24th expected that shelling would continue on October 16th, but throughout the day the situation remained quiet and uneventful. Night brought no change in conditions, the absence of hostile shelling and the comparative quiet of the German machine-guns greatly assisting when the 1st/5th Battalion of the Warwickshire Regiment came forward at 11.30 p.m. to relieve. Relief by an Imperial regiment meant that the Canadian Corps was on the move, and the men of the 24th Battalion, as they withdrew to Zivy Siding and were conveyed by light railway to Ottawa Camp in Bois des Alleux, discussed the Corps' probable destination. None could speak with knowledge or assurance of what lay ahead, but not a few, speculating shrewdly, prophesied that the streets of Ypres would echo again to the tramp of Canadian battalions and that the Salient would, for the third time, extend to the men from across the sea its usual bloody welcome.

CHAPTER X

PASSCHENDAELE

I

In the spring of 1917, when General Nivelle was dismissed from his post as Commander-in-Chief of the French Army, General Pétain, who succeeded him, visited Sir Douglas Haig and stated without equivocation that for the remainder of the year, or at least for some months, the burden of battle on the Western Front must be assumed by the British. The morale of the French Army had suffered appreciably as the result of General Nivelle's disastrous failure on the Aisne, and, though confident that his troops would eventually regain their former efficiency, General Pétain stated that, for a time, he must be freed from all danger of serious attack.

In reply to General Pétain's request for assistance, Sir Douglas Haig, as mentioned in a previous chapter, suspended operations on the Arras front and advanced preparations to strike with the whole weight of the Armies of the Empire in Flanders. His plan involved a series of battles designed to clear the Belgian coast of German submarine bases and to cut, or at least threaten seriously, enemy communications through the narrow bottle-neck of the Liége gap, which lay in a vital position between the impassable forests of the Ardennes to the south and the frontier of Holland to the north. In view of the situation outlined by General Pétain with regard to morale in the French Army, Sir Douglas knew before his attack was launched that, whether success accrued or not, pressure in the area would have to be maintained.

Protecting his right flank by seizure of the Messines-Wytschaete Ridge on June 7, 1917, the British Commander-in-Chief, with a small French force co-operating on his left, opened his Flanders Offensive at 5.50 o'clock on the morning of July 31st, striking again on August 16th and thereafter, for a month, fighting bitterly, as at the Somme in 1916, for positions whence the attack on a major scale could be resumed.

Meanwhile, in August, General Guillaumat attacked with French forces at Verdun and, in an operation conducted with brilliant tactical success, wrested Morte Homme and Hill 304 from the enemy. Despite this success, which gave proof that the spirit of the French Army was rapidly reviving, General Pétain asked Sir Douglas Haig to abate in no degree the force of his blows in Flanders. French morale, he stated, was practically restored, but time must still elapse before he could face with confidence the possibility of a large-scale German attack.

Impressed by the necessity to give to General Pétain the aid he required and also by the possibility that his strategic purposes might still be attained, Sir Douglas Haig resumed the operation on September 20th and 26th. In July and August, General Ludendorff had used effectively against the British a system of "elastic defence," but on September 20th and 26th tactics were improvised by the British to render this type of fighting unsatisfactory. Shallow objectives were assigned to the attacking divisions and provision was made to deal ruthlessly with counter-attacks. As a result, all objectives were reached in the two engagements and the enemy, in addition to losing 3,243 prisoners and some guns, suffered appallingly in killed and wounded.

Believing that he would deceive the British after their victories on September 20th and 26th, General Ludendorff reverted in part to his older methods of defence, but the result was not successful, for on October 4th the British drove into his reinforced front line, capturing 5,000 prisoners and, in addition, inflicting heavy losses on a number of his divisions which had been massed not far from the front line. Caught by concentrated artillery fire, these divisions suffered casualties so severe that, until opportunity to reorganize was afforded, their value in the line was far below the German average.

By this time, as in 1916, the ceaseless attack of the British Army had produced a situation which the higher officers of the German Staff viewed with increasing alarm, but, as in the previous year, heavy and continuous rain washed away all hope of substantial Allied success. In these circumstances, Sir Douglas Haig's decision to continue his attacks in October and early November has been bitterly criticized, more particularly during the War, when it was impossible to explain the situation that existed. General Pétain's appeals for continued support were made in strictest confidence and, so long as the War lasted, the lips of the British Commander-in-Chief were sealed. Even to his own Staff, who, perhaps, suspected that pressure had been brought to bear upon him, no explanation could be offered until the War was over.

After two days of steady rain, the British attacked at dawn on October 9th, with the French First Army, which had remained inactive for many weeks, co-operating. On the extreme right, the 2nd Australian Division drove through to its final objective and on the fronts of the French Army, the 29th British Division, and the Guards Division similar success was achieved, but elsewhere the attack, after capturing the first objectives, was held fast in the bottomless mud of the devastated district.

Three days later, the British renewed the attack, with Imperial, Australian, and New Zealand divisions in line, but, despite gallantry of a high order, the waves of the assault could make little progress and at noon orders to press the advance were cancelled. With the suspension of operations on this date, the last faint hope that the long and costly Flanders Offensive might yield major results vanished beyond recall. When the British attacked again on October 22nd, General Ludendorff was impressed by the valour and determination of the assault and says that in the awful fighting the horror of the shell-hole area at Verdun was surpassed. Little diminution in the violence of the attack could, therefore, have been perceptible, but the fact remains that the British had abandoned all thought of major success and were fighting only for positions in which a winter line could be established.

To secure a winter line which his troops could hold effectively, Sir Douglas Haig was forced to undertake the capture of Passchendaele Ridge and the operation presented difficulty which no Commander-in-Chief could contemplate without serious concern. The autumn was far advanced; the approach to the Ridge was through a wide sea of unbelievable mud; the Germans could not be taken by surprise; the enemy artillery was powerful and well supplied with shells; and the German commanders knew that, if they held the Ridge, the British would be forced to abandon the ground purchased in the bitter fighting of August, September, and early October.

In these circumstances, Sir Douglas Haig decided that no troops under his command could attack with greater hope of success than the Canadian Corps. In April, the Corps, under Lieut.-General Sir Julian Byng, had torn from German grasp the previously impregnable stronghold of Vimy Ridge; in August, under Lieut.-General Sir Arthur Currie, the 1st and 2nd Canadian Divisions had repeated their success at Hill 70; now, in October, success *must* be obtained and Sir Douglas believed that the Corps could accomplish what was required.

Lieut.-General Sir A. C. Macdonell, at that time commanding the 1st Canadian Division, has described the scene at Canadian Corps Headquarters when the British Commander-in-Chief, arriving unexpectedly, announced to the Canadian Divisional Commanders, after a private conference with the Corps Commander, the purpose of his visit: "Gentlemen, circumstances have arisen that render it imperative that Passchendaele Ridge must be taken at all costs. I know the Canadian Corps can take it, and my mission here is to ask the Corps Commander to do so. I feel I should tell you he was opposed to doing so. I have been able to meet his objections and to agree to what he considers necessary. I may say he has demanded an unprecedented amount of artillery to cover your advance; and this I have promised. I would like to be able to explain why this attack must be made and perhaps some day in the future I may be able to do so. At present, I simply ask you to take my word for it. The necessity is imperative."

And so the Canadian Corps moved from before Lens to the Ypres Salient and began the operations in which there *must* be no failure. Men might die and battalions be shattered, but the Corps, when its time of agony was completed, *must* stand where, at the time, the enemy stood, on the dominating crest of Passchendaele Ridge.

Coming into action, in conjunction with a British and French attack, on the morning of October 26th, the 3rd and 4th Canadian Divisions drove through deep mud, overcame bitter enemy resistance, and captured Bellevue Spur. Five days later, after fighting as savage as any in the Corps' experience, the Canadian line was driven forward for 1,200 yards on a front of 3,000 yards; then, on November 6th, the 1st and 2nd Canadian Divisions completed the task the 3rd and 4th Divisions had so splendidly begun and, sweeping over the crest of Passchendaele Ridge, justified Sir Douglas Haig's faith that the Corps would succeed in the awful task which circumstances had placed before it. Three thousand Canadian soldiers died in the attacks, a thousand disappeared forever in the mud and water-filled shell holes of the area, and twelve thousand were wounded, the total explaining why the name "Passchendaele" is to all Canadians a name revered because of untold sacrifice, and yet a name of accursed memory.

II

In the 24th Battalion, Victoria Rifles of Canada, preparation for transfer from the Lens to the Passchendaele front began on October 17, 1917, when, at Ottawa Camp in the Bois des Alleux, the men rested until noon and spent the remainder of the day cleaning equipment and getting ready to march on the following morning. Leaving Ottawa Camp at 8.25 a.m. on October 18th, the Battalion marched by way of Camblain l'Abbé, Cambligneul, and Villers Chatel to Bailleul-aux-Cornailles, arriving about 5 o'clock in the afternoon and taking over billets, which were to be occupied until October 24th.

On October 20th, the 5th Canadian Infantry Brigade paraded and was inspected by General Sir H. S. Horne, Commanding the First British Army. General Horne stated that the Canadian Corps was leaving his Army for special service in Belgium, but was, he understood, to return to his command as soon as its special duty had been accomplished. He then wished the Brigade good fortune in the days ahead and assured officers of the battalions that, when the time came to return, a warm welcome from the First Army would await them.

Two days later, an advance party of the 24th Battalion, under Lieut. W. E. Bidwill, left Bailleul-aux-Cornailles at 4 p.m. and proceeded to Pradelles in the Caestre area, the Battalion, less "D" Coy., following by train from Tinques Station at 6.40 o'clock on the morning of October 24th. "D" Coy. marched from Bailleul-aux-Cornailles at 7.45 o'clock that night, entrained at Tinques at 10.40 p.m., and rejoined the Battalion in the Caestre area at 8 o'clock on the morning of October 25th.

Soon after "D" Coy. arrived in Caestre, Lieut.-Col. C. F. Ritchie, M.C., and 15 officers of the unit left by bus for Poperinghe to study a plasticine model of Passchendaele Ridge and the area in which the Canadian Corps was to attack. On the following day, which was marked by the promotion to commissioned rank of Battalion Quartermaster-Sergt. J. A. Donovan, D.C.M., company and platoon commanders lectured to their units, the instruction being followed on October 27th by prolonged practice of platoons in attack. This practice was followed in turn on October 28th by Battalion practice over the area taped out to resemble Passchendaele Ridge. Again on the morning of the 29th, the Battalion practised over the taped area, joining that afternoon with the other battalions of the 5th Brigade in more extended manoeuvres, which, on the morning of October 31st, were repeated, with variation in accordance with changes which had occurred in the situation at the front.

Meanwhile, the 3rd and 4th Canadian Divisions were fighting their way forward in the Passchendaele area, securing a line from which the 1st and 2nd Canadian Divisions could launch the final attack with fair prospect of complete success. It was a struggle demanding the last ounce of courage and endurance and the 1st and 2nd Division battalions, training behind the lines, knew that before long they must take over the front and carry the work to completion.

On November 1st, a group of 24th Battalion N.C.O.'s travelled to Ten Elms near Poperinghe to study the plasticine model of Passchendaele Ridge, a larger group, which included a number of privates, travelling for the same purpose on the following day. The Commanding Officer and his Company Commanders, meanwhile, had been conveyed by bus to Ypres and, proceeding forward, had reconnoitred a bivouac camp near Potijze which the Battalion was soon to occupy. Exposure to shell-fire made this camp unattractive, but no other billets near the line were available.

Parading at 5 o'clock on the morning of November 3rd, the Battalion marched to Caestre station, entrained there at 6.45 a.m., and reached Ypres one hour and 55 minutes later. Detraining at Ypres, the men marched by platoons through the ruined streets and forward to Potijze, where tarpaulin shelters and shallow "funk holes" were occupied. Here, at 9 p.m., the unit was rejoined by its Transport, which, under Lieut. V. Curtis, had marched from the billets previously occupied in Caestre.

Even before the arrival of the Transport, the Battalion had experienced a measure of the welcome which, as veterans of the unit knew so well, the Salient might be relied upon to extend, for no sooner had the unit reached Potijze than German long range guns shelled the camp, forcing the men to scatter. Few casualties were inflicted, but bivouacs were blown high in the air and the incident revealed the manner in which the German artillery sought continually, by hammering the British rear, to weaken the fast tightening grasp of the British Army on Passchendaele Ridge.

By this time, it was known that, so far as the 5th Canadian Infantry Brigade was concerned, the attack in the final phase of the struggle for the ridge would be carried out by the 26th Battalion alone. The 24th Battalion, Victoria Rifles of Canada, would be holding the Brigade front line at the time and would, as soon as the attack of the 26th Battalion had passed through its lines from the rear, come into close support and afford the 26th Battalion such assistance as lay in its power. The right half of the 24th Battalion's trenches would remain as the British front line, for the attack of the 26th Battalion was to veer left against Passchendaele Village and positions nearby. For the operation, the trench strength of the 24th Battalion would be 21 officers and 542 other ranks, commands being held as follows:

Commanding Officer......Lieut.-Col. C. F. Ritchie, M.C.
Adjutant...............Major J. N. Bales
Lewis Gun Officer.......Lieut. T. S. Sanders
Signalling Officer........Lieut. N. W. Robins, M.C.,
                         M.M.
Medical Officer..........Capt. J. L. Jepson
Chaplain...............Hon. Capt. C. J. S. Stuart
Transport Officer........Lieut. V. Curtis
Asst. Transport Officer...Lieut. A. W. H. Arundell
Quartermaster..........Lieut. J. A. Donovan, D.C.M.

A. Coy.	B. Coy.
Capt. A. M. Dewar	Capt. J. D. MacIntyre
Lieut. E. C. Platt	Lieut. W. E. Bidwill
Lieut. C. B. Picken	Lieut. J. J. Kavanagh
Lieut. G. R. Grenough	Lieut. F. W. Stenson

C. Coy.	D. Coy.
Capt. G. G. Garvey	Major P. L. Hall, M.C.
Lieut. W. H. F. Ketcheson	Lieut. T. L. Foote
Lieut. H. M. Alexander	Lieut. P. E. R. Lockwood
Lieut. D. M. Wilson	Lieut. H. R. Tanner

At 4 o'clock on the morning of November 4th, "C" Coy. of the 24th Battalion reported to the 11th Field Company, Canadian Engineers, and was employed in laying a bath-mat track between Boethoek and Hamburg. No casualties were suffered in this labour, but the work was arduous in the extreme and the men were completely exhausted when, at 10 a.m., they reported back to their own Battalion.

Leaving the men of "C" Coy. to obtain a few hours' additional rest, the main body of the Battalion advanced from Potijze by platoons at 3 p.m. and, after following Bath-mat Track "H" across the deep mud, relieved the 19th Canadian Battalion in the front line at Vienna Cottages, with Headquarters at Hamburg and the left and right flanks held respectively by troops of the 29th Canadian Battalion and the Australian infantry. The bath-mat track ended at Battalion Headquarters and from that point forward direction could be maintained only by following through mud, in which it frequently disappeared, a tape leading to the battered front line trenches.

Despite the difficulty of relieving in such circumstances, the men of the 24th Battalion completed the task at 9.30 p.m., occupying the front line and immediate support positions without having suffered losses. For a time this good fortune continued, but before day broke on November 5th enemy shelling, which had been concentrated on gun positions to the rear, shifted to the Battalion area, where, in a short time, 7 other ranks were killed and 10 wounded.

All day on November 5th, the position of the 24th Battalion was subjected to heavy fire, Headquarters and the support trenches attracting more than their share of enemy attention, though the front line was also battered severely. Casualties could not be avoided and a number of other ranks were killed, or wounded, the list of wounded also including Lieut. F. W. Stenson, who was struck by a fragment of shell in the leg.

Meanwhile, at 3 p.m., Lieut.-Col. Ritchie had moved his Headquarters forward from Hamburg to a German concrete pill-box at Hillside Farm, where, at 5 p.m., he was joined by the Headquarters Staff of the 26th Battalion, which was arriving to form up in the 24th Battalion area and, early on the morning of November 6th, to launch its assault. The concrete pill-box, though almost impenetrable by shell fire, was not more than 12 by 7 feet in area, but no other headquarters could be found and the staff of each battalion, with genuine appreciation of the other's difficulties, strove to carry out the work to which it was assigned, at the same time helping the staff of the sister battalion when opportunity offered.

Coming forward on the night of November 5th, the 26th Battalion carried out a successful assembly in the 24th Battalion area. At 1.50 a.m. on November 6th, Lieut. J. J. Kavanagh, of "B" Coy., reported that a party of troops was visible in front of his left flank, but that identity of the group was uncertain. No men of the 24th Battalion had been sent forward from the front line and enquiry revealed that the party did not belong to the Canadian unit on the flank. Fire was accordingly opened from the front line trenches of the 24th Battalion and, following the disappearance of the party, whose strength could not be accurately estimated, assembly of the 26th Battalion was completed.

Some hours after the enemy party was sighted and dispersed, 3 flares rose from the German lines and, bursting into lights of brilliant green, called the enemy artillery into action. Shelling by the Germans was intense for a time, but died down at 5.30 a.m., twenty-five minutes before the British barrage broke on the slopes of Passchendaele Ridge and evoked in reply the fire of every battery and gun the Germans could bring to bear.

After five minutes of British artillery and machine-gun barrage more intense than men of the 5th Brigade had previously witnessed, the 26th Battalion moved forward through the left of the 24th Battalion lines and drove forward to the final objective, valuable assistance in the operation being rendered by a party of the 24th Battalion, under Lieut. J. J. Kavanagh, whose contribution to the success of the attack was later recognized by award of the Military Cross. Meanwhile the companies of the 24th Battalion remained in the old front line and support positions, where they suffered severely from enemy fire. Even before the attack was launched, "C" Coy., which had come forward from Potijze on the night of November 5th, was caught by a heavy bombardment and almost annihilated. Capt. G. G. Garvey was disabled by a shell soon after the bombardment started; another explosion wounded Lieut. D. M. Wilson in the thigh and broke two ribs; Lieut. W. H. F. Ketcheson suffering similar injury when a shell, bursting a few feet away, hurled him to the ground and piled over him a great mass of debris.

For a time, it seemed that no member of the company would survive, but at last the shelling died down and Lieut. H. M. Alexander, the only remaining officer, set his surviving men to work to carry out the dead and wounded. Shelling was renewed when the British attack was launched and Lieut. Alexander visited Battalion Headquarters to report the plight in which his company stood. No relief could be afforded for a time, but later, as shelling in his area seemed more severe than further forward, he was ordered to take the remnant of his men and report to Capt. A. M. Dewar, of "A" Coy., in the old front line.

All day on November 6th, particularly at 4.45 p.m., when the British artillery fired an "army barrage" and the enemy artillery answered, the positions of the 24th Battalion companies were torn and rent by frequent bursts of field and heavy gun fire. "D" Coy. on the right was fortunate and suffered few direct hits, but "A" and "B" Companies were forced to endure a fire which steadily reduced their strength and increased their heavy toll of killed and wounded. Battalion Headquarters also suffered from the heavy fire of the German guns, casualties including Lieut. N. W. Robins, M.C., M.M., the Signalling Officer, who was struck in the face by a flying fragment of steel.

Despite the wounding of Lieut. Robins, the Signal Section of the Battalion accomplished work on November 6th which reflected credit of a high order on the unit and on the courage of the men to whom the maintenance of its communications was entrusted. As soon as the attack of the 26th Battalion was launched, Sergt. A. Findlay, M.M., Lance-Corporal James Day, Private L. T. Bellhouse, and Private W. A. Chafe moved forward under heavy fire, laying out four lines of communication. Private Chafe was killed and Private Bellhouse wounded, but Lance-Corporal Day and Sergt. Findlay completed the vital work on which they were engaged and established communication back to the lines of their own Battalion, their work receiving recognition at a later date when Sergt. Findlay was awarded the Distinguished Conduct Medal and Lance-Corporal Day the Belgian Croix de Guerre. Private John McDowell, a Battalion Runner, whose work in maintaining communication was in quality equal to that of his comrades in the Signal Section, also received the Belgian Croix de Guerre.

Following a day of heavy shelling, which tested the endurance and courage of the men of the 24th severely, the Battalion remained in position on the night of November 6th, and on the 7th again endured the intense shelling of the German guns. No disaster similar to that which had reduced "C" Coy. to a remnant of 1 officer and 30 men occurred, but the Battalion suffered appreciably, the casualties including Lieut. E. C. Platt, a gallant and efficient officer, who was killed whilst supervising the disposition of his men.

That night, the main body of the 24th Battalion was relieved by "C" Coy. of the 25th Battalion and moved back to Brigade Support positions at Seine, but "D" Coy. under Major P. L. Hall, M.C., was ordered to remain in the position it occupied and to serve for an additional day as close support, under 25th Battalion command. The men of "D" Coy. were almost exhausted and had expected to be relieved at the same time as their comrades, but they received their orders without complaint and, following the example set by the officer who commanded them, carried out their duties to the entire satisfaction of all concerned. At night on November 8th, with the exception of a sentry post of 3 men, who remained for a further 24 hours in position, they were relieved by the 19th Battalion and made their way back to 24th Battalion Headquarters, where Lieut.-Col. Ritchie and Major Bales awaited them. With these officers of Battalion Headquarters, they then marched back to Potijze Camp, whither the main body of the unit had proceeded at 3 o'clock in the afternoon.

At Potijze, where the Battalion remained on November 9th and 10th, Major J. N. Bales checked the casualty returns for the engagement and reported to the Commanding Officer that Lieut. Platt and 61 other ranks had been killed, 16 other ranks were missing, presumed killed, 11 other ranks had died of wounds, and that, in addition to the disabling of Capt. G. G. Garvey by shell fire, Lieuts. W. H. F. Ketcheson, F. W. Stenson, D. M. Wilson and N. W. Robins, M.C., M.M., had been wounded. One hundred and forty other ranks had also been wounded, all having been removed from the forward area before the Battalion was relieved, despite the fact that, owing to the awful mud, 6 men were needed to carry a stretcher and hours of exhausting effort were required to get each wounded man back to where wheeled transport could be provided. In accomplishing this work, stretcher bearers of the Battalion, under Lieut. S. A. Rolland, had earned the commendation of their own Headquarters and that of the Staff of the 5th Brigade.

As soon as Major Bales's returns were complete, the Commanding Officer and Hon. Capt. Stuart, the Chaplain, who could speak with personal knowledge of what the Battalion had endured in the line, began the task of writing letters to the next-of-kin of those who had fallen in action. It was not possible to complete this voluntary service in a day, but both officers, as was their custom, made careful note of the names of the dead and, when personal knowledge of how the soldier had died was lacking, sought information in order that their tributes to the memory of the killed should be both accurate and complete.

At Potijze Camp, the Battalion attracted the attention of enemy aircraft on November 9th, the German pilots flying low and spraying the district with fire from their machine-guns. British anti-aircraft guns were for some reason silent on this occasion, but the Lewis guns of the Battalion engaged the Germans in a stirring duel, which, so far as could be judged, ended without serious losses to either of the forces concerned. A number of men in the Battalion were caught in showers of fire, but no bullet found a living mark, nor could the Lewis gunners advance proof that their fire had achieved more definite success. Again on November 11th, while marching through Ypres to entrain for the Brandhoek area, the Battalion came under fire, this time from long range guns, which pounded the shattered town in an effort to inflict losses on whatever troops were passing through. As on November 9th, however, the enemy fire found no living target and the Battalion reached the point where it was to entrain without having suffered losses.

By this time, the Canadian Corps, having accomplished in the Ypres Salient the work for which it had been summoned from Lens, was returning to the First Army to take over again the line vacated in mid-October. No thought of a major operation against Lens now remained, for the battle just completed had shorn the Corps of its splendid strength and time must elapse before it could attack again with the vigour and assurance, which, in succession, had carried Vimy, Hill 70, and Passchendaele Ridge. Arduous trench work lay immediately ahead; but, for the time being, the Corps' work in attack had been completed.

CHAPTER XI

THE MERICOURT AND LENS SECTORS

I

Soon after the conclusion of the Flanders Offensive in November, 1917, and the capture by the Canadian Corps of the dominating Passchendaele Ridge, Sir Julian Byng's Third British Army struck a heavy blow at the German defences before Cambrai. Contrary to the custom which had become established on the Western Front, no preliminary barrage revealed the British plan, Sir Douglas Haig and Sir Julian Byng being determined to reintroduce into the warfare they were conducting the element of surprise, which, as all military history taught, provided a factor invaluable to the commander who could successfully adapt it to his purpose.

The wisdom of the British Commanders' decision was amply demonstrated on November 20th, when 6 infantry divisions and 324 tanks, under Sir Julian Byng's command, crashed through the front of General von der Marwitz's army, penetrated to a maximum depth of $4\frac{1}{2}$ miles, and, by the end of the first day's fighting, captured more than 5,000 prisoners. Even more striking success appeared probable early in the day, but at Masnières a tank broke down the last remnant of a vital bridge across the Canal de l'Escaut and at Flesquières a German officer, bravely serving the sole remaining gun of his battery of field artillery, delayed the British advance appreciably. Even more important as a factor in the battle was the unexpected arrival on the scene from Russia of the 107th German Division. Using this division on the front between Rumilly and Crèvecoeur, General von der Marwitz strengthened his line at the moment when, without the additional strength, disaster would almost certainly have overwhelmed it.

For some days after the initial British effort, the battle continued and was marked by intense fighting at Fontaine and Bourlon. Then, on the morning of November 30th, the Germans launched a counter-attack in strength. On the front of the 29th British Division near Masnières and Marcoing, the enemy attack was stingingly repulsed, but further to the south it drove through the British front so successfully that by noon the position in the Cambrai Salient of General Byng's whole Third Army was seriously endangered. Summoned from a rest position north of Havrincourt Wood to avert the disaster which threatened, the Guards Division of the British Army responded magnificently and drove the enemy back. Through this counter-attack and through resolute fighting on subsequent days by other British divisions, a major disaster was avoided.

When the operation is considered as a whole, that is the British attack of November 20th and the enemy counter-attack ten days later, a substantial balance of success is found to be with the forces of Sir Julian Byng, nevertheless the result was disappointing, more particularly in view of altered circumstances on the Western Front which indicated that initiative had been wrested from the Allied Armies and that, in 1918, the ability to attack and to choose the time and place of attack would definitely rest with Germany.

As Sir Douglas Haig has observed in his *Despatches*, the elimination of Russia and other factors associated with the situation at the close of 1917 made it "necessary to change the policy governing the conduct of the operations of the British Armies in France. Orders accordingly were issued early in December having for their object immediate preparation to meet a strong and sustained hostile offensive. In other words, a defensive policy was adopted, and all necessary arrangements consequent thereon were put in hand with the least possible delay."

The defensive policy mentioned by Sir Douglas Haig should be borne in mind when considering the work of the battalions of the Canadian Corps in the winter of 1917-'18. The Corps was given the task of holding, and preparing the defences of, Vimy Ridge, the second of these duties explaining the endless working parties which, throughout the winter, toiled day and night, often under heavy fire and nearly always in conditions of mud and physical hardship harder to endure than words can easily convey. Statistics present an amazing total in miles of trenches dug and barbed wire erected, but perhaps the greatest reward of the troops who carried out the work lies in knowledge of the fact that in 1918, when the vast surge of Germany's final offensive had been broken, the British Army stood fast on Vimy Ridge, where it had stood in 1917. Realizing that the men of the Canadian Corps had converted Vimy Ridge into a fortress of almost unbelievable strength, the enemy refused to attack it from in front and, when flanking operations against it failed, left it to stand as the greatest physical barrier on the Western Front between the German Empire and military victory.

II

Immediately after completion of the operations at Passchendaele and a two days' rest in Toronto Camp, Brandhoek, the 24th Battalion, Victoria Rifles of Canada, moved back to the British front before Lens. Leaving Toronto Camp at 11.30 o'clock on the morning of November 13, 1917, the men were conveyed by bus to Robecq, reaching their destination at 4.30 p.m. and billeting for the night with the French inhabitants, who extended a warm and hospitable welcome.

Proceeding by bus on the following day, the Battalion moved to Lozinghem, where, on November 15th, busses again picked up the men and conveyed them, by way of Divion, Houdain, Estrée-Cauchie, and Camblain l'Abbé, to Villers au Bois, whence, a day later, they moved forward to Hanson Camp, Neuville St. Vaast. At Hanson Camp, where equipment was issued to make good the loss occasioned by the operations at Passchendaele, the Battalion received a draft of 101 reinforcements, and welcomed to duty Capt. V. E. Duclos, who had recovered from the wound received at Vimy Ridge, Lieut. G. A. McGiffin, who had similarly recovered from a wound received in the Battles of the Somme, Lieut. A. McBean, from the 244th Battalion, Kitchener's Own, and Capt. R. A. C. Kane, another officer of the 244th Battalion, who arrived to assume duties as the 24th Battalion's Paymaster.

For six days, the Battalion remained in Hanson Camp, the time being marked by no incident of outstanding importance, though interest was added to the routine by the arrival in Neuville St. Vaast of a number of former inhabitants of the town, under care of the French Military Mission, to dig for money they had concealed when they fled before the advance of the German Army in 1914. Parties from the 24th Battalion were ordered to assist the civilians by digging where they suggested and, as a result, some thousands of francs were found and restored to their rightful owners.

Leaving Hanson Camp at 9 o'clock on the morning of November 22nd, the Battalion, with a trench strength of 17 officers and 380 other ranks, moved up and relieved the 27th Canadian Battalion in support trenches of the Mericourt Sector. Six days were passed in the support positions, the Battalion then advancing, one company at a time, and relieving the 25th Canadian Battalion in the front line. On the day of the relief, the officer strength of the Battalion was increased when Lieuts. J. L. Cains, D. G. Campbell, E. T. Hart, J. C. Kelley, and E. Shamper reported for duty from England.

Undoubtedly, the chief incident of the front line tour that followed occurred on the early morning of December 2nd, when, after a heavy bombardment of "B" Coy.'s front and of Tot Communication Trench, a party of the enemy, about 20 strong, raided the Battalion lines at a point near Archer Post, the right post of the 5th Canadian Infantry Brigade's front. Soon after entering the Battalion lines, the Germans encountered a small group of Victoria Riflemen and a wild hand-to-hand fight followed.

In the encounter, the Germans were successful in overpowering and capturing Private E. R. Brown and in delivering such a blow on the head of Private G. V. England that the unfortunate victim fell dazed and half unconscious to the bottom of the trench. Leaping forward as Private England fell, a German soldier lunged at the Victoria Rifleman's prostrate body and drove a bayonet through his wrist. Simultaneously, a second German kicked at his head, the heavy boot finding its target, but the full force of the resulting shock being lessened appreciably through the protection afforded by England's steel helmet.

Satisfied that the fighting spirit of the Canadian had been subdued, the Germans were gloating over the capture of this second prisoner and were making preparations to bundle their victim back to their own lines, but Private England viewed the situation in a different light. His rifle had fallen from his grasp, but, sheathed in the boot of the sergeant-major who commanded the German party, he noticed the handle of a knife. With a jerk, he tore this weapon from its place, then leaped at the man who owned it, stabbed him deep in the chest, struck hard at another German who attempted to interfere, and escaped down a communication trench to the left, despite a bomb flung after him, which, exploding at his feet, grievously wounded him in the back and legs.

On escaping from the German party, Private England reached the section of front occupied by troops of the 4th Canadian Infantry Brigade and was despatched to No. 42 Casualty Clearing Station. At first, his story of the manner in which he had received his wounds was doubted by the Intelligence Staff of the 2nd Canadian Division, but evidence confirming his report accumulated rapidly, all doubt as to the accuracy of the story in its essentials vanishing when, not far from the point where the fight was said to have occurred, Canadian patrols found the dead body of a German sergeant-major, with an empty knife sheath in his boot and a great knife wound in his chest. This mute evidence was an important factor in gaining for Private England a prompt award, for bravery in hand-to-hand fighting, of the British Military Medal.

Two days after Private England's adventure in the line, the 24th Battalion was relieved by the 26th Battalion and marched back to Cubitt Camp, Neuville St. Vaast. In this position the unit remained for six days, supplying heavy working parties, drilling, voting in the Dominion election, and preparing to reoccupy the line.

Moving from Neuville St. Vaast on the afternoon of December 10th, the Battalion took over support positions in the Mericourt Section of the line from the 22nd French-Canadian Battalion. No unusual incident marked the relief, and by 7.30 p.m. the 21 officers and 456 other ranks of the unit had settled down and the men of the 22nd Battalion had moved off into reserve.

Throughout the six-day tour that followed, all men of the Battalion who could be spared from other duty were employed on working parties, the majority erecting heavy belts of protective barbed wire in front of Canada Trench. Enemy guns and aeroplanes were fairly active, several sharp bombardments striking near Canada Dump, where a number of other ranks were wounded, but no heavy losses had been incurred when, on December 16th, the Battalion was relieved by the 26th Battalion and, after marching to Bon Summit, proceeded by light railway to Villers au Bois.

After spending in Villers au Bois three days, on two of which strong parties were despatched for work in the forward area, the Battalion embussed at Chateau d'Acq on December 19th and proceeded to Estrée Blanche, where the men billeted in farm buildings and barns. These were not entirely comfortable, for snow lay deep on the ground and a cold wind blew through every crack in floor, wall, or roof, but in comparison with dugouts in the line they appeared luxurious and the men settled down in them with complete satisfaction.

Three days after the Battalion reached Estrée Blanche, Lieut.-Col. C. F. Ritchie, M.C., proceeded on a month's leave to England and command of the unit was assumed by Major P. L. Hall, M.C. At the time, it was presumed by the Battalion that Lieut.-Col. Ritchie, who had gained distinction at the Somme and had commanded the unit in all its major engagements in 1917, would return to the Regiment when his leave was completed, but, on December 28th, Brigadier-General J. M. Ross notified Major Hall that Lieut.-Col. Ritchie had been appointed to command a reserve battalion in England and that command of the 24th Battalion in the field would be assumed by Major W. H. Clark-Kennedy, D.S.O., who, at the moment, was serving as Brigade Major of the 5th Canadian Infantry Brigade.

Though regretting deeply the departure of a Commanding Officer who had crossed from Canada with the 24th Battalion and had served for more than two years in a manner reflecting marked credit upon the Victoria Rifles, officers and men of the 24th welcomed Major Clark-Kennedy whose record, first with the 13th Battalion, Royal Highlanders of Canada, of the 1st Canadian Division, and later on the Staffs of the 3rd Canadian Infantry Brigade, the 2nd Canadian Division, and the 5th Canadian Infantry Brigade, was such that the 24th Battalion's chain of distinguished leadership would remain unbroken.

Before Major Clark-Kennedy reported to assume command of the Battalion on December 30, 1917, the unit, at Estrée Blanche, had celebrated its third Christmas in France. The Companies and Details held their respective dinners at such time as opportunity offered between December 23rd and 27th, and the officers dined on Christmas night, the guests including Lieut.-Col. R. O. Alexander, a former Commanding Officer, Capt. F. T. Bown, and a number of others who previously had served on the Battalion's commissioned establishment. Following the Christmas celebrations, the unit, still at Estrée Blanche, resumed its routine training.

III

For the first sixteen days of January, 1918, the 24th Battalion, Victoria Rifles of Canada, remained at Estrée Blanche, under command of Lieut.-Col. W. H. Clark-Kennedy, D.S.O., carrying to completion the syllabus of training begun on December 20th. Little incident marked the period, though all ranks were pleased by the announcement that, for his services as Adjutant in the great engagements of the previous year, Major J. N. Bales had been awarded the Military Cross and that, for valuable work as Traffic Control Officer of the 2nd Canadian Division, Capt. F. T. Bown had received a similar award.

Some days after these honours had been announced, the Battalion welcomed back to its establishment Major E. M. Amphlett, M.C., who had completed a Senior Officers' Training Course in England, and bade farewell to Lieut. G. Earnshaw, who was leaving to join the United States Army as an instructor. Two days before Lieut.

THE SERGEANTS, 24TH BATTALION, C.E.F. AT ANICHE, 1918.

Front Row: left to right: Coy. Sergt.-Major P. G. Fournier, M.M., Sergt. M. A. Murphy, Arm.-Sergt. J. R. Bales, Coy. Q.-M.-Sergt. J. Donohoe, D.C.M., Coy. Sergt.-Major W. H. Boyd, R.Q.M.S. Robert Mitchell, M.M., Coy. Sergt.-Major G. W. Croll, D.C.M., Coy. Sergt.-Major J. C. Mackie, M.M., Coy. Q.-M. Sergt. E. W. Hughes, Coy. Q.-M. Sergt. L. Cade, M.M., Sergt. S. Arber, Sergt. E. F. Sloman, Sergt. John Barron. *Second Row:* Sergeants J. Stewart, A. J. Crabbe, M.M., ——, R. T. Dawson, D. Monteith, ——, J. P. Kelly, M.M., W. Croft, J. J. Donoghue, W. G. S. Egerton, A. E. Giles, Wood, R. C. Bliault. *Top Row:* Sergeants F. H. Sweeney, D.C.M., J. W. Kennedy, M.M., S. Bell, ——, J. N. Swift, ——, J. Jasper, R. W. Handren, D.C.M., D. E. Stewart, J. D. M. MacDougall, B. F. Fitchett, W. Innes.

Earnshaw left, Lieut. D. M. Matheson, who had recovered from a wound received in the Battle of Hill 70, reported for duty and was posted to "B" Coy.

Apart from the appointments and transfers of officers, the most interesting event of the training period at Estrée Blanche occurred on January 10th, when the Battalion and its Transport was reviewed by the Divisional Commander, Major-General H. E. Burstall. Despite a footing of clear and slippery ice, the Battalion marched past with a fair measure of order and assurance, but no effort could keep the horses and wagons in line. They approached the saluting base with difficulty and, encountering sloping ground, skidded until, at the feet of the inspecting General, horses, mules, and limbers piled up in woeful confusion.

Six days after Major-General Burstall's inspection, which, notwithstanding the Transport's misfortune, revealed the Battalion in a most satisfactory light, the unit moved from Estrée Blanche to Auchel, proceeding on the following day to Camblain l'Abbé, and on January 18th to familiar quarters in Hanson Camp, Neuville St. Vaast. Previous to the last of these moves, Lieut.-Col. Clark-Kennedy, his Company Commanders, and Scout Officer had proceeded by light railway to inspect the Mericourt Section of the front line, which the Battalion was to take over on the night of January 19th.

Marching from Hanson Camp at 3 p.m. on the 19th, the Victoria Rifles, with a trench strength of 22 officers and 541 other ranks, duly relieved the 72nd Battalion, Seaforth Highlanders, of the 4th Canadian Division, in the line. Deep mud forced the incoming and outgoing battalions to move overland instead of through the usual communication trenches, but this was accomplished without attracting enemy attention, and relief was completed at 9.45 p.m.

Following relief of the 72nd Battalion, the Victoria Rifles carried out in the line the customary 6-day tour. Shelling, heavy at times, damaged the Battalion front on a number of occasions and inflicted some losses, these including the Scout Officer, Lieut. Wallace Watson, who was wounded while returning from a patrol in No Man's Land on January 24th.

After completing the tour in the line, the Battalion moved back to support positions, whence, as always, strong parties were ordered out each day, or night, for service in the forward area. While in support, the Battalion took leave of Lieuts. A. W. H. Arundell and E. Shamper, who had transferred to the Royal Flying Corps, and welcomed Lieut. W. S. Dickson, an original member of the unit, who arrived to succeed Lieut. Watson as Scout Officer.

On the afternoon when Lieut. Dickson reported, January 29th, the Battalion took over from the 25th Battalion the right sub-section of the Mericourt front line and undertook at once the heavy work of clearing a number of trenches blocked by rain and the resulting mud. Shelling was heavy at intervals throughout the tour and a number of casualties occurred, the total being increased on the early morning of February 3rd when a Battalion patrol, under Lieut. H. R. Tanner, encountered a strong enemy patrol in No Man's Land and suffered the loss of 1 man killed and 2 wounded.

On the night of February 3rd, the Battalion was relieved and moved back into support, with three companies in Canada Trench and one company and Battalion Headquarters in the Railway Embankment. From these positions, strong working and salvage parties moved into the forward area on five successive days, an impression of the value of the work accomplished being conveyed by entries in the Battalion Diary which show that artillery ammunition worth $196,000.00 was collected and turned in to the Salvage Department of the Canadian Corps.

After working hard in the forward area, as the salvage figures indicate, the Battalion withdrew from support on February 8th to Cellars Camp, Neuville St. Vaast, whence strong wiring, digging, and carrying parties were supplied on the majority of the six days that followed. From Cellars Camp, the Battalion moved on February 14th to Camblain l'Abbé, proceeding thence on February 18th to Columbia Camp, near Souchez, and on the 19th into the right sub-section of the front line, Lens Sector, in relief of the 44th Battalion.

In this sector, the Battalion carried out a 4-day tour. Artillery and trench mortars were active and German snipers were troublesome, their victims including Sergt. Horace Firth, who, under the name "Jack Depledge," had served the Battalion well and, for bravery in action, had won the Military Medal. Sergt. Depledge, while studying the German line from a position in "C" Coy.'s front, was shot in the head by a sniper and died in hospital a few days later.

Following completion of the 4-day tour in the line, the Battalion moved back on February 23rd to the support area in Liévin; carried out there a 4-day tour, in the course of which the entire unit was on several occasions called out on working parties; and on February 27th marched by companies to Vancouver Camp, Chateau de la Haie. Here, on February 28th, the men of the Battalion attended bath parades and prepared to carry out a syllabus of training, which, it was announced, would continue for some weeks.

In accordance with these arrangements, the Battalion remained in reserve throughout the first three weeks in March, 1918, at Vancouver Camp, Chateau de la Haie, until March 11th, when the unit moved to Bruay, and thereafter in Lozinghem, which was reached on March 12th. In the period of service in reserve, drills or manoeuvres were carried out each day, and special attention was paid to improving the Battalion's standard of musketry and to the co-operation between attacking infantry and tanks.

With the second of these ends in view, "D" Coy., under Major P. L. Hall, M.C., demonstrated on March 6th the system to be used when co-operation with tanks was required. Demonstrations on subsequent days, lectures to officers and men, and practices, notably on March 21st, when manoeuvres were conducted under the orders of Capt. E. P. Denman and Lieut. D. M. Matheson, provided the men with training in tank liaison which was to prove of the greatest value later in the year.

While the 24th Battalion was in training in Lozinghem, Lieut.-General Sir A. W. Currie issued an order, notifying the battalions in the Canadian Corps of increased activity on the part of the German armies in France and instructing all units and formations to stand by, prepared for prompt and efficient action. In forwarding the order to the battalions of the 5th Canadian Infantry Brigade, Brigadier-General J. M. Ross stated that the number of men allowed on pass after each day's training must be reduced to a minimum, that no passes to men to proceed outside the Brigade Training Area should be issued, and that units undertaking a route march in the Brigade Area must notify Brigade Headquarters of the hour at which the march would start, the point of departure, and the exact route to be followed.

Realizing the significance of these orders, officers and men of the Battalion trained faithfully, knowing that before long the result of all their effort must be tested in the furnace of bitter and prolonged fighting. It was known throughout the Army that Germany was mounting on the Western Front an offensive on a major scale, and, on March 21st, the Battalion received news that the great battle had begun. At 3 p.m., an order was received warning the Battalion that a move on the morrow might be expected. At 9.30 p.m. the order was cancelled, but the unit realized that the cancellation was temporary and that soon action in the forward area must follow.

CHAPTER XII

GERMANY'S BID FOR MILITARY VICTORY

I

Early in January, 1918, the Prime Minister of Great Britain asked Field Marshal Sir Douglas Haig for an opinion regarding the operations which the German Army would undertake in the spring, and the British Commander-in-Chief replied that, almost certainly, the Germans would attack as soon as weather conditions would permit. He added that the blow would be delivered with all the strength the enemy could muster and that the British, for a time, must expect to lose ground, prisoners, and guns. Casualties might total 100,000 a month and this, Sir Douglas admitted, would strain the fabric of the British Army severely, nevertheless the Commander-in-Chief stated that in his opinion the Army, if adequately reinforced, would triumph in the bitter defensive fighting which the German attack would involve.

As February, 1918, drew to a close, all evidence that the British Intelligence Department could gather convinced Sir Douglas Haig and his Staff that the Germans were about to attack the junction of the Third and Fifth British Armies. The French Intelligence Department, however, did not endorse British opinion, and the French Commander-in-Chief justified a refusal to move troops into position to support the British front, as previously arranged, by stating his conviction that the main blow in the coming German offensive would strike against the French front at Rheims. Even on March 2nd, when the British Fifth Army was given the order "Prepare for battle," the French could not believe that on the Fifth Army front a serious German offensive was intended.

At 4.45 o'clock on the morning of March 21, 1918, a bombardment, surpassing in intensity any the war had previously witnessed, broke on the front of the Third and Fifth British Armies and some hours thereafter, under cover of a heavy fog, masses of German infantry attacked. Long before the end of the day, it was clear to the British Staff that Germany's supreme effort was under way; but the French command, for two-and-a-half days, maintained their belief that only a diversion on a major scale was intended.

By night on March 21st, the Germans had effected a serious penetration of the British front, the situation thereafter growing hourly more critical as, before the ponderous weight of the massed offensive, the Third and Fifth Armies gave ground. Retreat in perfect alignment was beyond the power of the British to effect and gradually a gap between the two armies was opened. Exploiting this situation with skill, the enemy drove a wedge into the gap in the British line and, as the waves of battle surged back almost to Amiens, strove mightily to encompass the Third and Fifth Armies' destruction, also that of French troops which were co-operating.

Even more serious than the reverse on the front of the Third and Fifth Armies was the situation that developed between the British and French Commanders-in-Chief. On the afternoon of March 24th, General Pétain announced to Sir Douglas Haig that, in the event of the Germans making further progress towards Amiens, General Fayolle, who with a number of French divisions was advancing to support the British front, had received orders to fall back south-westwards and use his force for the protection of Paris. These orders, which General Pétain refused to cancel, contemplated a possible separation of the British and French Armies, as a result of which the French, with Paris behind them, and the British, with their backs to the sea, must strive independently to avert irreparable disaster.

Believing that disunion of the Allied Armies represented a policy born of despair, which would present to Germany a real chance for military victory, and realizing that prompt action to escape this danger was essential, Sir Douglas Haig telegraphed at once to London, asking the British Secretary of State for War and the Chief of the Imperial General Staff to come to France, in order that General Ferdinand Foch might be appointed Generalissimo. Sir Douglas knew that to this proposal the French would eagerly agree; he knew equally that with General Foch in command all thought of dividing the Allied Armies would promptly be abandoned.

In reply to the British Commander-in-Chief's urgent message, Lord Milner and General Sir Henry Wilson crossed at once to France and proceeded to Doullens, where, at an Anglo-French conference on March 26th, the appointment of General Foch was signed. Unfortunately, he was authorized only to "co-ordinate the work of the Allied Armies," and General Pétain was left to direct the movement of French reserves. This situation proved anomalous and, on April 3rd, at Beauvais, a modification of the appointment order was effected, and General Foch was authorized to "direct the strategy of military operations." Though vague, this phrase achieved its purpose and eventually rendered the Commanders-in-Chief of the British, French, Belgian and American Armies amenable to Foch's "strategic directives"; at the same time it left to each full authority for the tactical control and guidance of his own armies in the field.

Even before the conference at Beauvais took place, the tide in the great battle on the British front had turned against the enemy. By nightfall on the 26th, the peak of danger had been passed; and on the 28th, the situation eased perceptibly. On this date, the Seventeenth German Army struck hard at General Sir H. S. Horne's First British Army on the 20-mile front from Puisieux to Oppy, with the intention of smashing the British line, capturing Arras, and rolling in behind Vimy Ridge. Beaten back with disastrous losses on the whole front of attack, the Germans were compelled to abandon the operation, though upon its success hinged the ultimate fate of the battle begun on March 21st. Twenty-four hours after General Horne's victory, the British line on the fronts of the Third and Fifth Armies began unmistakably to stablilize.

Throughout this fighting in the spring of 1918, possession of Vimy Ridge meant to the British more than a few words or paragraphs can convey. As the author of *Sir Douglas Haig's Command* has written: "Like a mighty tree, with its roots fast anchored to the great bastion of the Vimy Ridge, the British Army bowed to the fierce hurricane that swept upon it on March 21. Its branches were hurled back westwards, whipping and bending in the gale; but the trunk stood unbreakable and the grip of the roots could not be loosed."

Bearing witness to the truth of this description, General Ludendorff writes that by April 4th "it was an established fact that the enemy's resistance was beyond our strength and General Headquarters had to take the extreme and difficult decision of abandoning the attack on Amiens for good. Strategically, we did not achieve what the events of March 23rd, 24th, and 25th had encouraged us to hope for."

Abandonment of the attack on Amiens, however, did not mean that Germany had yielded the initiative. In attack lay the enemy's one hope of victory; to resume the offensive, as soon as possible and with all his strength, therefore, was a policy forced upon him by circumstances whether he would or no.

Accordingly, on April 9, 1918, he drove forward in the Lys Sector, shattering a division of the Portuguese Army Corps and thereafter involving many divisions of the British Army in prolonged and bitter fighting. As at Amiens, the waves of the German attack rolled forward for a time, and lapped eventually at the approaches to Ypres and the English Channel. Desperate fighting occurred at many places, but before April ended the enemy realized, beyond all doubt and despite substantial local success, that his second great effort to defeat the British Army had failed. Thereafter, until the Allied Armies assumed the offensive later in the year, he concentrated his attention on attempting to overwhelm the French.

II

When the German attack broke on the front of the Third and Fifth British Armies before Amiens on March 21, 1918, the 24th Battalion, Victoria Rifles of Canada, as mentioned in the previous chapter of this book, lay in billets in Lozinghem. News of the battle on the Amiens front arrived at a moment when the Battalion football team was engaged in a spirited contest with a team from the 2nd Canadian Divisional Signals. The game was not interrupted; but it was announced that orders had been received to move on the following morning. These were cancelled at 9.30 p.m., and on March 22nd the unit continued its training, until, at 4.30 o'clock in the afternoon, orders for a move on the morning of March 23rd were received and issued.

Parading at 10 a.m. on March 23rd, the Battalion began a march to Divion, but when more than half the distance had been traversed, the unit received orders to halt for lunch and to stand by, awaiting further instructions. In obedience to these orders, the men of the Battalion rested in a field until 8.30 p.m., when lorries arrived and conveyed them to York Camp at Ecoivres.

At York Camp, the Battalion rested on March 24th; but on the 25th, at 6.30 a.m., 22 officers and 560 other ranks were furnished as a working party to dig reserve trenches. Again on March 26th, the Battalion was employed to dig trenches in the forward area, the men returning at 3.30 p.m. to York Camp, where, forty minutes later, a message from the 5th Canadian Infantry Brigade ordered the unit to prepare at once for a move. At 5.10 p.m., Lieut.-Col. Clark-Kennedy notified Brigade that the warning order had been carried out and that the Battalion stood ready for whatever service should be required.

That evening, at 11.30 o'clock, the Battalion paraded and, marching all night, by way of Maroeuil, Louez, Dainville, Beaumetz les Loges, Basseux, Bailleuval, and Berles au Bois, arrived eventually in Bienvillers au Bois, where, at 9.30 a.m. on March 27th, the men billeted in cellars, or whatever accommodation they could find. The ten hour march, coming at the end of a day of heavy labour in the forward area, was exhausting to a degree and over and over men slept soundly throughout the hourly ten minute halts, or, falling asleep as they marched, staggered from the ranks and collapsed completely. All, however, realized that the service on which they were engaged was urgent in the extreme and few failed to reach Bienvillers au Bois with the company or detail to which they belonged.

By this time, the 2nd Canadian Division had left the area occupied by the Canadian Corps and was in Third Army Reserve. On March 28th, the Division was transferred to the British VI Corps. As this formation was part of the Third Army, the 2nd Canadian Division served in the days that followed under the orders of General the Hon. Sir Julian Byng, who formerly had commanded the Canadian Corps.

After resting in Bienvillers au Bois on March 27th, the Battalion received orders to advance on the night of March 28th and occupy support trenches in the Ficheux Sector of the line. Reaching these positions at 4 o'clock on the morning of March 29th, the Battalion took over and remained in position until 10 p.m., when it advanced and relieved the 2nd Battalion, Royal Scots, in the front line. The Royal Scots had suffered severely in the fighting of the previous week, but were encouraged by the arrival of fresh troops and the knowledge that the 2nd Canadian Division was to operate in the area.

As a whole, the first hours spent by the Battalion in the new sector of the front line were uneventful; but, at 9.15 o'clock on the morning of March 30th, the enemy opened an intense bombardment on positions occupied by the British Guards Division to the 24th Battalion's right and, after some hours of shelling, drove forward to the attack. Without hesitation, the Guards met the assault and, by concentrated rifle fire, destroyed it before it reached their line. A few Germans got into the British trenches, but the unfortunate few were promptly killed with the bayonet. On the 24th Battalion front, though no attack followed, the bombardment was at times intense and several men were wounded, the number including Lieut. S. A. Rolland, who was struck in the face by a flying piece of shell.

After their attack on the Guards Division on March 30th, the Germans remained inactive that afternoon and night; but at 2.30 p.m. on March 31st, their 77-mm. guns shelled the Headquarters of the 24th Battalion. Again on the afternoon of April 1st, Battalion Headquarters was heavily shelled; and at 9.30 p.m., following an S.O.S.

signal on the left section of the Brigade front, barrage fire struck the Battalion lines, damaging a number of trenches and wounding 5 other ranks severely.

Even more serious was the effect of an artillery concentration on the following day. At 6 o'clock in the morning the Battalion trenches were battered by intense fire and by 7.30 a.m., when the bombardment slackened, 2 other ranks had been killed and 23 wounded. The 22nd French-Canadian Battalion also suffered from this fire, among the killed being Hon. Capt. Crochetière, their Roman Catholic Chaplain. Rumours spread that Hon. Capt. C. J. S. Stuart, Chaplain of the 24th Battalion, had also been killed, but these reports were fortunately without foundation. The period, however, was disastrous to the front line chaplains, the number of seriously wounded including Hon. Capt. H. M. Shore, for whom many in the 24th Battalion cherished a most warm regard.

After the bombardment on the morning of April 2nd, the Battalion remained in the line until 8.30 o'clock that night, when units of the 29th Canadian Battalion arrived to relieve, the movement being completed at 12.15 a.m. on April 3rd and the Battalion then marching back to billets in Berles au Bois. Two days were spent in billets, after which, on April 5th, the Battalion paraded, with a trench strength of 23 officers and 666 other ranks, and marched to relieve the 20th Canadian Battalion in the Green Line and Telegraph Hill Switch Right Support.

In support, the Battalion remained for four days, the time being marked by fairly active artillery fire, by heavy rain, and by working parties, notably on the night of April 6th, when 10 officers and 300 men worked throughout the hours of darkness on construction and trench repairs. Some gas shelling featured the period, particularly on the early morning of April 8th, when several 8-inch gas shells fell in the Battalion lines, causing a number of casualties.

After completing four days in support, the Battalion moved up at 7.30 p.m. on April 9th and at midnight effected relief of the 25th Canadian Battalion in the Right Sector of the Neuville Vitasse front line (Green Line). One other rank was killed and 3 were wounded on the Battalion's first day in the new position, even more serious loss being suffered by the Rear Details at Beaumetz when, on the afternoon of April 10th, the positions they occupied were heavily shelled by enemy long-range guns.

For two hours gunfire played on Beaumetz and when it ceased the Rear Details of the 24th Battalion had suffered a total of 7 other ranks wounded and 8 other ranks killed, the dead including Sergts. C. F. Franklin, M.M., J. R. Irvers, and W. J. Milne, and Corporals G. K. Murray and J. W. Johnson. In addition to the loss occasioned by the death of these efficient and experienced N.C.O.'s, the shelling at Beaumetz deprived the Battalion of the services of a gallant officer, Major E. M. Amphlett, M.C., who was wounded in the leg. He had crossed with the Battalion from Canada, had received a commission after service in France in the ranks, and had risen until, at the time when wounded, he was serving as Lieut.-Col. Clark-Kennedy's Second-in-Command. News of his injury, reaching the Battalion in the line, was received with deep regret, and the good wishes of all ranks accompanied him as he was transferred from France to a hospital in England.

Meanwhile, in the front line, the Battalion was experiencing a period of pronounced activity. At 6 o'clock on the morning of April 11th, the enemy opened an intense bombardment of the Battalion's area, following this at 9.30 a.m. by a manoeuvre in which a battle patrol of the 8th Battalion of German Storm Troops, 80 strong, attempted to approach through saps and drive into a position on the left of "B" Coy.'s front. The German troops were in marching order, and seemingly expected to occupy the 24th Battalion line without serious opposition.

The men of the Battalion, however, had no thought of abandoning their trenches to the enemy, either on "B" Coy.'s front, or on that of "A" Coy., where a second battle patrol of the German Storm Troops attempted to force the Canadian line. On both sections of the front, the Victoria Riflemen drove the attacking forces back by concentrated rifle and machine-gun fire, which inflicted heavy losses, further casualties being suffered by the Germans when, in retreating, their broken formations were caught in the blast of the Canadian artillery barrage. So intense and accurate was this fire, that few of the Germans were able to reach the protection of their own trenches, and their dead, visible from the 24th Battalion lines, remained as mute evidence of the heavy loss the attacking waves had suffered.

Soon after the enemy battle patrols had failed to penetrate the Canadian line, the German artillery resumed the intense bombardment which the forward movement of the infantry had interrupted. All morning and in the early afternoon, gunfire played on the 24th Battalion lines, in an attempt to clear from the path of the German unit opposite the stubborn opposition which had held the enemy battle patrols from their objectives.

Believing that this purpose had been accomplished, a strong enemy party advanced at 2 p.m. on "B" Coy.'s front and, driving through the Canadian defences, plunged into the 24th Battalion's front line trench, other enemy parties advancing simultaneously to occupy saps about 60 yards from "B" Coy.'s front. Though successful in penetrating the Victoria Rifles' front, the ascendency of the Germans lasted for a few minutes only, as the men of "B" Coy. rallied and promptly bombed them out of the position they had fought so bravely to attain. In the 24th Battalion trench, they left the body of one man, and a few yards outside the trench the dead bodies of several more. From these, definite identification of the 8th Battalion of German Storm Troops was obtained.

When the broken waves of the German attack retreated from the Battalion's front line trench, they found immediate shelter in the line of saps, which, as mentioned previously, parties of their comrades had occupied while the assault was driving forward. Possession of these saps by the enemy presented a threat the 24th Battalion could not ignore. Accordingly, at 5.30 p.m., Stokes guns of the 5th Canadian Trench Mortar Battery were brought into action and these, with the help of "B" Coy.'s rifle grenadiers, drove the Germans back to the position they had occupied before the operation had begun.

Though the engagements on April 11th ended with the Victoria Rifles in possession of the entire front which the

Germans had attacked, the successful defence had not been accomplished without substantial losses. No officers had fallen in the heavy bombardments, or in the hand-to-hand fighting and bombing of the morning and afternoon, but the other ranks had suffered sharply, their casualties when the day ended having reached a total of 17 killed and 40 wounded.

Writing of the events of the day, a senior officer of the unit mentions to a brother officer in hospital that, throughout the engagements of the morning and afternoon, officers, non-commissioned officers, and men acted in a manner that enhanced the prestige of the Battalion. Confirmation of this statement is found in many private papers and in a report, compiled by Major J. N. Bales, M.C., and forwarded, on Lieut.-Col. Clark-Kennedy's orders, to Headquarters of the 5th Canadian Infantry Brigade.

In this report, or in other documents prepared at the time, the attention of higher authority was drawn to the outstanding work accomplished in the engagements by Lieut. D. M. Matheson, by Sergts. A. W. Cooke, M.M., and W. F. Gauld, by Corporal R. G. Hagen, by Lance-Corporal W. Divorty, and by Privates A. N. Withey, F. W. G. Botsford, L. Lareau, and C. E. Willis. Record has also been preserved of the devotion to duty of Lieut. A. McBean, Sergt. A. Findlay, D.C.M., M.M., Coy. Sergt.-Major Arthur Copeland, of "C" Coy., and Private T. M. Carey.

Referring to the conduct of Lieut. D. M. Matheson in the fighting on April 11th, Lieut.-Col. Clark-Kennedy's report stated that this officer, who was in charge of the section of trench attacked by the enemy in the morning and penetrated in the afternoon, had defended his position courageously and, when momentarily forced to yield a section of his line, had organized the counter-attack, which achieved immediate success. Throughout the whole operation, Lieut. Matheson's bearing and demeanour had served as a real inspiration to his men.

Similar in quality and effect was the work of Sergts. Cooke and Gauld. The former, when an enemy shell buried his machine-gun and its crew, dug the gun from the mud that engulfed it, organized a new crew, and,

THE COMMANDING OFFICERS, 24TH BATTALION, VICTORIA RIFLES OF CANADA, 1914-1919.

Above: Brigadier-General J. A. Gunn, C.M.G., D.S.O. (October 22, 1914—October 19, 1916), Lieut.-Col. R. O. Alexander, D.S.O. (October 19, 1916—July 18, 1917). *Below:* Lieut.-Col. C. F. Ritchie, D.S.O., M.C. (July 18, 1917—December 22, 1917 and September 5, 1918—May 18, 1919), Lieut.-Col. W. H. Clark-Kennedy, V.C., C.M.G., D.S.O. (December 30, 1917—August 28, 1918).

bringing the gun into action at a time when it was needed most, assisted in checking an advancing wave of German infantry. Sergt. Gauld, reorganizing a shattered platoon, occupied a post of danger and, directing the rifle fire of his men, contributed materially to the enemy's downfall. Private C. E. Willis, who brought a machine-gun forward under heavy shelling, organized a crew from a supporting platoon, and opened fire on the Germans as they approached his post, was also instrumental in checking abruptly the wave of the German attack.

While these events were taking place, Corporal Hagen, Lance-Corporal Divorty, and Private Botsford, of the Signal Section, had maintained the Battalion's telephone wires in working order. Again and again the wires were cut by shells, but, each time a break occurred, one or other of the Signallers soon reached the point where damage had been done and, without regard to personal safety, worked hard and fast until communication was restored. The fine example set by the Signallers, and their courage in moving without hesitation into the open, or wherever duty called, were factors contributing to the high morale which all ranks of the Battalion displayed.

Equally creditable was the work of Stretcher-Bearers Withey and Lareau. Private Lareau dressed the wounded of his platoon under heavy fire, encouraged his comrades by cool attention to the work in hand when danger seemed most imminent, and evacuated all his wounded with the least possible delay. In the words of the official report on his behaviour: "His cheerfulness and courage were a splendid example to his platoon."

Private Withey, too, earned similar commendation for his behaviour when Private W. Purves, a linesman, fell wounded in the open while repairing a broken wire. Private Withey, who saw Purves fall, left the shelter of the front line trench and, crawling under heavy fire to where the injured man lay, dressed his wounds and carried him to the nearest shell hole. By this time, fire was intense and return to the Battalion trenches was impossible. The shell hole where Withey crouched, with Purves in his arms, was waist deep in water, but for hours no opportunity to move was afforded. At last, when darkness had fallen, the stretcher-bearer and the man he had attended so bravely reached the shelter of the front line trench. Private Purves died soon thereafter; but Withey, though destined to fall eventually in action, suffered no injury at the time and lived to receive the Distinguished Conduct Medal awarded for his courageous work.

Tribute to Private Withey, who won distinction in the manner described above, is paid as follows in a letter written by an officer under whom he served: "I consider Withey's daily work deserving of special mention. He was not a young man, as you may remember, but over and again, when marching back after a hard tour in the line, I would find him plodding along at the rear of the platoon, carrying his own equipment and the bandoliers, or machine-gun ammunition, of men whom he felt were more weary than himself. Then again, when we reached billets, no matter how tired he was, he would go from man to man, checking up on the condition of their feet, and always willing to rub the feet of any man the mud, or tight boots, had affected. I consider that his work was of real benefit to the Battalion, and I can speak of the very genuine respect with which the privates regarded him. Behind their backs, officers might receive scant deference, but this stretcher-bearer was always referred to as 'Mr. Withey', the distinction being respectfully used and reflecting truthfully the measure of regard he commanded."

III

After the sharp actions in the line on April 11, 1918, the 24th Battalion was relieved on the night of April 12th. No incident marked the relief, which was completed at 12.15 o'clock on the morning of the 13th, the Battalion thereafter moving back to Wailly Huts, whence, after three days in reserve, it advanced once more and took over from the 20th Canadian Battalion the centre subsection of the front line.

As a whole, the 4-day tour that followed was uneventful. Patrols covered the front each night, but returned, in the words of the Battalion Diary, with "nothing to report." Probably the only incident that distinguished the tour from others in the same area occurred on April

19th when, at 3.30 o'clock in the morning, four soldiers of the 51st (Highland) Division, who had escaped from the German lines, were brought in by a 24th Battalion listening post. The Highlanders reported harsh treatment by the Germans, and were greatly relieved to reach the Canadian lines. After food and a hot drink had been given to them they were despatched as soon as possible to the rear.

On the day following, the 24th Battalion was relieved in the line by the 22nd Canadian Battalion and moved back to positions in the Purple and Intermediate Lines, proceeding thence on April 24th and taking over Divisional Reserve billets in Wailly Huts. Five days were spent in Divisional Reserve, the Battalion then advancing, with a trench strength of 26 officers and 570 other ranks, and relieving the 19th Canadian Battalion in the right sub-sector of the front line. Shelling west of the Arras-Bapaume Road was heavy during the relief, the Battalion encountering barrage fire at one point and suffering the loss of 1 other rank killed and 5 other ranks wounded.

Throughout the tour that followed, enemy artillery was active and German planes frequently bombed the Battalion front, a measure of revenge for the aerial attacks being obtained on one occasion when a Lewis gun of the 24th fired on a German plane and forced it down. This incident occurred on May 3rd, two days after Battalion Headquarters had been visited by Lieut.-General Sir Aylmer Haldane, K.C.B., who commanded the British VI Corps, to which the 2nd Canadian Division was at the time attached.

On completion of a 4-day tour in the front line, the 24th Battalion withdrew on the night of May 3rd to right support in Telegraph Hill Switch, whence strong parties were provided on subsequent days for work under the direction of the 6th Field Company, Canadian Engineers, and smaller parties for work on road construction under officers of the 18th and 20th Batteries, Canadian Field Artillery. At the time when the working parties were thus engaged, Lieut. W. A. Fowler reported to the Rear Details to act as Battalion Paymaster; and two non-commissioned officers, Coy. Sergt.-Major K. C. McIntyre and Coy. Sergt.-Major E. T. Lane, left the unit to study for commissions in England.

After six days in support in Telegraph Hill Switch, the Battalion proceeded to huts in Bretencourt on May 9th and there remained until May 15th, when it advanced and, without casualties, relieved the 20th Canadian Battalion in support in the Intermediate Line and Mercatel Switch. On the day of the move, Capt. G. L. Jepson, M.C., relinquished his post as Battalion Medical Officer and proceeded to duty with No. 3 Canadian General Hospital (McGill), being succeeded by Capt. R. B. Jenkins. Two days later, the Battalion strength was increased when Lieuts. D. A. Ewan and F. W. Stenson, both former officers of the unit who had recovered from wounds, reported for duty from England with a draft of 39 other ranks, a number of whom had also seen previous service with the Victoria Rifles in France.

On May 22nd, the Battalion, with a trench strength of 24 officers and 608 other ranks, moved forward from Mercatel Switch and, at 11.45 p.m., relieved the 25th Canadian Battalion in the left sub-section of the Mercatel front line. Raiding was a feature of the front at this time, and the Battalion scouts, under Lieut. J. L. Cains, sought in No Man's Land information on which plans for a successful foray into the German lines could be based.

As a result of reconnaissances on three successive nights, Lieut. Cains reported that enemy posts at a point just beyond the Arras-Bapaume Road presented an opportunity for a raid with excellent chances of success. Lieut.-Col. Clark-Kennedy, Major Bales, Major Hall, and senior officers of the Battalion studied the report with care and agreed that the possibility of a striking success existed. Accordingly, Lieut. Cains was instructed to complete plans for the operation and to carry these out on the early morning of May 26th.

Obeying these orders, Lieut. Cains arranged that two parties, each composed of 1 officer and 14 other ranks, should carry out the actual assault, he commanding and leading the party on the left and Lieut. G. V. O'Gorman the party on the right. These parties were to be protected respectively by covering parties, each composed of 10 other ranks with a Lewis gun, the left party to be commanded by Sergt. J. Goneau and the right party by Lieut. J. J. Kavanagh, M.C.

Leaving the Battalion lines at 11.20 o'clock on the night of May 25th, the attacking and covering parties assembled in accordance with the prearranged plan, the movement being carried out in silence and with success, despite the unforeseen obstacle presented by three rows of concertina barbed wire, which, in the previous 24 hours, the enemy had placed in position. No British artillery was firing at this time, as it had been agreed that the raiders should operate without barrage assistance.

At 12.16 o'clock on the morning of May 26th, the raiders jumped off from their assembly positions, shot 2 Germans in an enemy listening post, killed 1 and captured 3 in a post ten yards further on, and, sweeping forward, plunged into the main German position, where a garrison of approximately 15 members of the 161st German Regiment, 185th Division, was attacked and destroyed before serious opposition could be offered. An enemy machine-gun, which a crew attempted to serve, was also bombed and destroyed completely.

After eleven minutes in the enemy lines, the raiding parties of the 24th Battalion withdrew to their own trenches, escorting the prisoners they had captured, two of whom wore the ribbon of the German Iron Cross. The enemy barrage had fallen in No Man's Land by this time, but it struck with no great weight and the Victoria Riflemen, evading it successfully, reported to Lieut.-Col. Clark-Kennedy that their mission had been completed, with casualties in their own force totalling only 2 other ranks slightly wounded. For his outstanding part in the conduct of this successful operation, Lieut. Cains received the congratulations of all ranks in the Battalion and, from the King, the award of the Military Cross.

In retaliation, perhaps, for the losses inflicted on the enemy infantry in the raid, German artillery was active on May 26th, killing 1 man of the Battalion and wounding 10. British artillery also opened frequently on the enemy lines, a shoot in which success was observed occurring at 7 p.m., when parties of the enemy in marching order were dispersed by concentrated fire.

Dissatisfied with the results of the artillery duels, the Germans bombarded the front and support lines at 5 o'clock on the morning of May 27th and then, at 6 a.m., sent forward two parties, each approximately 45 strong, to raid the Battalion trenches. The parties approached determinedly, and simultaneously a supporting party, about 200 strong, moved forward from positions in the German rear, presumably to exploit any success the attacking parties might achieve. No opportunity for exploitation, however, was afforded. All three parties were subjected to heavy fire from rifles, rifle-grenades, machine-guns, or artillery, and retreated, leaving a number of dead or wounded in their wake.

For the remainder of the day, German artillery maintained a desultory fire on the Battalion's front line and support trenches, this shelling increasing in volume on May 28th, when Canadian troops to the Battalion's right raided the German front. As a whole, the German fire was accurate and casualties mounted accordingly, the number for the tour, when the Battalion was relieved that night, having reached a total of 7 other ranks killed and 37 wounded.

After relief on the night of May 28th, the Battalion marched back to huts in Wailly Woods, where, on May 30th, all Roman Catholics in the unit were addressed by Bishop Fallon, of London, Ontario. Training continued on the days following, a special feature occurring on June 1st, when an aeroplane flew at heights varying from 500 to 3,000 feet, the pilot signalling his altitude by coloured flares, so that the infantry might learn to estimate when machine-gun fire against aeroplanes would, or would not, be effective.

Soon after reaching Wailly Wood, all ranks in the Battalion were pleased when, in the honours list published on the birthday of His Majesty the King, Lieut.-Col. W. H. Clark-Kennedy, D.S.O., was appointed a Companion of the Order of St. Michael and St. George; and the Battalion Chaplain, Hon. Capt. C. J. S. Stuart, received a Mention in Despatches. Recognition of the work accomplished by other ranks was afforded some days later by awards of a number of Distinguished Conduct Medals and Military Medals.

Even before the last of these awards had been announced, the Battalion, on the evening of June 3rd, had relieved the 20th Battalion in the right sub-section of the Neuville Vitasse front line, two casualties as the unit marched in bringing the trench strength of the Battalion to 25 officers and 573 other ranks. This force, without suffering further loss, completed the relief at 12.40 a.m.

Three days after taking over the front, the Battalion welcomed Lieut.-Col. Lord Kensington and 5 officers of the 24th Welsh Regiment, who were attached for instruction. Lord Kensington and his officers had arrived on the Western Front after long service in Palestine and were anxious to know all details of how trench warfare in France was conducted. The Victoria Riflemen, in turn, were deeply interested to hear of battles in circumstances and surroundings widely different from any within the range of their own experience.

Less than 48 hours after the officers from Palestine reported, the Battalion front became the scene of pronounced activity when, at 9.45 p.m. on June 8th, the enemy barraged the forward area and soon thereafter drove a raid against the Canadian battalion to the left. No attack on the Victoria Rifles' front occurred, but as a result of the heavy shelling used to cover the raid, 1 other rank was killed and Lieut. E. Motton, Lieut. H. S. Johnson, and 9 other ranks were wounded.

Following the activity in the line on June 8th, the Battalion remained in position until midnight on June 9th and then moved back to support in the Intermediate Line. From this position, 8 officers and 216 other ranks moved on June 10th to carry gas projectors into the forward area, a party of 2 officers and 110 other ranks proceeding simultaneously to dig a communication trench to the right front line. Shelling was encountered by these parties, also by a digging party of 5 officers and 220 other ranks, furnished on June 14th, but for the most part the enemy fire struck to the right, or left, and casualties in the Battalion were avoided.

After completing a 6-day tour in the Intermediate Line, the Battalion marched to Bretencourt and there trained until June 21st, when the unit moved up once more and relieved the 18th Canadian Battalion in support.

Working parties of approximately 9 officers and 325 other ranks were furnished on the two nights that followed and parties almost as strong on the nights of June 24th and 25th. On the 26th, the Battalion, under Major P. L. Hall, M.C., who was in command during the absence on leave of Lieut.-Col. W. H. Clark-Kennedy, moved at 9.30 p.m. and at 11.50 o'clock completed relief of the 25th Battalion in the left sub-section of the front line.

Taken as a whole, the tour in the front line that followed was devoid of outstanding incident. Patrols of the Battalion, under Lieut. A. Findlay, D.C.M., M.M., who a few weeks previously had been granted a commission in the field, were active and brought in valuable reports concerning the conditions prevailing in No Man's Land and the position of enemy machine-gun posts. They also reported one night that enemy transport was in motion on the Neuville Vitasse-Henin Road. Artillery fire was thereupon concentrated on the road, apparently with success, for shouting was heard and the sound of limbers attempting desperately to escape.

On completion of the tour in the line, the Battalion was relieved on June 30th by the 2nd Canadian Mounted Rifles, and moved back to huts in Wailly, whence, on July 1st, 200 men were conveyed by bus to attend the Canadian Corps Sports at Tinques. At 4 o'clock that afternoon, the main body of the Battalion handed over their huts to the 43rd Canadian Battalion, under Lieut.-Col. H. M. Urquhart, D.S.O., and moved to a field nearby. At 7 p.m., the Battalion marched to Bridgewater Siding, there entrained on a light railway, proceeded to Lattre St. Quentin, and thence to billets in Beaufort and Blaincourt.

These moves marked the return of the 2nd Canadian Division to service with the Canadian Corps, which, at the time, lay in G.H.Q. Reserve. For three months the Division had served in the VI Corps of the Third British Army, there adding to the fighting reputation which all units of the Canadian Corps cherished and maintained. Lieut.-General Sir Aylmer Haldane, G.O.C. the VI Corps, wrote to express appreciation of the distinguished service the Division had rendered under his command;

and General Sir Julian Byng, the Third Army Commander, placed on record his satisfaction with the Division's work in the following terms: "I can only hope that they are as proud of their work as I was of again having them under my command."

IV

For the first thirteen days of July, 1918, the 24th Battalion remained in billets, carrying out a syllabus of training, participated in by Lieuts. G. H. Macario and P. G. Tucker, former non-commissioned officers of the unit, who reported for duty on July 3rd; and by Lieuts. W. McMurray, E. V. Power, and T. Redpath, who reported one day later. Sports featured this period; also a competition in which the brass band of the Battalion won the championship of the 5th Brigade. Another incident of the period occurred on July 2nd, when two senior officers of the unit were invited to Divisional Headquarters to dine with the Prime Minister of Canada, the Right Honourable Sir Robert Borden.

After training for thirteen days, the Battalion paraded in Beaufort on July 14th, under command of Lieut.-Col. W. H. Clark-Kennedy, who had returned from leave, and proceeded to Lattre St. Quentin. Near Avesnes le Comte, Lieut.-General Sir Arthur Currie, accompanied by a group of senior officers of the Overseas Military Forces of Canada, took the salute, the Battalion marching past in a manner and with an appearance which clearly revealed its marked efficiency and high order of discipline.

At Lattre St. Quentin, the Victoria Rifles resumed the training begun at Beaufort, continuing their work, until, in the last days of July, orders were received for a move to an unnamed destination. No one knew what the orders boded; but, to a man, the Corps believed that action was imminent. The German Army had attacked throughout the spring and early summer; the British Army's time to attack had come.

CHAPTER XIII

THE BATTLE OF AMIENS

I

On July 4, 1918, when Australian troops of the Fourth British Army attacked the enemy at Hamel, the Army Commander, General Sir Henry Rawlinson, was deeply impressed by the failure of the German forces opposed to him to launch the determined counter-attacks he had expected. From the manner in which the enemy accepted defeat in this minor action, he became convinced that operations on a larger scale might yield correspondingly satisfactory results. Accordingly, on July 18th, the day when French and American troops were counter-attacking successfully on the Rheims front and driving the enemy back in confusion from the Marne, he approached Sir Douglas Haig and suggested that, if the Canadian Corps were used to lead the assault, he believed that a highly successful blow could be delivered against the nose of the salient created by the German drive at Amiens in the previous March and April.

Explanation of the Fourth Army Commander's desire for the Canadian Corps to form the spear-head of the proposed attack lay in the fact that the Corps, at this time, was undoubtedly the most powerful striking force on the Western Front. Organized under Lieut.-General Sir E. A. H. Alderson, the Corps had developed remarkably under the skilled leadership of Lieut.-General the Honourable Sir Julian Byng, and, under Lieut.-General Sir Arthur Currie, had attained the outstanding position of 1918. In contrast to the divisions of the Imperial Army, which, owing to shortage of reinforcements, had been reduced from a 12-battalion to a 9-battalion basis, the four divisions of the Canadian Corps had been maintained at full strength; five divisional artilleries supported the infantry in action; and many highly effective auxiliary units served under the Corps' command. The formation was experienced in attack, and had suffered little in the awful fighting of the spring and early summer, its splendid strength, despite severe temptation, having been preserved from dissipation in defensive fighting against the inevitable day when the British Army should resume the attack.

To Sir Henry Rawlinson's suggestion that the Corps be now used to lead an attack by the Fourth Army at Amiens, Sir Douglas Haig gave immediate assent, the proposal corresponding in its main outlines with plans upon which the Commander-in-Chief had already decided. Success of the French counter-attack on July 18th confirmed the belief that the time for a major offensive had come, and a detailed plan for the British attack at Amiens was drawn up without delay.

In this plan complete secrecy was an important factor, surprise being an element which, it was hoped, would contribute greatly to overwhelming success. Infinite pains, accordingly, were taken to conceal from the enemy a concentration of 11 infantry divisions, 3 cavalry divisions, 2,000 guns, and 400 tanks, and to convince the German Commanders that the Canadian Corps, which they had cause to fear, was moving into the British line at Mont Kemmel.

Through the loyal co-operation of all ranks in the attacking forces, the Germans were deceived, and on the night of August 9th, thirty-six hours after the battle had begun, Sir Henry Rawlinson was able to note in his diary "two splendid days" of victory, unequalled up to that time in the whole history of Allied fighting on the Western Front. Substantiation of General Rawlinson's entry is found in records from the enemy's side of the line, for General Ludendorff has written that "August 8th was the black day of the German Army in the history of this war."

Continuing the attack, after the opening assault on August 8th, the British forces made further progress, but Sir Arthur Currie and the commanders of the other corps engaged reported that resistance on their respective fronts showed a definite inclination to stiffen. Despite these reports, Marshal Foch instructed Sir Douglas Haig to drive forward and, if possible, to push the enemy back across the famous battlefields of the Somme, a country seamed with old trenches, wherein machine-gun nests abounded and heavy losses to an attacking force would be unavoidable.

Impressed by these considerations, Sir Douglas Haig sought to dissuade Marshal Foch from the plan suggested and to induce him to authorize attack at some point where substantial success at infinitely lower cost might reasonably be expected. By August 14th, 22,000 prisoners, 400 guns, and approximately 2,000 machine-guns had been captured; the Paris-Amiens railway had been freed from German threat; the junction of the French and British Armies had been made secure; the enemy had been thrown back to his Roye-Chaulnes line of 1916; and the great German railway junction at Chaulnes had been brought within range of Allied gunfire. All this had been accomplished with casualties less than the total of German prisoners; and the British Commander-in-Chief was satisfied that no further action on this front was advisable.

Still more profound would Sir Douglas Haig's satisfaction have been could he have known how severely the drive forward of the British troops had shaken the confidence of the leaders of the German forces in the field. On August 14th, the Crown Council of Germany, under the presidency of the Emperor, met at German Great Headquarters and received from General Ludendorff a statement that diplomatic overtures for peace must be inaugurated without a moment's unnecessary delay. Defeat of the Allies was no longer to be hoped for; but military defeat by the Allies had loomed as a danger which prompt and skilful diplomatic intervention alone could avert.

Unaware of the proceedings of the German Crown Council, but with the belief forming in his mind that the Allies' day of reckoning with Germany was approaching, Sir Douglas Haig laid careful plans for further action. At first Marshal Foch objected to the operations the British Commander-in-Chief proposed, but, as will be seen in subsequent chapters of this book, he finally agreed, with the result that the Canadian Corps, before August ended, was withdrawn from the Amiens front to serve again as the spear-head of a British offensive at Arras.

II

In the Battle of Amiens on August 8, 1918, and the days immediately following, the 24th Battalion, Victoria Rifles of Canada, took an important part. On July 30th, at 6.45 p.m., the men marched from Lattre St. Quentin to a point between Hauteville and Fosseux, where busses awaited them. Boarding the busses at 8.30 o'clock, the Victoria Riflemen travelled throughout the night, reaching Briquemesnil at 5.30 a.m. on July 31st and proceeding to bivouac in a field between Briquemesnil and Floxicourt. That night, at 9.45 o'clock, the Battalion left its bivouacs and, marching for approximately three hours, arrived early in the morning on August 1st in billets at Picquigny, where, on August 2nd, the companies, under the eyes of the Corps and Brigade Commanders, carried out a series of practice attacks in co-operation with British tanks.

At 10 p.m. on the following day, the Battalion marched from Picquigny to billets in the grounds of an old chateau at Guignemicourt, where, on August 4th, the unit welcomed Brigadier-General J. A. Gunn, C.M.G., D.S.O., its original Commanding Officer, who was visiting the front in France after a period of service in England. Proceeding from Guignemicourt that night at 7 o'clock, the Battalion marched to Cagny and, at 2.30 o'clock on the morning of August 5th, bivouacked in a wood a quarter mile to the south.

Marching again at 9 o'clock that night, the Battalion advanced in pouring rain and, despite traffic which often forced the men off the roads into the mud-filled ditches at the side, reached its destination on the west edge of Bois de l'Abbé at 2.30 a.m. on August 6th. It was a hard and trying march, and progress in formation was often impossible, but at the cross-roads beyond Gentelles all stray parties were united and directed to the Bois de l'Abbé position, one mile north of the town.

Here the Battalion received Operation Order No. 247 from Headquarters of the 5th Canadian Infantry Brigade, with details of the engagement that now lay immediately ahead and of the duties therein that the divisions, brigades, and battalions of the Canadian Corps would be called upon to perform. In substance, the Brigade's orders and instructions were:

(1) *Information*—The Canadian Corps, in conjunction with troops on the right and left, is attacking the enemy's position between the Amiens-Roye Road and the Villers Bretonneux-Chaulnes Railway (both inclusive) at an hour and date to be notified later.
The 2nd Canadian Division will attack as the left division of the Corps.
The 1st Canadian Division will attack on the 2nd Canadian Division's right; and the 2nd Australian Division will attack on the left. The 5th Australian Division will pass through the 2nd Australian Division in the 1st Objective and continue the attack to the 2nd and 3rd Objectives.
The 3rd Cavalry Division, and probably one other cavalry division, will advance behind the 2nd Canadian Division.

(2) *Intention*—The 2nd Canadian Division will attack within the boundaries and to the objectives shown on the map issued to the battalions on August 3rd.
The 5th Canadian Infantry Brigade will attack to the Red Line, and consolidate that line.

(3) *Duties of 5th Brigade Battalions*—The 26th Canadian Battalion will attack on the right, and the 24th Battalion, Victoria Rifles of Canada, will attack on the left.
These battalions will go through to their forward objective and will not pause to systematically mop up frontage or battery positions.
The 25th Canadian Battalion will follow 500 yards in rear of the 26th and 24th Canadian Battalions, with one company behind the 26th Canadian Battalion and three companies behind the 24th Canadian Battalion. They will push straight through to the

eastern edge of Guillaucourt and the valley to the south. They will be responsible for the mopping up of Guillaucourt. The 24th Battalion will detail a special force to advance to the 3rd Objective and consolidate in conjunction with the division on our left.

The 22nd Canadian Battalion will follow 500 yards in rear of the 25th Canadian Battalion, on a two-company frontage, and will be responsible for the mopping-up of Wiencourt and battery positions to the south of Wiencourt.

(4) *Support*—The attack of the 5th Canadian Infantry Brigade will be supported by 2 companies of the 14th Tank Battalion, 2 mobile brigades of the 2nd Canadian Divisional Artillery, 2 mobile Newton trench mortars, and 1 company of the 2nd Battalion, Canadian Machine-Gun Corps.

(5) *Assembly*—At zero hour the 5th Canadian Infantry Brigade, and attached troops, will be assembled. Detailed instructions regarding the assembly will be issued later.

(6) *The Attack*—The 4th Canadian Infantry Brigade will capture Marcelcave (the Green Line). The 5th Canadian Infantry Brigade will then pass through the 4th Canadian Infantry Brigade, will capture Wiencourt and Guillaucourt and will consolidate 1,500 yards beyond (the Red Line).

(7) *Liaison*—Major C. G. Porter, D.S.O., of the 26th Canadian Battalion, will report for liaison duty to the 1st Canadian Infantry Brigade on the right.
Major P. L. Hall, M.C., of the 24th Canadian Battalion, will report for similar duty to the 15th Australian Infantry Brigade on the left.

All day on August 7th, the 24th Battalion remained in position on the edge of the Bois de l'Abbé, north of Gentelles. It was clear that the Battle of Amiens was soon to open and eventually orders arrived stating that the zero hour of the attack had been placed at 4.20 a.m. on August 8th.

Even before these orders were received, an officer from the Australian unit which was to operate on the 24th Battalion's left flank had visited Lieut.-Col. Clark-Kennedy's Headquarters and discussed how liaison between the two battalions might best be maintained. As a railway line formed the inter-battalion boundary, it was arranged that a platoon of each battalion should operate on the side away from its own unit, thus interlocking the two forces securely. The Australian officer favoured the plan, but was uneasy lest the Canadian troops, with whom he had never previously co-operated, should not maintain the speed of advance which the Australians would set. Lieut.-Col. Clark-Kennedy assured him that the Canadians had no thought of advancing slowly, and suggested that the 24th Battalion would be willing to race to the final objective and would promise the Australian unit a stiff competition from the moment of jumping off until the final objective was captured and held. Well pleased with this suggestion, the Australian officer returned to his own unit, which, in the ensuing engagement, raced the 24th Battalion as agreed, and lost a close contest only when heavy German machine-gun fire delayed its forward drive a few minutes more than had been expected.

Meanwhile, at 9.45 o'clock on the night of August 7th, the 24th Battalion had marched to its jumping-off position in front of Villers-Bretonneux. Some shelling occurred as the unit advanced and 7 other ranks were wounded, but by midnight the Battalion had reached its destination and stood ready for action. At 3.10 a.m. on August 8th, Major Hall notified 5th Brigade Headquarters that the attacking troops of the 15th Australian Brigade on the left were in position, ready to go, and that all on the Australian front was quiet. Quiet prevailed on the Canadian front, too, the enemy apparently being unaware of the storm that in another hour would sound the knell of German military victory.

Sharp at 4.20 o'clock, the British guns opened their barrage and the infantry of the first attacking waves moved simultaneously from their trenches. For an hour, as the 4th Canadian Brigade drove forward, the 24th Battalion, Victoria Rifles of Canada, remained in position, then, with the 26th Canadian Battalion moving at the same time, the unit advanced to its final jumping-off point in the Green Line near Marcelcave. A mist lay heavily over the area and some parties of the Battalion lost their way. All, however, discovered their error before harm had resulted and reached their destinations safely, a number being picked up by Lieut. A. Findlay, D.C.M., M.M., and guided by compass to the positions they were seeking.

By 7.45 o'clock, when the 4th Canadian Infantry Brigade reported the capture of its final objective, the 24th Battalion had formed up and was ready to carry the attack forward. In the front line of the Battalion's formation were "B" and "D" Companies, commanded respectively by Capt. V. E. Duclos and Capt. P. I. Walker, M.C., who were experienced in leading the waves of an assault and could be relied upon to permit no surmountable obstacle to hold the attack from its final objectives. In support of the front line companies were "C" and "A" Companies, under Lieut. K. S. Drummond, M.C., and Capt. J. D. MacIntyre. These officers, too, had served with distinction in many of the Battalion's previous engagements, their courage and proved ability giving assurance that failure in the forthcoming attack would not accrue through faulty leadership of the supporting companies.

At 8.20 a.m., with Lieut.-Col. W. H. Clark-Kennedy leading, the Battalion advanced from the Green Line and, leaving the 4th Brigade to consolidate, drove the Canadian attack deeper and deeper into the enemy lines. Reaching Pierret Wood, sharp opposition was encountered from a number of enemy machine-gun posts, but, with the assistance of a supporting tank, the German garrisons were soon overcome and the Battalion, sweeping forward without serious losses, overwhelmed a number of German battery positions, capturing four 4.2-inch howitzers, two 5.9-inch guns, several anti-tank guns, and a substantial batch of German prisoners.

By 8.50 a.m., the Battalion had driven its way through Pierret Wood and was approaching Wiencourt. Some fighting in this village occurred, but the Germans had been dismayed by the speed of the Canadian advance and, as a whole, fought less stubbornly than usual, surrendering frequently when the leading waves of the Battalion's attack approached, or when a supporting tank lurched forward and threatened to crush on top of them the bricks and mortar of the houses wherein they lurked.

By 9.20 o'clock, Wiencourt was definitely in 24th Battalion hands and the forward companies were attacking Guillaucourt. Opposition in this village was severe and the Battalion lost heavily in the house-to-house and hand-to-hand fighting, but the unit would brook no denial and by 9.50 o'clock the Germans had been defeated. A number of them, including an officer and 25 other ranks, attacked in Guillaucourt Chateau by Lieut. Findlay and 5 scouts, were captured and despatched to the Canadian rear.

Soon after the capture of Guillaucourt, enemy resistance stiffened appreciably, and in the 1,500-yard advance from the village to the final objective, the Battalion suffered severely, particularly by fire from a small quarry and a nearby wood, which the Germans defended stubbornly and well. It was in this stage of the operation that the Battalion lost four gallant and capable officers when Lieut. K. S. Drummond, M.C., who had returned to duty though only half recovered from a grievous wound, Lieut. J. J. Kavanagh, M.C., Lieut. E. V. Power, and Lieut. R. B. Hingston were killed, while leading their men determinedly against the Battalion's final objective. When less than a hundred yards from the objective, Lieut. A. Findlay, D.C.M., M.M., was also struck by a shot from a German sniper which wounded him severely in the chest and arm.

Despite the loss of these officers, and of Lieut. H. G. Macario, who was also wounded, the Battalion drove steadily forward to its final objective, the Red Line. This position was reached and captured on scheduled time, excellent work at this stage being accomplished by Lieut. F. S. Leach, who had succeeded Lieut. Drummond in command of "C" Coy., and by Company Sergt.-Major G. W. Croll. Opposition was fierce as the Battalion fought its way into the Red Line, and cavalry, which came up from the rear to exploit the infantry's success, could make little progress. The horsemen rode through the 24th Battalion lines and attempted to gallop out "into the blue," but machine-gun fire was intense and the effort was checked abruptly, the survivors being forced to dismount and establish themselves a short distance in front of the Red Line. That night the cavalrymen were relieved in their positions when troops of the 6th Canadian Infantry Brigade passed through the Red Line and carried the Canadian attack forward.

When the 6th Brigade had passed through the Red Line and the 24th Battalion had an opportunity to check the statistics of its gains and losses, returns showed that, in addition to the officers whose names have been mentioned, casualties amongst the other ranks totalled 27 killed, 4 missing, presumed killed, and 152 wounded. In relation to the results achieved, this loss was not severe, though it included the death or wounding of a number of men whose faithful service and devotion to duty had marked them for promotion to commissioned rank as soon as vacancies in the officer establishment should occur.

After spending the afternoon and night of August 8th in position in the Red Line, the 24th Battalion, Victoria Rifles of Canada, received orders from the 5th Canadian Infantry Brigade to take part in a further attack by the 2nd Canadian Division on the morning of August 9th. At 8.15 a.m., Major A. L. Walker, D.S.O., an original officer of the Battalion, who at this time was serving as Brigade Major, issued verbal orders for the operation that was to follow. The 5th Brigade, he said, was to move into the 2nd Brigade area and to attack, through the 2nd Brigade, in co-operation with the 6th Brigade, which was to attack on the left half of the 2nd Canadian Divisional front. The 22nd and 25th Canadian Battalions were ordered to assemble forthwith in rear of the Amiens Defence Line, immediately east of Caix, and to attack at 11 a.m., with the 24th Battalion, Victoria Rifles of Canada, in support and the 26th Canadian Battalion in reserve.

On receipt of these orders, which Major Walker delivered on behalf of Brigadier-General J. M. Ross, Lieut.-Col. Clark-Kennedy ordered his companies to move to the assembly area forthwith. They moved at once, but, before reaching their destination, were notified that the hour set for their advance in support had been changed and now stood at 1 p.m. No notice of this change, it would seem, reached the 6th Brigade, which attacked at 11 a.m. The left company of the 22nd Battalion moved forward 45 minutes later to protect the 6th Brigade's exposed flank, the right company of the 22nd Battalion and the attacking companies of the 25th Battalion following at 12.30 p.m.

Half an hour after the attacking waves of the 25th Battalion had advanced, the 24th Battalion moved forward in support. The attacking formations encountered stiff machine-gun opposition throughout the operation, particularly in the village of Vrély, which was stormed by the 22nd Battalion, with "C" Coy. of the 24th Battalion co-operating. The remaining companies, arriving some time later, carried out the duty of mopping-up. Proceeding forward from Vrély, many machine-gun posts were out-manoeuvred and captured, some by tanks, which joined in the assault at this time, and some by direct action of the infantry. After clearing these posts from their path, the troops of the 5th Brigade pushed forward rapidly and reached Meharicourt at approximately 5 p.m. Sharp opposition was encountered near Meharicourt, but the German defences were eventually overwhelmed and by 5.30 p.m. the Brigade had penetrated through the village to a line some 500 yards beyond. At this point the attack of the 22nd and 25th Battalions was halted, as it had outstripped the advance on both flanks.

Though the infantry halted, an effort was made by the British cavalry to drive the attack still deeper into the enemy lines. Forming up in rear of the 24th Battalion's positions near Meharicourt, the horsemen flashed their swords and charged gallantly forward. It was an impressive sight, which all who witnessed it will ever remember, but it was not a military success. Caught in a concentration of enemy machine-gun fire, horses and riders were shot down and little was gained of permanent advantage.

After witnessing the magnificent charge and the heartbreaking repulse of the cavalry, the men of the 24th Battalion settled in their support positions to the north

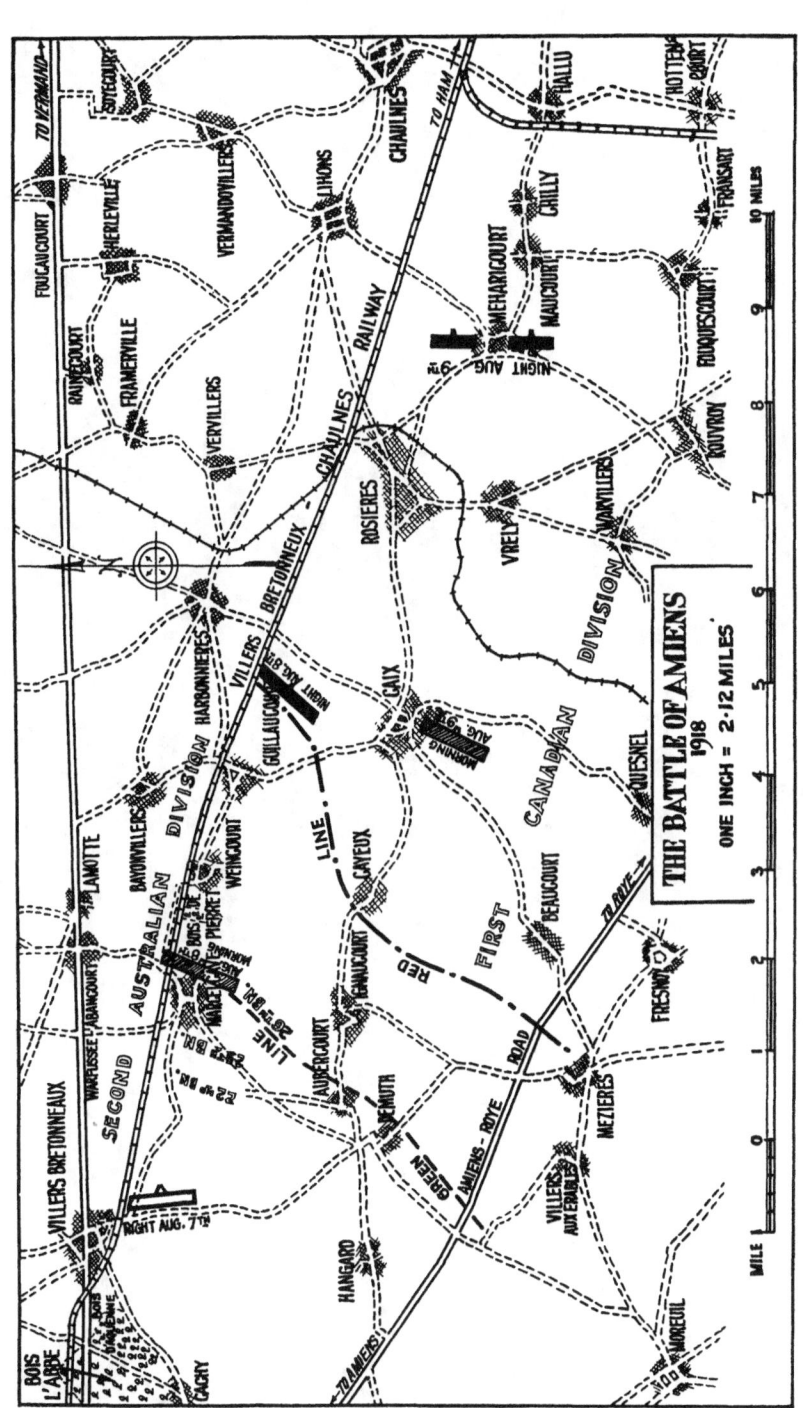

and south of Meharicourt and, for the second time in as many days, checked their roll of killed and wounded, the process receiving a strange interruption on "A" Coy.'s front when a German soldier, who had lost his way, rode into the Canadian lines on a bicycle. No officers of the 24th Battalion had fallen, it was found, but 12 other ranks had been killed and 47 wounded. The Battalion had also lost an original member through the death at Brigade Headquarters of Major A. L. Walker, D.S.O., who was killed by a shell, which also wounded Brigadier-General J. M. Ross and killed or wounded a number of his Staff. On receipt of the news that Brigadier-General Ross had been wounded, Lieut.-Col. T. L. Tremblay, of the 22nd Battalion, assumed command of the 5th Brigade.

By this time, the extent of the British victory was becoming apparent, and some impression of the whole may be gained from the 2nd Canadian Divisional Narrative, which states that between August 8th and 11th the Division advanced approximately 18,000 yards, captured 6 villages, defeated 4 German divisions (the 41st, 109th, 117th and 225th), captured 57 officers and 1,589 other ranks, and buried more than 1,000 enemy dead. All this had been accomplished with dead in the Division totalling 29 officers and 345 other ranks; and an aggregate of 88 officers and 1,990 other ranks wounded. For the whole Battle of Amiens, the Division's grand total of casualties, killed, wounded, and missing, is stated to have been 130 officers and 2,643 men.

So far as the 24th Battalion is concerned, few of the casualties in the 2nd Canadian Division's summary were incurred after August 9th; though on the 10th, as the Battalion maintained its positions to the north and south of Meharicourt, shell fire became heavy at one time, killing 8 other ranks and wounding 5. Lieut. G. W. Jones, an original member of the Battalion, who had received a commission after service in the unit's ranks in France, and Lieut. J. L. Cains, who had received his Military Cross for leadership in the Battalion's successful raid in the Mercatel Sector, were also wounded.

Following the shell fire on August 10th, the Battalion stood fast in position until the night of August 11th and then moved to positions about 500 yards east of Vrély.

In these trenches, the whole Battalion remained until the night of August 14th, when "C" Coy., under Capt. R. H. Lamb, moved forward to near Chilly, in close support to the 25th Canadian Battalion, and with the additional duty of selecting jumping-off positions for an attack in which the 24th Battalion was to participate. Little prospect for a successful attack could be found by Capt. Lamb, or by Major Hall and Lieuts. Stenson, Grenough, Matheson, Johnson, and McMurray, who carried out careful reconnaissances, only to discover that heavy belts of barbed wire would be met before the advance could proceed far, also a great ditch, which would present a serious obstacle. In these circumstances, all with knowledge of the situation were profoundly relieved on August 15th when the proposed attack was cancelled. Following the cancellation, "C" Coy., which had suffered some losses from low-flying German aeroplanes, was ordered to rejoin the main body of the Battalion, which had advanced to trenches in front of Meharicourt.

Following a trail marked by tapes previously placed in position, the men of "C" Coy. marched back as ordered on the night of August 15th. Some shelling harassed the move, but no serious losses were inflicted, nor were any incurred up to the early morning of August 18th, when the Battalion was relieved by the 75th Canadian Battalion and marched back to a wood one mile north-east of Caix. From this position, on the night of August 19th, the unit marched to bivouacs in the Bois de Blangy.

When the unit reached Blangy Wood and bivouacked, at 4.30 o'clock on the morning of August 20th, its part in the striking British success at Amiens stood completed. On August 20th, the 2nd Canadian Division was transferred from the Canadian Corps to the XXII British Corps, but before the month ended it had returned to Sir Arthur Currie's command and, under his leadership, had gained great honour in heavy fighting at Arras.

Even before the transfer to the Arras front, the troops had been gratified by a Special Order, dated August 13, 1918, in which the Corps Commander, Lieut.-General Sir A. W. Currie, K.C.B., K.C.M.G., paid tribute to the work they had accomplished. In this Special Order, the Corps Commander said:

"The first stage of this Battle of Amiens is over, and one of the most successful operations conducted by the Allied Armies since the war began is now a matter of history.

"The Canadian Corps has every right to feel more than proud of the part it played. To move the Corps from the Arras front and in less than a week to launch it in battle—was in itself a splendid performance. Yet the splendour of that performance pales into insignificance when compared with what has been accomplished since zero hour on August 8th.

"On that date the Canadian Corps, to which were attached the 3rd Cavalry Division, the 4th Tank Brigade, and the 5th Squadron, R.A.F., attacked on a front of 7,500 yards. After a penetration of 22,000 yards, the line to-night rests on a 10,000 yards frontage. Sixteen German divisions have been identified, of which 4 have been completely routed. Nearly 150 guns have been captured, while over 1,000 machine-guns have fallen into our hands. Ten thousand prisoners have passed through our cages and casualty clearing stations, a number greatly in excess of our total casualties. Twenty-five towns and villages have been rescued from the clutch of the invaders, the Paris-Amiens railway has been freed from interference, and the danger of dividing the French and British Armies has been dissipated. . . .

"From the depths of a very full heart I wish to thank all staffs and services—and to congratulate you all on the wonderful success achieved. Let us remember our gallant dead, whose spirits shall ever be with us, inspiring us to nobler efforts, and when the call again comes, be it soon or otherwise, I know the same measure of success will be yours."

Officer Casualties—August 8-10, 1918

Killed in Action

Lieut. K. S. Drummond, M.C.   Lieut R. B. Hingston
Lieut. J. J. Kavanagh, M.C.   Lieut. E. V. Power

Wounded

Lieut. A. Findlay, D.C.M., M.M.   Lieut. H. G. Macario
Lieut. J. L. Cains, M.C.   Lieut. G. W. Jones

CHAPTER XIV

THE SECOND BATTLES OF ARRAS, 1918

I

In January, 1918, when Sir Douglas Haig reported to the British Government that the enemy would almost certainly attack with all the strength available in the spring and early summer, he added the significant remark that failure of the massed enemy offensive must lead to disaster for the whole German cause. By August, he reported, if the great German offensive had failed, the enemy would be found in a highly vulnerable situation. Testing this belief, Sir Douglas allowed General Sir Henry Rawlinson to use the British Fourth Army in the great Battle of Amiens, and the result, in conjunction with the success achieved earlier by the French and American forces at Rheims, deepened his conviction that the time for a major Allied offensive had come.

On August 14, 1918, Marshal Foch expressed to the British Commander-in-Chief his desire that the Amiens Battle should continue and that attack on the German Roye-Chaulnes line of 1916 should proceed forthwith. Sir Douglas Haig replied that reports from his commanders opposed such action and that a personal visit to the front had convinced him that little would thereby be gained, though casualties would undoubtedly be enormous. He suggested, therefore, as he had suggested before, that the Amiens attack be abandoned and that operations on a major scale be undertaken elsewhere.

Marshal Foch refused to consider this suggestion and a sharp conflict of opinion followed. Some heat was engendered by the discussion, which was brought to a climax when the Generalissimo ordered the British Commander-in-Chief to attack the Roye-Chaulnes line forthwith. Regretfully, but quite adamantly, Sir Douglas Haig maintained his argument that such action was unwise and unsound. He knew that the attack would dissipate his strength without compensating gain and would, in all probability, render abortive the vast plan of operations which was slowly but surely maturing in his mind.

Faced with the British Commander-in-Chief's determination, the true greatness of Marshal Foch appeared. When the great French soldier realized that no argument, no persuasion, no threat would avail, he yielded and gave Sir Douglas Haig his way. He not only yielded the point immediately at issue, but agreed to support, with the whole weight of the French and American Armies, the main British attack, which Sir Douglas Haig proposed. Marshal Foch has deserved the gratitude of the Allied nations for the services he rendered on the Western Front in supreme command, but for this, his greatest and perhaps his most difficult, it is doubtful if adequate honour has ever been paid to him.

Seven days after the assent of Marshal Foch to Sir Douglas Haig's plan of campaign, the British Third Army, under General Sir Julian Byng, opened the Second Battles of the Somme, 1918, and on the same day, August 21st, the French Army struck hard at the enemy on the Aisne. Within a few days of the opening of the Second Battles of the Somme, Sir Douglas Haig's wisdom in refusing to attack the Roye-Chaulnes line stood revealed, for Sir Julian Byng's forces turned the German positions from the north and enabled troops of the British Fourth Army, in co-operation with the French, to advance across the old battlefields of the Somme with losses trifling in comparison to those a frontal attack would inevitably have involved.

Three days after the Germans had suffered a severe blow in the opening engagements of the Battles of the Somme and had recoiled before the vigour of Marshal Foch's offensive on the Aisne, Sir Douglas Haig extended his line of battle to the north and launched against the German line at Arras the British First Army, under General Sir H. S. Horne. In this operation the Canadian Corps, under Lieut.-General Sir A. W. Currie, again served as the spear-head of the British attack; and the 24th

Battalion, Victoria Rifles of Canada, gained distinction through the valour of its assaults and the measure of its heavy sacrifice. When it is realized that the Battle of Amiens opened on August 8th, that the first stages of the Battles of Arras, 1918, were undertaken little more than two weeks thereafter, and that before the month ended the 24th Battalion had entered the Battle of Arras and emerged in a shattered state, it becomes clear why August, 1918, is a month equalled by none and rivalled by few in the whole story of the Battalion's experience in France.

II

At 7 o'clock on the evening of August 21, 1918, the 24th Battalion, Victoria Rifles of Canada, marched from bivouacs in Blangy Wood to a point on the Amiens-Villers Bretonneux Road and there embussed for Herlin le Sec, arriving at 2 o'clock on the morning of August 22nd and marching to billets in Buneville. On the following morning, the unit marched to Petit Houvin Station and entrained for Maroeuil, reaching this destination at 5 o'clock in the afternoon and marching to comfortable billets in Wanquentin. From these billets, the Battalion marched at 7 p.m. on August 24th to positions in Wailly Woods. Enemy aircraft bombed the roads as the Canadians advanced, but the Battalion was fortunate and reached its destination at midnight without having incurred losses.

Soon after the Battalion reached Wailly Woods, the 5th Canadian Infantry Brigade was notified of an attack to be carried out astride the Arras-Cambrai Road on August 26th, with the 2nd and 3rd Canadian Divisions in line and in which the Brigade would take an active part. Assembly would be carried out near the Brickworks between Arras and Beaurains and would be completed early on the morning of August 26th. After attending a church parade in Wailly Woods at 11 a.m. on August 25th, the Battalion prepared for battle and, at 9.15 p.m., marched by way of Track "A" to the assembly area north of Beaurains. Beating rain, unusual darkness, and a heavy bombardment with gas shells complicated the move, but, despite the difficulty of groping their way forward with box respirators in use, the men reached the positions assigned to them, the companies reporting to Lieut.-Col. Clark-Kennedy before midnight that their assembly was complete.

Three hours later, the attack of the British Army began; and at 4.45 a.m. the 5th Brigade was informed by the Staff of the 2nd Canadian Division that, so far as could be judged, all was going well. In the 2nd Canadian Division, at this time, the attack was being conducted with the 6th Canadian Infantry Brigade on the right and the 4th Canadian Infantry Brigade on the left. The 5th Canadian Infantry Brigade lay in its assembly trenches in support.

At zero plus 2 hours, orders for the 5th Brigade to move forward were issued and soon thereafter, with the 26th, 24th, and 22nd Battalion in line and the 25th Battalion in Brigade Support, the formation got under way. In the 24th Battalion, "C" Coy. on the right was commanded by Capt. R. H. Lamb and "A" Coy. on the left by Major A. M. Dewar; behind them on the right was "B" Coy., under Capt. G. A. McGiffin, and on the left "D" Coy., under Capt. P. I. Walker, M.C.

Some shelling was encountered shortly after the Battalion moved from its assembly positions, but casualties were few and progress was uninterrupted. Accordingly, at 7 a.m., "C" and "A" Companies reported that they had reached and occupied positions in Nova Scotia Trench, "B" and "D" Companies reporting simultaneously that they were established in close support. For the rest of the day, the companies remained in the positions occupied at 7 o'clock. Light shell fire struck the Battalion's lines at intervals, but few casualties were suffered and, at night, Major J. N. Bales, M.C., the Adjutant, was able to note in the Battalion War Diary a quiet and uneventful day.

At 9 o'clock that night, the 2nd Canadian Division notified the 5th Canadian Infantry Brigade that the attack would be resumed on the following morning, August 27th. It was suggested that the zero hour would be 4 a.m., but this was amended, owing to the impossibility of assembling the battalions in time, and 10 a.m. was substituted. Verbal orders were thereupon issued to the battalions of the Brigade, with emphasis on the desirability of hastening the assembly as much as possible.

In substance, the orders to the battalions of the 5th Brigade stated that the 2nd Canadian Division would attack on a 2-brigade front, with the 5th Canadian Infantry Brigade on the right and the 4th Canadian Infantry Brigade on the left. The frontage of the 5th Brigade would be 2,600 yards, the first objective to be the line of the Sensée River and the second general objective the Drocourt-Quéant Line and the village of Cagnicourt. The 5th and 4th Brigades would launch their attack from the line reached by the 6th and 4th Brigades on August 26th. This was in the old British support system just east of the crest of the Wancourt Tower ridge. The Brigade, it was ordered, would attack with 3 battalions, the 26th, 24th, and 22nd, in line, with the 25th in support. The 29th Battalion, of the 6th Canadian Infantry Brigade, would be attached to the 5th Brigade and would serve as Brigade Reserve.

At 3.30 o'clock on the morning of August 27th, the 24th Battalion received definite orders to move at 4 a.m. to its assembly area behind Egret Trench, a position which the 6th Brigade had attacked and captured during the night. As on the previous day, some shelling struck the area as the Battalion advanced, but casualties were light and, by what seemed a miracle, the unit formed up in Crow Trench in broad daylight without serious misadventure.

At 10 a.m., the British barrage opened, playing for 3 minutes on a line 200 yards from the jumping-off positions of the 5th Brigade and thereafter lifting 100 yards every 4 minutes. With the first crash of the barrage, "C" and "A" Companies moved from their assembly positions, with "D" and "B" Companies in close support. Orders had instructed the companies to wait in position for 3 minutes after zero, when the British barrage would lift, but, as the barrage was playing accurately on the German line 200 yards away, officers decided that it would be safer to advance at once and led their men forward accordingly.

Despite this procedure, which was adopted in a well-considered effort to avoid the first blast of enemy artillery and machine-gun fire, the waves of the Battalion's attack suffered severely as soon as they climbed over the parapets of their jumping-off trenches. A hail of machine-gun fire and heavy gas shelling struck the companies in the first minutes of their assault and the attacking formation of the Battalion was quickly broken, but the spirit of the men was unsubdued and small groups, each under an officer, or N.C.O., moved undauntedly forward.

Before these determined groups, the enemy steadily gave ground, though he rallied as the Victoria Riflemen approached Mallard Trench and defended this position stubbornly with machine-guns. Trench mortars also came into action at this point, but the attack of the Battalion was not to be denied and the trench was carried, partly by machine-guns, which subdued the enemy fire, partly by bombing operations, and partly by the direct assault of a number of men, who, driving their way into the position, bayoneted the German gun crews who resisted them. These crews, in conjunction with the German artillery, provided the main factor in the enemy defence. They fought bravely and well, in contrast to the German infantry, who, at some other points, revealed evidence of approaching demoralization.

When the machine-gun garrisons in Mallard Trench had been routed, the attack of the 24th Battalion moved forward against the village of Chérisy. Machine-gun opposition had been reduced by the capture of the guns in Mallard Trench, but artillery fire was becoming heavier and the troops were having difficulty both from high explosive shells and "Blue Cross" shells, containing gas. Casualties from this shelling added appreciably to the list suffered through the previous machine-gun fire, but the ardour of the troops was undiminished and Chérisy was captured shortly before noon. No hand-to-hand fighting occurred in the village, which most of the garrison had abandoned and which, as the 24th Battalion approached, was the target for scattered fire from the supporting German guns.

Immediately after capturing Chérisy, the waves of the Battalion's attack reached the dry bed of the Sensée River, and crossed without serious resistance, capturing on the crest of the steep opposite bank a row of machine-guns, which the enemy crews had been forced to abandon. At noon, Lieut.-Col. A. E. G. McKenzie, D.S.O., of the 26th Canadian Battalion, reported to 5th Brigade that his troops were crossing the Sensée River bed, that he was in touch with the Royal Scots on his right and the 24th Battalion on his left, and that a number of prisoners were being passed by the attacking battalions to the rear.

After crossing the Sensée River bed, the 24th Battalion halted for half an hour, while the barrage played on Occident Trench beyond, the pause affording the Victoria Riflemen an opportunity to reorganize their shattered and broken lines. Accurate information with regard to losses was impossible to obtain at the time, but it was clear, even at a glance, that "A" and "C" Companies had suffered sharply and that the supporting companies had not come through unscathed. In "C" Coy., Capt. R. H. Lamb had been wounded and command had been assumed for a time by Lieut. P. E. McLaughlin, but this officer had later been wounded, leaving the command to Lieut. H. M. Alexander, M.C. Before the day ended, Lieut. Alexander was also wounded and the company command passed to Lieut. W. McMurray.

Meanwhile, when the barrage lifted from Occident Trench, the reorganized waves of the 24th Battalion's attack swept up the slope, and, despite the opposition offered by German field guns which fired at point blank range, captured the position and advanced to within 150 yards of Ulster and Union Trenches. Here the movement was definitely checked by heavy fire from in front and from both flanks. The attack by this time had reached a point beyond the range of the supporting field guns and had outstripped the assault of the battalions on the flanks. Accordingly, Lieut.-Col. Clark-Kennedy gave orders to the unit to halt and establish a line of resistance in Occident Trench.

When this had been done, Lieut.-Col. Clark-Kennedy visited Brigade Headquarters and reported on the situation in which his Battalion stood. He stated that the 26th, 24th, and 22nd Battalions were in touch with one another, but were not in touch with units on their flanks. Major Dubuc, Officer Commanding the 22nd

Battalion, had been severely wounded and Lieut.-Col. Clark-Kennedy, at the time his report was made, was co-ordinating the action of the companies of the 22nd Battalion as well as his own.

Just as Lieut.-Col. Clark-Kennedy completed his report, the leading batteries of the Canadian field artillery reached Brigade Headquarters, whence, on information which the Commanding Officer of the 24th Battalion supplied, fire was opened on the enemy guns south of Upton Wood and on parties of German soldiers moving on the Hendecourt Road. This fire was effective in silencing German guns, which had been engaged by the 24th Battalion's Lewis guns, but had outranged the Victoria Riflemen and, from positions in full view, had harassed the Battalion severely.

Soon after the Canadian guns had opened fire, Major J. C. Kemp, the 5th Brigade's Brigade Major, carried out a careful reconnaissance of the formation's right flank; and somewhat later Lieut.-Col. T. L. Tremblay, O.C. the Brigade, went forward with Col. MacParland, of the Canadian Field Artillery, to see if the battalions in the line could attack, with Unicorn Trench as their objective, provided a good barrage were fired in support. It was found that no attack would be possible until after dusk and, as a night operation offered little chance of success, the battalions were ordered to stand fast and prepare to resume the attack on the morrow.

Obeying these orders, the 24th Battalion carried out the reorganizations made necessary by the death in action of Capt. G. A. McGiffin, who had fallen while bravely leading "B" Coy. forward, and the wounding of 9 other officers, including Major J. N. Bales, M.C., the experienced and capable Adjutant, Major A. M. Dewar, commanding "A" Coy., and Capt. R. H. Lamb, the officer commanding "C" Coy. In addition to these senior officers, whose loss to the Battalion cannot easily be exaggerated, the list of wounded included Lieuts. G. V. O'Gorman, A. Briggs, T. Redpath, E. G. O'Brien, P. E. McLaughlin, and H. M. Alexander, M.C., the majority of whom had seen long service in the Battalion's ranks and had been awarded commissions for the faithful and courageous manner in which their work had been performed. Amongst the other ranks of the Battalion, losses had been equally severe, a check of casualties showing that 19 men had been killed, that 33 were missing, and that 190 had been wounded. To the regret of all ranks, the killed included Regimental Sergt.-Major James Hennessy, M.M., who had sailed with the Battalion from Canada and had earned promotion by long and valuable service in France.

III

When the battalions of the 5th Canadian Infantry Brigade were halted by enemy resistance on the late afternoon of August 27, 1918, plans were at once drawn up for a resumption of the attack on August 28th. At 4.15 a.m. on that date, Lieut.-Col. T. L. Tremblay, over the signature of his Brigade Major, Major J. C. Kemp, issued Operation Order No. 269, written in pencil on a Field Service Message pad, which stated that the 2nd Canadian Division would attack at 12.30 p.m., with its first objective the Fresnes-Rouvroy Line, and its second objective the Drocourt-Quéant Line. The 5th Brigade was ordered to attack, as on August 27th, with the 26th Battalion on the right, the 24th Battalion in the centre, the 22nd Battalion on the left, and the 25th Battalion in Brigade Support.

This formation, though it included in the first line of its assault the 22nd and 24th Battalions, which had suffered severely in the fighting on the previous day, was found advisable, as the front was too wide to permit a 2-battalion attack and, in any event, the movement necessary to replace the 22nd Battalion, or the 24th Battalion, by the 25th Battalion was a manoeuvre which the enemy could not fail to observe and deal with. The strain on the 22nd and 24th Battalions would be severe, but both were willing to assume the burden that would be theirs and to attack with all the strength they could muster.

At 11 o'clock on the morning of August 28th, a barrage opened on the front of the 3rd Canadian Division to the left and some retaliatory fire struck the area occupied by the battalions of the 5th Brigade. For approximately ten minutes, this fire threatened to inflict serious losses, but before many casualties had actually been incurred it died down, or was shifted to strike against the division to the left. At 12.30 p.m., the barrage on the 2nd Canadian Divisional front opened and at once the Canadian troops, leaving the trenches in which they had passed the night, resumed the attack of the previous day.

In the 24th Battalion, Victoria Rifles of Canada, "C" and "D" Companies, under Lieuts. R. B. E. Wilson, M.C., and Capt. P. I. Walker, M.C., formed the first wave of attack, with "A" and "B" Companies, under Lieuts. F. H. Morgan, M.C., and W. Watson, advancing in close support. No tanks were to accompany the 24th Battalion, but 8 guns of No. 1 Company, 2nd Battalion, Canadian Machine-Gun Corps, were ordered to report to the unit and serve under Lieut.-Col. Clark-Kennedy's orders.

From the beginning, the attack of the 24th Battalion on this occasion encountered bitter artillery and machine-gun resistance, the casualties in the early stages of the advance including the Commanding Officer, who fell with a shattered leg, but continued to direct the operations of the unit from a shell-hole nearby. Officers and men fell fast thereafter under the heavy fire of guns and machine-guns, but the Battalion pushed forward, until the barbed wire in front of Ulster and Union Trenches was reached. Again and again, parties of the Battalion strove to penetrate this wire, but great belts had remained uncut by the artillery barrage and each party that attempted to get through was cut to pieces, or thrown back, by the concentrated fire of the enemy machine-guns.

At 3.30 p.m., knowledge of this situation was brought to Brigade Headquarters by Sergt. J. N. Swift, of "D" Coy., 24th Battalion, who reported that the unit was definitely held up some 200 yards short of the first objective. Sergt. Swift added that casualties had been severe, but that the Commanding Officer, though badly injured and quite unable to move, was in touch with the situation and was carrying out his duties to the full extent that circumstances would permit. Soon after hearing Sergt. Swift's verbal report, the 5th Brigade received information that the attack of the 4th Brigade had been held up in front of Ocean and Opera Trenches, in the same manner that, on the 24th Battalion front, the drive had been brought to a standstill by the defending wire and machine-guns of Ulster and Union Trenches.

By this time, the front line strength of the 24th Battalion, Victoria Rifles of Canada, had been reduced to a total of 3 officers and approximately 150 other ranks, the losses, in addition to Lieut.-Col. Clark-Kennedy, who, from the shell hole where he lay, was still exercising command, including amongst the killed Capt. P. I. Walker, M.C., who had been struck down while leading the attack of "D" Coy., Lieut. J. C. Shipway, an original member of the Battalion, who had rejoined as an officer after being wounded in the Ypres Salient in June, 1916; and Lieut. P. G. Tucker, M.C., another original, who had suffered wounds in the autumn of 1915. Capt. Walker, who had sailed with the unit from Canada, was an officer who, throughout the long period of his service in France, had set an example of devotion to duty unsurpassed in the fine record of the Battalion's career. Three times he had suffered wounds, but on each occasion he had rejoined as soon as his injuries were healed and had continued to serve with marked bravery and skill.

In addition to the deaths in action of Capt. Walker, Lieut. Tucker, and Lieut. Shipway, the Battalion had suffered severely through the wounding of Lieuts. R. B. E. Wilson, M.C., W. Watson, D. A. Sutherland, N. W. Robins, M.C., M.M., T. G. Courtenay, and C. E. Riley, all experienced officers, the majority of whom had rejoined the unit after recovering in hospitals from wounds received in previous engagements. Nine other ranks had been killed outright in the day's fighting, 18 were missing, presumed dead, and 125 had been wounded.

Despite these losses and the fact that many men of drafts received after the Battle of Amiens were fighting in their first engagement, the 24th Battalion clung tenaciously to the positions taken up on the afternoon of August 28th. At 5.30 p.m., Lieut.-Col. Clark-Kennedy realized that the situation had stabilized on his front and consented to be carried back from the shell-hole whence, for hours, he had exercised command. On his departure, command of the Battalion was assumed by Lieut. F. H.

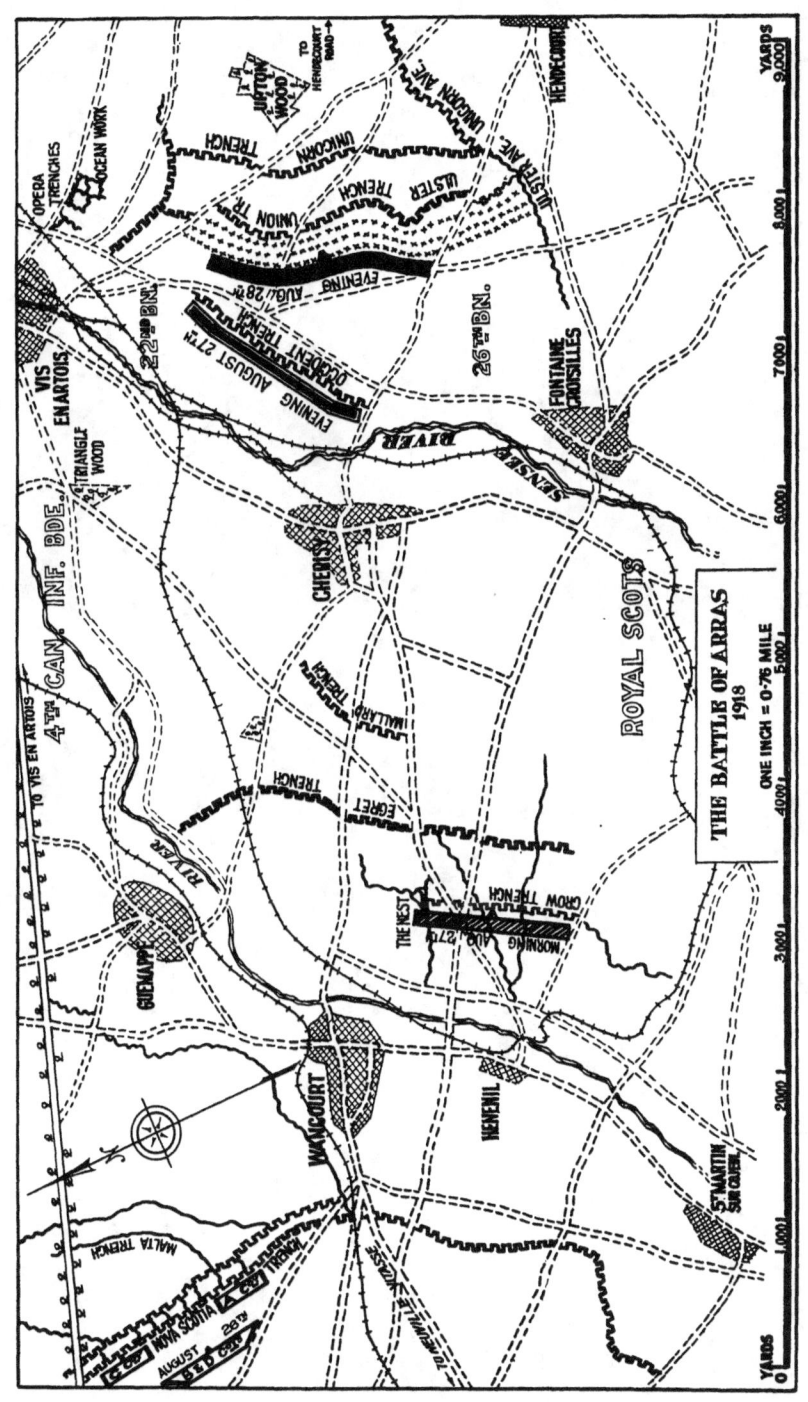

Morgan, M.C., who, with the assistance of Lieuts. H. R. Tanner and W. McMurray, carried out this duty until the arrival of Major P. L. Hall, M.C., who, after serving as Liaison Officer with the 4th Brigade, had been ordered to take command of the 24th Battalion and the shattered remnant of the 22nd Battalion.

On reaching the front and assuming command of the 24th Battalion, or what was left of it, Major Hall established touch with the 26th Battalion on his right and attempted to reach the 22nd Battalion on his left. This was difficult to do, for the 22nd Battalion, as a battalion, no longer existed, all officers having fallen, killed or wounded, together with the great majority of their N.C.O.'s and men. Small parties could be found, clinging determinedly to a ditch, or shell-hole, but no organization remained. In the 24th Battalion, through the magnificent work of the Commanding Officer, the presence of Lieuts. Morgan, Tanner, and McMurray, and the survival of a number of well-trained N.C.O.'s, complete disorganization had been avoided, nevertheless the task of relieving the men in the exposed and widely scattered positions they had occupied presented serious difficulty. Even the problem of securing knowledge of the exact situation that existed was not capable of easy solution, but Major Hall and his officers, with valuable co-operation on the part of Lieut. Donald Deeks, of the Canadian Field Artillery, and noteworthy assistance from Private Davidson, of the 24th Battalion Scout Section, gradually mastered the details of the positions their troops occupied and gave orders for the defensive measures that the situation demanded. Reports forwarded to Lieut.-Col. Tremblay by Major Hall, and acknowledged with the comment "most valuable, you have done very well," helped the Brigadier to form an impression of the situation that existed, and verbal explanation, presented by Lieut. F. H. Morgan, who had carried Major Hall's reports, also proved of the greatest value.

At 6 p.m., the 5th Brigade had been notified that the 3rd Brigade, of the 1st Canadian Division, would carry out relief that night, the 13th Battalion, Royal Highlanders of Canada, relieving the 24th Battalion, Victoria Rifles of Canada. As it was impossible to carry out relief in the usual manner, the troops of the 3rd Brigade occupied a line to the rear of the most advanced line held by the 5th Brigade and, from this position, sent forward parties to take over the shell-holes, trenches, ditches, and dugouts which the men of the 5th Brigade had captured and were consolidating. There was no established "line" and the relief was most difficult, but at last it was completed and the men of the 5th Brigade marched back to a position approximately 1 mile east of Neuville Vitasse.

When the men of the 24th Battalion reached the assembly position of the 5th Brigade near Neuville Vitasse, they found a hot meal waiting for them, also a ration of army rum, the combination of food and stimulant helping them to recover from exhaustion and to rest quietly until, in the afternoon, they were roused to march by way of Neuville Vitasse, Beaurains, and Achicourt, to billets in Dainville. At Dainville, the Battalion was joined by Capt. J. D. MacIntyre and 60 other ranks, who, throughout the unit's tour of duty in the line, had been employed as an evacuation party and, in co-operation with the Medical Officer, Capt. R. B. Jenkins, and the Chaplain, Hon. Capt. C. J. S. Stuart, had accomplished work of a high order. Here, also, on August 30th, the unit was visited by the Brigade Commander, Lieut.-Col. T. L. Tremblay, C.M.G., D.S.O., who expressed to Major Hall his appreciation of what the Battalion had accomplished and his sorrow at the losses it had been forced to endure. Some measure of the loss can be gained from the list and table given below:

Officer Casualties—August 25-29, 1918

Killed in Action

Capt. G. A. McGiffin, M.C.
Capt. P. I. Walker, M.C.
Lieut. P. G. Tucker
Lieut. J. C. Shipway
Lieut. C. E. Riley (died of wounds)
Regt. Sgt.-Major J. Hennessy, M.M. (W.O.1)

Wounded

Lieut.-Col. W. H. Clark-Kennedy, C.M.G., D.S.O.
Major J. N. Bales, M.C.
Major A. M. Dewar
Lieut. E. G. O'Brien
Lieut. P. E. McLaughlin
Lieut. H. M. Alexander, M.C.

Capt. R. H. Lamb
Lieut. G. V. O'Gorman
Lieut. A. Briggs
Lieut. T. Redpath
Lieut. T. G. Courtenay

Lieut. R. B. E. Wilson, M.C.
Lieut. W. Watson
Lieut. D. A. Sutherland
Lieut. N. W. Robins, M.C., M.M.

Battalion Casualties—August, 1918

Officers		Other Ranks	
Killed	8	Killed	67
Wounded	20	Wounded	516
	——	Missing	55
	28		——
			638

Total 666

CHAPTER XV

THE PURSUIT TO MONS

I

After the Battle of Amiens, the Second Battles of the Somme, and the opening stages of the Battles of Arras in August, 1918, it is now evident that Field Marshal Sir Douglas Haig decided definitely to strike with the full weight of the Armies of the Empire in an effort to defeat the German Army before the year ended. Exactly when realization of the possibility of victory dawned in the mind of the British Commander-in-Chief remains a matter of opinion, and must so remain until the private papers of Earl Haig are published, but there is no doubt that Sir Douglas perceived the opportunity before it was recognized by the French or British Government, or even by Marshal Foch.

Tribute to this foresight on the part of the British Commander-in-Chief is paid in the journal of Sir Henry Rawlinson, on the day when the Armistice crowned the long years of Allied suffering and sacrifice. "We owe victory", Sir Henry wrote, to the spirit of the troops, to Foch's work in co-ordinating the Allied effort, "and to Douglas Haig's faith in victory this year. He believed in it long before I did, and when all the people at home were talking about plans for 1919. He not only believed in it, but went 'all out' for it, and he must be a proud and thankful man to-day."

Confirmation of Sir Henry Rawlinson's statement is found in the writings of Brigadier-General John Charteris, Chief of the British Intelligence Service in France, who describes the scene at G.H.Q. as Sir Douglas Haig outlined on a map the objectives which Marshal Foch desired to reach in 1918. The Staff were viewing respectfully these lines, whence the Allies would resume the offensive in 1919, but the thrill of the conference was to come, for suddenly the strong fingers of the Commander-in-Chief swept beyond the line of the Generalissimo's objectives to Cambrai, St. Quentin, and Le Cateau, even to Hirson, a point essential to a continuance of German resistance on the Western Front. These, Sir Douglas explained, were the remote, but vital, objectives he would attempt to attain.

Obviously, to reach such objectives, sustained and bitter fighting would be involved. Large scale operations on wide fronts by the Armies of France and the United States were an integral part of Sir Douglas Haig's plan. The British Commander-in-Chief realized that these, though extensive, would not compare otherwise with the intense fighting which the existing concentration of German divisions would force upon the British. Believing, however, that the Armies of the Empire would not fail in this supreme test of their courage, ability, and endurance, Sir Douglas Haig had decided to commit them to battle.

First, though, he had to convince Marshal Foch that his plan was sound; and this was no easy task, for acceptance of the British scheme meant that the Generalissimo must seriously modify plans upon which he and the French Staff had spent long weeks of earnest and profoundly skilled endeavour. These plans could not lead to victory in 1918; but Marshal Foch had faith only in a campaign for victory in 1919. Sir Douglas Haig's plan, therefore, though interesting, seemed to breathe a hope, inspiring as such, but otherwise worthy of little more than academic consideration.

Meanwhile, the attack of General Sir H. S. Horne's First British Army had been launched at Arras, the French Army had attacked on a broad front, and the American Army was preparing to reduce the St. Mihiel Salient and thereafter, in conjunction with the French, to undertake operations of even greater significance. With knowledge of the situation on the British, French, and American fronts, Sir Douglas Haig wrote to Marshal Foch on August 27th, urging him to amend the plan of action so that the French and American attacks should converge at Mezières, the amendment involving the substitution of definite strategic objectives for the vague destinations to be attained by random blows without co-ordinated purpose. In his Directive No. 3537, issued on September 3rd, Marshal Foch accepted Sir Douglas Haig's plan.

By this time, the attack of the British First Army at Arras had captured more than 16,000 prisoners and 200 guns and had brought General Horne's troops, among them the divisions of the Canadian Corps, approximately into line with the Third and Fourth British Armies, in contact with that vast defensive work, known to the Germans by different names in different sectors of the front, but familiar to the Allies throughout its entire length as "The Hindenburg Line." Back of this line and protected by its enormous strength, lay the railway communications vital to the maintenance of the German Army in France.

Knowing that the position throughout its entire length was strong, and that on the British front it attained a strength unequalled, or even approached, by any line of enemy resistance on the entire Western Front; knowing, too, that behind the British section of the line the enemy had massed his divisions, including an overwhelming majority of those classed as the best in the German Army, the British Government became alarmed at Sir Douglas Haig's obvious determination to attack. On September 1st, Sir Henry Wilson, Chief of the Imperial General Staff, telegraphed to Sir Douglas to warn him that, should his projected attack fail, he must assume full and unqualified responsibility.

This telegram, though carefully worded, conveyed to the Commander-in-Chief the knowledge that dismissal would follow should his opinion on the wisdom of attacking prove wrong. On September 7th, Sir Douglas issued a Special Order to all ranks, mentioning that 75,000 prisoners and 750 guns had been captured and appealing confidently for loyal co-operation in seizing and turning to the utmost advantage the opportunity which the splendid fighting since August 8th had created. Two days later, he travelled to London to convince the Secretary of State for War and the members of the British Cabinet that an opportunity really existed.

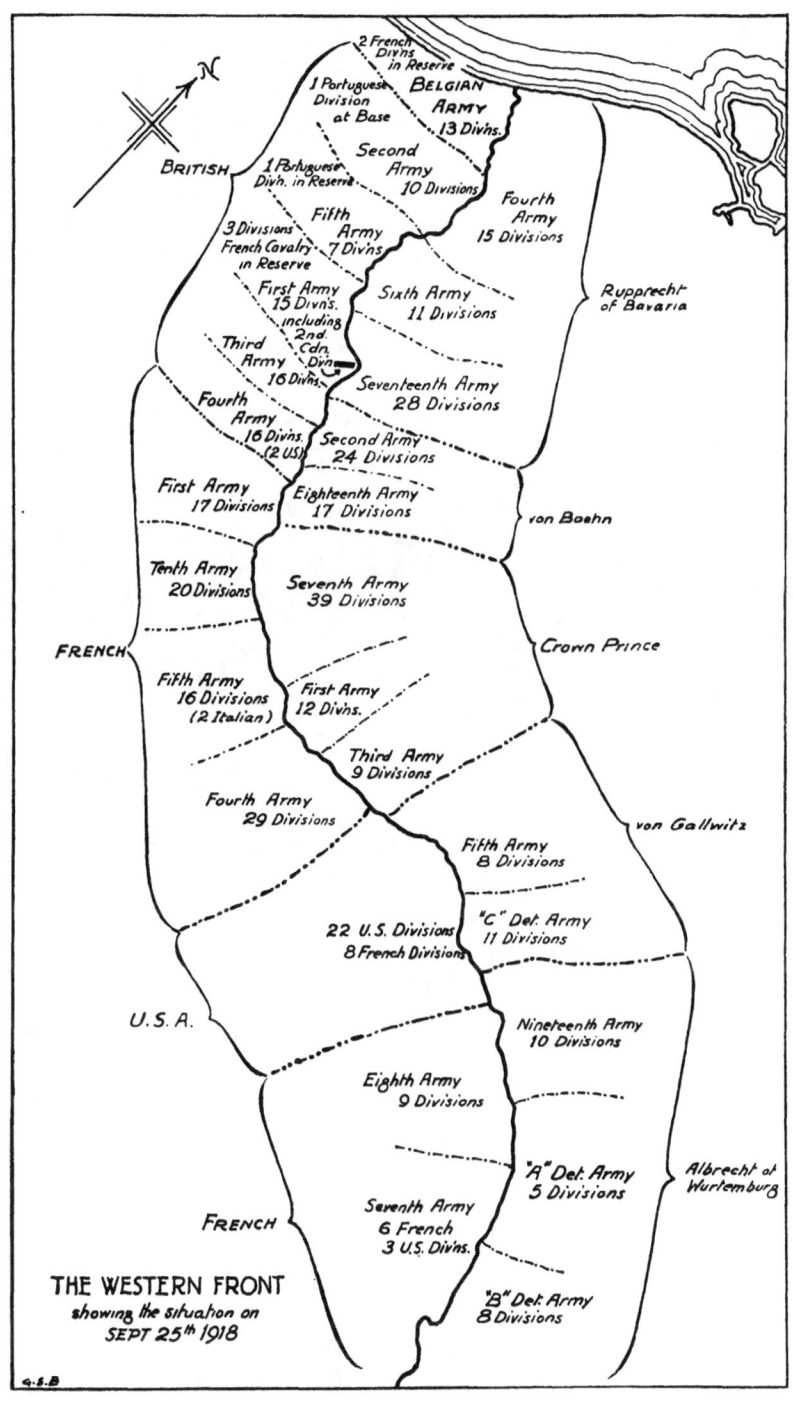

This Sketch, based upon Official Information, clearly reveals the massing of German Divisions on the British Front at the time of the

In London, Sir Douglas received scant encouragement. He pleaded that the end was actually in sight, provided the Allied Armies struck, and continued to strike, with all their strength; but the Government, convinced that the crisis of the war would occur in the summer of 1919, considered his arguments absurdly optimistic and entirely unconvincing. He was not forbidden to attack the Hindenburg Line, but it was impressed upon him that responsibility, more particularly if heavy losses should accrue, must be his and not the Government's.

Undismayed by the lack of confidence in London and undeterred by responsibility greater, perhaps, than had ever been placed upon a British commander in the field, Sir Douglas Haig returned to France and unhesitatingly announced to those concerned his decision to commit the Armies of the Empire to the great attack. As Brigadier-General Charteris has observed, no weightier decision can be imagined, nor one which yielded greater results.

While Sir Douglas was in London, the United States First Army, augmented by an experienced French corps of three divisions and aided by the French Independent Air Force, was completing preparations to attack the St. Mihiel Salient. At 5 o'clock on the morning of September 12th, nine divisions of American infantry advanced through dense fog to assault the enemy, who, to quote General Pershing, the American Commander-in-Chief, were demoralized by the surprise and the intensity of fire by the French artilleries in support. When the action ended, 16,000 prisoners and 443 guns had been captured, and the Americans had suffered but 7,000 casualties. Losses amongst the co-operating divisions of French infantry are probably not included in this total, quoted from General Pershing's report, but they were not sufficiently severe to alter the character of the striking success achieved.

Six days after the opening of the action in the St. Mihiel Salient, the Third and Fourth British Armies attacked on a 17-mile front and, driving the enemy back, seized positions whence an assault on the Hindenburg Line would be possible. Blow after blow was thereafter delivered and, by September 30th, the whole Hindenburg Line north of St. Quentin had been broken. In the breaking of the line at its most formidable point, the divisions of the Canadian Corps took a part in keeping with the fighting reputation established by the 1st Division in 1915 and maintained by all divisions of the Corps thereafter.

As the great battle waged in the centre of the British line, heavy blows were struck, under Marshal Foch's direction, by the French and American Armies and, in the north, by a combined Franco-Belgian force, under the personal command of the Belgian King. By September 30th, this force had regained all territory abandoned during the German offensive in the spring and, advancing still further, had driven beyond the point reached by the British Army in the Flanders Battle of 1917.

Meanwhile, in the Meuse-Argonne area, the American Army had advanced from three to seven miles; and on the long French front the forces of General Pétain had everywhere made progress, driving the Germans from territory occupied for years and adding daily to the enormous Allied captures of men, guns, and material. On October 4th, the attack of the American Army in the Meuse-Argonne was renewed; and on November 1st the final attack in this area was launched, the operations, in conjunction with those in September, capturing 32,000 German or Austrian prisoners and 911 guns. American losses to November 18th totalled 50,280 killed, 205,690 wounded, and 4,526 taken prisoner.

While the Americans were battling forward in the Meuse-Argonne and the French were driving the enemy from mile after mile of the soil of France, Sir Douglas Haig was exerting on the vital British front the decisive pressure which gave assurance that the splendid co-operative efforts of the Allied Armies would not be put forth in vain. As a result of fighting subsequent to September 25th, General Ludendorff was compelled to order the withdrawal of his forces on the whole front from Ypres to Cambrai; but hardly had the resulting movement begun when, on October 8th, there descended upon his fast crumbling line a crushing attack delivered with the whole weight of the First, Third, and Fourth British Armies. A few days later, General Plumer's Second British Army and the entire force under command of the King of the Belgians drove against the enemy to the north and advanced in triumph to Courtrai.

By mid-October, the Belgian Coast and the great industrial region of France had been cleared of the enemy, who had been driven back to the line of the Rivers Scheldt, Selle, and Aisne. No rest, however, was afforded the Germans in these positions, for on October 17th the British Fourth Army again attacked, followed by the Third Army and one division of the First Army on October 20th. These attacks drove the enemy headlong from the line of the Selle and from positions where the Germans had hoped against hope that a stand might successfully be effected.

A fortnight later, on the same front, Sir Douglas Haig launched his armies in the final and decisive blow of the war. Driving forward, they advanced the British line more than twenty miles in ten days, and, seizing the enemy's lateral communications, divided the German Army so effectively that further resistance, without months given for opportunity to reorganize, was beyond the power of the enemy to offer.

Though the fighting subsequent to November 1st produced the actual rupture of the German communications and is, therefore, referred to as decisive, it was in the attacks previous to this date that the spirit of the German Army was broken, more particularly in the battles of late September and early October, when the British Army shattered the Hindenburg Line, the French crushed the forces opposing them on the formidable front in Champagne, and the Americans drove forward in the great battle of the Meuse-Argonne. All the Allied nations, therefore, shared in the triumph achieved under the brilliant leadership of Marshal Foch and rejoiced when German envoys, admitting defeat, sought the Generalissimo to ask on what conditions an armistice would be granted them.

II

When the 5th Canadian Infantry Brigade was relieved after participation in the opening stages of the Battle of Arras in the last days of August, 1918, the 24th

Battalion, Victoria Rifles of Canada, under Major P. L. Hall, M.C., proceeded to Dainville to reorganize and re-equip, the process starting on September 1st, when Lieut. J. L. Cains, M.C., and a draft of 19 other ranks reported for duty from England. The arrival of this draft preceded by twenty-four hours the announcement that, for gallantry and devotion to duty in operations subsequent to August 7th, 17 non-commissioned officers and men of the Battalion had been awarded the Military Medal. The majority of the recipients were in hospitals recovering from wounds on the day when the awards were announced, but a number, at duty with the Battalion, received the congratulations of the Officer Commanding and of their comrades in the ranks.

The next day, at 1.45 p.m., the Battalion left Dainville and proceeded into the forward area, billeting late in the afternoon in old trenches not far from Neuville Vitasse. In these positions the Victoria Riflemen spent the night and the morning of September 4th, but in the afternoon orders for a move to near Chérisy were received and carried out, the unit bivouacking in old trenches, with Battalion Headquarters in one of the solid concrete pill-boxes which the Germans had used to defend this front.

At Chérisy, on September 5th, the 24th Battalion welcomed back to duty in France Lieut.-Col. C. F. Ritchie, M.C., who reported from England to assume command in place of Lieut.-Col. W. H. Clark-Kennedy, C.M.G., D.S.O., whose wounds meant that months must elapse before he could hope to carry out duty in the field. Simultaneously with the arrival of Lieut.-Col. Ritchie, 60 other ranks reported as reinforcements from England, these being followed on September 7th by Capt. J. R. Simard and Lieut. R. L. Weaver, officers who had recovered from wounds received while serving previously with the unit in France.

In the afternoon on September 7th, at 2 o'clock, the Battalion marched from Chérisy to relieve a unit of the 63rd (Royal Naval) Division in old trenches outside Croisilles, where, in the following five days, training was carried out, several reinforcing drafts were received, and announcement was made that, for splendid service in recent engagements, Corporal O. P. Long had been awarded a Bar to his Military Medal. Two days after this announcement, the Battalion vacated its positions near Croisilles and relieved the 21st Canadian Battalion in old trenches and dugouts at Cagnicourt, where, on September 14th, the unit was strengthened by the arrival of 43 other rank reinforcements and by that of Lieuts. Arthur Beck, M.M., G. H. P. Coneybeare, and N. T. Hammett, M.M., all of whom had served the unit previously as N.C.O.'s.

Next day, the Battalion moved at 2.30 p.m. to Croisilles, arriving at 5 p.m., entraining an hour and a half later, proceeding to Acq, and marching thence to Agnez-les-Duisans, where billets were occupied at 2 o'clock on the morning of September 16th. At Agnez-les-Duisans, where the Battalion remained for two days, the commissioned establishment received reinforcement when Lieuts. E. T. Lane and K. C. MacIntyre, M.M., former N.C.O.'s, and Lieut. W. R. Kingsford, who had served in France with the Royal Canadian Dragoons, reported from reserve battalions in England. On the following day, as the Battalion was retracing its route from Agnez-les-Duisans to Acq and thence by train to Croisilles, the strength was again increased when 93 other ranks reported to Lieut.-Col. Ritchie and were taken on the unit's roll.

Accompanied by the men of the new draft, the Battalion marched forward from Croisilles and took over trench positions from the 29th Canadian Battalion, proceeding forward again at 5.30 p.m. on September 19th and, at 10.55 p.m., relieving the 7th Battalion, Highland Light Infantry, in close support positions in the Inchy-en-Artois Sector. Here the Battalion remained for a week, supplying strong working parties, enduring shelling and bombing from the air, which killed 4 men and wounded 14, and assimilating the men of the draft from England. While the unit was still in support, it was announced that Lance-Corporal J. W. Kennedy and Private H. Cairns had each been awarded a Bar to the Military Medal and that the Military Medal had been granted to twenty of their comrades. At the same time the officer strength was increased, when Lieut. S. A. Rolland reported back for duty after recovering from wounds in England.

On September 25th, two days after the honours had been announced, the Battalion was relieved at 10.30 p.m. by the 50th Canadian Battalion and marched to bivouacs in trenches outside Hendecourt, whence, at 2.15 p.m. on September 27th, it moved to trenches near Bullecourt. On this day, the Canadian Corps was engaged in the mighty task of storming and crossing the famous Canal du Nord, but, as the 2nd Canadian Division lay in Corps Reserve, the 24th Battalion took no active part in the resulting operations, until, on September 30th, it received orders to advance and relieve troops of the 9th Canadian Infantry Brigade in the newly-established front line.

III

Advancing in battle order at 2 o'clock on the morning of October 1, 1918, the 24th Battalion, Victoria Rifles of Canada, proceeded from Hobart Trench in the Inchy-en-Artois area, west of the Canal du Nord, to the assembly area of the 5th Canadian Infantry Brigade, northwest of Bourlon. Arriving in this position at 5 a.m., the Battalion occupied a field until 8 o'clock at night, when it marched to relieve the four battalions of the 9th Canadian Infantry Brigade in front line positions east of Tilloy. On reaching the front, "A" and "B" Companies occupied the outpost line, "C" Coy. and Battalion Headquarters took over cellars in the village of Tilloy, and "D" Coy. was established along the railway embankment west of Tilloy. Despite the fact that the troops of the 9th Brigade had attacked that morning and that the situation of their foremost positions was, consequently, not entirely clear, the relief was effected most satisfactorily, no casualties in the incoming or outgoing battalions being incurred.

Dawn on October 2nd witnessed an awakening of activity on the part of the German gunners, who severely shelled the village of Tilloy and the outpost line, occupied by "A" and "B" Companies, maintaining their fire throughout the day. Casualties from this bombardment and from sharp machine-gun fire were unavoidable, one of the first occurring at an early hour in the morning when Lieut. R. L. Weaver, who, after recovering from wounds, had rejoined the Battalion less than a month before, was killed in action.

At 5.30 o'clock that afternoon, a German patrol of 1 officer and 6 other ranks approached a 24th Battalion outpost and succeeded in capturing the garrison of 2 men. The Germans were about to retire with their prisoners when Lieut. G. H. P. Coneybeare realized what had happened and, without hesitation, leaped to the rescue. Before the Germans could offer effective resistance, four of their number had been wounded, the prisoners had been released, and the officer leader of their patrol had been disarmed and captured. At this stage of his very gallant exploit, Lieut. Coneybeare became aware that an enemy force, approximately 200 strong, was forming up in the German lines with the obvious intent of driving into the 24th Battalion positions. At once, Lieut. Coneybeare ordered an S.O.S. call to be relayed to the supporting artillery, but even before the guns responded and barrage fire crashed on the Battalion front, the unit's machine-guns and rifle fire had checked the attack completely. Lieut. Coneybeare was wounded in the operation, but his injury was not severe and he refused to consider hospital treatment, stating, in the circumstances existing, that he preferred to remain at duty with the Battalion.

That night passed quietly, but morning on October 3rd was marked by a renewal of German activity. All day gas and heavy calibre shells and machine-gun fire fell in Tilloy and elsewhere in the Battalion's area, the resulting casualties including Lieut. H. S. Johnson, an original member of the Battalion, who was killed early in the day. The death of Lieuts. Weaver and Johnson on consecutive days was deeply regretted by all ranks in the unit, particularly by those who had served with the dead officers in the Battalion's ranks and knew of the devoted service they had so faithfully rendered.

On the day when Lieut. Johnson was killed, the Battalion's commissioned strength was further reduced through the departure of Major P. L. Hall, M.C., the Second-in-Command, to attend a Senior Officers' Course at Aldershot, England. Simultaneously, however, there arrived from reserve units Lieuts. R. S. Egan, David Colville, and E. M. Styles, Lieuts. Egan and Colville being original members of the unit who had received commissions after long service in the ranks.

Not long after the new officers reported to Lieut.-Col. Ritchie from England, a Special Order, dated October 3rd, was issued by the Canadian Corps Commander, Lieut.-General Sir A. W. Currie, K.C.B., K.C.M.G., and communicated to all troops under his command. In this Special Order, the Corps Commander said in part:

"I wish to express to all troops now fighting in the Canadian Corps my high appreciation of the splendid fighting qualities displayed by them in the successful battle of the last five days.

"The mission assigned to the Corps was the protection of the flank of the Third and Fourth Armies in their advance, and that mission has been carried out to the complete satisfaction of the Commander-in-Chief.

"In your advance you overcame the very formidable obstacle of the Canal du Nord, you carried by assault the fortified Bourlon Wood, the Marcoing line, and seized the high ground extending along the Douai-Cambrai road. . . . Your patrols have entered Cambrai itself.

"How arduous was the task assigned to you can be judged from the fact that whereas in the operation of the First, Third, and Fourth British Armies thirty-six enemy divisions have been engaged to this date, twelve of those divisions, supported by eleven independent machine-gun units, have been met and defeated by the Canadian Corps . . . .

"You have taken in this battle over seven thousand prisoners and two hundred field and heavy guns, thus bringing the total captures of the Canadian Corps since the 8th of August of this year to twenty-eight thousand prisoners, five hundred guns, over three thousand machine-guns, and a large amount of stores of all kinds . . . .

"In the short period of two months the Canadian Corps—to which were attached the 32nd Division for the Battle of Amiens, the 4th and 51st Divisions for the Battle of Arras, and the 11th Division for this Battle of Cambrai—has encountered and defeated decisively forty-seven German divisions—that is nearly a quarter of the total German forces on the Western Front. . . .

"The victories you have achieved are the fruit of the iron discipline you accepted freely and of the high standard you have reached in the technical knowledge of your arms and the combined tactical employment of all your resources.

"You must therefore with relentless energy maintain and perfect the high standard of training you have reached, and guard with jealous pride your stern discipline.

"I am proud of your deeds and I want to record here my heartfelt thanks for your generous efforts, and my unbounded confidence in your ability to fight victoriously and crush the enemy wherever and whenever you meet him."

Two days after Sir Arthur Currie's Special Order was issued from Canadian Corps Headquarters, recognition of work accomplished by the 24th Battalion, Victoria Rifles of Canada, was afforded in a list of honours and awards to officers for their services in the Battle of Amiens. To the gratification of all ranks in the Battalion, the gallant and capable leadership of Lieut.-Col. W. H. Clark-Kennedy, C.M.G., D.S.O., was recognized by the award of a Bar to the Distinguished Service Order. All realized that Lieut.-Col. Clark-Kennedy must in due course receive further honour for gallantry at Arras when, despite a shattered leg, he had exercised command through long hours of pain and intense anxiety, but this award for his leadership at Amiens was appreciated none the less.

In addition to the Commanding Officer, the list of honours published on October 5th included the names of Capt. V. E. Duclos, Hon. Capt. C. J. S. Stuart, Lieut. G. H. Macario, Lieut. W. McMurray, Lieut. F. W. Stenson, and Lieut. J. A. Donovan, D.C.M., who received the Military Cross. A similar honour was granted to Lieut. P. G. Tucker, who, after winning the decoration by gallant fighting in the Battle of Amiens, had been killed in action at Arras on August 28th.

Not long after the Amiens honours were gazetted, gallantry of a number of 24th Battalion officers in the subsequent fighting at Arras received recognition when Lieuts. H. M. Alexander and F. H. Morgan were each awarded a Bar to the Military Cross; and the Military Cross was granted to Capt. R. H. Lamb and Lieut. H. R.

Tanner, and to the Battalion Medical Officer, Capt. R. B. Jenkins. In the same list of honours, it was announced that Sergt. R. W. Handren had been awarded the Distinguished Conduct Medal.

On the day when the above awards proved that the fine fighting of the 24th Battalion in the actions subsequent to August 7, 1918, had commanded appreciation, "C" and "D" Companies of the unit relieved "A" and "B" Companies in the front line east of Tilloy. No striking incident marked the relief, nor was there any noteworthy event on October 6th and 7th, but on the 8th, at 10.30 o'clock in the morning, an enemy party of 6 men approached the Battalion lines, one being captured and the others wounded by troops under the command of Lieut. S. A. Rolland.

Meanwhile, Warning Order No. 294, dated October 7, 1918, had notified troops of the 5th Canadian Infantry Brigade that, on a date and at an hour to be named later, the Third British Army was to resume the advance south of Cambrai, and that the Canadian Corps would co-operate by carrying out an artillery demonstration north of Cambrai. In addition to the artillery demonstration, the 2nd Canadian Division was to co-operate by seizing bridge-heads on the Canal de l'Escaut, with a view to advancing and establishing contact with troops of the Third Army east of Cambrai.

It was further stated in Warning Order No. 294, that the operation by the 2nd Canadian Division would be carried out in two phases. In the first of these, the 5th Canadian Infantry Brigade on the right would establish bridge-heads on the east side of the Canal de l'Escaut at Morenchies, Pont d'Aire, and Ramillies. The 6th Canadian Infantry Brigade on the left would conform to the advance of the 5th Brigade to safeguard the left flank of the Division. The second phase of the operation, which would involve a crossing of the Canal, an advance north of Cambrai, and the securing of contact with the troops of the Third Army, would be carried out by the 4th Canadian Infantry Brigade.

In the 5th Canadian Infantry Brigade, the Warning Order stated, the attack would be carried out by the 26th and 25th Battalions, with the 22nd Battalion following in support, with the duty of forming a defensive flank on the right of the 26th Battalion. The 24th Battalion would hold the front line and, when the 22nd Battalion had passed through in support, would become Brigade Reserve. In the confirmation of Warning Order 294, issued on October 8th, the duty of mopping up the Brigade Area from the jumping-off line to the Canal and within stated boundaries was also allotted to the 24th Battalion.

In obedience to the instructions in the Warning Order and the confirmation issued later, the 25th and 26th Canadian Battalions formed up behind the outpost lines of the 24th Battalion on the early morning of October 9th and, at 1.30 o'clock, launched their attack. Success attended the effort, the battalions establishing bridgeheads across the Canal at Morenchies and Pont d'Aire as ordered, capturing the town of Escaudoeuvres, and establishing a line along the railway north-east of Cambrai. Throughout the operation the 24th Battalion remained in position as Brigade Reserve. Shell and machine-gun fire were unusually light, as the Germans were fully employed in evacuating and setting fire to Cambrai, and casualties in the Battalion were consequently almost negligible.

The next day, at 7 p.m., the Battalion moved by companies from its positions near Tilloy to an area along the Ramillies-Morenchies road, two companies bivouacking in the open and two occupying ruined buildings and cellars in Ramillies. Soon after reaching these destinations, Battalion Headquarters and the companies were subjected to a brisk bombardment with enemy gas shells, but all ranks were alert to the danger and, through the use of gas helmets, avoided serious consequences.

October 11th passed uneventfully, but at 15 minutes after midnight Lieut.-Col. Ritchie was instructed to report to Brigade Headquarters for orders. Returning at 6 o'clock on the morning of October 12th, Lieut.-Col. Ritchie summoned his company commanders and stated that the Battalion would move from Ramillies to an assembly area north of Iwuy, would attack and capture the village of Hordain, and establish a line to the north.

Marching from Ramillies in fighting order at 8 a.m., the Battalion proceeded to the area mentioned and formed up for the assault, the company commanders, at 11.30 o'clock, reporting to Battalion Headquarters, which had been established in Iwuy Chateau, that assembly was complete. Half an hour later the Canadian barrage opened on what was believed to be the German front line, played heavily on this position for ten minutes, and then, lifting 200 yards each five minutes, rolled ponderously forward into enemy territory.

Following immediately in the wake of the barrage, the waves of the 24th Battalion's attack left their assembly area and flowed steadily towards the village of Hordain. Sharp opposition had been expected and the men had steeled themselves to endure punishment similar to that which the unit had borne so devotedly in the fighting of late August, but, to their surprise, the enemy remained inactive and the attack, sweeping forward almost as a sham manoeuvre might do, reached and captured Hordain without difficulty and with minimum losses.

Beyond Hordain, however, the advance was more seriously hampered. German machine-guns opened fire and the troops found difficulty in evading the supporting barrage, casualties from these sources, and from German artillery fire, increasing as the attack approached its final objectives and, before these were attained, reaching a total of 49, the wounded including Lieut. G. H. P. Coneybeare, who had remained at duty after suffering a less serious injury little more than a week before.

On reaching the final objectives beyond Hordain, "A" and "B" Companies of the 24th Battalion established a main line of resistance, with "A" Coy.'s right flank resting on the embankment of the railway which ran northward from Iwuy and "B" Coy.'s left flank on swampy ground which stretched as far as the Canal de l'Escaut. Beyond the railway embankment to the right, the unit established contact with the 4th Battalion, Seaforth Highlanders, of the 51st (Highland) Division.

After "A" and "B" Companies had taken position in the final objectives of the day's attack, "C" Coy. passed through the new front line and established a series of outposts some distance beyond. "D" Coy., meanwhile, moved up and occupied positions to the right of the

Battalion front in immediate support of "A" Coy. In these positions, the companies endured frequent bombardment with gas and heavy shells throughout the afternoon and night of October 12th. Battalion Headquarters in Hordain was also shelled, but the damage effected was slight and the Battalion suffered no serious inconvenience.

After passing an uneventful night in the positions beyond Hordain, the companies of the 24th Battalion received orders on the morning of October 13th to advance in conjunction with troops of the 51st Division on the right and, when the men of the 51st had captured Lieu-St. Amand, to attack Basse Ville and establish a bridgehead at Bouchain. At 9 a.m., the 51st Division advanced against Lieu-St. Amand in accordance with this plan, but little success resulted. The troops advanced with all the courage and determination that had gained for their formation an enviable place in the history of the Great War, but concentrated machine-gun fire tore the gallant waves of their attack and forced them back to the positions from which their assault had been launched.

Meanwhile, "A" and "D" Companies of the 24th Battalion had attempted to move forward to the outpost line occupied by "C" Coy. Heavy machine-gun fire, however, was encountered from the moment the companies left their positions, and before long two officers, Lieuts. G. R. Grenough and David Colville, had been wounded and 28 other ranks had been killed or wounded. As the attack on the right had by this time been repulsed and as further casualties in a continuation of the operation would be inevitable, without compensating advantage, "A" and "D" Companies were ordered to abandon the forward move and to reoccupy their original line.

Following the carrying out of these orders, which was effected by 11 a.m., the Battalion was notified that it would be relieved by the 18th Canadian Battalion on the night of October 14th. Meanwhile, the unit remained in position and Lieut.-Col. Ritchie prepared a report on the operations his men had carried out. In this report, he mentioned the outstanding work of the Battalion Signal Section, under Lieut. Arthur Beck, M.M., which maintained communication between Headquarters and the companies under circumstances of great difficulty and danger; also the co-operation afforded by the 16th Battery, Canadian Field Artillery, commanded by Major R. F. Baker, which had served under 24th Battalion orders and had effectively silenced many enemy machine-guns.

As arranged beforehand, the companies of the 24th Battalion were relieved in the line on the night of October 14th and moved back to bivouac positions in a field some distance to the rear. Relief was completed early at night and by 9.30 p.m. the Battalion was clear of Hordain village. Battalion Headquarters, however, remained to receive official notification of relief from the incoming battalion and endured severe discomfort and danger when, from 9.30 to 10 o'clock, the village was bombarded heavily with mustard gas and sneezing gas shells. No serious harm resulted, but the experience is recalled by many of the Headquarters personnel as more disagreeable than some in which far greater damage was inflicted.

IV

After passing the night of October 14th in bivouac positions well back of the front line, the 24th Battalion embussed at 7.45 o'clock on the morning of October 15th and proceeded to Marquion, where the companies billeted, "B" and "C" in cellars and "A" and "D" in old trenches in the open fields. In the afternoon, the main body of the Battalion paraded to baths which had been established at Barelle and there washed away the mud and dirt accumulated during the tour in the line.

Refreshed by the bathing, which was completed on the morning of October 16th, and pleased by a parade for pay, the men of the Battalion were in high spirits when, at 11 a.m., His Royal Highness the Prince of Wales visited the unit, had presented to him at Battalion Headquarters a number of the senior officers, and thereafter carried out an informal tour of inspection. Three days later, the Battalion, including the Transport, paraded and was formally inspected by the Corps Commander, Lieut.-General Sir A. W. Currie.

On the morning after this inspection, the Battalion was to have paraded for Divine Service at 10 a.m.

Holy Communion was celebrated at Battalion Headquarters at the appointed hour, but all routine church parades were cancelled, for a move had been ordered to Sancourt, whither the unit marched at 1.30 p.m., arriving at 4.30 o'clock and billeting in old cellars, ruined buildings, or whatever accommodation of a similar nature could be found.

From Sancourt, the Battalion marched at 10 o'clock on the morning of October 22nd to billets in Fressain. A party, 300 strong, proceeded from this spot for work near Aubigny-au-Bac, but soon returned, as the task on which it was to have been employed had been cancelled.

After passing the night in miserable billets in Fressain, the Battalion paraded at 9 o'clock on the morning of October 23rd and proceeded to Aniche, where it remained until November 4th, carrying out a syllabus of routine training. As a whole, the period in Aniche was uneventful, but some incidents, recorded in the Battalion Diary, are worthy of passing notice.

On October 24th, Lieut.-Col. C. F. Ritchie, M.C., left the unit to assume temporary command of the 5th Canadian Infantry Brigade, command of the 24th Battalion, Victoria Rifles of Canada, passing in his absence first to Capt. E. P. Denman and then, on October 28th, to Capt. V. E. Duclos, M.C., who returned from leave and continued to command until, on November 3rd, Lieut.-Col. Ritchie completed his duties with the 5th Brigade and again took over his own Battalion. Previous to the Commanding Officer's return, Capt. G. C. Graham had reported for duty as Medical Officer in relief of Capt. R. B. Jenkins, M.C., who was proceeding on leave to England; and Lieut. H. M. Alexander, M.C., had reported as a reinforcement after recovering from the wound received in the Arras battle late in August.

When the training period at Aniche had been completed, the Battalion embussed at 10 o'clock on the morning of November 4th and was conveyed to Anzin, the troops being cheered again and again in the towns and villages along the route by the inhabitants, who were stirred by their own release from virtual captivity and by the fact that the Germans, after years on French soil, were being hurled back in disorder. In Anzin, the

Battalion billets were repeatedly shelled by a German high-velocity gun, but good fortune attended the men, and, though narrow escapes were frequent, casualties were avoided.

After the Battalion had rested overnight in Anzin, Lieut.-Col. Ritchie, over the signature of his Adjutant, Lieut. E. T. Hart, issued an operation order, in obedience to which the unit, at 7 o'clock on the morning of November 6th, marched through the city of Valenciennes to St. Saulve, where the men found shelter from heavy rain in the local seminary. In this building were packed the personnel of the four battalions of the 5th Canadian Infantry Brigade and the congestion was severe, nevertheless the kitchens served a satisfactory hot meal, packs and blankets were stored, bombs and ammunition were issued, and the men, excited by the prospect of battle with the fast retiring enemy, prepared eagerly for whatever adventure the hours immediately ahead might bring.

After dinner had been eaten, the Battalion marched at 2.30 p.m. and, in battle equipment, moved to the village of Rombies, with the Transport following in the rear. The roads were fairly good and the troops on foot progressed without serious difficulty, though great craters at every crossroad marked the destructive path of the retiring enemy and afforded obstacles which the Transport could pass only after protracted effort. Rombies, where the Battalion halted for the night, was packed with troops and two casualties were incurred from the fire of enemy guns, but, at approximately 9 p.m., the German artillery withdrew, or ceased fire, and the remainder of the night passed uneventfully.

At dawn on November 7th, the 25th Canadian Battalion, which was in the van of the 5th Brigade's pursuit of the enemy, resumed the advance from the positions occupied overnight and at noon the companies of the 24th Battalion followed in support, marching independently and moving, not in accordance with a hard-and-fast time-table, but as the situation and circumstances would permit. On reaching the River Honnelle, the men of the 24th found that the enemy had destroyed the only available bridge, but the 25th Battalion had thrown a plank bridge over the stream and on this, in single file, the Victoria Riflemen crossed without misadventure to the east bank. The Battalion kitchens were halted by the destruction of the main bridge, but food was prepared and carried in dixies to where the men had assembled on the far bank.

In Baisieux, east of the River Honnelle, the men of the 24th Battalion were distributed in cellars and in the adjoining fields. The village had been heavily bombarded with enemy gas shells not long before the Battalion arrived and many of the civilian population had been wounded, or overcome by the fumes. Four other ranks of the Battalion were wounded in renewed shelling, which continued until approximately 9 o'clock at night, these men and a number of the distressed civilians receiving the attention of Capt. G. C. Graham, the relieving Medical Officer, who dressed their injuries and supervised their evacuation to the rear.

At 8 p.m., Brigadier-General T. L. Tremblay notified Lieut.-Col. Ritchie by telephone that the 25th Battalion had reached the main road running north and south through the town of Elouges and that the 24th Battalion, passing through this position at 8 o'clock on the morning of November 8th, would become the van of the 5th Brigade's pursuit, with the 25th Battalion acting as support. All ranks of the 24th Battalion were warned that, should German peace envoys under a white flag be encountered, no delay must occur in escorting such delegations to the British rear. On the whole, these orders provoked amusement and were attributed to a form of humour possessed by brigade, divisional, and higher staffs. Though the enemy was flying before the Allied advance, front line opinion agreed surprisingly that the retreat would halt abruptly when a line suited to the German needs had been reached and occupied.

Believing only that long and hard fighting would continue in the months that lay ahead, "A" Coy. of the 24th Battalion, under Capt. J. D. MacIntyre, M.C., moved from Baisieux at 3 o'clock on the morning of November 8th and took position in Elouges on the left flank of the Battalion's assembly area. Half an hour later, "D" Coy., under Lieut. J. L. Foote, moved into position on the right flank, being followed at 4 a.m. by "C" and "B" Companies, commanded respectively by Lieut. D. M. Matheson, M.C., and Capt. E. P. Denman, which moved simultaneously into right and left support. At 5.30 o'clock, Battalion Headquarters moved to a road crossing, where the 25th Battalion had established a report centre, and prepared to take over from the 25th Battalion the duty of advancing the Brigade front line.

Two and a half hours later, the 24th Battalion passed through the front line established by the 25th Battalion on the night of November 7th, Nos. 16 and 13 Platoons, of "D" Coy., working their way without serious opposition through the Bois d'Epinois and into the country beyond. No. 14 Platoon, working along the southern edge of the wood, came under machine-gun fire from the right flank. An enemy post in the buildings of a brewery was engaged at this stage of the operation and, with appreciable difficulty, was swept out of the Battalion's path. Thereafter, the attack of "D" Coy. progressed steadily, until checked by heavy machine-gun fire from slag heaps near the village of Dour.

Advancing from the assembly position simultaneously with "D" Coy., "A" Coy. moved steadily forward, No. 1 Platoon across open country on the left, No. 4 Platoon, Company Headquarters, and No. 2 Platoon along parallel roads running east. No opposition was encountered by "A" Coy. until the eastern outskirts of Dour were reached, when machine-gun fire from Fosse St. Catherine, Fosse Frederick, and nearby positions checked the advance abruptly. Strict orders against the incurring of heavy losses through attacking strong positions without artillery support had been issued before the day's advance began. "A" Coy., therefore, halted when the machine-gun fire became intense and established contact with the 26th Canadian Battalion on the left and "D" Coy. on the right.

Meanwhile, "B" and "C" Companies of the Battalion had advanced in close support, No. 9 Platoon, under Lieut. H. M. Alexander, M.C., working along the line of railway in the area as far as Fosse No. 8, then along the southern edge of the Bois d'Epinois to a position not far from the brewery previously mentioned. No. 10 Platoon, under Lieut. J. C. Kelly, and No. 11 Platoon, under Lieut. H. E. Rose, advanced through the Bois d'Epinois; and at 10 a.m., when the advance of the front line companies had been checked, No. 9 Platoon, under Sergt. S. Arber, was thrown in to form a defensive flank from the brewery position to the eastern outskirts of Dour.

At 10.45 o'clock, Battalion Headquarters advanced to Fosse No. 4, the 17th Battery, Canadian Field Artillery, moving simultaneously and, later, coming into action against the enemy machine-gun posts which were holding up the Battalion's advance. A special shoot, arranged through the Headquarters of the 5th Brigade, opened at 7.30 p.m. and achieved noteworthy success as, in half an hour, the enemy machine-guns had been silenced and on "D" Coy.'s front a way had been cleared for further action.

Taking advantage of the opportunity afforded, "D" Coy. advanced without delay and pushed patrols into the village of Warquignies, which the enemy had evacuated. Somewhat later, "A" Coy. was also able to advance, continuing to do so until, at 8 o'clock on the morning of November 9th, the 21st Battalion relieved the 24th Battalion in the front line and carried the attack forward. When the relief was completed, "A" and "D" Companies of the 24th were withdrawn to the village of Petit Wasmes, where "B" and "C" Companies had already billeted.

In reporting upon the actions subsequent to November 6th, Lieut.-Col. Ritchie drew to the attention of the higher command the skilled leadership of his company and platoon commanders, the outstanding work accomplished by his signallers and runners, under Lieut. Arthur Beck, M.M., by his scouts, under Lieut. J. L. Cains, M.C., by the Battalion Report Centre, under Major V. E. Duclos, M.C., by his Quartermaster, Capt. J. A. Donovan, M.C., D.C.M., and by the Battalion Transport, which, under Lieut. V. Curtis, had overcome many serious difficulties. The Battalion Signallers, too, had encountered unusual difficulties, not the least of these being furnished by eager civilians, who, seeing the Canadians rolling up German telephone wires, joined whole-heartedly in the work, but, failing to distinguish enemy from British wire, joyously rolled up and delivered with pride whatever wires they could lay hands on. In concluding his report, Lieut.-Col. Ritchie stated that the operations had been carried out with a loss of only 2 other ranks killed and one officer, Lieut. J. L. Bérubé, and 24 other ranks wounded.

In Petit Wasmes, on November 10th, the Battalion attended Divine Service in the Protestant Church; and welcomed Major J. N. Bales, M.C., who had recovered from the wound received at Arras and reported to assume duty as Second-in-Command. There, too, on the morning of November 11th, the unit received word that an armistice had been signed and that the war with Germany was over. The news seemed too good to be true and the men of the companies, on parade, heard the Commanding Officer's announcement with strangely contrasting emotions. Far from the front, the news evoked hysteria and unrestrained rejoicing; at the front, the men received it, deeply conscious that the shadow of death had passed for the time being from their lives, with joy, because the enemy had been defeated, but quietly on the whole, as though in tribute to the memory of the fallen, who, through the measure of their ungrudging sacrifice, had brought that day to pass.

CHAPTER XVI

THE MARCH TO THE RHINE

I

Of all the documents dealing with the operations of the Allied Armies in the Great War, none are perhaps of deeper interest than the "Advance to Victory" and the "Final Despatch," in which Sir Douglas Haig, as Commander-in-Chief of the Armies of the Empire on the Western Front, summarized for the British Government the accomplishment of his troops in the period now known as the "Hundred Days" and pointed out the decisive part they took in compassing Germany's military downfall. In these Despatches, destined to hold an imperishable place in the proud records of the British Army, Sir Douglas Haig wrote, in part:

"In three months of epic fighting the British Armies in France have brought to a sudden and dramatic end the great wearing-out battle of the past four years. . . . In the fighting since the 1st November our troops had broken the enemy resistance beyond possibility of recovery, and had forced on him a disorderly retreat along the whole front of the British Armies. Thereafter, the enemy was capable neither of accepting nor refusing battle. The utter confusion of his troops, the state of his railways, congested with abandoned trains, the capture of huge quantities of rolling stock and material, all showed that our attack had been decisive. . . .

"In the decisive contests of this period [August 8 to November 11, 1918] the strongest and most vital parts of the enemy's front were attacked by the British, his lateral communications were cut, and his best divisions fought to a standstill. On the different battle fronts 187,000 prisoners and 2,850 guns were captured by us . . .

[This record] "is a proof also of the overwhelmingly decisive part played by the British Armies on the Western Front in bringing the enemy to his final defeat. . . .

"We have been accustomed to be proud of the great and noble traditions handed down to us by the soldiers of bygone days. The men who form the Armies of the Empire to-day have created new traditions which are a challenge to the highest records of the past and will be an inspiration to the generations who come after us."

In the published edition of Sir Douglas Haig's Despatches, Marshal Foch presents a foreword which contributes to an understanding of what the British Army, in co-operation with the French and American Armies, had accomplished. In part, this foreword says:

"Never at any time in history has the British Army achieved greater results in attack than in this unbroken offensive lasting 116 days, from the 18th of July to the 11th of November. The victory gained was indeed complete, thanks . . . above all to the unselfishness, to the wise, loyal and energetic policy of their Commander-in-Chief, who made easy a great combination, and sanctioned a prolonged and gigantic effort. . . .

"In order to estimate the ardour and endurance of these troops during this final stage, it will be enough to mention the dates and importance of the main events:—

Battle of Amiens: Fourth Army: August 8-13: 22,000 prisoners, 400 guns.

Battle of Bapaume: Third Army and Left Wing of Fourth Army: August 21—September 1: 34,000 prisoners, 270 guns.

Battle of the Scarpe: First Army: August 26—September 3: 16,000 prisoners, 200 guns.

Battle of Havrincourt and Epéhy. Fourth and Third Armies: September 12-18: 12,000 prisoners, 100 guns.

Battle of Cambrai and the Hindenburg Line: Fourth, Third, and First Armies: September 27—October 5: 35,000 prisoners, 380 guns.

Battle of Flanders: Second Army: September 28—October 14: [11,000 prisoners, 310 guns].

Battle of Le Cateau: Fourth, Third, and First Armies: October 6-12, [12,000 prisoners, 250 guns].

Battle of the Selle: Fourth and Third Armies: October 17-25, 20,000 prisoners, 475 guns.

Battle of the Sambre: Fourth, Third and First Armies: November 1-11: 19,000 prisoners, 450 guns."

II

Having taken a major part in many of the great engagements described in Sir Douglas Haig's "Advance to Victory," and "Final Despatch," and outlined in the table by Marshal Foch, the Canadian troops were deeply gratified when, soon after the Armistice, it was announced that the Canadian Corps, under Lieut.-General Sir A. W. Currie and composed for the time of the 1st and 2nd Canadian Divisions, would form part of the Second British Army in its advance to the Rhine. The 3rd and 4th Canadian Divisions, it was stated, would not move into German territory, but would billet in Belgium and there await demobilization, or whatever service the situation following the Armistice might demand.

On November 16th, the General Officer Commanding the 5th Canadian Infantry Brigade issued "Instructions for Advance to German Frontier No. 1" in which it was stated, in part:

(1) In accordance with the terms of the Armistice, the occupied portions of France, Belgium, and Luxembourg are being evacuated by the enemy by November 26th. The further withdrawal to the East of the Rhine will take place at a later date.

(2) The advance of the Allied Armies to the German frontier begins on November 17th.

(3) The country through which the advance will be carried out is divided into three zones. The enemy is to be clear of these zones on the day preceding the entry of the Allied Armies into that zone.

(4) The British advance is to be carried out by the Second and Fourth Armies. The Canadian Corps is in the Second Army. The Second Army is advancing with the Canadian Corps on the right, the IInd Corps on the left, and the Cavalry Corps (less one division)

in front. The cavalry will always be one march ahead of the infantry.

(5) On November 18th the Canadian Corps is advancing with the 2nd Canadian Division on the right and the 1st Canadian Division on the left. The 2nd Canadian Division is moving in three columns, with the 6th, 5th and 4th Brigade Groups in line from right to left.

(6) The 5th Canadian Infantry Brigade Group is composed of H.Q. the 5th Brigade; the 6th Brigade, Canadian Field Artillery; No. 1 Coy, 2nd Battalion, Canadian Machine-Gun Corps; the 5th Battalion, Canadian Engineers; one troop, Canadian Light Horse; one platoon, Canadian Corps Cyclist Battalion; 5th Canadian Field Ambulance; and No. 3 Coy., 2nd Canadian Divisional Train.

(7) Units will march in full marching order, with steel helmet on the back of pack, and with box respirator on top of the pack. Transport is being provided for blankets.

(8) All units will halt the last ten minutes in each clock hour. There will be no smoking on the march except at halts.

Even before the above instructions were received by the 24th Battalion, officers and men had attended a number of celebrations in honour of the Armistice and had made many private preparations for the march to the Rhine. All ranks were deeply pleased at the thought of marching victoriously to German soil, also by the return, in time to join in the march, of Capt. A. M. Dewar, M.C., Lieut. R. B. E. Wilson, M.C., Lieut. A. Gunnell, M.M., Lieut. H. G. Macario, and Lieut. D. H. Sutherland, the majority of whom had recovered in England from wounds received in the pre-Armistice fighting. Lieut. J. G. LeBlanc, who had been wounded while serving in France with the Royal Canadian Regiment, was also taken on the strength at this time.

On November 14, 1918, the Chaplain of the unit, Hon. Capt. C. J. S. Stuart, M.C., conducted a special service of thanksgiving for victory in the Protestant church at

Petit Wasmes, which was banked with chrysanthemums, brought by the civilians to express the depth of their gratitude for release from the bondage they had endured for long months and years. On the day following this impressive service, Lieut.-Col. Ritchie, two officers, and 66 other ranks proceeded to Mons, as part of a special battalion, under Lieut.-Col. Ritchie's command, formed to represent the 2nd Canadian Division in the official entry into that city of the British First Army Commander, General Sir H. S. Horne.

Even before this event, the 24th Battalion had moved, at 1.45 p.m. on November 14th, to billets in Frameries, where a large group of men were taken on strength from reserve and from the 5th Canadian Trench Mortar Battery, which had been disbanded. Lieut. V. R. Spearing, M.C., also returned to the Battalion at this time after service with the 5th Trench Mortar Battery.

With the additional strength provided by these reinforcements, the Battalion paraded on November 18th and marched from Frameries to Houdeng-Geognies, the civilians along the way according the men a rousing reception and those at the destination expressing their welcome by providing in the billets every comfort and convenience that their means and circumstances would allow. Again on November 19th, the citizens of Houdeng-Geognies celebrated their release from German oppression by giving a civic reception with all officers of the 24th and 26th Battalions as guests, and by speeches, in which deep emotion was revealed. Vengeance upon the Germans was beyond the power of the citizens to wreak, but a number of them, with bitter recollection of suffering and wrongs, stormed the houses of neighbours, whom they accused of friendly relations with the departed enemy, and flung the goods and chattels they found into the street.

In return for the civic reception, the officers of the 24th Battalion invited the citizens and ladies of Houdeng-Geognies to a dance on the evening of November 20th, the invitation being accepted eagerly by many representative members of the commune's personnel. The band of the Battalion played well, particularly when called upon for the waltz airs the citizens preferred, and the evening passed most agreeably.

Next day, the Battalion paraded at 9 a.m. and resumed the march to the Rhine, passing before the Corps Commander, who took the salute, and reaching Pont-à-Celles at 4 o'clock in the afternoon. It was a hard march, but the men found compensation on their arrival in billets which were as comfortable and roomy as any they had up to this time occupied.

For two days, the Battalion remained in Pont-à-Celles, where Lieut. R. J. McLean was taken on the strength, then, on November 24th, it joined the Advance Guard of the 5th Canadian Infantry Brigade Group and, in company with the 16th Battery, Canadian Field Artillery, under Major Baker, D.C.M., and one section of Canadian Engineers, marched approximately 16 miles to Tongrinne. Accommodation in this village was crowded and poor, despite the fact that "D" Coy. took position in the outpost line some distance east of the town.

Marching again on November 25th, the Battalion reached St. Servais at 4 p.m. Fine weather prevailed in the first hours of the march, but heavy rain in the afternoon soaked the roads and obscured the attractive scenery. As a diarist wrote, "it would have been a lovely trip in summer, but as things were we arrived in St. Servais cold, wet, and fairly miserable." Despite these trying conditions, another diarist noted that the men were sticking cheerfully to their work, instancing a private, older than the majority of his comrades, "who swears he will finish the march, in spite of badly swollen feet, if only so that he can say he marched to Germany."

To have taken part in that historic march was, indeed, an experience which a man would recall with pride all his life. A great army was on the move, some impression of the miles of roadway it covered and of the tremendous effort required to keep it moving being furnished by the following table of the space in yards taken by the units of the 5th Canadian Infantry Brigade Group, one of the many groups plodding steadily forward to German soil:

Unit	Space Covered	Interval	Total
5th Brigade H.Q...	260 yards	100 yards	360 yards
22nd Battalion....	1,180 yards	500 yards	1,680 yards
24th Battalion....	1,230 yards	500 yards	1,730 yards

25th Battalion	1,200 yards	500 yards	1,700 yards
26th Battalion	1,150 yards	500 yards	1,650 yards
6th Brigade, C.F.A	2,680 yards	500 yards	3,180 yards
No. 1 Coy. 2nd Bn., C.M.G.C.	750 yards	500 yards	1,250 yards
5th Bn. Can. Engineers	1,410 yards	500 yards	1,910 yards
5th Can. Field Ambulance	430 yards	500 yards	930 yards
7 Motor Ambulances	50 yards	50 yards	100 yards

Grand Total.....................14,490 yards
(8¼ miles)

After halting in St. Servais on November 26th and 27th, the 24th Battalion paraded at 9.05 o'clock on the morning of November 28th and accomplished a long march to Strud, reaching this hamlet at 5 p.m. and billeting round about, with Battalion Headquarters at Haut Bois. In the morning, the unit marched in fine weather through the city of Namur, crossing the River Meuse to Jambes and proceeding for some miles thereafter along the bank of the stream. Rain fell heavily when the unit turned inland from the Meuse and the final stage of the march was accomplished in cold discomfort.

Marching again at 9 a.m. on November 29th, the Battalion passed Sir Arthur Currie, who took the salute at Havelange, and billeted for the night in Jeneffe. It had been announced that the Battalion would remain in Jeneffe on November 30th, but orders were suddenly changed and the unit, parading at 11.30 a.m., marched steadily until, long after night had fallen, billets were occupied in Bomal.

Leaving Bomal at 8.20 o'clock on the following morning, December 1st, the Battalion marched in beautiful weather through wooded and hilly country to Malempré. The thermometer indicated the approach of frost, but the sun shone brilliantly from a cloudless sky and the men enjoyed the march, including the mid-day halt on the bank of a lovely stream. Billets in Malempré were poor and crowded, but all ranks, finding shelter of some description, welcomed orders which stated that the unit might rest on December 2nd and 3rd and resume the march on December 4th.

In Malempré, amid scenery not unlike that in the Highlands of Scotland, the unit rested as ordered for two days, the men taking advantage of the halt to care for their feet which, in many instances, were sore and swollen as a result of the hard and wet marches of the previous two weeks. At this time, a discouraging rumour stated that the battalions of the Canadian Corps would not return to Canada as battalions, but would be broken up and shipped home, as one veteran bitterly expressed it, "like cattle, or a bunch of anti-war draftees." The men at first were concerned by this rumour, but decided eventually that it was a rumour and that to demobilization by categories, or districts, the Corps Commander would never agree.

With the condition of the men's feet improved appreciably by the halt in Malempré, the Battalion marched at 7.20 o'clock on the morning of December 4th and, mounting to the height of land in the district, proceeded to billets in Courtil, a total distance of $15\frac{1}{2}$ miles. Again the weather was wet and cloudy, but at intervals the mists and rain cleared, revealing the beauties of the mountains of the Ardennes through which the route lay. In the morning, not far from the highest point of the road, the unit marched past the Divisional Commander, Major-General Burstall, who congratulated Lieut.-Col. Ritchie on the Battalion's fine marching and appearance.

Leaving Courtil at 7.40 o'clock next morning, December 5th, the Battalion proceeded for two hours and then, with colours unfurled, marched across the German border at Beho. No unusual incident marked the occasion, but all ranks were conscious of an historic moment and of the stimulation that followed when their feet trod German soil. For five hours and twenty minutes after crossing the border, the Battalion moved steadily forward, completing a march of $15\frac{1}{4}$ miles to Wallerode at 3 o'clock in the afternoon. At St. Vith, a point en route, the unit was joined by Capt. R. H. Lamb, M.C., who had recovered in hospital from the wound received at Arras.

After halting overnight in Wallerode, the Battalion proceeded on December 6th and, covering 15 miles of a hilly and difficult route, reached Manderfeld at 3 p.m. Good accommodation in this town was provided, the inhabitants carrying out the billeting orders they received with care and attention. They were not enthusiastic hosts, and were not expected to be, but, if their feelings were hostile, they concealed their emotion and did as they were told without question.

On December 7th the Battalion, for the fourth time on successive days, completed a 15-mile march, from Manderfeld to Schmidtheim. The roads were muddy, rain fell at intervals, and the Transport had serious difficulty on a number of steep hills, nevertheless the unit, though weary, arrived in good condition at 3.30 p.m. In addition to the completion of the unit's fourth consecutive march, the day was marked in the Battalion's history by announcement in London that the inspiring leadership, devotion to duty, and great bravery shown by Lieut.-Col. W. H. Clark-Kennedy, C.M.G., D.S.O., in the Battle of Arras had been recognized by His Majesty the King, who had awarded to the former Commanding Officer of the 24th Battalion the Empire's highest military honour—the Victoria Cross. At the time when this distinction was announced, Lieut.-Col. Clark-Kennedy was in England recovering from his serious wound. News of the honour, however, reached the Battalion, together with favourable reports regarding Lieut.-Col. Clark-Kennedy's progress towards a full recovery, and was received by all ranks with deep satisfaction.

On the day following the march from Manderfeld, the Battalion remained in Schmidtheim, about 200 of the men attending a church parade, which the Chaplain conducted in the courtyard of the local chateau. After this service, which took place in the morning, the men rested in the agreeable sunshine, or devoted themselves to preparation for a resumption of the march on the morrow.

With all preparation completed, the unit paraded in Schmidtheim at 8.30 o'clock on the morning of December 9th and marched 16 miles, up hills and down valleys, to the old walled town of Munstereifel, where the whole Battalion billeted in a convent. Proceeding again through less hilly country on December 10th, the Battalion passed the Divisional Commander, who took the salute, and, at 4 p.m., in fine weather, completed a march of 16½ miles to Meckenheim. Again on December 11th, in glorious sunshine, the unit continued on its way, completing a short march of approximately 8 miles to Godesberg at 11.45 o'clock in the morning. From Godesberg, a number of officers made their way forward for about a mile and stood for the first time on the bank of the Rhine.

All day on December 12th, the Battalion remained in Godesberg, preparing for the march of the 2nd Canadian Division through Bonn and to the east bank of the Rhine. The occasion was regarded as even more historic than the crossing of the German frontier and the troops were determined that their appearance and bearing should reflect to the credit of Canada and the British Empire. Accordingly, they spared no pains in shining and polishing their equipment and in repairing, so far as was possible, the wear and tear to clothing resulting from the long march just completed.

The staffs of the formations of the Canadian Corps, equally anxious that the march across the Rhine should reveal the Corps' magnificent discipline and training, issued careful orders regarding the manner in which the operation would be conducted. Summarized, the orders to the units of the 5th Canadian Infantry Brigade were:

(1) On December 13th, the 2nd Canadian Division is marching through Bonn and across the Rhine. The Division is marching past the Corps Commander en route.

(2) The Divisional Starting Point is the junction of Meckenheimer Allee and Poppelsdorfer Allee.

(3) The Saluting Base will be near the eastern end of the Rhine Bridge.

(4) The route from the Divisional Starting Point to the Saluting Base will be: Poppelsdorfer Allee—Kaiser Platz—Martins Platz—Munster Platz—Windeck Strasse—Friedrich Strasse—Drucken Strasse—Rhine Bridge.

The 24th Battalion, Victoria Rifles of Canada, Crossing the Rhine Bridge at Bonn, December 13, 1918.

(5) The order of march of the 5th Canadian Infantry Brigade Group will be as follows:

> 5th Brigade Headquarters
> 22nd Battalion
> 24th Battalion
> 25th Battalion
> 26th Battalion
> 6th Brigade, C.F.A.

(6) Units will march with fixed bayonets and with colours flying. Bayonets will not be unfixed until units are at least 1,000 yards past the Saluting Base.

(7) Bands will march at the head of their battalions and, on reaching the Saluting Base, will fall out on the sidewalk opposite the Saluting Base and play their units past. They will then fall in immediately behind the last company and in front of the Battalion Transport.

(8) After crossing the Rhine there will be no long halt until units are clear of the main road Beuel-Siegburg.

(9) Steel helmets will be worn by all ranks (the bands excepted) with the strap on the point of the chin. Packs will not be worn. No greatcoats, or raincoats, will be worn by officers or men while passing through Bonn, or over the Bridge.

(10) Billeting and advance parties must all be east of the Rhine Bridge before 8.30 o'clock on the morning of December 13th.

Bearing in mind the above instructions, as well as many details given in the original operation order, but not quoted here, the 24th Battalion, Victoria Rifles of Canada, paraded on the morning of December 13th and took position in the column of the 5th Canadian Infantry Brigade Group for the march across the Rhine. Assembling as ordered, the Battalion marched through the city of Bonn and, at 11.40 a.m., Lieut.-Col. Ritchie led the way on to the Rhine Bridge. Rain fell in sheets as the Battalion approached the point where Sir Arthur Currie stood to take the salute, but the band played superbly and the men, inspired by an historic occasion, marched past in a manner that left nothing to be desired. A small body of German civilians witnessed the event in silence. No man can voice the thoughts that were theirs; but the proud battalions, when compared with the disorganized and defeated German troops, who had withdrawn across the Rhine some days before, must have stirred sombre and poignant reflection.

After the Battalion had swung past Sir Arthur Currie on the Rhine Bridge and had tendered its salute, the band fell into position ahead of the Transport and the unit proceeded to Birlinghoven. From this village, "B" and "C" Companies moved to Rauschendorf, and there took position in the outpost line of the centre brigade sector, 2nd Canadian Divisional area. As all ranks had been soaked by the heavy rain of the morning, the afternoon was passed in drying wet clothing and settling quietly in the new positions.

III

For six weeks after the memorable march across the Rhine at Bonn on December 13, 1918, the 24th Battalion, Victoria Rifles of Canada, remained on German soil. As a whole, the period was marked by no events of outstanding importance, but a number of incidents occurred, not without interest in the Battalion's story. The first of these took place on December 16th, when the Commander of the Second Army, General Sir Herbert Plumer, visited the Battalion lines; and the second on the following day, when it was announced that, for able leadership of the unit in the last two months of the fighting, Lieut.-Col. C. F. Ritchie, M.C., had been awarded the Distinguished Service Order. For valuable and gallant service while in command of a company in the same period, Capt. E. P. Denman was awarded the Military Cross.

For some days after the announcement of these awards, the Battalion carried out routine training and the administrative duties resulting from the occupation of enemy soil. No serious difficulty was encountered, but a number of civilians were arrested and fined for breach of regulations, more particularly those which forbade movement between the area of British occupation and territory under German control.

On December 21st, after the whole Battalion had been paid, "A" Company moved from Birlinghoven to Bonn, being followed on December 22nd by the remaining companies, which had been relieved by the 25th Battalion. In Bonn, all other ranks of the 24th Battalion were billeted in the infantry barracks and officers were provided with accommodation nearby. At this time, the unit took on its commissioned strength Lieut. J. G. Ross, who had crossed from Canada with the 1st Canadian Tank Battalion and had served as A.D.C. to the G.O.C. the 2nd Canadian Division.

Soon after taking over the barracks in Bonn, all ranks of the 24th Battalion prepared to celebrate their first Christmas on German soil. "C" Coy. dined at 3 o'clock on the afternoon of December 24th and from that time until the same hour on December 27th, when "A" Coy.'s dinner was held, festivity was the order of the day. On Christmas, church parades were held in the morning for Protestants and Roman Catholics, and the Battalion Chaplain celebrated Holy Communion for all who desired to attend. In the afternoon, a number of dinners were held, and at night, with Major-General Burstall as their guest, the officers joyously celebrated what all believed would be their final Christmas in the armed forces of the King.

On December 28th, Sir Arthur Currie inspected the Battalion and the barracks in which it was quartered at 11 a.m., afterwards addressing the men and complimenting them on the appearance and bearing of the unit, which revealed the high state of their morale. Two days after the Corps Commander's inspection, the Battalion marched from Bonn and took over Brigade Reserve billets at Menden.

In Menden, the Battalion welcomed the New Year. No formal celebrations were held on January 1, 1919, but routine parades were cancelled and, as the day was fine and clear, the men enjoyed a series of football games, including a match in which a Battalion team defeated a team from the 5th Squadron, Royal Air Force, by the close score of 1 to nil. In addition to the football matches, the day was marked by the return to duty of Major P. L. Hall, M.C., who reported to Lieut.-Col. Ritchie on completion of the Senior Officers' Course he had attended in England.

Two days after Major Hall's arrival, educational classes in the Battalion were started, English, farming, and geography and history being taught respectively by Lieuts. R. S. Egan, J. L. Foote, and R. B. E. Wilson, M.C. From the beginning, these classes were popular and so continued throughout the Battalion's stay in Germany and the later period in Belgium. In part, the popularity of the classes rested upon the fact that attendance won release from routine fatigues and drill, but many of the men, aware of defects in their elementary, or more advanced, education, attended in a genuine effort to gain knowledge applicable in the civilian life to which demobilization would soon be leading them.

For ten days after the inauguration of the educational classes, the Battalion remained in Menden in Brigade Reserve. Then, on January 14th, it paraded, under Major P. L. Hall, who had assumed command on the departure of Lieut.-Col. Ritchie on leave to England, and marched, with a strength of 43 officers and 781 other ranks, to relieve the 22nd French-Canadian Battalion in the Brigade Outpost Line, with Battalion Headquarters at Geistingen.

Throughout the subsequent period of outpost duty, difficulty arose frequently in governing the civil population and in enforcing military law. Over and again, German civilians attempted to pass through the outpost line, or moved about at night without permission. At last it was found necessary for a court of summary justice to sit and for the Officer Commanding the Battalion to impose fines and prison sentences, varying from a minimum of 20 marks, in cases of ignorant or unintentional breach of rules, to a maximum of 500 marks, with from 4 days' to 2 months' imprisonment, when the offence was deliberate and committed in defiance of known regulations.

While this court was still in operation, the Battalion welcomed as a guest Lieut.-Col. W. H. Clark-Kennedy, V.C., C.M.G., D.S.O., who had recovered sufficiently from the serious wounds received in August to permit a visit to the Canadian forces in Germany. All ranks were deeply pleased to greet the former Commanding Officer and to realize from his appearance that his shattered leg had healed and would not seriously hamper him, either as a soldier, or in the civil life that lay ahead.

On the evening of the day following Lieut.-Col. Clark-Kennedy's arrival, the 15th Battalion of the Argyll and Sutherland Highlanders marched in to Geistingen, each company billeting with the corresponding company of the 24th Battalion. Next morning, at 11 o'clock, Major Hall and the Commanding Officer of the Highlanders rode around the line of the 24th Battalion posts, completing the circuit at approximately 5 p.m. and returning to Battalion Headquarters in Geistingen. Meanwhile, the Argyll and Sutherland companies and details had relieved the corresponding elements of the 24th Battalion and had assumed responsibility for the line.

This relief marked the conclusion of the 24th Battalion's active employment in Germany. On January 23rd, the morning was spent in preparing for a move and the afternoon in sport, the feature being a football match in which teams from the Argyll and Sutherland Highlanders and the 24th Battalion battled keenly to a 3-all draw. Next morning "A," "C" and "D" Companies marched to Siegburg, being followed by Battalion Headquarters and "B" Coy., with the pipe band of the Argylls leading, a compliment which officers and men of the 24th duly appreciated.

At Siegburg, the 24th Battalion, Victoria Rifles of Canada, entrained in box-cars, and at 4.30 p.m. the train pulled out of the station. That night the train, rumbling slowly westward, crossed the German border and the men of the Battalion, with their service on enemy soil completed, gazed in the morning at the snow-clad fields of Belgium and wondered how long a time must elapse before the unit might hope to see the shores of Canada. No one could answer this question. All that was known was that the Battalion must detrain at Auvelais, Belgium, there, presumably, to await transfer to England and, later, demobilization in Canada.

CHAPTER XVII

THE END OF THE ROAD

I

On completion of its service with the British Army of Occupation in the Rhineland of Germany, the 24th Battalion, Victoria Rifles of Canada, moved by train to Auvelais, Belgium, as related in the previous chapter of this book, and there remained in billets for ten weeks. It was a difficult period for officers and men, as all ranks were anxious to return to Canada and resume their civil occupations. Demobilization, however, could not be accomplished in a day and the troops, realizing this, trained, attended educational classes, and took part in varied programmes of sport with highly creditable enthusiasm. On the signing of the Armistice, or, perhaps it would be more accurate to say, upon the return of the unit from German soil, the major incentive to first class military endeavour vanished, but the men were proud of the record established by the Battalion in the field, and, with negligible exceptions, co-operated with their officers in maintaining a high morale and a conspicuous esprit de corps.

Reaching Auvelais at 9 o'clock on the night of January 25th, the men detrained and immediately took over billets in the town. These were uncomfortable and not outstandingly clean, but were improved on January 27th when the greater part of the unit was set to work to make them more habitable and convenient. With this work accomplished, educational classes were promptly resumed, under the officers who had lectured in Germany, and Capt. J. R. Simard, who filled a much desired vacancy by giving instruction in French. In addition to formal instruction, a number of lectures of general interest were delivered at this time, one of the most absorbing being presented on January 31st by a British Naval officer, who lectured on "Submarines."

Some days before the delivery of this popular lecture, all ranks of the unit had been pleased by the announcement in Divisional Orders that the Belgian Government had conferred on Major P. L. Hall, M.C., and on Private D. M. Morrison, of the 24th Battalion, the Belgian Croix de Guerre. At the time of the announcement, Private Morrison was in England, recovering from wounds, but Major Hall, who was commanding the Battalion during the absence on leave of Lieut.-Col. Ritchie, received the congratulations which the honour deserved.

Approximately a week after the announcement of the Belgian Government's awards, three officers of the Battalion, Lieuts. Paul Emard, W. R. Kingsford, and P. E. R. Lockwood, proceeded to England for demobilization. These were the first to go, but they were followed three days later by Lieuts. J. C. LeBlanc, J. C. Kelley, N. T. Hammett, and H. E. Rose, M.M., and on February 11th by Capt. J. R. Simard. Four days after Capt. Simard's departure, the unit welcomed Lieut.-Col. C. F. Ritchie, who returned from leave in England and again assumed the command.

From the time of Lieut.-Col. Ritchie's return on February 15th, until the end of the month, no outstanding incident occurred, the time being filled by routine, educational classes, entertainments, to which the citizens were frequently invited, and sports. In the last of these categories, a fine long distance road race aroused much enthusiasm. Fast teams from the 22nd and 25th Battalions offered sterling opposition, but the 24th Battalion team carried off the prize, Private W. J. Gover running a plucky race and breasting the tape well ahead of his nearest rival.

On March 1, 1919, Lieut.-Col. C. F. Ritchie proceeded on command to the battlefields of Verdun, being followed three days later by his Second-in-Command, Major P. L. Hall, who handed over command of the 24th Battalion to Major J. N. Bales, M.C. Previous to Major Hall's departure, the majority of the Battalion personnel had attended Divisional Sports at Namur on March 3rd and had witnessed some keen competition. In the road race, Private Gover again broke the tape in front of all opposition, but the Battalion team could not rival his speed and the team prize passed to the 31st Battalion. In the finals for the Divisional football championship, the 31st Battalion also scored a splendid win, defeating the 24th Battalion by a score of 1 to nil.

On March 8th, the unit bade farewell to Capt. R. B. Jenkins, M.C., the Medical Officer, who was proceeding to England and thence to Canada for demobilization. Four days later, with a strength of 19 officers and 412 other ranks, the Battalion paraded, under Major J. N. Bales, M.C., and was inspected by the Fourth Army Commander, General Sir Henry Rawlinson, G.C.B. Sir Henry cast an experienced eye along the ranks and, noting that the period in billets had not been permitted to affect the men's bearing, complimented Major Bales on the unit's smart appearance.

For ten days after Sir Henry Rawlinson's inspection, the Battalion, under Lieut.-Col. Ritchie, who returned from Verdun on March 13th, continued to carry out the routine of life in billets and the process of turning in equipment, without noteworthy interruption. Plans for demobilization were proceeding at the time and 8 other ranks, who intended to marry in England before returning to Canada, were permitted to proceed to England for this purpose on March 21st, being followed on March 25th by 15 other ranks, who had accepted employment as military police at Bramshott Camp, under Canadian Corps Headquarters. In offset to these losses, the Battalion strength was increased on March 25th when 1 officer and 70 other ranks, who wished to be demobilized in Montreal, reported for duty from the 19th, 20th, and 21st Battalions and from the Canadian Machine-Gun Corps.

On the days immediately following, regrouping of troops from units of the 2nd Canadian Division continued, the 24th Battalion taking on strength approximately 50 additional other ranks, who left the 27th, 28th, 29th, and 31st Battalions to join a unit which would be demobilized in Montreal. As it was not convenient to absorb these drafts into the existing companies of the Battalion, they were eventually grouped in a special formation, referred to in regimental orders as "E" Company.

Early in April, 1919, the men of the 24th Battalion received with deep satisfaction definite information that the unit would entrain in Auvelais for le Havre on the morning of April 3rd. At 9.30 o'clock on the morning of April 2nd, Lieut.-Col. Ritchie held a muster parade and thereafter, until the hour of departure, at noon on the following day, all ranks were employed in preparations for the journey. When the Battalion marched to the station to entrain, the good people of Auvelais gathered to wish the men farewell, and being emotional, as one diarist has written, "were most affectionate and demonstrative." The same diarist reports, however, that "the men were far too excited to reciprocate much and left the town without a shadow of real regret."

Steaming from Auvelais at noon, the train carrying the 24th Battalion proceeded to Mons and thence, on the morning of April 4th, through Arras and across the old battlefields on which the Battalion, in the autumn, had won enduring distinction. From their box-cars, which were not uncomfortably crowded, the men viewed the sites of their engagements with deep and ever-increasing interest. It was hard to realize that areas, traversed by the train in a few moments, were those which, a few months before, had been torn from the enemy's grasp only after days, or even weeks, of bitter and costly fighting.

Though peace now reigned in the fields of former action, the Battalion's journey was marked by one event, awakening memories of the days when tragedy was ever close at hand. No enemy now opposed the unit's movement to its appointed destination, but one name remained to be added to the roll of the Battalion's fallen, the tragic total being completed when Lieut. R. J. McLean, the Officer on Train Supervision Duty, slipped on the wet platform of a wayside station and, to the deep regret of his brother officers and to that of the other ranks over whom he held command, died from injuries inflicted by the wheels of the moving train.

After crossing the historic battlefields near Arras, the train proceeded and reached le Havre at 3.30 o'clock on the afternoon of April 5th, the troops then marching at once to quarters in the Canadian Embarkation Camp. This camp was a model of comfort and efficiency, the second quality being demonstrated on April 6th when the entire Battalion was put through a steam de-lousing process, after which the men, clean as to person and clothing, were sent to fresh billets and declared ready for the crossing to England.

II

Proceeding from the Canadian Embarkation Camp at le Havre on the afternoon of April 7th, "A" and "B" Companies and Headquarters of the 24th Battalion, Victoria Rifles of Canada, embarked on the S.S. *Prince George*, which sailed at 7 p.m. and, after an uneventful crossing of the English Channel, docked in Southampton about 12.30 o'clock on the morning of April 8th. Disembarking at 8 a.m., the men entrained at 11.30 o'clock and, reaching Milford some two and a half hours later, marched to Witley Camp, where accommodation had been provided. At Witley Camp, the main body of the Battalion was joined by "C," "D" and "E" Companies, which reported from le Havre at 5 o'clock on the afternoon of April 9th.

After bathing parades and medical boards had been held on April 10th and 11th, approximately 20 officers and 300 other ranks proceeded on leave on April 12th, being followed by 15 officers and 300 other ranks on the morning of April 13th. For a week thereafter the Battalion Diary contains no entry other than the simple phrase "Battalion away on leave," but, on April 20th, some 18 officers and about 250 other ranks reported back for duty and the Battalion, as a battalion, began to function once more.

On April 23rd, 18 officers proceeded to London to attend the 2nd Canadian Divisional Dinner at the Savoy Hotel; and on the 26th the unit paraded for presentation by its Honorary Colonel, Field Marshal His Royal Highness the Duke of Connaught, of the King's Colour. At this ceremony, the Duke of Connaught was received at Witley Camp by Major-General Sir Henry E. Burstall,

K.C.B., and conducted to a position near the Portsmouth Road, where the 18th, 20th, and 24th Canadian Battalions were drawn up on three sides of a square. After receiving the Royal Salute, the Duke of Connaught stood by while the colours for the three battalions were consecrated by Bishop Taylor Smith. Rain fell at intervals, but the impressive ceremony was not seriously marred, nor were the subsequent manoeuvres when, after His Royal Highness's presentation address, the battalions formed in line, the colours received the general salute, the colour parties rejoined their respective units, as the band played *God Save the King*, and the three battalions, with their new colours flying proudly in the breeze, carried out a splendid march past.

On the occasion of the presentation of colours, His Royal Highness spoke with deep feeling of the part taken by the troops before him in the great battles of the war. Addressing the officers and men of the battalions, he said:

"It gives me the greatest pleasure and pride to see you on parade, and to present you with these colours, which are the symbol of loyalty to King and Country. May you ever carry them to the honour and glory of Canada. You represent three battalions of the great Second Canadian Division that fought so splendidly in France. I would weary you were I to repeat the names of the engagements in which you took so prominent a part, but perhaps the great attack on Vimy Ridge, where the Second Division fought with such bravery, will recall to you many who fell on the bloody field.

"My son, who is with me here to-day, saw the Second Division go into action at Vimy Ridge, and he says he will never forget it as long as he lives. I do not suppose I shall have the pleasure of seeing you again, certainly not in the Old Country. I am proud to think of the splendid way you have maintained the good name of Canada throughout France and Belgium. May you carry back to the great Dominion the gratitude and respect of all your fellow-countrymen.

"You leave England bearing with you the affection and respect of the whole British Army and of the whole British Nation. May God bless you, may you always honour and respect those colours which are carried before you, and may you teach your children to look upon them as a symbol of the splendid services which their fathers performed. I am glad to have the opportunity of being with you once again. I invoke the blessing of God upon you, and wish you a happy return to your country."

A week after the Duke of Connaught had honoured the three battalions of the 2nd Canadian Division by presenting to each a King's Colour, Lieut.-Col. C. F. Ritchie, Capt. R. H. Lamb, Lieut. F. W. Stenson, Lieut. A. McBean, and 120 other ranks of the 24th Battalion proceeded to take part in a march of the troops of His Majesty's Overseas Dominions through the streets of London. Leave to witness the event was granted to other officers and to a large number of men.

As the occasion was unique in the history of the Empire, no pains were spared by the staffs of the units participating to see that their respective troops knew exactly what procedure would be expected of them. To the battalions of the 5th Canadian Infantry Brigade, on May 1st, was issued an order, containing, in substance, the following instructions:

(1) A detachment of the 5th Canadian Infantry Brigade will take part in a march of Dominion troops through London on Saturday, May 3rd.

(2) The detachment will be under the command of Brigadier-General T. L. Tremblay, C.M.G., D.S.O., G.O.C. the Brigade.

(3) Each battalion of the Brigade will send:
1 battalion commander
1 company commander
2 subalterns
120 N.C.O.'s and privates
2 N.C.O.'s for battalions with King's Colours.

(4) Dress: Battle order, with caps instead of steel helmets. Officers will wear Sam Browne belts, without revolvers or field glasses. No sticks will be carried.

(5) The detachment will move from Witley Camp to London by train. On reaching London, troops will march to the concentration area in Hyde Park, near the Marble Arch.

His Royal Highness the Duke of Connaught Presenting the King's Colour to the Battalion, April 26, 1919.

(6) The starting point will be Stanhope Gate. The head of the Canadian Corps Column will pass this point at 1.48 p.m.

(7) His Majesty the King will inspect the troops at Buckingham Palace. The head of the Canadian Corps Column will pass this point at 2 p.m.
Two bands of the Brigade of Guards will play troops past the saluting point. Other bands will not play within 200 yards of the saluting point.

(8) The Brigade detachment will march in two parallel columns. The right column will consist of the 22nd and 25th Battalions, and the left column of the 24th and 26th Battalions.

(9) Battalion detachments will march in column of route, each detachment being divided into two equal platoons, with the colour party between, 4 yards in rear of the front platoon and 4 yards in advance of the rear platoon.

(10) Troops will march at ease except past Buckingham Palace.

(11) Watches will be synchronized at Grosvenor Gate at 1.15 p.m.

(12) Horses for Commanding Officers will be at Grosvenor Gate and will be handed over at the same point after the march. Horses will be labelled with officers' names.

(13) Route:
    Grosvenor Gate (1.48 p.m.)
    Ring Road (inside the Park)
    Hyde Park Corner
    Constitution Hill
    Buckingham Palace Road
    Victoria Street
    Whitehall
    Strand
    Round Australia House
    Aldwych
    Kingsway

High Holborn
New Oxford Street
Oxford Street
Marble Arch
Hyde Park

In addition to the above orders, the attention of all units to march under Sir Arthur Currie's command was directed by the Corps Comander to six points which, in substance, were as follows:

(1) Sizing of the men chosen, to secure a measure of uniformity.
(2) The carrying of the rifle, with elbow close to the side and forearm straight to the front.
(3) The pipe-claying of equipment and the polishing of all brass.
(4) The wearing of the haversack high on the shoulder.
(5) The care to be taken in dressing of ranks.
(6) The wearing of the cap square on top of the head, not on the side of the head, or at the back.

In conclusion, Sir Arthur remarked that, as the occasion would be the first in the war, and probably the last, on which a large body of Canadian troops would parade in London, march discipline must be strictly maintained, in order that the Canadian claim to the highest position amongst the troops of the Overseas Dominions might be adequately supported.

Parading in accordance with the above orders and instructions, Lieut.-Col. Ritchie led his detachment from Hyde Park, past His Majesty the King at Buckingham Palace, and through the streets of London by the route laid down. Never before in the age-long history of Britain's capital had such a pageant of Empire taken place. More brilliant displays the old city had witnessed in abundance, but this march of the khaki-clad battalions, though triumphal, stirred memories of Ypres, Gallipoli, and the Somme, and the citizens, in tribute to the troops who had fought on those stricken fields, cheered the units at all stages of the march. It was a magnificent

HOMEWARD BOUND. OFFICERS OF THE BATTALION ON BOARD H.M.T. "OLYMPIC," MAY, 1919.

Front Row: left to right: Capt. J. D. MacIntyre, M.C., Lieut. A. Beck, M.M., Hon. Capt. C. J. S. Stuart, M.C., Lieut. G. H. Macario, M.C., Lieut. H. M. Alexander, M.C., Lieut. J. L. Foote, Lieut. J. G. Ross. *Second Row:* Capt. P. E. McLaughlin, Major V. E. Duclos, M.C., Major P. L. Hall, D.S.O., M.C., Lieut.-Col. C. F. Ritchie, D.S.O., M.C., Major J. N. Bales, M.C., Major A. M. Dewar, M.C., Capt. W. E. Bidwill, Capt. E. P. Denman, M.C. *Third Row:* Lieut. D. H. Sutherland, Lieut. Urquhart (attached), Capt. J. A. Donovan, M.C., D.C.M., Lieut. E. T. Lane, Lieut. F. H. Morgan, M.C., Lieut. F. J. Montle, Lieut. A. Gunnell, M.M., Lieut. W. McMurray, M.C., Lieut. E. M. Styles, Lieut. A. McBean. *Top Row:* Lieut. K. C. McIntyre, M.M., Lieut. W. Watson, Lieut. D. M. Matheson, M.C., Lieut. V. Curtis, M.C., Lieut. S. A. Rolland, Lieut. H. R. Tanner, M.C., Lieut. F. S. Leach, Lieut. R. B. E. Wilson, M.C., Lieut. F. W. Stenson, M.C.

military spectacle and stirred the hearts of all who were privileged to take part in, or witness, it.

In a Special Order of the Day, issued when the march was over, Lieut.-General Sir Arthur Currie congratulated the troops under his command and stated: "I have never seen the troops of the Canadian Corps bear themselves more soldierly. . . The marching and march discipline were excellent. . . Although one could have wished that representatives of all units of the Canadian Corps had participated in the parade, yet those who had that distinction were worthy representatives of that splendid organization which, in all the severe tests to which they were subjected on the battlefields of Europe, fought so magnificently and victoriously."

Before reviewing the march of the troops of his Overseas Dominions on May 3rd, His Majesty the King had held an investiture in Buckingham Palace and had presented to a number of officers of the Overseas Forces orders and decorations won by them in France. Among those who appeared before the King on this occasion and received their honours from his hand were the following officers of the 24th Battalion:

Lieut.-Col. C. F. Ritchie, Distinguished Service Order
Capt. V. E. Duclos, Military Cross
Capt. A. M. Dewar, Military Cross
Capt. E. P. Denman, Military Cross
Lieut. W. McMurray, Military Cross and Bar
Lieut. F. H. Morgan, Bar to the Military Cross
Lieut. H. G. Macario, Military Cross
Lieut. D. M. Matheson, Military Cross
Lieut. H. M. Alexander, Bar to the Military Cross

Following the break in routine caused by the ceremonies in London, the 24th Battalion, at Witley Camp, resumed preparations for demobilization in Canada. Thousands of documents were completed, medical boards sat each day, and the men, when not engaged in supplying information for documents, passed the time in routine fatigues, in packing equipment for transportation to Canada, and in the carrying out of an extensive and varied programme of sport.

Though the camp life was not without attraction, the men soon wearied of it and eagerly awaited orders to sail for home. Rumours that orders were expected spread rapidly in the early days of May and on the 8th were confirmed when it was announced that the 5th Canadian Infantry Brigade would move to Southampton on the night of May 9th and there embark on His Majesty's Transport *Olympic*, which would sail for Halifax forthwith.

Entraining in accordance with these orders, the 24th Battalion reached Southampton, embarked on the *Olympic*, together with the 22nd, 25th, 26th, and 29th Battalions, and on May 10th, exactly four years after sailing from Montreal, left the shores of England behind. Six days later, after a voyage marked by no outstanding incident, the Battalion disembarked in Halifax and, in two trains, proceeded to Montreal.

On the trains, as they sped westward through the Maritime Provinces and then through Quebec, all was bustle and excitement, as the men polished their equipment and prepared for their final march through the streets of Montreal; and in the city excitement was no less intense, for the people, having welcomed battalions of the 1st and 3rd Canadian Divisions, were determined that the 24th Battalion, representing the 2nd Canadian Division, should receive an equal tribute. Officers and men of the 3rd Regiment, Victoria Rifles of Canada, took an eager part in the resulting preparation and, assembling at the Regimental Armoury on Cathcart Street, marched to the Place Viger Station, of the Canadian Pacific Railway, where the troop trains were due to arrive.

Steaming into the station within a few minutes of one another on the afternoon of May 18th, the trains bearing the 24th Battalion came to a stop and the men of the unit, tumbling from the cars, were overwhelmed by a great wave of cheering comrades and citizens, the former group including a guard of honour composed of 3 officers and approximately 100 men of the Victoria Rifles of Canada, and Brigadier-General J. A. Gunn, C.M.G., D.S.O., the original Commanding Officer of the Battalion, who had travelled from Toronto to welcome his old unit home. Admission to the station was granted only to a limited

THE BATTALION'S LAST PARADE.

The unit crossing the Champ de Mars, Montreal, May 18, 1919, on its return from service overseas.

number of civilians and to those who, through official connection with the Battalion, were entitled to witness the unit's return, but to the men it seemed that, in the cheering and excited throng, all Montreal was represented.

After receiving a warm welcome in the station, Lieut.-Col. C. F. Ritchie, D.S.O., M.C., issued orders in response to which his men, wearing steel helmets and with bayonets fixed, formed up to march through the streets of the city to the Peel Street Barracks, whence the unit had marched to sail for overseas service on that memorable night in May, 1915. Four years had passed since that time, four momentous years, and the Battalion paraded with the knowledge that the city's tribute was paid not alone to those who had survived, but equally to the men of 1915 whose graves in France and Belgium marked the unit's path to victory.

Of the officers who had marched with the unit in 1915, three remained on the strength when the Battalion returned to Montreal, Lieut.-Col. C. F. Ritchie, D.S.O., M.C., Major P. L. Hall, D.S.O., M.C., the Second-in-Command, and Major V. E. Duclos, M.C., commanding "B" Coy. The other companies were commanded by Capt. A. M. Dewar, M.C., Capt. E. P. Denman, M.C., and Capt. W. E. Bidwill, the two former being original members of the unit who had sailed in the ranks from Montreal. In the position of Adjutant, which he had filled with distinction for so many months in France, was Major J. N. Bales, M.C., who also, in the ranks, had been with the unit when it had sailed for service overseas.

Marching from Place Viger Station, Lieut.-Col. Ritchie led the Battalion across the Champ de Mars, where Major-General E. W. Wilson, G.O.C. Military District No. 4, a former Commanding Officer of the Victoria Rifles of Canada, took the salute. Proceeding by way of St. James Street and Beaver Hall Hill, the unit turned west on St. Catherine Street and then north to the Peel Street Barracks. Wheeling to the right, the men marched up the steps of the barracks, where command passed from Lieut.-Col. Ritchie to the staff officers entrusted with demobilization. There was no ceremony and no prolonged process of farewell. Instead, the men of the 24th Battalion, Victoria Rifles of Canada, after a few words of grateful thanks from their Commanding Officer, laid down their arms and, almost without delay, turned their thoughts from war to the insistent demands of peace. They had served with marked distinction in the armed forces of His Majesty the King; to-day, eleven years later, they are serving Canada, in accordance with the country's needs. Tried in the furnace of bitter fighting overseas, and not found wanting, they serve now with no small measure of the indomitable courage and high morale which, at the Somme, Vimy Ridge, Hill 70, Passchendaele, Amiens, and Arras, enshrined in Canadian military history forever the number "24" and the proud title "Victoria Rifles of Canada."

APPENDICES

(Compiled from data furnished through the courtesy of the Records Section, Department of National Defence, Ottawa.)

APPENDIX A

24th Battalion, Victoria Rifles of Canada

HONOUR ROLL

KILLED IN ACTION OR DIED OF WOUNDS

OFFICERS

Buchanan, Lieut. Reginald H. B.

Campbell, Hon. Capt. Harry Davies (Quartermaster)

Cowan, Lieut. Stewart

Davis, Lieut. Harry A. (while serving with the Canadian Machine Gun Corps)

Donald, Lieut. John

Drummond, Lieut. Kevin Stewart, M.C.

Durman, Lieut. Arthur, M.C.

Duthie, Lieut. Wilfred Alexander (while seconded to the Canadian Machine Gun Corps)

Fair, Lieut. Robert McCamus (while seconded to the 5th Canadian Trench Mortar Battery)

Fairweather, Capt. Frank Russell (while serving with the 26th Canadian Battalion)

Green, Capt. Carleton Carroll (while serving with the 13th Battalion, Royal Highlanders of Canada)

Haddock, Lieut. Geoffrey

Hallam, Lieut. Frank Harold

Hastings, Capt. William Roy (while serving with the 16th Battalion Canadian Scottish)

Hawkins, Lieut. Kenneth Belmont

Hingston, Lieut. Reginald Basil

Johnson, Lieut. Hugh Stanley

Kavanagh, Lieut. Joseph John, M.C.

Laing, Lieut. Murdoch

Laird, Lieut. John Hewitt

LeMesurier, Lieut. George Stuart

Murray, Capt. Harcourt Amory

MacArthur, Lieut. James McPherson

MacNaughton, Lieut. Ian Robert R.

McGiffin, Lieut. George Allan

McLean, Lieut. Robert John (accidentally)

McMurtry, Major Eric Ogilvie (while on command Royal Flying Corps)

Parr, Major Clayton Bowers

Platt, Lieut. Edward Cuthbert

Power, Lieut. Edward Victor

Riley, Lieut. Charles Edward

Ritchie, Lieut. Hubert Sydney

Ross, Major John Alexander, D.S.O.

Scott, Lieut. Howard Elliot (while serving as Brigade Grenade Officer)

Scougall, Lieut. Walter Mowbray

Shipway, Lieut. John Cecil

Smith, Lieut. Cecil Parker

Smyth, Lieut. George Crawford

Tucker, Lieut. Percival George, M.C.

Walker, Major Arthur Leslie (while serving as Brigade Major, 5th C.I.B.)

Walker, Capt. Philip Ilderton, M.C.

Weaver, Lieut. Ralph Lincoln

Wilkins, Lieut. John Fox

HONOUR ROLL

OTHER RANKS

Adams, Private Charles
Adams, Private Guy Kinsman
Adams, Private Victor
Albright, Lance-Corp. Charles Albert
Alden, Private Edgar
Aldrich, Private Merrill Stanley
Alger, Private George Walter
Allen, Private Frank James
Alley, Private Eric Elgin
Anderson, Private John
Anderson, Private William Carson
Andrews, Private Reide
Anthony, Private James Bray
Arbing, Private Harry Spurgeon
Armburg, Private Frank James
Ash, Sergt. Francis
Ashcroft, Private Albert Edward
Astels, Private Herman
Astle, Private George Esmonde
Atkinson, Lance-Corp. James Watson
Aveling, Private Charles

Bacon, Private Albert
Bagge, Private Sydney Charles J.
Bailly, Private Debney Byron
Baker, Private Percy Irvine
Barclay, Private Alexander
Barlow, Lance-Corp. Ronald
Barnes, Lance-Sergt. Edward Ernest
Barnwell, Private Frederick William G.
Barth, Corporal Robert L.
Bartlett, Sergt. James B.
Bates, Private Charles
Bates, Private Eric Nye
Batt, Private Stanley
Batten, Private Frederick
Baverstock, Private Ernest
Baxter, Private Allen
Baxter, Sergt. Richard James
Beard, Private Archie Warren
Beaton, Private Duncan
Beazley, Corporal Vincent Levi
Belcourt, Private George Albert
Bell, Private Leo
Berryman, Private Harvey Charles
Bickerdine, Private Robert Shearley
Bilton, Private Oliver
Birdseye, Private Francis James
Birne, Corporal James

Birnie, Private Charles Henry
Biron, Private Joseph
Blake, Private Christopher Edward
Blanchard, Private John
Blanchette, Private Guy
Blough, Lance-Sergt. Stanley Roy
Bockus, Private Henry
Bolduc, Private Thomas
Booth, Private Gardner
Borthwick, Private James M.
Bosse, Private Henri
Bosee, Private Joseph Albert
Boudreau, Private John Angus
Boulay, Private Emile
Boutin, Private Adelard
Bowden, Private William C.
Boyle, Private Louis
Brackenridge, Lance-Corp. Max
Braden, Private Clarence George
Bremner, Private Stewart
Brennan, Private George
Brennan, Private Harold Vincent
Brereton, Lance-Sergt. John Lamb
Brett, Private Walter George
Brewer, Corporal Christopher Robert
Brigden, Private Samuel
Brisson, Private Xavier
Brochu, Sergt. Joseph
Brooks, Private Francis Hiram
Broom, Private Charles Sidney
Brophy, Private Frank Lawrence A.
Brophy, Private Lawrence Walter
Brown, Private Frederick Young, M.M.
Brown, Lance-Corp. Medes
Brown, Private Peter
Brown, Private Robert Donald
Brown, Private Thomas
Brown, Private William (No. 65124)
Brown, Private William (No. 171045)
Brownell, Private Frank
Bruce, Private Robert
Brundage, Lance-Sergt. Claude Lionel
Bryenton, Private Vernon James
Buckley, Private William
Buels, Private John Frank
Bullard, Private Merle Frederick
Bullock, Private Thomas
Burgess, Private Victor George
Burns, Private John

Burns, Sergt. John Edward
Burns, Corporal William
Burton, Private Arnold Morley
Burton, Private David
Burton, Private Frank
Burton, Private William
Butler, Private Charles Andrew
Butler, Private Martin

Cairns, Private John Arthur
Calbeck, Private Lindsay
Calderley, Private Edward
Callaghan, Private Edison
Callaghan, Private Richard Patrick
Callaghan, Private Frank (No. 919604)
Cameron, Sergt. Alexander
Cameron, Private Louis Coutney
Camire, Private Ludger
Campbell, Lance-Sergt. Lachlin C., M.M.
Campbell, Private Michael
Cannon, Private John Richard
Cantwell, Private Walter Thomas
Carey, Private Patrick
Carlsen, Private Henry Carl
Carmenson, Private Robert
Carmichael, Private John
Carmichael, Private Robert
Carroll, Private James
Carson, Private James
Carter, Private Clarence
Carter, Private Richard
Carter, Private Roland
Casey, Private John
Cave, Lance-Corp. Louis
Chaese, Sergt. Francis Stuart
Chafe, Private William Ambrose
Chapman, Private Jack
Chappell, Private Frank
Charbonneau, Private Armand
Charbonneau, Private Rock
Charrel, C.Q.M.S. Alexander Robert
Chesley, Private Roger Bert
Churchill, Private Arthur Joseph
Clark, Private Joseph Leonard
Clendinning, Private William
Clift, Private Edwin Alfred
Clourey, Private John
Clunie, Private William
Coakley, Private Maurice

Coapland, Private Glenn
Coates, Private Frank
Cochrane, Private Norman Jasper
Colclough, Private Wilfred George
Cole, Private William James
Colebrook, Private William
Coleman, Private Francis
Collins, Private Daniel
Collins, Private Henry
Collins, Private James
Collyer, Private Frank
Conlan, Private Patrick
Conley, Private Joseph
Conlon, Private Mike
Conlon, Sergt. Thomas
Connolly, Private John
Cook, Corporal Arthur
Cook, Corporal Frank
Cook, Private Harry
Cook, Private Robert Mackenzie
Cook, Private Samuel
Cooke, Private Charles William
Cooke, Corporal Thomas Henry
Cooper, Private James
Cooper, Private William
Copeland, Sergt. Arthur
Copeland, Private George
Corcoran, Private Lawrence
Cording, Private George
Cornish, Private Ernest
Cottingham, Sergt. William
Coulthard, Private Lewis William
Cound, Private Michael William
Couture, Private Ovila
Craine, Private Laurence
Crawford, Private Stanley
Croft, Private John
Cronkwright, Private George
Crosby, Private Keith Bruce
Crowell, Private George
Crozier, Private Andrew
Cullen, Lance-Corp. William E.
Cutler, Private James Joseph

Daigle, Private Arthur
Dakers, Private Albert
Dakin, Private Chester B.
Dalton, Private Thomas
Dalzell, Private James
Daniel, Private Reginald H. H.

HONOUR ROLL

Darlison, Private Albert
Darrell, Private Robert
Davies, Private George
Davies, Private Herbert
Davis, Private Alfred
Davis, Private Robert
Davis, Private William George
Day, Private Aca
Dayton, Corporal Robert Maurice
Deane, Private Jeffrey
DeGarmendia, Private Vincent
Denis, Private George Albert
Dennis, Private William Henry
Dent, Private William Charlie
Depledge, Sergt. Jack, M.M. (True name Horace Firth)
Deradour, Private Thomas
Derynck, Private Patrick
Deville, Private Clyde Burton
Dewitt, Private Harry
Dias, Private William
Dibley, Private Ernest
Dingwall, Private McLaren
Dion, Private Joseph Alexandre
Diver, Private Charles J.
Dodd, Private William
Doherty, Corporal Joseph
Dolphin, Sergt. James
Doucette, Private Felix
Doucette, Private Renie
Dowling, Private John Bowes
Dowling, Private John Daniel A
Downton, Lance-Corp. Clifford H.
Doyle, Private Arthur Cornelius
Doyle, Private Frank
Doyle, Private Michael, M.M.
Draper, Private Frank
Driscoll, Private Reginald Henry
Dudley, Private Griffith Ernest
Duffy, Private William Patrick
Duggan, Private William John
Dumaresk, Private Amedee
Dumas, Private Delos
Dunbar, Private William John
Duncan, Private William Cameron
Dunn, Private John
Dunne, Corporal Thomas
Dupuis, Private Arthur
Dupuis, Private Ernest
Durman, Private Fred

Dutka, Private Peter
Dyke, Private Owen

Easson, Private Robert
Eastland, Private William Henry
Easton, Private Clifford G.
Eberwein, Private George James
Eccles, Private Hilton B.
Ecclestone, Corporal Arthur A.
Edgley, Private Ernest Lloyd
Eldridge, Private George
Elford, Private Stephen
Elliott, Private Leonard William
Elliott, Private Richard
Ellis, Private James Hudson
Ellis, Corporal William J. W.
Ettinger, Private Elroy
Evans, Private Caleb
Ewens, Private William

Fahey, Private Percy Edward
Fairbairn, Private Harold Peter
Fales, C.S.M. Archibald William
Farewell, Private Thomas William
Farrell, Private James (No. 65321)
Ferguson, Private Gordon Henry
Ferguson, Private James (No. 841282)
Ferguson, Private Laurence
Ferguson, Sergt. Alpine, M.M. (True name, Albert Halliwell)
Ferrier, Private George Watt
Field, Private Joseph Ernest
Finney, Private Wilfred John
Fitzpatrick, Private Lawrence
Flannery, Private Frederick Victor A.
Fleming, Private William
Flynn, Private Fred Charles
Forbes, Private Elliston
Ford, Private John Condon
Ford, Private Frederick
Fosbre, Private Patrick Gordon
Fournier, Private Raoul
Fox, Private George
Fox, Private George Alfred
Frampton, Sergt. George Henry
Francis, Private Philip Edward
Franklin, Sergt. Charles Frederick, M.M.
Fraser, Private John
Fritzgarlds, Private Frank (True name, Norman Storring)

Fudge, Private Stanley Joseph
Fuller, Private Alexander Smart
Furze, Private Frank

Gagnon, Private Arthur
Gagnon, Private Joseph
Gagnon, Private Wilfred George L.
Gale, Private Joseph
Gallagher, Private Eugene Thomas
Garbutt, Private John Thomas
Gardner, Private Frank Robert
Garephy, Private Nelson Putvah
Garland, Private Leonard Herbert
George, Private Joseph
Gervais, Private Omer
Gibbons, Private John Joseph
Gibson, Private James
Gilbertson, Sergt. William
Gilker, Private Clifford James
Gillard, Private James E.
Gillespie, Private William James
Gilmore, Private James Alec
Gilmour, Private Oswald
Gilson, Corporal Allen
Girard, Private Donat
Girard, Private Joseph
Girvan, Private William Coleman
Glennon, Private Joshua
Godman, Private Walter Williams
Godsoe, Private Hector
Godwin, Private Albert
Godwin, Private Harold Albert
Gogarty, Sergt. Christopher
Goldie, Private Alexander Joseph
Golding, Private Frederick James
Goodin, Private Joseph F.
Gopsill, Private James Joseph
Gore, Private Alfred Francis
Gorem, Private Mitchell
Gorman, Private Frank (True name Frank Lionel Reid)
Gosselin, Private Amede
Gosselin, Private Rene
Goudrau, Private Henri
Gougersing, Private Sunta (True name Gunga Singh)
Grasswell, Private Andrew
Gray, Private Charles
Green, Private Arthur (No. 267434)
Greenwood, Private Arnold Kye

Gregoire, Private Arthur
Gregory, Private William Hugh
Grenier, Private Adolphe
Griffith, Private James Peter
Grundy, Private Gordon
Guerin, Private Albert
Guertin, Private Percy Edward
Gunn, Private Gordon
Gunn, Private Robert Adam

Haines, Private Frederick Ernest
Haley, Private Jay Bolton
Halford, Private Isaac
Halkyard, Private Samuel (Accidentally)
Hamilton, Private Daniel
Hamilton, Private James
Hammond, Private Thomas John
Harden, Private Percy
Hardie, Private Thomas
Harding, Private Alan Wilfred
Harding, Private Charles Arthur
Hardman, Private Charles L.
Hards, Private Brian
Hardy, Corporal Lawrence
Hare, Sergt. Robert
Harris, Private John (No. 645415)
Harris, Private Ralph Claudian W.
Harrison, Private Stanley
Harsh, Private James
Hartley, Private Harold
Hartley, Private Sydney
Harvison, Corporal Reiding Alexander
Haselton, Private Milton Simon
Haselton, Private Robert Cecil
Hawley, Private William
Hayes, Private Francis Joseph
Hayes, Private James
Heather, Private George Ernest
Hedderson, Private Harry
Hempson, Private James
Hendry, Corporal Fred George
Hendy, Private Joseph
Heney, Private Ernest
Hennessy, R.S.M. James, M.M.
Hewson, Private Howard Samuel
Hill, Private Alfred Ernest Perrin
Hill, Private Cyril
Hill, Private Horace
Hillans, Private Samuel

Honour Roll

Hinds, Private William
Hobday, Private Walter James
Hocking, Private Charles Carlyon
Hodgin, Private Bert
Hodgson, Private Archie
Hodson, Private Joseph
Hogan, Lance-Corp. Thomas Joseph
Hogg, Private James
Holbrook, Private Charles
Holliday, Private Robert Edward
Hollowood, Private Herbert
Holmes, Private George Burton
Hooker, Private Frederick George
Horn, Private Frederick
Horsefield, Private Russell Newman
Horsley, Private Joseph
Horsley, Private William
Houle, Private Frank
Hourd, Corporal William
Howell, Lance-Corp. Arthur James
Hudson, Private Albert
Hughes, Private Edward (True name Edgar Hugh Rowley)
Hughes, Private Herbert
Hunt, Private C. J. B.
Hunt, Private William
Hunter, Private Henry George
Hurley, Private Cornelius James H.
Hutchings, Private William John

Ingalls, Private Carl Daniel, M.M.
Ingersoll, Private Ralph Adrian
Innes, Corporal John (Jr.)
Inverarity, Sergt. James Arthur Ross
Irvers, Sergt. John Robert

James, Private Edward (No. 65487)
James, Private Russell Charles
Jarvis, Carporal Fernleigh
Jeans, Private Alexander
Jell, Private Robert
Johnson, Private Chester O'Dell
Johnson, Private Edward
Johnson, Private Ernest Edward
Johnson, Private Frederick
Johnson, Lance-Corp. John William
Johnson, Private Ole
Johnston, Private Alfred Charles
Johnston, Private Thomas John
Johnstone, Private Henry

Jolly, Private Albert
Jones, Private Arthur
Jones, Private Frederick Lowther N.
Jones, Private John (No. 412392)
Jones, Private John (No. 66159)
Jones, Private John Michael
Jones, Private Norris Hugh Elliott
Jones, Corporal Trevor Prys
Juteau, Private Felix P.

Kane, Private Patrick Joseph V.
Keating, Private Thomas
Keefe, Private Michael Joseph (True name, Michael Joseph Mullaney)
Kennedy, Private Edmund Joseph
Kennedy, Private James Gordon
Kennedy, Private Joseph Peter
Kensenhauser, Private Charles Albert
Kent, Private George
Keough, Private Harold Samuel
Kerr, Private James
Ketch, Lance-Corp. Albert Harold W., M.M.
Kevany, Private Patrick
Kimball, Private Harold C.
Kinchin, Private Harold
King, C.S.M. Ernest Fred Henry
King, Private John Ferguson
King, Private Lloyd Nixon
King, Private Peter
Kinsella, Private John Joseph
Kinson, Private Samuel Thomas
Kirk, Private Arthur Harold
Kirk, Sergt. Walter
Krivoruk, Private Justin
Kristiensen, Private Albert
Kuchar, Private Wasili
Kydd, Sergt. Robert Ewart G.

Laberge, Private Leon
Lacroix, Private Alfred
Lambert, Private William
Lamontagne, Private Alfred
Lamoureux, Private Philip
Landry, Private John
Langille, Private Eben Nelson
Laviolette, Private Joseph
Law, Lance-Sergt. Alden Leonard
Lawler, Private William (No. 187619)
Lawlor, Private William (No. 701005)

Lawton, Private Thomas Christopher
Lea, Private Christopher
Leach, Private Albert
Leadbeater, Private Charles Joseph
Learie, Private John W.
Leaver, Private Samuel Edward
LeBoutillier, Private Leo B., D.C.M.
L'Ecuyer, Private Amedee
Lee, Private William John
Leggett, Private Ernest William
Lemeire, Private Edgar
Lenihan, Private Frank Patrick
Lepine, Private Wilfred
Leslie, Private Donald Young
Lessard, Private Henri
Levesque, Private Leopold
Lewis, Sergt. Frank
L'Heureux, Private Victorien
Libby, Private Loftus Mason
Liddle, Private Alfred
Lingard, Private John Joseph
Livernois, Private Hormidas
Livett, Private Edward
Lockwood, Private Gordon
Lockyer, Private Sidney
London, Private David
Long, A/Corporal Harry Ireland
Longhurst, Private Cecil Frank (Accidentally)
Longmore, Private Thomas David L.
Loose, Private Alfred Smith
Lowe, Private Arthur
Lowe, Private Samuel Ernest
Lucas, Private James
Luck, Lance-Sergt. Frank
Luckett, Private Frank
Lynott, Private James Edward
Lyon, Private Robert Henry

Mack, Private James
Mackie, Private Walter Lock
Mainland, Private Thomas Gavin
Manseau, Private Ovila
Mansell, Private Ernest Samuel
Marchand, Private Adolphe
Marchand, Private Willy
Marchington, Private John Douglas
Marcoux, Private Wilfred
Margeson, Private James William
Marsh, Private James

Marshall, Private Samuel (No. 841336)
Martin, Private Alfred
Martin, Private William
Martin, Private William Henry
Mather, Private Robert John
Matheson, Private Douglas Cameron
Matzukievich, Private Anton
Maxwell, Private James Gilbert
Mayle, Private Henry William
Meadows, Private Cecil
Meanwell, Private George Henry
Mehan, Private Charles Henry
Melvin, Private Norman Edward
Miller, Private Albert
Miller, Private Cam Reay
Miller, Private Clarence Willard
Miller, Private John Mathias
Miller, Private Laurie Merton
Milne, Sergt. William James
Mitchell, Private Henry
Mobey, Private Alfred
Moisan, Private Ephraim Waterford
Molloy, Private John Herbert
Monahan, Private Daniel
Monahan, Private Roy Frederick
Moody, Private James
Moore, Private Herbert
Moore, Private John Lewis
More, Private John Stewart
Morris, Private Stanley
Morrison, Private Adrienne
Morrison, Private Hector
Mortimer, Private Harold
Morton, Private Henry D.
Mott, Private Edgar Andrew
Moxham, Sergt. Ernest
Muise, Private Charles Edward
Mullin, Private Walter Edward
Mullins, Private Edward John
Munroe, Private Edwin
Murch, Private Clarence Egbert
Murphy, Private James
Murphy, Private Peter Algeron
Murray, Corporal George Kenneth
Myers, Private George
McAllister, Private David Dunn (Accidentally)
McAulay, Private George Hugh
McBride, Private James Santo
McCaig, Private Ivan Frederick

HONOUR ROLL

McCallum, Sergt. Neil
McCann, Sergt. Clark Wallace
McCann, Private William (No. 457872)
McCaul, Private Redvers
McCaw, Private Edward
McClare, Private Percy Winthrop
McClellan, Private Angus Joseph
McCubbin, Sergt. Alexander
McCullough, Sergt. Wallace Scott
McDermott, Private Joseph
McDonald, Private Alexander
MacDonald, Private Kenneth
MacDonald, Private William Douglas
McDonnell, Private John
McDowell, Private John (Belgian Croix de Guerre)
McElmon, Private Arthur Rupert
McEwan, Private David M.
McGartland, Private William
McGillaway, Private James
McGillivray, Private John Alexander
McGonnigal, Private Gordon
McGrath, Private Terence
McGraw, Private William
McIlwham, Private Alfred
McIntyre, Private Ernest Roy
McIntyre, Private Frank
McIvor, Corporal John (No. 187658)
McIvor, Corp. John Angus (No. 841548)
McKay, Private James
McKay, Private Linden Robert
McKay, Private William Arthur
McKay, Private William Stuart
McKee, Lance-Sergt. Andrew Goff
McKenna, Corporal Adrien
McKenzie, Private Kenneth
McKenzie, Private Rod A.
McKim, Private James
MacKinnon, Private Neil J.
McKitrick, Private Leonard Patrick
McLachlan, Private Arthur
McLachlan, Private Sidney James, M.M
McLeod, Private Archibald
MacLeod, Private John
McLoughlin, Private Charles
McMorran, Private Waldron William
McNulty, Sergt. Thomas
McPherson, Private Charles, M.M.
McPike, Private George
McRae, Private Duncan Harry

McRae, Private Roderick
McRae, Private Wesley

Nairn, Lance-Corp. Thomas
Nakelis, Private Anton
Nares,..........Leslie Mowbray
Nash, Lance-Corp. John
Naylor, Lance-Corp. Lewis
Neill, Private George Alexander
Newman, Private Walter
Newton, Lance-Corp. Thomas William
Nicholson, Private Frederick S.
Nolan, Private James
Nolan, Private Thomas Francis
Norris, Private Robert William

O'Brien, Private Bernard
O'Brien, Private Georges
O'Brien, Private Michael
O'Brien, Private Thomas Joseph
O'Connell, Private Michael
O'Connor, Private Charles E.
O'Connor, Private William
Ogden, Private Chris
Ogilvie, Private Walter
O'Hara, Private Lester Conwell
O'Keefe, Private Oney
Oliphant, Private William
Olsen, Private Herbert Hugh
O'Malley, Private Charles
O'Neil, Private Patrick
O'Riley, Private Neil
Osablink, Private Anton
Owen, Private William Griffith

Pageau, Private Joseph
Paine, Corporal Charles
Palmer, Private Edwin
Palmer, Private Harry
Parker, Private George
Parkes, Private Arthur Austin
Parkin, Private Whyte Burnett H.
Parlee, Private Eric R.
Parliament, Private Harold Stanley
Parsons, Private George Cecil
Parton, Private William
Patenaude, Private Olier
Paterson, Private Bryce Martin
Paterson, Private George Burt
Patterson, Private Leonard

Payne, Sergt. Frederick Thomas
Peacock, Private James Edward
Peake, Private Christopher
Pearce, Private Ernest Bottrell
Pedder, Private John S.
Peever, Lance-Corp. Gordon
Pelletier, Private Francois, M.M.
Perrin, Private John Percy W.
Perron, Private Edgar
Peters, Private Stanley Wallace (No. 842161)
Peters, Private Stanley (No. 470467)
Peterson, Private Charles Alfred
Peturson, Private Magnus
Phillips, Private Frank Ernest
Phillips, Private Joseph Reginald
Piche, Private Arthur
Plant, Private Percy Wilfred
Plante, Private George
Plante, Private Leo
Plante, Private Louis R. H.
Poitras, Private John William E.
Ponton, Private Maitland A. (Drowned)
Porteous, Private Arthur
Porter, Private John Thomas
Presswood, Private John
Price, Private Charles William
Price, Private Lionel Glen
Proctor, Private Charles George
Proudfoot, Corporal Alexander
Proulx, Private Rene
Purves, Private William

Quackenbush, Private George
Quigley, Private Charles Valentine
Quinn, Private Thomas

Rabey, Private William
Racine, Private James Windsor
Rae, A/Sergt. Alfred Hamilton
Raindal, Private Leo
Rainey, Private Hilliard
Rainville, Private Urgel
Ralston, Private Donald
Redgrave, Private George
Redmond, Sergt. Walter Henry
Reeve, Private Cecil Harry
Regan, Private Cornelius Adrian
Reid, Private Robert John
Renaud, Private Xavier

Renaud, Private John Phillip
Rhiner, Private Albert
Ricard, Private Arthur
Richards, Lance-Corp. Edwin R.
Richardson, Private Julius J. G.
Rickner, Private William
Ridge, Private Percy (Accidentally)
Riley, Sergt. Charles Gordon
Ringland, Private George William
Risk, Private William Alexander
Roberts, Private William O.
Robertson, Private David
Robertson, Private David Allan
Robertson, Private Charles Wesley
Robins, Private Ernest
Robinson, Private Chester
Robinson, Private Charles Elvin
Robinson, Private Donald
Robinson, Private Levi
Robson, Private Arnold
Rollo, Sergt. Andrew
Romea, Private Frank
Romhild, Private Fred
Rose, Private Henry
Rose, Private Samuel
Rose, Lance-Corp. Svend Owen
Ross, Lance-Corp. David M.
Ross, Private James
Ross, Private Robert M.
Rothnie, Private William
Round, Private George
Rouse, Private James
Routledge, Private Harold E.
Rowe, Private Edward
Rowe, Private Walter
Roy, Private Albert
Roy, Private Joseph Delphis
Roy, Private Ovila
Ruddick, Private George
Rudman, Private Frederick
Russell, Private Edward
Rutter, Private Morley
Ryals, Private John Bryan
Ryan, Private Mathew William

Sadrowski, Private Stanislaw
Sale, Private Charles William
Saillant, Private Aldard
Salvidge, Private Edward
Sanborn, Private Oscar

HONOUR ROLL

Sandell, Private Charles
Sanders, Private Arthur
Sanders, Private Edwin Francis
Sansoucie, Private Ovie Louis
Savoie, Private Gedeon
Savord, Private David
Sawyer, Private Arthur
Sayers, Private John William
Schooling, Private Joseph
Schuh, Lance-Corporal Albert Otto
Scolnuck, Private Harry
Scott, Private Grant Robert
Scroggie, Lance-Corp. William
Shannon, Private John
Sheridan, Private Albert
Shopland, Lance-Sergt. Albert Henry
Shorrock, Private Richard
Shortliff, Private Lloyd Clifton
Shorts, Lance-Sergt. Roy
Silvester, Private Arthur
Sime, Private John Carron
Simpkins, Private Henry Ernest
Sims, Private George Henry
Sinclair, Private Hugh Cameron
Singer, Private Joseph Hines
Singer, Private Maurice
Smart, Private Harry William
Smith, Private Alexander
Smith, Private Donald
Smith, Private Frank Joseph
Smith, Private Harry
Smith, Private James
Smith, A/Corporal Stuart
Smith, Private Thomas Grant
Smith, Private Victor
Smyth, Private Thomas John
Sosnowchik, Private Nicolas
Spalding, Private James A.
Spiring, Private Oliver Arthur
Spray, Private George Bertram
Squires, Private Francis William
Squires, Private Jack
Stagg, Private Hedley Charles
Stanistreet, Private William George
Stanley, Private Frank
Staples, Sergt. Arthur
Stephens, Private Frederick William
Stewart, Private Ernest
Stewart, Private Lawrence Douglas
Stewart, Private Robert

St. John, Private Christopher
St. Marie, Private Adrian
Stockall, Lance-Sergt. George
Stockall, Private Thomas
St. Pierre, Private Alexander
St. Pierre, Private Paul
St. Pierre, Private Romeo
Strachan, Private William, M.M.
Street, Private Daniel Thomas J. W.
Stroud, Private Frank
Sturgeon, Private Joseph
Sullivan, C.S.M. Herbert Percy
Sullivan, Private James R.
Sullivan, Private William C.
Sweeney, Private Herbert Joseph
Sweeney, Private Harold
Sweeney, Private Martin
Swift, Corporal Albert Arthur
Sydenham, Private William
Syder, Private James
Symonds, Private Frederick Ernest
Synski, Private Stevin

Talbot, Private Louis
Taunton, Private Charles H.
Taylor, Lance-Corp. Alexander
Taylor, Sergt. George Grant R.
Taylor, Corporal James (No. 65968)
Taylor, Private Robert Henry
Terentiev, Private Samuel
Terrault, Private Julius Daniel
Terreau, Private Archie
Tessier, Private Felix
Thain, Private Robert
Thayer, Private Charles Orrin
Therien, Lance-Corp. Charley
Thibault, Private George
Thistlethwaite, Private Robert
Thomas, Private David John
Thomas, Private Harvey Matthew
Thomas, Private William
Thompson, Private John Bell
Thomson, Private Hugh
Thomson, Private John
Tice, Lance-Corp. Percy Wallace
Timmons, Private James
Tinsley, Private Arthur
Torrance, Private Donald Fraser
Tovey, Private Frank George
Townsley, Private William Osborne

Tracey, Private Weldon
Treadwell, Private Albert Edward
Trevor, Private Ralph
Tunley, Private Harold
Turnbull, Private John Love
Turner, Private Edgar Douglas
Turner, Private William
Tweedley, Corporal Feil
Tyo, Private Arthur
Tyrie, Private James

Valois, Private John
Van Der Hayden, Private Florian
Vernon, Private Albert
Vickers, Corporal Sidney B.
Vickery, Private Cory Ferman
Viens, Private Henri
Vincent, Private Orrin Foster
Vusachenko, Private Demian

Wade, Private Robert
Waldron, Lance-Corp. Frank
Walinck, Private James
Walker, Private Andrew
Walker, Private William H.
Wallace, Lance-Corp. William John
Walsh, Private Michael
Walsh, Private Roy
Walsh, Private Silas
Walsh, Private William
Walter, Sergt. George Hugh
Walter, Private Michel
Walton, Private William
Walton, Private Walter Frank
Ward, Private James
Ward, Private John
Ward, Private Walter A.
Ward, Private William Edward
Wardell, Private Harry Thomas
Wass, Lance-Corp. Seth, M.M.
Watson, Private James
Watson, Private Thomas William
Watts, Private Henry C.
Webb, Private George Albert
Weinberg, Private Samuel
Welding, Private Charles Philip

Wellington, Private Thomas John
Wherry, Private Burt Alfred
Whiley, Private William Ernest G.
White, Corporal Archie
White, Private Clarence Joseph
White, Private Frederick George
White, Private Harry
White, Lance-Corp. Jasper Ray, M.M.
White, Private Philip Henry
Whitford, Private George
Whitty, Private Walter Jones
Wightman, Private William
Wilcox, Corporal Thomas A.
Wilkinson, Sergt. Willlam James
Williams, Private Harold
Williams, Private William
Williams, Private William Arthur
Williams, Private Walter William
Williamson, Private Albert
Williamson, Sergt, John
Willis, Private John Henry (Accidentally)
Wilson, Private Charles
Wilson, Private George
Wilson, Private John Henry
Wilson, Sergt. Lawrence
Wilson, Private Robert Wesley
Winsper, Private George
Withey, Private Albert N., D.C.M.
Wood, Lance-Corp. William
Woodroofe, Private William Turton
Woods, Private George
Wren, Private Arthur
Wright, Private Alfred
Wright, Private James Edward
Wright, Private Samuel Kerr

Yolland, Corporal Henry L.
Young, Private Howard
Young, Private Harley Ernest
Young, Private Robert Charles
Young, Private Weldon
Yull, Private Thomas Henry

Ziepowski, Lance-Corp. Peter
Zinkoi, Private Kost

HONOUR ROLL 309

DIED OF SICKNESS

Allardyce, Private William
Bell, Private Allen William
Bessig, Private George Washington
Branney, Private William
Chambers, Private Thomas
Conway, Private George Emery
Crawford, Private John
Fry, Private Howard
Gorman, Private Frederick Leonard (True name Frederick Leonard Reid)
Grant, Private Alexander
Henderson, Private William (No. 624091)
Ion, Private Clifford
Kennedy, Private William
Kerry, Private Arthur
Kinloch, Private William
Laing, Private John Daniel
Law, Private Richard
May, Private Herbert Stephen
Rollins, Private Ernest Lee
Royer, Private Adelard
Smith, Lieut. Allen Dale (while serving with the 259th Battalion).
Wall, Private Edward Joseph
Wigston, Private Charles Henry

KILLED IN ACTION AFTER TRANSFER TO OTHER UNITS OF THE C.E.F.

Allabush, Private George
Bernard, Private Eugene
Bowie, Gunner W. E. P.
Boyd, Private Mathew
Bullough, Private A. T.
Burchell, Sergt. George (Accidentally)
Burns, Private James
Carey, Private Alfred
Currall, Private Frederick (Accidentally)
Donald, Lieut. W. J.
Gorman, Private John (True name, John Reid)(Accidentally)
Hannaford, Capt. A. C., M.C.
Hill, Private T. H.
Hipkins, Sergt, F. G.
Jean, Private Napoleon
Lampron, Private Dalph
Lepine, Private Henri
Livingstone, Private Claud
Marcoux, Private Philip
Mattingley, Private Harry
Milroy, Lance-Corp. A. M.
Mitchell, Armourer-Sergt. James
Moulton, Private Morris
McNamara, Private B. T.
Oldfield, Private Edward
Pacey, Private F. E. (Accidentally)
Peters, Lieut. G. H.
Porteous, Sapper George
Scotland, Private James
Singleton, Private Frank
Slater, Corporal Herbert
Sloan, Corporal John
Thompson, Private James
Torrance, Capt. S. G.
Vallett, Private Joseph
Wilson, Private Herbert
Withrow, Corporal C. E., M.M.

APPENDIX B

24th Battalion, Victoria Rifles of Canada

HONOURS AND AWARDS

(The following honours and awards were granted for service with the Battalion.)

THE VICTORIA CROSS

Lieut.-Col. W. H. Clark-Kennedy

COMPANION OF THE ORDER OF ST. MICHAEL AND ST. GEORGE

Lieut.-Col. W. H. Clark-Kennedy

BAR TO THE DISTINGUISHED SERVICE ORDER

Lieut.-Col. W. H. Clark-Kennedy

THE DISTINGUISHED SERVICE ORDER

Brigadier-General John Alexander Gunn
Lieut.-Col. Ronald Okeden Alexander
Lieut.-Col. Charles Frederic Ritchie
Major Patterson Lindsay Hall
Major Arthur Lennox S. Mills
Major John Alexander Ross

OFFICER OF THE ORDER OF THE BRITISH EMPIRE

Lieut. Donald Chipman Skinner

THE MILITARY CROSS AND BAR

Capt. Frederick Henry Morgan
Lieut. Harry McNeven Alexander
Lieut. William McMurray

THE MILITARY CROSS

Lieut.-Col. Charles Frederic Ritchie
Major Edgar Montague Amphlett
Major James Nunn Bales
Major Victor Eugene Duclos
Major Patterson Lindsay Hall
Capt. Frank Thompson Bown
Capt. Alexander Bruce Campbell
Capt. Edward Percival Denman
Capt. Alexander Montgomery Dewar
Capt. Herbert D'Olier Kingstone
Capt. Reginald Heathfield Lamb
Capt. Norman Lisle LeSueur
Capt. George Ross Robertson
Capt. Philip Ilderton Walker

HONOURS AND AWARDS

THE MILITARY CROSS—*Continued*

Hon. Capt. John A. Donovan (Quartermaster)
Hon. Capt. Cecil J. S. Stuart (Chaplain)
Lieut. John Lighthall Cains
Lieut. John Cecil Carling
Lieut. Francis deLancey Clements
Lieut. George H. P. Coneybeare
Lieut. Vladimir Curtis
Lieut. Kevin Stewart Drummond
Lieut. Arthur Durman
Lieut. Joseph John Kavanagh
Lieut. George Herbert Macario
Lieut. Daniel McIntosh Matheson
Lieut. John Donald MacIntyre
Lieut. Norris Williams Robins
Lieut. Vernon Robert Spearing
Lieut. Francis Wilfred Stenson
Lieut. Harold Richard Tanner
Lieut. Percival George Tucker
Lieut. Robert Benjamin E. Wilson

THE DISTINGUISHED CONDUCT MEDAL

Donovan, Hon. Capt. John A. (Quartermaster)
Findlay, Lieut. Alexander

Abbey, Private Arthur Edward
Adam, C.S.M. Hector
Baillie, Sergt. Frederick James
Bradley, Sergt. George Loraine
Carpenter, Sergt. Sydney Harold
Cooke, Sergt. Arthur William
Croll, C.S.M. George Wood
Donohoe, C.Q.M.S. John
Gauld, A/C.Q.M.S. William
Grogg, Private Charles Henry
Handren, Sergt. Ralph Waldo
LeBoutillier, Private Leo B.
McNeill, Sergt. George Henry
O'Toole, Corporal James Christopher
Scott, Lance-Corp. George Douglas
Sweeney, Sergt. Fred Howard
Wilson, Private James
Withey, Private Albert N.

THE MILITARY MEDAL AND BAR

Gunnell, Lieut. Alfred

Cairns, Corporal Hubert
Coughlan, Lance-Sergt. Gerald Diomede
Draycott, Sergt. Arthur Francis
Gillard, Sergt. John William
Keating, Corporal Edward
Kennedy, Sergt. James Wesley
Long, Lance-Sergt. Arthur Philip
Quirk, Sergt. George

THE MILITARY MEDAL

Beck, Lieut. Arthur
Findlay, Lieut. Alexander
Hammett, Lieut. Nathan Thomas
McIntyre, Lieut. Kenneth Cameron
Mott, Capt. Arthur Frederick
Robins, Lieut. Norris William
Rose, Lieut. Howard Edwin

Adelson, Private Henry Jasper
Baldwin, Private Charles
Berkin, Corporal Joseph
Bethune, Private Samuel John
Bishop, Sergt. Laurie L.
Botsford, A/Sergt. Frederick W. G.
Brown, Private David
Brown, Private Frederick Young
Buck, Lance-Corp. Barrett
Burden, Private Frank
Cade, C.Q.M.S. Leonard
Campbell, Lance-Sergt. Lachlin Collin
Cassidy, Lance-Corp. Alexander J.
Chase, Corporal William H.
Collins, Private Edgar Guy
Cooke, Sergt. Arthur William
Cooper, Private Claude
Crabb, Sergt. Abraham John

THE MILITARY MEDAL—*Continued*

Cree, Sergt. Samuel
Cross, Sergt. Gordon
Crowell, Corporal W.
Davidson, Private Charles Smith
Davidson, Private Harry
Dawson, Private H.
Depledge, Sergt. Jack (True name Horace Firth)
Devan, Sergt. John Francis
Divorty, Corporal William
Dodsworth, Lance-Corp. George Edgar
Doyle, Private Michael
Duley, Lance-Corp. Edgerton Edmund
Edgar, Private John James
England, Private George Vincent
Evernden, Sergt. Frederick James
Ferguson, Sergt. Alpine (True name Albert Halliwell)
Ferguson, Private James
Feilde, Lance-Sergt. Edmund Ralph
Finlayson, Lance-Sergt. Alexander
Fournier, C.S.M. Philippe J.
Francis, Corporal Frederick Albert
Franklin, Sergt. Charles Frederick
Gardner, Private John Henry
Gauld, A/C.Q.M.S. William
Gaunt, Corporal Thomas Lopton
Gautby, Private Leonard
Giguere, Private Balthazar
Gillespie, Corporal Andrew
Godsell, Private Henry John
Gow, Private John
Grey, Corporal Harry
Hagen, Sergt. Ray G.
Hansen, Corporal Alfred Emil
Henderson, C.Q.M.S. William
Hennessy, R.S.M. James
Hillerby, Private James
Hogan, Private William James
Hurst, Sergt. George
Hutchinson, Lance-Corp. Thomas
Ingalls, Private Carl Daniel
Jones, Corporal John
Kelly, Lance-Corp. Frank John
Kelly, Lance-Sergt. James Patrick
Kennaugh, Sergt. William Henry
Kennedy, Lance-Corp. George Wilfred
Ketch, Lance-Corp. Albert Harold W.
Lamarre, Private Henri
Lanctot, Private Medard
Lareau, Private Leopold
Mackie, C.S.M. James C.
Marcel, Private Laurent
Marsh, Private George Stanley
Marshall, Sergt. Hugh
Matatall, Sergt. James Danford
May, Corporal Frank
Merrian, Lance-Corp. Kerr H.
Metzger, Lance-Sergt. Albert
Mitchell, R.Q.M.S. Robert
Murphy, Lance-Corp. Harry
McCormick, Private Percy
McDonald, Sergt. Samuel
McLachlan, Private Sidney James
McPherson, Private Charles
Naylor, Private Donald Benjamin
Naylor, Sergt. Harry Starbuck
Noakes, Corporal Joseph Walter G.
O'Brien, Corporal Arthur James
Oliver, Lance-Sergt. John
Owens, Corporal Bert
Pelletier, Private Francois
Pellow, Private William Henry
Prince, Private John Wesley
Proctor, Corporal Victor
Rae, Sergt. William Ferguson
Robertson, Corporal John H.
Samson, C.S.M. Arthur Leslie
Sandford, Private Jack
Spinney, Corporal George E.
Stobie, Private James Henry
Strachan, Private William
Styles, Sergt. Edward Charles
Tarrant, Private Lawrence Ernest
Telfer, Sergt. Robert
Thompson, Corporal James
Tracey, Sergt. Arnold Samuel
Tyo, Private George
Vickers, Private Wilfred Hugh
Walden, Corporal James Perry
Walker, Corporal Frederick Lewis
Wass, Lance-Corp. Seth
Watkins, Corporal Ernest George
Watson, Private Oscar Everett
Webb, Lance-Corp. Ernest Arthur
Westwater, Sergt. W.
White, Lance-Corp. Jasper Ray

Honours and Awards

THE MILITARY MEDAL—Continued

Wilde, Sergt. Thomas Herbert
Williams, Corporal Gerald Frederick
Willis, Lance-Corporal Ellison
Woodley, Private Benjamin
Wooffinden, Sergt. Walter
Young, Lance-Corporal Mark

THE MERITORIOUS SERVICE MEDAL

Crotty, Lieut. William Harold

Carter, Corporal John
Drew, Sergt. John Herbert
Edwards, Sergt. L. M.

Hutcheon, Lance-Corp. Alexander Wales
Kemp, Sergt. George Ricardo
Lawrence, Sergt. J. T.
Pattison, Sergt. Richard Stanley

MENTIONED IN DESPATCHES THREE TIMES

Hon. Capt. Cecil J. S. Stuart (Chaplain)

MENTIONED IN DESPATCHES TWICE

Lieut.-Col. W. H. Clark-Kennedy
Major John Alexander Ross
Capt. Herbert Smith McGreevy
Lieut. Donald Chipman Skinner

MENTIONED IN DESPATCHES

Gunn, Brig.-General John Alexander
Alexander, Lieut.-Col. Ronald Okeden
Ritchie, Lieut.-Col. Charles Frederic
Bales, Major James Nunn
Hall, Major Patterson Lindsay
Mills, Major Arthur Lennox S.
Dewar, Capt. Alexander Montgomery
Lamb, Capt. Reginald Heathfield
LeSueur, Capt. Norman Lisle
Robertson, Capt. George Ross
Campbell, Hon. Capt. Harry Davies (Quartermaster)
Briggs, Lieut. Alfred
Jones, Lieut. George William
Leach, Lieut. Frederick Sydney
Macario, Lieut. George Herbert
Morgan, Lieut. Frederick Henry
McBean, Lieut. Arthur
MacIntyre, Lieut. John Donald
Rigg, Lieut. Harold Thornley
Tanner, Lieut. Harold Richard
Campbell, Sergt. H.
Connelly, Sergt. J.
Gauld, A/C.Q.M.S. William
Innes, Sergt. Walter
Lougheed, Private Harold John
Mackie, Sergt. J. C.
Meredith, Sergt. J. E.
Stewart, Sergt. James
Yuill, Lance-Corp. Don

BROUGHT TO THE NOTICE OF THE SECRETARY OF STATE FOR WAR

Moore, Private Frederick Godfrey

FOREIGN DECORATIONS

MEDAILLE MILITAIRE (French)
Quirk, Sergt. George

CROIX DE GUERRE (French)
Robertson, Corporal John H.

CROSS OF ST. GEORGE—4th CLASS (Russian)
Steele, Private Edwin Williard

ORDER OF ST. STANISLAS—3rd CLASS WITH SWORDS AND BAR (Russian)
Kingstone, Capt. Herbert D'Olier

CROIX DE GUERRE (Belgian)

Hall, Major Patterson Lindsay   Coneybeare, Lieut. George H. P.

Day, Lance-Corp. James
Morrison, Private Daniel Murdo
McDowell, Private John

APPENDIX C

24th Battalion, Victoria Rifles of Canada

HONOURS AND AWARDS
NON-REGIMENTAL

(The following honours and awards were granted to members of the Battalion following their transfer to other units.)

COMPANION OF THE ORDER OF ST. MICHAEL AND ST. GEORGE

Brigadier-General John Alexander Gunn, D.S.O.
Lieut.-Col. Stancliffe Wallace Watson

THE DISTINGUISHED SERVICE ORDER

Lieut.-Col. Claude Hardinge Hill
Lieut.-Col. John Stephen Jenkins
(Medical Officer)

Lieut.-Col. Stancliffe Wallace Watson
Major Arthur Leslie Walker

OFFICER OF THE ORDER OF THE BRITISH EMPIRE

Hon. Major Allan Pearson Shatford (Chaplain)

MILITARY CROSS AND BAR

Capt. Alfred Crawford Hannaford

MILITARY CROSS

Major Ronald Douglas Sutherland
Major Arthur Leslie Walker
Capt. Andrew Stuart Boa
Capt. Bernard Dysart Coombes
Capt. H. E. Cummins, C.A.M.C.
Capt. George Hagar Gilchrist
Capt. George Hobson
Capt. R. B. Jenkins, C.A.M.C.

Capt. G. L. Jepson, C.A.M.C.
Capt. Arthur Hawley A. Morphy
Capt. A. H. Taylor, C.A.M.C.
Lieut. A. C. Bowles
Lieut. Harry Alexander Dawson
Lieut. Mitchell Hartt Doig
Lieut. Warren Davidson Nelson

MILITARY MEDAL

Capt. George Hobson
C.S.M. William Nicholson
Corporal Edward Flynn
Corporal Robert McAskill
Corporal Calvin E. Withrow
Private William Godwin Brown
Private Ralph Griffin
Private Lawrence Fearus Donnelly
Private John Frederick Gardner
Gunner Edgar A Leach
Sapper Thomas McDonald
Private Harold George Stapley
Private John Gordon Wallace
Private John Henderson Weiss
Private William Wells
Private Edmund Marshall Zeller

MERITORIOUS SERVICE MEDAL

Sergt. Victor Burke
Sergt. Bernard Blyth Wones
Corporal John Joseph Elton
Private Edward John Harned

MENTIONED IN DESPATCHES FOUR TIMES

Lieut.-Col. Stancliffe Wallace Watson

MENTIONED IN DESPATCHES TWICE

Lieut.-Col. Ronald Okeden Alexander, D.S.O.
Lieut.-Col. Claude Hardinge Hill
Lieut.-Col. John Stephen Jenkins, C.A.M.C.
Major Arthur Leslie Walker

MENTIONED IN DESPATCHES

Hon. Major Allan Pearson Shatford (Chaplain)
Capt. Bernard Dysart Coombes
Capt. Arthur Frederick Mott
Sergt. A. L. Garvin
Private Isidore Ouellett
Private Frederick Arthur Taylor

BROUGHT TO THE NOTICE OF THE SECRETARY OF STATE FOR WAR TWICE

Brigadier-General John Alexander Gunn, D.S.O.

BROUGHT TO THE NOTICE OF THE SECRETARY OF STATE FOR WAR

Major Ronald Douglas Sutherland

FOREIGN DECORATIONS

CROIX DE GUERRE (Belgian)

Lieut. Hugh Mackay Patterson
Lance-Corporal Walter Bate

APPENDIX D

COMMISSIONS

COMMISSIONS IN THE 24th BATTALION

(The following officers of the 24th Battalion, Victoria Rifles of Canada, received commissions after service in the Battalion's ranks.)

Alexander, Lieut. H. M., M.C.
Amphlett, Major E. M., M.C.
Arundell, Lieut. A. W. H
Bales, Major J. N., M.C.
Beck, Lieut. Arthur, M.M.
Briggs, Lieut. Alfred
Bushe, Lieut. G. S.
Colville, Lieut. David
Coneybeare, Lieut. G. H. P., M.C.
Crichton, Lieut. A. F.
Crotty, Lieut. W. H., M.S.M.
Denman, Capt. E. P., M.C.
Dewar, Capt. A. M., M.C.
Dickson, Lieut. W. S.
Dolphin, Lieut. Charles
Donald, Lieut. John
Duckett, Lieut. G. S.
Durman, Lieut. Arthur, M.C.
Egan, Lieut. R. S.
Ewan, Capt. D. A.
Findlay, Lieut. Alexander, D.C.M., M.M.
Grenough, Lieut. G. R.
Haddock, Lieut. Geoffrey
Hallam, Lieut. F. H.
Hammett, Lieut. N. T.
Hobson, Capt. George
Johnson, Lieut. H. S.
Jones, Lieut. E. E.
Jones, Lieut. G. W.

Kavanagh, Lieut. J. J., M.C.
Lamb, Capt. R. H., M.C.
Lane, Lieut. E. T.
Leach, Lieut. F. S.
Lidstone, Capt. E. G. N.
Lockwood, Lieut. P. E. R.
Macario, Lieut. G. H., M.C.
Matheson, Lieut. D. M., M.C.
Morgan, Capt. F. H., M.C.
McIntyre, Lieut. K. C., M.M.
McMurray, Lieut. William, M.C.
Picken, Lieut. C. B.
Redpath, Lieut. Thomas
Rigg, Lieut. H. T.
Riley, Lieut. C. E.
Ritchie, Leiut. H. S.
Robins, Lieut. N. W., M.C., M.M.
Rose, Lieut. H. E., M.M.
Scobie, Lieut. Arnold
Sewell, Lieut. L. A.
Shipway, Lieut. J. C.
Smith, Lieut. A. D.
Smyth, Lieut. G. C.
Stenson, Lieut. F. W.
Styles, Lieut. E. M.
Sutherland, Lieut. D. H.
Tucker, Lieut. P. G., M.C.
Walker, Capt. P. I., M.C.
Wilson, Lieut. D. M.

COMMISSIONS IN THE C.E.F.

(The following other ranks of the 24th Battalion, Victoria Rifles of Canada, were granted commissions in units of the C.E.F.)

Allen, C.Q.M.S. Henry J.
Ardagh, Private R. C.
Balfour, Sergt. George
Barry, Private G. A.

Binmore, Sergt. L. R.
Boa, Sergt. A. S.
Butteris, Sergt. H. L.
Chambers, Private F. G.

Coombes, Private B. D.
Coughlan, Lance-Sergt. G. D., M.M.
Craig, Sergt. Charles
Cross, Sergt. Gordon
Dawson, Private H. A.
Dewar, Sergt. W. H.
Ditton, Private T. A.
Dodsworth, Lance-Corp. G. E., M.M.
Doig, Private M. H.
Donald, Private W. J.
Duley, Lance-Corporal E. E.
Eldridge, Private V. E.
Ferguson, Sergt. H. J.
Fraser, Private Gordon
Freeman, Corporal Edwin
Gauthier, Private J. A.
Gilchrist, Lance-Corp. G. H.
Goneau, Sergt. N. E.
Grenough, Corporal E. R.
Hagen, Sergt. Ray G., M.M.
Hannaford, Lance-Corp. A. C.
Hart, C.S.M. Albert
Heward, Private R. B.
LaMothe, Private A. P.
Larue, Private E. W.
Law, Corporal F. A.
Lyon, C.Q.M.S. Reuben N.

Medhurst, Sergt. Thomas
Mott, Private A. F., M.M.
MacDonald, Lance-Corp. A. deL.
MacDonald, Sergt. D. A.
Macleod, Private G. W.
Nares, Private L. M.
Naylor, Sergt. H. S., M.M.
Neil, Corporal John
Nelson, Private W. D.
Newsam, C.Q.M.S. Benjamin W.
Patterson, Corporal H. M.
Peters, Private G. H.
Rae, Sergt. W. F.
Roodhouse, Lance-Corporal A. E.
Rose, Sergt. James
Samson, C.S.M. Arthur L., M.M.
Sewell, Corporal R. L.
Simpson, Lance-Corp. C. L.
Torrance, Private S. G.
Tozer, Lance-Corp. W. P.
Tracey, Sergt. A. S., M.M.
Waters, Private J. S.
Watson, Sergt. David
White, Private W. A. (Cadet)
Wilson, Corporal G. S. (Cadet)
Wooffinden, Sergt. Walter, M.M.

COMMISSIONS IN THE IMPERIAL ARMY

(The following other ranks of the 24th Battalion, Victoria Rifles of Canada, were granted commissions, or cadetships, in the Imperial Army.)

Beckett, Private W. C.
Bell, Lance-Corp. John W.
Birch, Private J. F.
Bisset, Lance-Corp. L. A.
Botsford, Private F. W. G., M.M.
Church, Private S. A.
Colvin, Private A. G.
Cronopulo, Private D. W.
Davis, Private G. J.
Denne, Sergt. Vincent A.
Fick, Lance-Corp. D. R.
Fraser, Sergt. Hugh
Fuller, Private Percy
Grant, Private J. B.
Hewson, Private R. S.
Hunter, Sergt. H. G.
Hurley, Lance-Corp. R. P.
Johnston, Private N. C. T.
Jones, Private Joseph

Mangin, Private F. C.
Mitchell, Arm. Sergt. James
McBoyle, Private K. C.
McGoun, Corporal D. M.
McLeod, Corporal J. A.
Nicholson, Private Fitzroy
Pearson, Private William
Pickering, Private P. L.
Richardson, Private M. M.
Sedgwick, Lance-Corp. E. F.
Shaw, Private Barclay
Shelley, Private J. A.
Smith, Sergt. Andrew
Smiley, Private Sterling
Stewart, Private C. W.
Taylor, Lance-Corp. J. W.
Thorne, Sergt. V. R.
Turnbull, Lance-Corp. D. T.

APPENDIX E

24th Battalion, Victoria Rifles of Canada

STATISTICS

Total of the Nominal Roll.	4,827
Officers Who Served.	219
Other Ranks Who Served.	4,608
Officers Killed.	34
Other Ranks Killed.	950
Other Ranks Died of Sickness.	22
Total Dead All Ranks.	1,006
Officers Wounded.	83
Other Ranks Wounded.	2,302
Total Wounded All Ranks.	2,385
Total Battle Casualties.	3,369

HONOURS AND AWARDS

Honour	24th Battalion	After Transfer	Total
V.C.	1	0	1
C.M.G.	1	2	3
O.B.E.	1	1	2
D.S.O.	6	4	10
Bar to D.S.O.	1	1	2
M.C.	33	15	48
Bar to M.C.	3	1	4
D.C.M.	20	0	20
M.M.	126	16	142
Bar to M.M.	8	0	8
M.S.M.	6	4	10
M. in D. (4 times)	0	1	1
M. in D. (3 times)	1	0	1
M. in D. (twice)	4	4	8
M. in D.	28	6	34
Brought to Notice (twice)	0	1	1
Brought to Notice	1	1	2
Foreign Decorations	9	2	11
Total	249	58	307

www.ingramcontent.com/pod-product-compliance
Lightning Source LLC
Chambersburg PA
CBHW071811230426
43670CB00013B/2420